AMSTERDAM

The Virago Woman's Travel Guides

Series Editor: Ros Belford

Amsterdam
London
New York
Paris
Rome
San Francisco

forthcoming:

Athens and The Greek Islands
Great Britain

VIRAGO WOMAN'S GUIDE TO

AMSTERDAM

CATHERINE STEBBINGS

Published by VIRAGO PRESS Limited March 1994
20–23 Mandela Street, Camden Town, London NW1 0HQ

A CIP catalogue record for this book is available from the
British Library

Printed in Great Britain by Cox & Wyman Ltd, Reading, Berkshire

CONTENTS

ACKNOWLEDGEMENTS

This book is dedicated to Jonathan Stebbings and our daughters Imogen and Polly.

Thanks to Els Wamsteeker at the Amsterdam Tourist Office, Julia Britchford at British Midland, Russell Stenhouse for Sally Ferries, Steven Fletcher of the Amsterdam Travel Service, the Netherlands Tourist Board, the Agora Hotel, Prinsengracht Hotel, Swiss Hotel Ascot and the Memphis Hotel.

Thanks for information and practical assistance to Sandra van Beck, Tony Garcia, Dineke Stam, Julia Bigham, Agnes at De Graaf Stichting, Bernhard Scholten, Tilly Vriend and all the staff at the IIAV. Thanks for everything to Jonathan Stebbings, John and Felicity Cripwell, Jeanette Stebbings, Sophie Matthews, Jo Oldham, Tessa Kerwood, Martin Nield, Richard Cripwell and Emma Coles.

Disclaimer

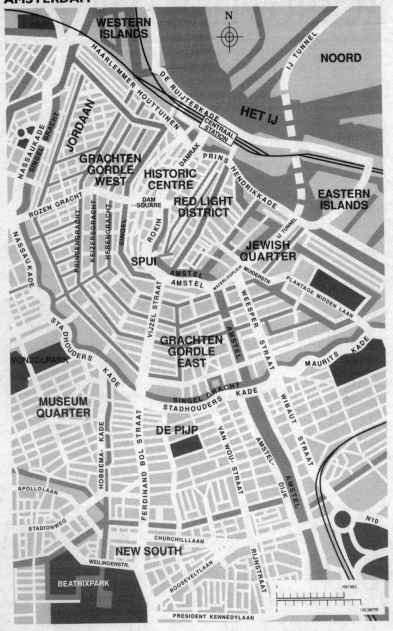

CENTRAL AMSTERDAM

N

WESTERN ISLANDS

NOORD

HAARLEMMER HOUTTUINEN

DE RUIJTERKADE

IJ TUNNEL

HET IJ

CENTRAAL STATION

JORDAAN

NASSAUKADE

SINGEL GRACHT

GRACHTEN GORDLE WEST

DAMRAK

PRINS HENDRIKKADE

HISTORIC CENTRE

DAM SQUARE

RED LIGHT DISTRICT

EASTERN ISLANDS

ROZEN GRACHT

PRINSENGRACHT

KEIZERSGRACHT

HERENGRACHT

SINGEL

ROKIN

NASSAU KADE

SPUI

VLIZEL STRAAT

AMSTEL

AMSTEL

JEWISH QUARTER

IJ TUNNEL

WATERLOOPLEIN MUIDERSTR

PLANTAGE MIDDEN LAAN

WEESPER STRAAT

STADHOUDERS KADE

VONDELPARK

GRACHTEN GORDLE EAST

AMSTEL

MAURITS KADE

SINGEL GRACHT

STADHOUDERS KADE

MUSEUM QUARTER

HOBBEMA-KADE

FERDINAND BOL STRAAT

DE PIJP

VAN WOU-STRAAT

AMSTEL-DIJK

WIBAUT STRAAT

APOLLOLAAN

N10

STADIONWEG

CHURCHILLLAAN

NEW SOUTH

WEILINGENSTR.

ROOSEVELTLAAN

RIJNSTRAAT

BEATRIXPARK

0   HALF MILE

0   1 KILOMETRE

PRESIDENT KENNEDYLAAN

INTRODUCTION

Amsterdam is a friendly city where tram drivers crack jokes across the intercom and where tramps dance for children in the playground, where cars give way to bicycles and where animals have their own ambulance service. The same old man turns the wheel on his barrel organ year after year, housewives buy armfuls of tulips every morning and cheese comes in bright yellow rounds.

A compact city, its narrow alleys, cobbled streets and wide canals radiate like a cobweb from the historic centre. By day cafés spill onto the streets, over bridges and alongside murky canals. Open air markets sell anything from Afghan coats to sequinned sofas, from soap to wheelchairs, from old stamps to antique prams. Buskers from around the world entertain the passing crowd; a couple of music students from St Petersburg sound trumpets beneath the vaults of the Rijksmuseum, an elderly French man sings the songs of Edith Piaf in the courtyard of the old city orphanage, jugglers toss multicoloured balls for children in Vondelpark and puppets dance to Dutch folk music in Kalverstraat. A stream of tourist boats cut swathes in the city's waterways, cats lounge on warm wooden decks of brightly painted houseboats while huge cranes pull discarded bikes from the murky depths. Students chat on the steps of beautiful canal houses, old ladies gossip on canalside benches and dope dealers make new acquaintances against a constant background of carillon bells, cement mixers, boat horns and bicycle bells.

By night fairy lights stretch across canals, define humped-back bridges and reflect in sleeping waters. People gather to eat in restaurants serving food from almost every continent of the globe and a seething mass of men and tittering tourists head for the Red Light District to make what they will of the city's prostitutes. By midnight the night life is just beginning. Teenagers pull on body suits in preparation for a night of acid house and laser beams, a more soporific crowd crams into smoke-filled bars for live jazz and crisply coutured businessmen burn their fingers in the Casino. A drove of gay men, like leather clones, strut to hip clubs for sweaty dance floors and darkroom encounters.

However cosmopolitan it may seem, Amsterdam and the people

that make it so are unselfconscious. The city thrives on the diverse and transient nature of its population. For centuries refugees have fled to the city where tolerance of opposing political and religious ideas made it the melting pot of European non-conformity. The liberal attitude to soft drugs, prostitution, pornography and independent spirits continued this tradition in the psychedelic 60s, attracting hippies from all over Europe. The unique conditions that encourage self discovery remain secure. Women are neither subversive nor special. As a woman you have no need to feel threatened by anyone or anything here. Amsterdam is an open, accepting city, think of yourself as part of it and you will enjoy it.

Observe the city and you may find it baffling in its contradictions: children are given sweets in shops, yet are barred from many hotels; one minute you are being chatted up by a fair-skinned beer-soaked soccer fan, the next you are talking to a transvestite about the colour of her lipstick.

But there's no need simply to observe Amsterdam; immerse yourself in a city life that is impulsive and addictive. Don't shy away from dope dealers, sex shops, prostitutes, buskers and the unknown. See them as a challenge – a chance to overcome instinctive fears and break down a lifetime's inhibitions; with no one in a position to judge you for doing just that. Amsterdam is one of the few cities in the world where you can discover yourself, affirm and test your beliefs, and find out what you really enjoy.

You may think from their uniform of jeans, casual shirts and leather jackets that the Dutch are laid back, but after you have been here a few days you will start to appreciate the efficiency of every aspect of Dutch life; the postman is never late, trains run on time, appointments are kept and you can be fined for putting your rubbish out too early or too late. However, their efficiency is neither clinical nor soulless. It just means things work when you want them to. City life is clearly defined; queuing systems operate in banks and supermarkets, every flat, house, room and their inhabitants are entered on the police computer. There are clinics, crisis centres and help lines for everyone in need; and even the prostitutes have their own union, a PR department and an archive.

The city's historical and cultural heritage is intimate and manageable. There are many interesting buildings but few imposing ones. The canal houses are pretty but not magnificent, the churches are impressive but not inspiring and most of the museums are easily visited in a couple of hours. Of course the exceptions are the Rijksmuseum where the wealth of Dutch art could keep you transfixed for weeks, and the Van Gogh Museum where brilliant images from a mind on the edge of sanity can captivate you for hours.

The quaint brick façades of gabled houses, tree-lined canals and cobbled streets reflect the glories of the 17th century Golden Age yet belie the sufferings of darker, more recent times when Jewish families hid from Nazi oppressors and Dutch families risked their lives trying to support them; as the people move back to a Jewish Quarter razed by the Germans the city's Jewish community is now more remembered by memorials than represented by members.

It is worth remembering that Amsterdam, the capital of the Netherlands, is not far from the sea, undulating sand dunes and shell covered beaches. A short train journey will take you across flat open countryside, neatly divided by narrow ditches and punctuated with windmills. In spring the fallow turf transforms into a mass of colour as acres of tulips in brash, bright colours fade into the distance. Within an hour you can be in the country's political centre at the Hague, sipping coffee in a sleepy fishing village or cycling round a national park furnished with some of this century's greatest sculpture.

PRACTICALITIES

WHEN TO GO

Don't be put off by reports of bitterly cold winds and driving rain in the winter or hot, humid, mosquito-ridden summer nights. Amsterdam is always fun. The climate can be unpredictable, but the city is built to cope with it. Cafés hide behind doors and curtains in winter and spill onto the pavements in summer; tourists enjoy the streets, canals and parks in fine weather and simply drop into galleries and museums when clouds loom overhead. You should take an umbrella and a warm sweater at all times, but don't be disheartened by wet weather. There is always plenty to do.

Spring is an exciting season; the streets are filled with noise and laughter as people stop to talk in the morning sun. Boat owners slap a new layer of bright paint on their vessels, light breezes whip at the clear canals and the abundance of fresh flowers is breathtaking. By **summer** the city is often hot and always crowded. Clubs, bars and restaurants throb with new found friends. Locals flock to the parks to while away an afternoon watching jugglers and puppet artists as tourists consume gallons of cool frothy beer. Everyone enjoys the cultural festivals that take place in June and July. All too quickly the summer is over and the city returns to relative calm. The **autumn** is cool but pleasant. Canal houses reflect in the waters once again after a summer behind foliage and the Vermeers and Rembrandts at the Rijksmuseum emerge after a season behind tourists. You can enjoy the city at a leisurely pace and take part in the run up to Christmas which seems to start in September.

Rain is a constant threat and showers and storms can occur at any time of the year. The **winters** can also be bitterly cold. Ferocious winds sweep off the North Sea bringing with them hail, snow and driving rain. This is the season when you really enjoy the comforts of hot chocolate and apple pie in a typical Dutch café. The canals rarely freeze, but when they do everyone puts on their skates, leaves the streets and takes to the ice. If you are lucky enough to be part of this your winter visit will be spectacular. New Year is also celebrated with great panache: on New Year's Eve the whole city seems to party and the sky is full of cascading, rainbow-hued fireworks.

FESTIVALS AND EVENTS

The year is punctuated with street parties, fairs and arts festivals. The biggest party of the year happens on **Konninginnedag** (Queen's Day) on 30 April when up to three million people invade the streets, enjoy the free market and make merry. Theatre, dance and opera are taken to their limits in the **Holland Festival** which lasts for the whole of June.

February A **Carnival** is held as the preamble to Lent and in celebration of the coming of Spring. A chance for last minute partying, drinking and dressing up. Information from *Stichting Carnival Mokum*, tel. 623 2568. On 25 February a solemn **Commemoration of the February Strike** in which dockers led a general strike in protest at the rounding up of Jews by the Nazis in 1941 takes place on J.D. Meijerplein around the statue of the *Dokwerker*. (see p.192).

March There is usually a rally for **International Women's Day** on 8 March. Call the *Vrouwenhuis* for details, tel. 625 2066. The *Stille Omang* (Silent Procession) is held on the Sunday closest to 15 March. Roman Catholics walk along the Heiligeweg to St Nicolaaskerk in celebration of the Amsterdam Miracle of 1348. (see p.107) For information tel. 023 245415 after 7 p.m.

April During **National Museum Weekend** museums are crammed with people taking advantage of the free entrance or concessionary rates. Usually held on the third weekend of the month. 30 April **Konninginnedag** everyone makes the most of the national holiday to celebrate Queen Beatrix's official birthday. Amsterdam declares a 'free market' where anyone can set up a stall in the city and all bar and restaurant takings are tax free. The party runs from midnight to midnight and the population of Amsterdam is quadrupled for the day. For family entertainment head for Vondelpark and the Jordaan where adults and children flog ancient belongings, sing, dance and entertain the passing crowd. Many bars erect outdoor stages for bands – try Leidseplein, Egelantiersstraat and Spui for street bopping. Warning: avoid Dam Square, Muntplein, Rembrandtsplein, Leidseplein and Leidsestraat in the middle of the day, they get very crowded so use smaller streets to get from A to B. Fairgrounds are usually to be found in Nieuwmarkt, Dam Square and Museumplein. **World Press Photo Exhibition**, showing the best of the preceding year's international newspaper and magazine photographs, takes place in Nieuwe Kerk around the last weekend in April, tel. 626 8168.

May On **Herdenkingsdag** (Remembrance Day) Queen Beatrix lays a wreath at the national monument in Dam Square at 8 p.m. which is followed by two minutes' silence, in honour of those who lost their lives in the Second World War. **Bevrijdingsdag** (Liberation Day) heralds street parties and a free market, concentrated around Vondelpark and Leidseplein.

June The **Holland Festival** attracts theatre, dance and opera enthusiasts to Amsterdam and the Hague throughout the month. Like Edinburgh it is mainly repertory and has a fringe, the Off Holland Theatre for bright new talent. Tel. 627 6566 for details. The second Sunday of the month joggers take to the streets on the **Echo Grachtenloop**, a three, six, and thirteen-mile run around the city's canals.

Anyone can take part; register at Stadsschouwburg or Leidseplein; race begins 11 a.m. or watch from Prinsengracht or Leidseplein. Tel. 585 9222 for information. **Kunst RAI**, an international contemporary arts fair takes place at the end of the month, tel. 549 1212. The *Melkweg* Media Centre (see p.288) puts on a twelve-day **World Roots Festival** of dance, film and theatre from Africa and non-western countries, tel. 624 1777.

July The **Summer Festival** a festival of avant-garde theatre takes place in selected venues for most of the month. Ask at AUB (see p.13) for details, tel. 621 1211.

August Theatre groups and musicians from all over the Netherlands stage free performances in theatres, parks and squares in the *Uitmarkt* (Entertainment Market) in an attempt to gain publicity for the coming season. **Dammen Op De Dam** is an open air draughts tournament held on the Dam some time in the middle of August. Entry forms are available at any branch of the Rabobank. **Prinsengracht Concert,** an open air concert, takes place on the canal opposite the Pulizer Hotel (Prinsengracht 315–331) on the last weekend of the month, tel. 626 8485.

September For the **Bloemen Corso** (Flower Parade) a delightful parade of floats make their way from Aalsmeer to Amsterdam on the first Saturday of the month. Watch from Leidseplein, Leidsestraat, Spuistraat and the Dam. **National Monument Day** on the second Saturday in September is a great time to see inside canal houses, windmills and national monuments that are usually closed. For details tel. 626 3947. An animated street party is held in the lively Jordaan area in the *Jordaan Festival*. Usually held around the second and third weeks of September. Ask the Tourist Information Centre (see page 13) for dates.

November In mid November St Nicolaas (Father Christmas) arrives by steamboat at Central Station and parades through the city astride a trusty white steed. He receives the keys to Amsterdam on Dam Square and disappears into the mist. Ask VVV (The Tourist Information Centre) (see p.13) for dates.

December Most people stay at home on 5 December for **Pakjesavond** (Parcel Evening), the traditional day of present giving instead of Christmas Day. *Oudejaarsavond* (New Years's Eve) wild parties, street sing songs, fireworks and national cameraderie is enjoyed by locals and thousands of tourists. Dam Square gets very crowded. If you enjoy a street party and can't make Queen's Day on April 30th this is the next best thing.

Getting There

Amsterdam is a popular destination and most travel agents will be able to help plan your trip. It is easily accessible by plane, coach, train and ferry – each has its own advantages. Air travel is convenient but expensive for families who get only small, if any reduction for all children over two. Coach and train journeys with a break on the ferry are popular options. For independent travellers, particularly students, Student Travel Association **STA Travel** (see box) can arrange travel and accommodation at competitive rates. Numerous package tours are available through travel agents, but if you are looking for a specialist tour (art, architecture etc.) you will have to contact the companies direct (see below), look for them in the classified ads in the Sunday papers. Prices fluctuate enormously throughout the year according to the season and school holidays. There are lots of bargains about, so shop around.

Travelling by **rail and coach** is time consuming and not much cheaper than flying, Self-drive packages are expensive by the time you have paid for petrol, insurance and parking and having a car in Amsterdam is more of a headache than an asset (see p.9). Travelling by air is most popular because it is quick, easy and there is a greater choice of departure points. The Amsterdam Travel Service uses nineteen different airports within the UK.

Amsterdam by air

Scheduled and charter flights leave daily for Amsterdam from most international airports in the UK throughout the year. All fly into Schipol Airport where a regular train service carries you to Central Station in fifteen minutes. The main companies offering regular flights to Amsterdam are **British Airways, KLM, British Midland,** and **Transavia**. Prices vary according to the airport you use and the time of year. They are competitive so shop around. Check the travel pages of the national papers and city newspapers for travel agents offering a good deal. **Charter flights** start around £69 return and scheduled around £120. You will always pay more if you buy direct from the airline so look to your travel agent for the best rates. It is only a short flight, about an hour depending on the wind. Most airlines ask you to check in thirty minutes in advance.

When booking a flight give any special requirements concerning meals, seating, disability and children. Remind them of this when you check in.

Pregnant women and children   Most airlines carry pregnant women up to their 34th week. You will have to present a doctors certificate after your 28th week of pregnancy stating that you are fit and well. Confirm the requirements with your travel agent when booking.

Prices for babies and children vary, as does the terminology. 'Baby' usually refers to the under twos who have to share your seat. Sometimes they travel free but usually cost 10% of the adult fare. Children from two to twelve cost between 25% and 65% of the full fare and over twelve they pay the full whack. **Single mothers** with two babies will find it virtually impossible to fly as most airlines stipulate one adult per child. Sort this out with the airline before leaving or they may turn you away at the airport. (If you have trouble with an extra child at the check in, pluck up courage and find someone in the queue who is willing to hold your baby for the trip!)

Most airlines provide children's play packs and are happy to show youngsters the flight deck if they have time. Ask the stewardess.

PRACTICALITIES

Baby food, milk, nappies and **carry cots** are usually available, but ask for them when you book. Carry cots are very useful for small babies and must be booked in advance. Make sure you reserve an appropriate seat for yourself at the same time so that there is room for the cot at your feet.

Packages

Packages offering **travel and accommodation** are often the cheapest way to visit the city and are easy to book through your local travel agent. The **Amsterdam Travel Service** (tel. 0920 467444) offers a wide range of city breaks with prices ranging from £99 for two nights, travelling by rail and ferry, to £336 flying out and staying for three nights in a five-star hotel. They use good hotels, have a rep in Amsterdam and offer an imaginative selection of excursions and tours. An evening bike ride and a guided walk through the Red Light District are excellent for lone travellers. Thomsons (tel. 071 431 1950) and Sovereign Cities (tel. 0293 599900) are slightly more upmarket, offering a good range of breaks in well-chosen hotels.

Cheaper packages may use hotels in the Red Light District; always check when booking. Most tour operators tend to use large international hotels but packages to Amsterdam offer some notable exceptions. The Pulitzer, Canal House, Agora and Owl Hotel, all hotels of quality and character, are used by the companies mentioned.

Most packages offer cheap rates for children and a nominal fee for babies. Cots can be provided at most hotels for around £5 per night.

Single travellers and specialist tours

Nearly all package holidays require people travelling alone to pay a single supplement on the advertised price. The enterprising company **Solo's** (tel. 081 202 0855) offers breaks to the Netherlands for single people (over 30) where you are not penalised for travelling alone. Another company, **Travel Companions** (tel. 081 431 1984), can help if you are looking for someone to travel with.

For those looking for an educational trip, guided cultural tours are offered by **Inscape** (tel. 0993 891 726) and **Ace Study Tours** (tel. 0223 835 055) among others. For other specialist tours see the annually updated *Independent Guide to Real Holidays* (published by the *Independent* newspaper annually) and the travel pages of the weekend broadsheets.

Overland to Amsterdam

Travelling by coach to Amsterdam is both easy and the cheapest way to get there for under 25s. **National Express Eurolines** (tel. 071 630 8132) run a daily service (day and night) from Victoria, London to Centraal Station, Amsterdam for £53 return. Under 25s enjoy reduced fares and children under four travel free if they share an adult seat. The journey takes twelve hours. If business is bad they have been known to stop running trips in the winter.

Trains are a little more expensive and you do have to carry luggage on and off the ferry. Trains leave daily on the eleven-hour journey from Liverpool Street and Victoria. Night-time travellers can book single-sex couchettes for £10 or reclining seats for £5. Children under four go free.

Don't drive to Amsterdam unless you really need your car for exploring elsewhere on the holiday. Free parking is impossible to find, public car parks are expensive, car theft and break ins are common. Your route will be dictated by the ferry crossing you choose; Ramsgate-Dunkerque (Sally Line, tel. 089 4955522), Sheerness-Vlissingen (Olau, tel. 0795 666666), Dover-Calais/Boulogne (Hover Speed, tel. 0304 240241), Felixstowe-Zeebrugge, Dover-Ostend (P&O, tel. 0304 203388), Harwich to Hook of Holland (Stena Sealink, tel. 0233 647 033), Hull-Rotterdam (North Sea Ferries, tel. 0482 77177); Boulogne is the longest drive of 254 miles and the Hook of Holland is a short 40 miles.

All train and coach trips obviously include a ferry trip and the ferry companies also offer special excursions at competitive rates. **Ferry fares** vary considerably according to the time of year (Sally Line normal return for two adults and car ranges from £115 to £234). Note that it is usually cheaper to take a package than book a ferry and accommodation independently.

Ferries are now well equipped for families. Baby changing facilities include free nappies if you ask and children are well catered for in the play area, TV lounge or buffet. Sally Line offers a crèche for over twos.

USEFUL PHONE NUMBERS

AA European Routes tel. 0272 308 242
Ace Study Tours tel. 0223 835 055
Amsterdam Travel Service tel. 0920 467444
Air UK tel. 0279 680146
British Airways tel. 081 897 4000
British Midland tel. 071 5895599
Eurotrain tel. 071 730 3402
Hoverspeed tel. 0304 240202
Inscape Fine Art Tours tel. 0993 891 726
KLM tel. 081 750 9000
National Express Eurolines tel. 071 630 8132

North Sea Ferries tel. 0482 77177
Olau tel. 0795 666666
P&O Ferries tel. 081 863 2787
Sally Ferries tel. 0843 595522
Solo's tel. 081 202 0855
Sovereign Cities tel. 0293 599900
STA Travel tel. 071 937 9921
Stena Sealink tel. 0233 615915
Thomson Citybreaks tel. 081 200 8733
Transavia tel. 0293 538181
Travel Companions tel. 081 202 8478

PRACTICALITIES

Passports and Permits At the time of writing all you need is a valid passport to visit the Netherlands for up to three months, this applies to both EC and North American nationals. Remember to allow at least a month when applying for a full passport, though if time is not on your side buy a visitor's passport at your local Post Office.

If you intend to stay for longer than three months you need a full passport and should register with the local **Aliens Police Bureau** (*Vreemdelingenpolitie*) at Waterlooplein 9, open Mon–Fri 8.30 a.m.–12.30 p.m., tel. 559 9111 within eight days of arrival. You will need to apply for a Residence Permit (*Verblijfsvergunning*) from the same office after three months. A permit is normally free and available the same day but get there early as queues start around 7 a.m. You will be asked to show some form of ID, proof of an address (hotel will do) and proof that you have sufficient money to stay on (which usually means a job!). See working in the Netherlands p.44.

Insurance It is wise to take out private insurance to cover for cancellation or delay of your holiday, and the loss of luggage, money or valuables. It may seem a ridiculous expense to add to a cheap weekend away, but Sod's law is that you will lose everything the one time you decide not to fork out. It is also important to cover yourself for personal liability and accidents and make sure the policy includes treatment and repatriation in case of illness. Relying on an E111 (see Health) is not recommended; although it covers basic health care there is a lot of red tape to cope with if an accident does occur. Your travel agent should be able to advise you on the policies available.

If driving out remember to get a Green Card to insure your car overseas from your insurance company – the chances are that you will need it as foreign cars are prime targets for break-ins. Car owners must take the following with them: international identification disk, registration certificate, proof of the vehicle having passed a road safety test and insurance papers.

Money Dutch currency is the guilder, which divides into 100 cents. Within the Netherlands the guilder is also referred to as a florin abbreviated to *f*, f, fl or H*fl*. At the time of writing the exchange rate is around f2.65 to the pound (sterling). Shops and restaurants may be reluctant to accept the higher denominations of notes because of the increasing number of counterfeits in circulation. Many phone booths accept the tiny 25c (*kwartje*) pieces so don't throw them away on tips. The 5c coin is referred to as a *stui-*

ver, the 10c coin is a *dubbeltje* and the f2.50 coin is known as a *rijksdaalder*. The notes have raised symbols on them so that they can be used by blind people.

DENOMINATIONS
COINS 5, 10, 25 cents
1, 2.5, 5 guilders
NOTES 5, 10, 25, 50, 100, 250, 1,000 guilders

Changing Money Traveller's cheques or Eurocheques are the most useful means of money in Amsterdam; they are easily changeable in banks and *bureaux de change* dotted around the city, as long as you remember to take your passport with you. Amsterdammers prefer to use cash for most transactions although the big hotels, shops and restaurants usually take credit cards. It is however advisable to check before you tuck in to a meal. Few places will take credit cards for bills under f50 and, surprisingly, very few banks will give cash advances against credit cards.

By far the easiest way to manage your money in Amsterdam is to take a Eurocheque card or a credit card with a PIN number and use the cash dispensers outside banks all over the city. This way you can avoid carrying huge sums of money, passports and traveller's cheques which are easy prey for pickpockets. You also won't be tied by the opening hours of banks and bureaux de change. That said, if a machine swallows your card (as they so frequently do) you are stuck, so it is best to have some traveller's cheques stashed away at your hotel just in case anything should happen.

Most banks are open 9 a.m.–4 p.m., Monday to Friday and some stay open till 7 p.m. on Thursday. They will buy and sell foreign currency and exchange traveller's cheques at similar rates to the bureaux de change but usually charge less commission. If you are using **Eurocheques** transactions are limited to f300. You will find bureaux de change all over the city centre especially along Damrak, Leidseplein and Rokin; most stay open at weekends and late at night. Avoid using Hotel and Tourist bureaux exchange facilities as they are usually more expensive, while many, like Chequepoint, advertise 'no commission' they offer less competitive rates.

BANKS AND EXCHANGE OFFICES
ABN AMRO
Vijzelstraat 68–78, Mon–Fri 9 a.m.–4.45 p.m.
Dam 2, Mon–Fri 9 a.m.–5 p.m.
Leidseplein 25, Mon–Fri 9 a.m.–5 p.m.

Rombrandtsplein 47, Mon–Fri 9 a.m.–5 p.m.
Foreign bank head offices for business enquiries only:
Barclays Bank
Weteringshans 109, tel. 626 2209
Citibank NA
Herengracht 545, tel. 551 5911
Lloyds Bank
Leidseplein 29, tel. 626 3535
Bureaux de Change:
GWK
Central Station open 24 hours daily
Schipol Airport open 24 hours daily
Change Express
Damrak 86, 8 a.m.–11.30 p.m. daily
Leidsestraat 106, 8 a.m.–midnight daily

If you exchange traveller's cheques at a company branch there is no commission charge:
American Express
Amsteldijk 166, Mon–Fri 9 a.m.–5 p.m.
Damrak 66, Mon–Fri 9 a.m.–5.30p.m. Sat noon–5 p.m. Sun 11 a.m.–4 p.m. 24-hour cash dispenser for card holders and an automatic traveller's cheque refund service.
Koningsplein 10, Mon–Fri 9 a.m.–5 p.m.
Thomas Cook
Dam 23–25, 9 a.m.–6 p.m. daily
Damrak 1–5, 8 a.m.–8 p.m. daily
Leidseplein 31a, 9 a.m.–7 p.m. daily

Cost of Living

Amsterdam tourist office was keen to announce the results of a survey by the Bank of Switzerland which declared the city as one of the least expensive in Europe. In reality the cost of living is similar to Britain, though some things are cheaper and some more expensive; eating out can be very cheap, public transport, wine and books tend to be expensive. Museum entrance costs from around f2–f10, but the Museum Card is a good buy at f40 for anyone who wants to do everything. The Holland Leisure Card entitles you to discounts on theatre, transport, car hire and lots more for f25 and if you are under 26 the CJP or young persons card entitles you to discounts for cultural events and venues. All discount cards are available from the **VVV** and the **AUB Uitburo** (see below).

Like the rest of Europe in the 90s the Netherlands is going through economic recession and prices are unstable. All the prices in this book were correct in late 1993.

If you stay in a hostel with dormitory accommodation and breakfast thrown in, have a sandwich and a beer for lunch and a cheap meal in the evening you can manage on around f50 a day – you'll need more if you intend to go clubbing or drinking into the night. Once you move into hotel accommodation prices rise substantially and single travellers get stung for travelling alone. A night in a two star hotel in a shared room with a bathroom, a gallery visit, snack lunch and boozy dinner will put the daily rate around f150, not to mention what you might spend in the shops in the afternoon. If you are doing the city in style in a four star hotel, using taxis, eating at the city's classiest restaurants and enjoying the night life you will be spending over f500 a day. If money is no object enjoy the Amstel Hotel, take a helicopter tour, buy diamonds, eat oysters and dance the night away.

Information

The London branch of the Netherlands Board of Tourism has been so inundated with calls that they now refer you directly to the Vereniging voor Vreemdelingenverker or VVV in Amsterdam. Pronounced 'Fay Fay Fay', the national tourist information organisation has two offices in Amsterdam and a further 450 offices scattered around Holland.

VVV TOURIST INFORMATION OFFICES

Stationsplein10, tel. 626 6444. Open October–Easter Mon–Fri 9 a.m.–6 p.m. Sat. 10 a.m.–1 p.m. Sun 2 p.m.–5 p.m. Easter–June & Sept, Mon–Sat 9 a.m.–11 p.m., Sun 9 a.m.–9 p.m. July and Aug, daily 9 a.m.–11 p.m.
Leidsestraat 106, tel. 621 1211. Open as above except October to Easter, Mon–Fri 10.30 a.m.–5.30 p.m., Sat 10.30 a.m.–9 p.m.

Information on Cultural Events
AUB Uitburo
Leidseplein 26, tel. 621 1211. Open Mon–Sat 10 a.m.–6 p.m.

If you need information from Amsterdam before you leave it is virtually impossible to make contact with either office as they have a ludicrous telephone waiting system on which you can wait for hours before anyone talks to you, while the recorded message politely tells you that you are paying 50c per minute for the call. For information on cultural events ring AUB Uitburo (see above). If you need hotel accommodation, car hire and general information when you get there call into the VVV and expect to wait. Staff are overworked but always friendly and speak English, German and French. They guarantee to fix you up with accommodation (fee f3.50) even if this means having to send you to neighbouring towns if the city's hotels are full. They are not however in a position to recommend individual hotels. All those on their books have passed the basic test of being clean, safe and fairly priced.

Be warned: men hang around the tourist office aggressively hounding women about cheap accommodation. Don't listen to them, you would do better to wait your turn in the queue. Likewise there are a number of accommodation/tourist information offices in the city which have nothing to do with the VVV and are best avoided because the accommodation is often shabby, expensive or in a nasty area.

The VVV produces a fortnightly *What's on in Amsterdam* listing the main sights, useful addresses and listings for f3.50, but it is fairly incomplete and often inaccurate. They also sell maps and leaflets guiding you around various areas of the city which are quite fun to do; *Jewish Amsterdam, The Historical Centre* and *The Jordaan* are all good. All these publications are available in newsagents and museums around the city so there is no need to join the queues here if this is all you want. For **transport information** go to the transport office next door to the Tourist Office on Stationsplein by the metro entrance.

While the VVV do carry information on cultural events, as most people need this information in advance it is best to deal with the independent organisation AUB Uitburo at Leidseplein 26 (tel. 621 1211, Mon–Sat 10 a.m.–6 p.m. They provide information on all cultural events in the city and will book tickets in advance for a small commission: f5 by phone and f2 if you drop in. No credit cards.

Maps Amsterdam's street plan may look simple but be assured you will need a map. Ours will do for basic purposes but if you really want to explore, it is advisable to buy one. Most of the free maps available in hotels and restaurants only show the historic centre which is next to useless. The most manageable map is the *Falk* fold out plan which is sold in most newsagents and at the VVV for f5.50. For a more detailed but heavier version you may prefer the *Falk* pocket book map or the *Hallwag* map of Amsterdam and environs which is great if you are driving into the city and need information on one way streets, car parks and motorways.

What's On If you rely on the VVV *What's On* weekly listings guide for information you will be bound to miss the most important gigs in town. The extensive listings in the English monthly *Time Out Amsterdam* are far more comprehensive and reliable, available at most newsagents for f4. The free monthly *Uitkrant* (from AUB, VVV, libraries, museums and theatres) holds good listings which, despite being in Dutch, are fairly easy to understand. *Agenda* is to be found littered around the trendy cafés and is good on live music listings while *Oor*, the Dutch equivalent of *New Musical Express* will alert you to any spectacular events scheduled for Amsterdam.

Most of the city's cafés and bars rely on posters and information sheets for their decor so information gathering is something of a doddle. The AUB carries all the latest information on theatre, ballet, gigs, classical concerts, exhibitions and lots more and will book you tickets if you care to drop in. For details of **women and lesbian events** ring the Gay and Lesbian Switchboard for the most up to date information (tel. 623 6565). The women's bookshops Xantippe at Prinsengracht 290 or Lorelei at Prinsengracht 495 usually have plenty of information, as does the IIAV (women's archive) or the gay and lesbian HQ at COC. (See p.44.)

Communications

Post The postal service, **PTT Post**, is highly efficient. Red post boxes with the logo written in white are to be found all over the city. If you are posting mail to go out of the city use the *overige* slot. Post offices are generally open from Monday to Friday 9 a.m. to 5 p.m. for sending letters, telegrams and express post items or buying stamps and postal orders. Stamps (*postzegeten*) are also sold in many tobacconists and souvenir shops.

Parcels can only be sent from the main Post Office and the Centraal Station, both of which are very easy to find. Other post offices around the city will not deal with parcels.

If you need a **poste restante** address in Amsterdam ask for mail to be sent to: Poste Restante, Hoofdpostkantoor ptt, Singel 250, 1012 SJ, Amsterdam, Netherlands. You can pick it up from the main Post Office provided you show some form of ID with a photo. Passport is best.

USEFUL ADDRESSES

Post Offices
Main Post Office
Singel 250, tel. 655 6331. Open Mon–Wed, Thurs 8.30 a.m.–8.30 p.m.,
Fri 8.30 a.m.–6 p.m., Sat 9 a.m.–noon. No credit cards.
Centraal Station Post Office
Oosterdokskade 3, tel. 555 8911. Open Mon–Fri 8.30 a.m.–9 p.m. Sat 9 a.m.–noon.
A few minutes walk east of the station.

Poste Restante
Hoofdpostkantoor ptt, Singel 250, 1012 SJ, Amsterdam, Netherlands.

Telephones Most bars and cafés have public pay phones but if you are trying to hold a decent conversation look for a phone booth or better still go to a phone centre. The phone booths are mainly glass with a green trim and carry the white PTT logo. There are so few that they are usually recognisable by the queues outside. Coin booths take 25c, f1 and f2.50 coins and if you wish to avoid the queues you are better off using the card phones. Phone cards are available for f5, f10 and f25 from post offices, phone centres and some souvenir shops.

For long distance calls use the phone centres which work out much cheaper than phoning from hotels. The time for off peak rates is generally 8 p.m.–8 a.m. but it does change so check at the phone centre first, it also varies according to where you are phoning. The international dialling code is 09 followed by the country code (44 for Britain) and then omit the first zero from the area code in Britain. The dialling tone is a low hum, the ringing tone in the Netherlands is long beeps and the engaged tone is similar to Britain. When phoning information services, taxis and train stations you will probably be greeted with a recorded message telling you how many people are ahead of you in the queue – frustrating it may be but it is one way of learning how to count in Dutch. You will hear '*Er zijn nog drie* (three) *twee* (two) *een* (one) *wachtenden voor u*'.

USEFUL INFORMATION

To call numbers in this book from outside Amsterdam you will need to dial the area code 020 before the number given. If the number is outside Amsterdam the area code is given. Any numbers beginning with 06 are freephone numbers.

Directory Enquiries 008

International Operator 06 0410

International Directory Enquiries 06 0418

Direct dailling codes UK 0944; USA and Canada 091, Australia 0961, New Zealand 0964. Omit 0 from area code.

Emergencies 0611

Phone centres

Telehouse, Raadhuistraat 46–50, C tel. 673 3654/fax 626 3871/626 5326.

Open 24 hours daily

Teletalk Centre, Leidsestraat 101. IS, tel. 620 8599/fax 620 8559

You will find phone booths at Spui, Dam Square, Waterlooplein, Rembrandtsplein, Muntplein, Central Station and elsewhere.

Telegrams, Fax and Telex Telegrams can be sent from the Post Office and the phone centres. Faxes can be sent and received at both the Phone Centres listed in the box above. If someone is sending a fax they must write your name, address and phone number on the page. Telehouse also has a Telex Service.

Most of the larger hotels have a fax machine available to customers at a charge, but few can give you access to a personal fax. Businesswomen on longer stays may prefer to hire a machine from Particuliere Telefoon Dienst (tel. 686 6660, Mon–Fri 9 a.m.–5 p.m.). Rent is around f100 per month with a f500 deposit.

Media

Television and Radio

The Netherlands has had its own broadcasting system since 1928, but it is unique in leaving the programme making in the hands of private organisations. This means that all three TV channels and five radio channels are shared between different companies which is incredibly confusing for the viewer. For example, the Nederland 3 station will have three different identities depending on who is providing the programme. For the user it means that you can rarely be sure of what you are tuning into as the frequency may be pop one minute and religious discussion the next – the end result is that more and more Dutch people tune into cable stations and the BBC. Amsterdam's cable network has over twenty channels, in addition you may tune into lots of programmes from neighbouring countries and satellite stations. So while teenagers sit glued to MTV, parents enjoy EastEnders and grandparents are still trying to fathom out what's on in Dutch. While Dutch national broadcasting (known as 'Hilversum' after the town where it is based) remains strictly non commercial, since 1992 a number of commercially funded stations have gone on the air and both local and national stations look set to follow. Commercials are only allowed to take up 5% of the air time and cannot interrupt programmes.

If you can be drawn away from the cable channels you will find very conservative documentaries and drama on Nederland 1. According to which of the three organisations is showing a particular programme, Nederland 2 ranges from chat shows, subtitled US programmes, family entertainment and soft porn while Nederland 3, shared between another three organisations, ranges from sport to quality entertainment and trashy game shows. It will probably be easier and more fruitful to go back to BBC for both news and entertainment.

On the radio tune into Radio 3 (96.8 mHz) for pop, Radio 4 (98.9mHz) for classical music and Radio 1 (747 kHz) for the news. New stations are frequently popping up in Amsterdam; recent additions are Amsterdam Extra/AFM (105.9 MHz cable) for chart sounds, club music and a few English shows, and Radio Amsterdam (107.9 MHzFM/105.5 MHz cable) for news and pop. You will find a smattering of English programmes on SALTO Kanaal 3 (106.8 MHzFM/103.8 MHz cable) which between 6 and 9 p.m. is run by the **gay station MVS**. If you want to be sure of something in English or need an update on the **Archers** BBC Radio 4 is clear on 106.6MHz/198kHzAM and the **BBC World Service** is on 101.3MHz/648kHzAM.

Newspapers and Magazines

You will have no difficulty finding British daily and Sunday papers in Amsterdam – most are in the shops by lunch time on the day of publication. The same goes for the *International Herald Tribune* and *Wall Street Journal*. For the most comprehensive selection of papers and magazines in English try W.H. Smith, Kalverstraat 152.

If you can read Dutch try the conservative daily paper *De Telegraaf*. It was the only paper allowed to publish during the Nazi occupation because it didn't seem to have a view on the situation. Its coverage of pop stars, scandals and tragedies makes it the most popular paper in the country; more usefully it carries accommodation ads on Wednesday. *Algemeen Dagblad* is similarly sensationalist. *NRC Handelsblad* is the most intellectual paper and is worth buying on Thursdays for its cultural supplement and national listings. *Het Parool* (The Password) started life as a Resistance Paper and is now seen as Amsterdam's quality, intelligent local paper. *De Volkskrant, De Trouw* and *De Parool* published by the same company represent the left. For business news the *Het Financieele Dagblad* has a summary in English and good coverage of Dutch business affairs though at the expense of its coverage of international business.

Apart from the usual monthly glossies like *Elle* and *Vogue*, Dutch women enjoy numerous publications: *Magriet* is hugely popular with Dutch housewives offering hints on cooking and husband tending; *Viva* is equally popular with younger women; *Elegance* is aimed at wealthy, cultured and mature ladies, as is the glamorously produced *Avenue*. *Opzijds* is the most widely read **feminist** monthly magazine with a circulation of over 50,000, *Savante* is a women's studies magazine and *Lover*, produced quarterly by the IIAV, its name notwithstanding is a good literary review of feminist publications and current women's issues with an English summary. Other literary journals include *Chrysallis, Lust* and *Gratie* and *Surplus*. *Brjllantine, Dynamier* and *Pheme* are popular undergraduate women's study journals. The **gay magazines** *Sekstant* and *Gay Krant* carry information and listings for both gay men and lesbians, *Homologie* is a good gay/lesbian cultural mag. COC, the national gay organisation, (see p.44) produces *Ma'dam* specifically for lesbians. They also publish *Wildside*, produced for and by SM dykes.

LANGUAGE

The Dutch almost all speak some English and many are fluent so it is easy to expect them to speak your language. However, they do appreciate it if you try to speak some basic Dutch and a friendly *'dag'* as you go into a shop or café will improve the service and the atmosphere. If you meet someone for the first time shake hands and say your name clearly. Good friends exchange kisses – three is currently the fashionable number but friends will always tell you if you get it wrong.

If you want to come to grips with the language before you go, *Dutch in Three Months*, produced by Hugo, is a sound if pedantic start with a book and three cassettes, but the best way to learn is to spend some time in the Netherlands, enrol on a language course (see p.46) and speak to the locals.

'Dutch', the English name for the language and people of the Netherlands, derives from the medieval language of the Low Countries called *Duutsc* which, like the German *Deutsch*, means the 'language of the people', distinguishing it from the Latin of priests, scholars and bureaucrats. It is an earthy language; imagine English reduced to its Anglo-Saxon vocabulary without the civilising influence of Norman French and you will get the flavour of Dutch. It shares with its German cousin a lot of words and syntax so if you speak some German you will find that, after wrestling successfully with the mysteries of pronunciation, you can invent a reasonable pidgin Dutch from the more familiar tongue.

If you don't speak any German don't worry. If you meet anyone in Amsterdam who doesn't speak any English they are likely to be foreign, too, and the person next to them is certain to be almost fluent. The ability to speak other languages is not so universal outside the cities, but you will seldom find yourself unable to make yourself understood in English. However, it is worth getting to grips with some basic Dutch for the sake of politeness and because life is more fun if one is not completely illiterate and inarticulate.

Pronunciation

Dutch is spelt phonetically so once you have mastered the sounds of each letter in each context you should be able to read or spell any word without any thought. It is generally pronounced like English although there are some exceptions.

Consonants are pronounced as in English. None are hidden so roll all your rs. The following are different:

v	like f in fat
w	like v in vat
j	like y in yak
ch, g	like ch in Scottish loch

PRACTICALITIES

ng	like ng in bring
nj	like ni in onion
sj	like sh in ship
tj	like ch in chip

Apart from ch, ng, nj, sj and tj above, all double consonants express their individual sounds, as in the antelope 'gnu'.

In English single vowels are short, double vowels are long; but vowel sounds are not always the same as those in English:

a	like a in hat
aa	like ar in start
e	like e in vet
ee, y	like a in gate
ie	like ee in been
o	like o in hop
oo	like o in hope
u	like ou in could
ui	between oa in boat and ow in cow
uu, oe	like oo in food
au, ou	like ow in cow
ei, ij	like i in wine
eu	like u in fur

BASICS

Mr	Meneer ⎫ (both can be used for
Mrs	Mevrouw ⎭ addressing a stranger)
Miss	Mejuffrouw
Hello	Hallo, dag
Good morning	Goede morgen
Good afternoon	Goede middag
Good evening	Goedenavond
Good night	Goede nacht
Hi (informal)	Hoi
Goodbye	Tot ziens
Bye (informal)	Doei
Yes	Ja
No	Nee
Please	Alstublieft
Thank you/Thanks	Dank u/bedankt
How are you?	Hoe maakt u het?
Fine, thanks	Heel goed, dank je
Do you speak English?	Spreekt u Engels?
I don't speak Dutch	Ik spreek geen Nederlands
I don't understand	Ik begrijp het niet
Excuse me	Pardon
May I?	Mag ik?

I'm sorry	'T spijt me
Morning	Morgen
Afternoon	Middag
Evening	Avond
Night	Nacht
Today	Vandaag
Tomorrow	Morgen
Next week	Nast week
Last week	Laatst week
Yesterday	Gisteren
Now	Nu
Immediately	Onmiddelijk
Ready	Klaar
Wait	Weet
Here	Hier
There	Daar
Everywhere	Overal
Good	Goed
Bad	Slecht
Big	Groot
Small	Klein
Cheap	Goedkoop
Expensive	Duur
Early	Vroeg
Late	Laat
Near	Dichtbij
Far	Ver
How far is it?	Hoe ver is her aar?
Free/vacant	Leeg
Occupied/busy	Bezet
I'm busy	Ik ben bezig
With	Met
Without	Zonder
More	Meer
Less	Minder
Enough	Genoeg
Hot	Heet
Cold	Koud
Open	Open
Closed	Gesloten
Entrance	Ingang
Exit	Uitgang
Children	Kinderen
Boy	Jongen
Girl	Meisje
Men	Mannen
Women	Vrouwen
Ladies/Gents toilet	Damen/Heren
Where is the lavatory?	Waar is het toilet?

PRACTICALITIES

Push	Duwen
Pull	Trekken

QUESTION WORDS

Where?	Waar?
Where is?	Waar is?
What?	Wat?
Who?	Wie?
When?	Waneer?
Why?	Waarom
How?	Hoe?
How much?	Hoeveel?

STREET DIRECTIONS

Left	Links
Right	Rechts
Straight ahead	Vooruit/echtuit gaan
Opposite	Tegendeel
Corner	Hoek
Street	Straat
Canal	Gracht
Square	Plein
House	Huis
Church	Kerk

HOTELS

Hotel	Hotel
Room	Kamer
Single room	Eenpersoonskamer
Double room	Tweepersoonskamer
For one night	Voor een nacht
For one week	Voor een week
With a shower	Met douche
With a private bath	Met prive bad
Do you have a cot?	Hebt u een bedje?
How much is the room?	Wat kost de kamer?
Can I see the room?	Mag ik de kamer zien?

USING PUBLIC TRANSPORT

Timetable	Dienstregeling
Monday–Saturday	Maandag–Zatedag
Daily	Dagelijks
Sundays and holidays	Zondag en feestdag
A ticket please	Een kaartj, alstublieft
Bus	Bus
When does the next bus leave for...?	Wanneer vertrekt de volgende bus naar...?
The first bus to...	De eerste bus naar...
The last bus to...	De laatste bus naar...

Tram	Tram
Train	Trein
I want to go to...	Ik wil naar...
How can I get to...?	Hoe kom ik bij...?
Thief	Dief
Pickpocket	Zakkenroller

IN A CAFÉ OR RESTAURANT (see also menu box)

A coffee please	Een koffie alstublieft
Can I have the menu?	Mag ik het menu (zien)?
I'd like...	Ik wil graag
A quarter litre of white/red wine	Een kwart liter witte/rode wijn
Do you have?/Is there?	Heeft u ?/Is er?
Could I have the bill please?	Mag ik de rekening alstublieft?
Could you telephone for a taxi please?	Kunt u een taxi voor me bellen?
Can I telephone from here?	Kan ik hier bellen (or telefoneren)?
Out of order	Defect

MEETING PEOPLE

How do you do?	(say your first and last names clearly)
How are you?	Hoe maakt u het?
Fine, thanks	Heel goed, dank je
Do you have a light?	Hebt je een vuurtje?
My name is...	Mijn naam is...
May I get you a drink?	Mag ik u ets te drinken aanbieden?
How nice	Wat leuk
Really?	Echt?
I won't be long	Ik ben zo terug
America	Amerika
USA	VS (Verenigde Staten)
UK/Great Britain	Groot-Brittannie
England	Engeland
Scotland	Schotland
Ireland	Ierland
Australia	Australie
Canada	Canada
New Zealand	Nieuw-Zeeland
Netherlands	Nederland
Africa	Afrika
France	Frankrijk
Germany	Duitsland
Italy	Italie

NUMBERS

Nought	Nul
One	Een
Two	Twee
Three	Drie

Four	Vier
Five	Vijf
Six	Zes
Seven	Zeven
Eight	Acht
Nine	Negen
Ten	Tien
Eleven	Elf
Twelve	Twaalf
Thirteen	Dertien
Fourteen	Veertien
Fifteen	Vijftien
Sixteen	Zestien
Seventeen	Zeventien
Eighteen	Achttien
Nineteen	Negentien
Twenty	Twintig
Twenty-one	Eenentwintig
Twenty-two	Tweeentwintig
Twenty-three	Drieentwintig
Twenty-four	Vierentwintig
Twenty-five	Vijfentwintig
Twenty-six	Zesentwintig
Twenty-seven	Zevenentwintig
Twenty-eight	Achtentwintig
Twenty-nine	Negenentwintig
Thirty	Dertig
Thirty-one	Eenendertig
Thirty-two	Tweeendertig
Forty	Veertig
Fifty	Vijftig
Sixty	Zestig
Seventy	Zeventig
Eighty	Tachtig
Ninety	Negentig
Hundred	Honderd
Two hundred	Tweehonderd
Three hundred	Driehonderd
Four hundred	Vierhonderd
Thousand	Duizend
Two thousand	Tweeduizend

SEASONS, MONTHS, DAYS AND TIME

Year	Jaar
Month	Maand
Day	Dag
Next	Naast
Last	Laatst
Spring	Lente

Summer	Zomer
Autumn	Herfst
Winter	Winter
January	Januari
February	Februari
March	Maart
April	April
May	Mei
June	Juni
July	Juli
August	Augustus
September	September
October	Oktober
November	November
December	December
Monday	Maandag
Tuesday	Dinsdag
Wednesday	Woensdag
Thursday	Donderdag
Friday	Vrijdag
Saturday	Zaterdag
Sunday	Zondag
Today	Vandaag
What time is it?	Hoe laat is het?
One o'clock	Een uur
Noon	Middag
Midnight	Middernacht
Three o'clock	Drie uur
Half past one	Half twee [sic]
A quarter to two	Kwart voor twee
A quarter past two	Kwart over twee
Twenty past two	Tien voor half drie
Twenty to three	Tien over half drie

TERMS OF ABUSE

Get lost	Rot op
Leave me alone	Laat me met rust (alleen)
Creep (whore walker)	Hoereloper
Bitch	Trut
Arsehole	Lul
Idiot	Idioot

Police and Crime

Dutch police are about to become the most fashionable police force in Europe. As part of the recent unification of the *Gemeente Politie* (Urban Police) and the *Rijkspolitie* (Country Police) the national Police force will be donning a new logo and uniforms in 1994. Surprisingly, the new design seems to have gone to the anti-establishment designer Gert Dunbar who is all set to kit out the user friendly police force in leather jackets and casual trousers.

Don't be fooled by the low profile and laid back approach of the Amsterdam Police (all armed). You may not encounter many on the streets, but cars cruise round the centre day and night. The number of women in the force, at present 18%, is increasing due to the provision of a crèche and 24-hour child care facility – the police were one of the first organisations in the Netherlands to make provisions for women. If you do have problems in Amsterdam you will almost always have access to female officers. The police force, and the many factions within it, in general have a good public image – the most irritating group are the rubbish police who post fines through your letter box if you deign to put your rubbish out on the wrong day or before the allocated time. Be warned: if you rent a flat in the city always check the day and times when garbage can be left on the street.

On the beat you are more likely to come across the Neighbourhood Watch, who wear casual French blue uniforms. They have nothing to do with the police force but are employed by the municipal council on surveillance duties. This 'guardian angel' force is made up of unemployed citizens who are given one year's paid work to get them back on the payroll. They have no authoritarian power but are a great help to lost tourists and alerting the police to any problems.

Safety

Amsterdam is one of the safest places in Europe. You are very unlikely to come to any harm in the city if you take reasonable care of yourself. Many women feel very uneasy walking alone at night and the dark alleys of the Red Light District can be intimidating but are not usually unsafe. The most common harm to tourists is by self-inflicted drug overdose. Laws regarding drinking and driving, under age drinking and wearing seatbelts in cars are frequently overlooked by the police but they do exist. A blind eye is turned to possession of small amounts of drugs but the police are cracking down heavily on hard drugs (see below).

Opportunist crime in the city is something of a problem; theft from cars, pickpocketing and stealing bicycles are rife. Cars with foreign plates are likely to be broken into anywhere in the city, even if there is nothing inside to take. Lots of people plaster notices to their windows declaring that there is nothing inside and this does seem to deter thieves from smashing the glass. Pickpocketing is common in crowded streets, trams, queues and in the galleries. Bag and purse snatching is frequently reported and often involves a violent struggle. It usually happens when someone, waiting in a queue to pay, in a shop or tram, opens their bag to sort out their money and a thief – usually a junkie – appears from nowhere and takes off with the lot. Junkies have no fears; we witnessed an elderly American woman being dragged across a road because she didn't let go of her bag (the man involved was in fact quickly pinned to the ground by passers by). Some advice: don't carry money or a purse in your back pocket, carry a bag (if you have to) across your chest and keep your hand on it, wear a bum bag (fanny pouch) and don't flash credit cards or money until you actually need to pay for it. In pavement cafés keep hold of your bag or slip the strap under the chair leg.

A number of highly convincing con men (mainly English speaking and often British junkies) work the streets and cafés in Amsterdam. If anyone asks you for money accompanied by a tragic and well researched story of no money, no home – 'I only came here for a holiday' – don't believe them. If you are concerned for their safety direct them to the police station, but don't give them any money – the chances are you will see them doing the same to another tourist an hour later. They tend to hang around the station, opera house and the main museums. Con men are easily distinguishable from beggars and buskers because they only accept quantities upwards of f10, whereas the others are happy with a few coins.

EMERGENCY
For Police, Ambulance and Fire call 0611

Police Stations
Main Police Headquarters
Elandsgracht 117, tel. 559 9111
Kloveniersburgwal 26, nr Nieuwmarkt, tel. 559 3260
Linbaansgracht 219, nr Leidseplein, tel. 559 23 10
N.Z. Voorburgwal 118, tel. 623 93 14
Warmoestraat 44–50, Red Light District, tel. 559 22 10

Reporting Stolen Property and Street Crime
Report thefts to the nearest police station. If you are left with no money, passport or credit cards go to the Tourist Assistance Service ATAS where staff are efficient and sympathetic. They will not give you money, but will help you to cope with the problem. Your Consulate will help you if you have serious troubles, but try ATAS first. ATAS, N.Z. Voorburgwal 118 (in police station), tel. 559 4251

Lost Credit Cards
American Express, tel. 624 4488
Diner's Club, tel. 627 9310
Mastercard, tel. 010 457 0887
Visa, tel. 520 5534

Sexual Crime
If you wish to report it go to the nearest police station who will refer you to the Department for Sexual Abuse, Elandsgracht 117, tel. 559 9111.
Helpline
Telefonische Opvang Seksueel Geweld, tel. 612 7576. Open daily 10.30 a.m.–11.30 p.m. English-speaking staff give information and advice on sexual abuse and can refer you to the relevant clinics.

PRACTICALITIES

The liberal attitude to drugs in the Netherlands is considered to be enlightened by some, inconceivably stupid by others and highly confusing to foreigners who wish to indulge but abide by the law. In theory drugs are illegal, but the authorities tolerate possession up to 30g soft drugs and up to ½g hard drugs for personal consumption. Trafficking is not allowed, but the police admit someone has to supply the drugs in the first place and so they tolerate the existence of **smoking coffeeshops** for the sale and use of soft drugs.

This tolerance means that you will certainly witness drug taking in Amsterdam and probably be offered dope on the streets. There is no need to find this intimidating as no one will pursue the issue if you don't want to be involved.

The smoking coffeeshops (see p.254) are the best place to buy soft drugs as they have a reputation to maintain. Ask over the bar and they will show you a menu of what is available, usually sold in 25f lots. Soft drugs means cannabis (also known as pot, grass, hash, dope, puff, weed, marijuana and shit). It comes as grass, resin or oil and varies according to its country of origin. Coffeeshop owners will be pleased to explain the differences. Common reactions to smoking or eating it include hilarity, euphoria, talkativeness, relaxed inhibitions and increased appetite (the munchies). Too much can make you behave irrationally, but is more likely to send you to sleep and give you a hangover. The fairly harmless looking space cakes sold from the cookie tin on most coffeeshop counters are often more powerful than they look – about eighty tourists a year end up in hospital having overdosed on space cake. Remember, it takes longer for the dope to have an effect if you eat it, rather than smoke it. If there is no sign to say what is in them it is advisable to ask the assistant before you indulge. Misuse by tourists is not good news for drug users or outlets so many shops are withdrawing space cake altogether.

Heroin and cocaine are the most common hard drugs sold in Amsterdam and though you may find it disturbing to see people injecting and 'chasing the dragon' in public they pose no real threat. It is addicts without drugs who can become aggressive and irrational. Despite avid attempts by the police to clean up the city the main area for hard drug users is the Red Light District, particularly along the street Zeedijk.

Both heroin and cocaine are addictive and potentially fatal drugs if overdosed. Heroin (also known as smack, scag, junk, H, horse, harry, elephant, tiger 765 and stuff) causes euphoria, drowsiness, slow breathing, nausea and is easily recognisable in someone by constricted pupils. Cocaine (also known as coke, snow, nose candy and, in its powerful and more addictive form, crack) causes excitement, euphoria, alertness, racing pulse, insomnia and loss of appetite, recognisable outwardly through dilated pupils and dry lips.

Never share needles. 30% of drug users in the city carry the AIDS virus (see p.34). If you need needles contact the drug abuse helpline on 570 2335 and they will direct you to the nearest needle exchange. Should you be arrested by the police or be with someone who overdoses, always tell the police if you/they are drug users. The victim will be treated confidentially by a doctor at the police station. This can save lives.

Warning: It is best to confine dope smoking to smoking coffeeshops. If you are unsure ask the management. Many hotels state 'no drugs' – this is not necessarily because they disapprove but more likely to be because dope smoke sets off fire alarms. It is not advisable to buy or use cannabis outside the city and remember to remove all traces of drugs before leaving the Netherlands.

DRUG RELATED PROBLEMS

The **Drug Advice Service**, Keizersgracht 812, tel. 623 78 65 for help and advice, Mon–Fri 1–3 p.m.

Drug abuse helpline, tel. 570 2335

Drugs Vrouwen Crisis Centrum, Stadhouderskade 125, tel. 6750741. Help centre for women addicts in crisis.

Sexual Crime

Around 200 cases of rape are reported in Amsterdam each year and the attacker is usually known to the victim. Around 180 people report cases of sexual harassment. Tourists are rarely involved in either.

Victims are advised to report sexual crime at the local police station who will contact the department for sexual abuse at the main Police Headquarters on Elandsgracht 117 (see p.27). Ask for a female officer if you prefer. The staff will see you through the paperwork, medical tests and put you in touch with counselling services in the city. Women have found the treatment of officers in the local police stations unsympathetic at times, but they speak very highly of the staff at the department for sexual abuse. If you do not wish to report it to the Police or just want help call *Telefonische Opvang Seksueel Geweld*, tel. 612 7576. Open daily 10.30 a.m. –11.30 p.m. English-speaking staff give information and advice on sexual abuse and can refer you to the relevant clinics.

PRACTICALITIES

Sexual harassment in Amsterdam is pretty lukewarm. Men are attentive but not persistent and are usually more interested in selling you something than asking you out. A large proportion of the male population is gay so they are not interested anyway. Male attitudes to women can be flippant and disrespectful. It is up to the individual to interpret it for themselves.

Most harassment comes from people wanting money or trying to sell you something, whether it be dope or a room for the night. The 'hotel' men around the station are notorious for their aggressive and abusive sales techniques. They home in on women with backpacks leaving the station and heading for the tourist office. Whether you have somewhere to stay or not they will tell you that everywhere is full, expensive, dangerous and dirty. It is best to tell them to 'Rot op', meaning get lost. Around Centraal Station, Damrak and the Red Light District you are likely to be greeted with 'hello', 'hi, English?' by men who generally are more interested in selling you dope than picking you up.

It is perfectly normal for women to sit alone in bars and restaurants where you can expect little unwanted attention from fellow customers and waiters alike, unless you choose to dress provocatively and sit in the prime pick-up areas, like Rembrandtsplein, Leidseplein and Spui where you will be joined by cruising males in a matter of minutes.

You may be surprised on your first visit to a *proflokaal* (drinking house) when the barman fills the glass of genever to the brim and tells you to bend over with a glint in his eye. While they obviously enjoy the charade it is perfectly normal practise for all clients to take one sip before picking the glass up and it is not merely an excuse to peer down your cleavage. Customers who disobey and spill it all over the bar can expect a gruff response so it is best to play the game.

Curb crawlers are so spoilt for choice in Amsterdam that it is not unusual to find cars stopping if you walk on your own along the main highways running across the top of the city or particularly behind the station. Don't be offended; a quick 'no' will move them on – there is nothing like being turned down!

Dress   At the turn of the century an enterprising Amsterdammer, Margaretha Meyboon (1857–1927) founded a co-operative making casual, comfortable reform clothes. De Werker (the alarm clock) as it was known, produced dresses, shirts and skirts that did not require tight corsets underneath, liberating both women's bodies and Dutch fashion.

The Dutch are still into the comfortable casual look – even bank clerks wear T shirts and jeans to work. Foreign business-women often feel overdressed in Amsterdam and tourists can get away with anything. If you want to impress the locals, jeans, jackets and boots are very important. That said, if you intend to go club-bing you may be as outrageous as you like – leather is popular, body suits are cool and the more flesh you reveal the better.

During winter months it can be both cold and wet so take a thick jumper, a waterproof coat, good shoes and an umbrella. Fur coats are not recommended or seen in the city. In the summer shorts and a T shirt are the basic uniform. In the evenings some of the more up-market bars around P.C. Hooftstraat, Spui and Leidseplein fill with elegantly dressed, beautifully made-up women where fig-ures are as well cut as the clothes. What you wear depends on where you are going and how you are going to get there. Miniskirts attract a lot of looks and if you wear one to the Red Light District you can expect to be propositioned. Wear what you feel good in.

Danger Spots   Amsterdam is so safe that even the police have dif-ficulty pinpointing no go areas. The suburb of Bijlermeer and the residential area around Oosterpark in the East are not recom-mended for solo women, but you are unlikely to go to either unless you are visiting or staying with friends. You may feel uneasy wan-dering around the city at night, particularly in the Red Light District. Many women find their first solo trip through the area frightening, but as long as you avoid eye contact with anyone, know where you are going and walk purposefully you will come to no harm. You would be wise not to wander there alone after midnight.

It is always a good idea to have a map with you even if you think you know the way. The narrow streets in the centre are very confusing and they look different by night and day. However pur-poseful you look it is easy to seem vulnerable when lost. Maps come in very handy when you find yourself in a dark alley full of guys shooting up or a client fumbling with a prostitute. This may sound alarmist, but it does go on and it is no threat to you if you leave well alone and know the quickest way out.

Health and Sex

EC members are entitled to the same health care benefits as Dutch nationals provided they have an E111 available from the Department of Social Security and the Post Office. To apply, simply fill in the form at the Post Office (family members can be included on the same application) giving them your NI number. For non-EC nationals private insurance is a good idea in case you have to go to hospital, but there are a number of voluntary medical organisations working in Amsterdam who deal with your basic needs free of charge. (Many of these initially set up in the Red Light Area for the illegal immigrants who work as prostitutes.)

If you need urgent medical attention it is best to go to the casualty department at the nearest hospital (see list). For referral to a doctor or dentist or details of late night chemists ring the freephone 24 hour **Central Medical Service** (tel. 0606 350 32042). Another 24-hour medical referral service, the **Tourist Medical Service** (tel. 673 7567) is specifically geared to the needs of foreigners. If you have an E111 form always take it with you and it is a good idea to take a photocopy of it so that you can leave the form with the doctor. Most Dutch doctors speak English, but it is best to specify what you want with the medical referral services listed above. The cost of treatment and prescriptions will vary. There are a number of voluntary medical groups working in Amsterdam who can offer free consultation and treatment to people without medical insurance. Most are run by Christian associations who originally set up to help prostitutes, but they seem to serve the needs of both locals and tourists alike. The Tourist Medical Service (as above) has a number of volunteer doctors on its books and a free service at its daily clinics. **De Witte Jas** (tel. 624 9031) is an excellent voluntary organisation offering basic health care to people without insurance and for anyone wanting alternative health care or health information; the staff includes homeopaths, physiotherapists, acupuncturists and practitioners of natural medicine.

Chemists (*drogisteri*) sell toiletries, vitamins, non-prescription drugs (pain killers, cold remedies etc.) as well as tampons and condoms. For prescription drugs you have to go to a pharmacy (*apotheek*). Staff in both are usually helpful and prescription costs vary according to the drug prescribed.

Tampons, Tampax, sanitary towels and nappies are all available in chemists and supermarkets. They are generally cheaper in supermarkets. Tampon and sanitary towel dispensers can be found in the ladies loos in the main galleries and museums and the occasional restaurant.

Euthanasia

Contrary to popular opinion euthanasia is not yet legal in the Netherlands, but in reality it is tolerated providing the doctor in charge of your case follows a series of guidelines recommended by the government. The case is then reported to the Coroner who refers it to the public prosecutor. The prosecutor decides whether to drop the case or prosecute.

At the time of writing doctors in the Netherlands are faced with about 9000 requests a year for the termination of a patient's life, of which in 1992 around 2,300 cases of euthanasia were granted and

400 cases of assisted suicide. Out of an annual death toll of 130,000 the number is significantly small and it also shows that doctors more often than not refuse to comply with the patient's wishes. Unbearable suffering or the patient's natural desire to die peacefully and with dignity are the only reasons doctors consider when deciding to carry out euthanasia.

In February 1993, the Lower House of Parliament decided to include the procedure for reporting euthanasia in the law relating to the disposal of the dead. This would allow the prosecutor to consider the reports and their compliance with the government's guidelines while applying the homicide laws in each case. Foreigners wishing to go to the Netherlands to die with the help of a doctor would be very unlikely to find a doctor willing to take on the case. For an update of the law contact the **Netherlands Ministry of Justice**, Information Department, PO Box 20301, NL 2500 EH, The Hague (tel. 70 370 6850).

Contraception and Sexually Transmitted Diseases

The world's first birth control clinic opened in Amsterdam in 1882, long before many Europeans even knew about safe sex. The candid attitude to sex in the Netherlands has paid off over the AIDS crisis with teenagers and adults alike being conscientious condom wearers. Prostitutes will rarely work without one and even some of the gay clubs now insist that condoms are sold and used in the dark rooms.

Condoms are available in most chemists and are usually on display. Femidoms haven't taken off yet in the city but you will find them at the NVSH shop, Blauwburgwal 9. For a range of exotic and erotic condoms try the **Condomerie** on Warmoestraat (not a raunchy sex shop). If you are on the Pill remember to take a good supply with you. If you need a repeat prescription fix an appointment at the **Aletta Jacobshuis**, Overtoom 323 (nr Vondelpark), tel. 616 6222. Consultation costs f30. They also provide Morning after Pill for the consultation fee plus f17.50, fit IUD for f120 and Diaphrams for f90, and arrange smear tests for f65.

The most common STD in the city is chlamydia, which like gonorrhoea can lead to infertility if left untreated. Genital warts and herpes are common and irritating because they can recur. Syphilis and Hepatitis B are serious but less common. The Dutch are not keen on using Dental Dams for oral sex and they are not easy to find. They are only available from the NVSH shop or COC, the national gay organisation at Rozenstraat 14. If you think you may have contracted an STD go to the **VD Clinic**, Groenburgwal 44 (tel 625 4127) for free consultation and treatment of STD and sex related problems. The morning clinics tend to be a free-for-all so expect to wait. (It is better to arrange an appointment.) Women are usually seen by women unless they are very busy, but ask to make sure. Staff and clients maintain a kind of club atmosphere which is quite entertaining given what you have in common.

AIDS

You should *always* use a condom and *never* share needles in Amsterdam. Around half of the reported cases of AIDS in the Netherlands are people living in Amsterdam but the Dutch aversion to mass screening, because it alienates minority groups and is an invasion of privacy, means few statistics are available on the number of people with the HIV virus who have not yet developed AIDS.

'In the Netherlands, it is no longer acceptable to speak of *high risk groups*. Nowadays you can only refer to *high risk acts*' (Roel Coutinho speaking for the Amsterdam Public Health Department). Amsterdam's AIDS policy is very much one of educating the public, setting up help schemes and counselling services and making the people understand that it is up to them to adapt their own behaviour to avoid contracting the virus. Like AIDS itself, HIV infection is prevalent among gay men and to a lesser degree among intravenous drug users. At present only a tiny number of heterosexuals who have never had drugs intravenously or sexual contact with homosexuals are HIV positive. Safe sex campaigns continually alert people to the problem and a highly successful needle exchange system whereby addicts swap old needles for new hands out over a million needles each year. That said, around 30% of the intravenous drug users in Amsterdam carry the virus. Prostitutes who are not addicts rarely carry the virus but there are many drug-addicted prostitutes in the city who do have AIDS.

Women, as far as they know, have been little affected by the virus in Amsterdam but, as is the case with heterosexual men, few have actually been tested so we don't really know. Be safe; if you have sex with a new partner in Amsterdam always use a condom and don't take their word for it if they say they haven't got the virus – they may well not know.

The Dutch desire for patients to remain anonymous to respect their privacy has certainly averted the direct discrimination experienced in other countries. Systematic testing of employees, prisoners and people wanting life insurance was not thought feasible in Holland for some time. However, since 1988, anyone wishing to take out life insurance over f200,000 or a private disability policy for more than f40,000 will be asked to take an AIDS test first. HIV-positive individuals are refused a policy or have to pay a higher premium. Employers have been allowed to request a test since 1990 only if it is needed to assess suitability for a specific job.

Pregnancy

If you think you may be pregnant the quickest way to find out is to buy a self-predictor kit from the chemist or pharmacy. They sell all the recognisable brands like *Clear Blue* and *Predictor* which give you results in a matter of minutes. Just check when you buy it that there are instructions in English or you might end up with a choice between Japanese and Dutch and at f30 a time you don't want to make mistakes. If you are likely to be in the Netherlands for the duration of your pregnancy contact your doctor who will put you in the care of a midwife, '*Vroed Vrouw*', who will arrange prenatal tests and check-ups for you and advise you on amniocentiesis (*punctie*) and scans (*echoscopie*). Home birth is popular in Holland and you will only be referred to a hospital if complications are feared or you specifically want it.

If you need an abortion contact the **Stimezo Clinic MR70** (tel. 624 54 26).

Abortion

The Netherlands has the lowest abortion figures in the world, which is largely attributed to the pragmatic attitude of most Dutch people towards contraception. Unlike most other countries, the liberalisation of abortion policies preceded any change in the law. Abortion was declared a capital offence in 1886 and in 1911 the jurisdiction was extended to make it an ethical offence as well. Contraception was widely used in the Netherlands by the 1920s, but abortion didn't really hit the headlines until the 60s. The Dutch Organisation for Sexual Reform (NVSH) encouraged women to go to Britain for abortions until the abortion law at home could be changed. For the women's liberation groups of the 1960s and 70s abortion was a major issue. The women's group, Dolle Mina (see p.105), had a slogan 'Boss of our own bellies' which became a household word in Amsterdam. The establishment of STIMEZO (The Foundation for Medically Responsible Abortion Care) in 1969 was one of the most significant moves for abortion rights in the Netherlands. Their aim to open a non profit making, public, abortion clinic openly challenged the law. Within a month they had over 3000 supporters – their position was so strong that the authorities made no attempt to close the first clinic which opened in 1970. Abortion was finally legalised in 1981 and the private Stimezo clinics carry out 70% of the abortions done in the country today; only 10% are done in hospital, the rest in private clinics.

By law abortion in the Netherlands may only be carried out in a licensed clinic. Applicants must wait five days between seeing a doctor and termination and hospitals and clinics are obliged to register all cases anonymously. Foreign women may have abortions in the Netherlands; around 30,000 abortions are carried out each year, of which only about 18,000 are for Dutch women. Foreign women are not, however, entitled to free abortions – they cost around f500. Clinics performing abortions in the second trimester must conform to a number of extra conditions.

USEFUL ADDRESSES

Hospitals with outpatients departments open 24 hours a day:
Academisch Medisch Centrum, Meibergdreef, OE, tel. 556 9111; Boven Ij Ziekenhuis, Staten Jachtstraat 1, OE, tel. 634 6343; Vu Ziekenhuis, e Boelaan 1117, OE, tel. 548 9111; Lucas Ziekenhuis, Jan Tooropstraat 164, OW, tel. 510 8911; Onze Lieve Vrouwe Gasthuis 1E Oosterparkstraat 179, tel. 599 9111.

24-Hour Medical Referral Services, offering advice on doctors, dentists and late night chemists.
Central Medical Service, tel. 0606 350 32042
Tourist Medical Service, tel. 673 7567

Free Surgeries run by voluntary Christian organisations:
Kruispost (GP) O.Z. Voorburgwal 129, tel. 624 90 31. Open Mon–Fri 10 a.m.–12.30 p.m.
Kruispost (Emergency), O.Z. Achterburgwal 100, tel. 622 4159. Open daily 24 hours.
De Witte Jas, De Wittenstraat 29, tel. 688 1140. Open Mon noon–5 p.m. & 7 p.m.– 9 p.m., Tues & Thurs noon–5 p.m.

Help with Health
Stichting Vrouwen 40–60, Nicolaas Witsenkade 27, OS, tel. 626 8080. Open Mon–Fri 10 a.m.–5 p.m. for women in crisis aged 40–60.

Women's Healthcentre, Obiplein 4, OE, tel. 693 4358. Open Tues 9 a.m.–noon, Thurs 7 p.m.–10 p.m., Fri 1 p.m.–4 p.m. Offers advice on health and referral to doctors, clinics etc, but a tramride from the centre (catch nos 3, 6 or 14).

RIAGG, Sarphatipark 63, tel. 671 0468. Open Mon–Fri 9 a.m.–5 p.m. Help for people living in Amsterdam with psychological problems. Deals with people of all ages, domestic violence, child/parent problems, AIDS counselling. Other offices in different areas of the city.

Family Planning
Aletta Jacobshuis, Overtoom 323, tel. 616 6222. Open by appointment Mon–Fri 9 a.m.–4 p.m. 7.15 p.m.–9 p.m. Consultation fee.

Family Planning and Abortion
MR70 Saphatistraat 620–626, tel. 624 5426. Mon–Thurs 9 a.m.–4 p.m, Fri 9 a.m.–1 p.m. Fee charged; appointment needed.

STD Clinics and helplines
AIDS Helpline, tel. 06 022 2220. Open Mon–Fri 2–10 p.m.

VD Clinic, Groenburgwal 44, tel. 625 4127. Open Mon–Fri 8.30 a.m.–5 p.m. Also offers free AIDS tests.

Schorer Stichting, P.C. Hooftstraat 5, tel. 662 4206 AIDS information and counselling for gays and lesbians.

HIV Vereniging, P.C. Hooftstraat 5, tel. 664 4076. AIDS information and introductory service for women with AIDS.

Riagg, Women's helpline for AIDS related problems, psychological problems and other trauma, tel. 644 6911.

Sexual Counselling
NVSH, Blauwburgwal 9, tel. 623 9359. Runs regular sessions to help people with sexual fetishes and sexual education programmes for schools. Also has a shop for sex aids, condoms, femidoms and dental dams.

Dentists *(tandarts)*
Phone the *Central Medical Service* for names of dentists or try: *AOC*, Wilhelmina Gasthuiplein 167, OW, tel. 616 1234. Open Mon–Fri 8 a.m.–midnight, Sat 8 a.m.– 9 p.m., Sun 1–5 p.m. Minimum cost f50, but unlikely to exceed f100.

Opticians *(Opticien)*
EYES, Weteringshans 165, tel. 620 6911
York International Optical, Leidsestraat 32, tel. 618 2102

Pharmacies *(apotheek)*
Usually open week days 9.30 a.m.–5.30 p.m. Call the Central Medical Service for information on late night opening. A list of apotheeks open late is also published in *Het Parool* (see p.18).

Dam Apotheek, Damstraat 2, tel. 624 43 31

USEFUL VOCABULARY;

Headache	Hoofdpijn
Stomach ache	Maagpijn
Period/menstruation	Menstruation
Throat	Keelpijn
Hot flush	Opcliegers
Menopause	Meno-pauza
Temperature	Koorts
Pain	Pijn
Cystitis	Blaasonstekyng
Thrush	Schimmel
I think I am pregnant	Lle deuk dat in zwanger ben
Pregnancy	Zwangerschap
Labour	Weeen
Breastfeeding	Borstvoeding
Sanitary towels	Maand Verband (monthly bandage)
Tampons	Tampons
Nappies	Luiers
Incontinency pads	Incontinentie Verband
Abortion	Abortus
Condom	Condoom
The Pill	Pil
Morning after Pill	(use English)
Laxative	Laxeemiddel
Children's Aspirin/Calpol	Sinaspril and Kinderfinimal are both good

In terms of integration into the labour force, state support for child care and the general professional acceptance of women, the Netherlands is among the most backward countries in Western Europe, on a par with Ireland and Luxembourg. Paradoxically, the country boasts a feminist movement that is well integrated, politically active and intellectually alive; it has a long history of government support. Amsterdam's women have been largely responsible for this and the abundance of women's groups, archives, cafés and shops you are likely to find in the city overshadows the somewhat depressing reality elsewhere in the country. National awareness of women in history has been greatly improved by the recent introduction of Women's History in the national curriculum in schools.

Dutch feminism falls into two distinct movements: the political fight for equal rights and suffrage at the end of the nineteenth century and the more radical social movements of the 1960s and 70s. The fight for equal rights gained momentum in the 1860s, encouraged by improved education for women. Growing support led to the formation of the Association for Women's Suffrage (*De Vereniging voor Vrouwenkiesrecht*) in 1894. Inspired by pioneering women like the doctor Aletta Jacobs (see p.149) and pacifist Wilhelmina Drucker (see p.105) women fought for the freedom to work, better health care and the right to vote. Interestingly, industrialisation did not result in a sharp rise in female labour. Instead it produced two groups of women; middle-class wives struggling for the right to work and working-class wives struggling to be at home to look after the kids. When Dr Jacobs opened the world's first birth control clinic in Amsterdam in 1882 she substantially improved women's health and the quality of their lives in the city. The fight for suffrage was a long one, the vote eventually being granted in 1919. Fortunately the struggles, perseverance and achievements of the first wave of feminism in the Netherlands are well documented in the IIAV (International Information Centre and Archives for the Women's Movement). The IIAV was founded in 1935 in Amsterdam by the feminists Johanna Naber, Rosa Manus (see p.99) and Willemijn Posthumus-van der Goot. The archive miraculously survived the Second World War and has been an invaluable source of information for feminists ever since.

Open discussions on sexuality, love and marriage in the 60s, opened the debate on the social position of women and encouraged the subsequent foundation of women's groups and lesbian associations who represented the second feminist movement. Social Democrat Jok Kool Smit wrote an article entitled 'The Discontent Among Women' which resulted in the foundation of MVM (*Man

Vrouw-Maatschappij), meaning Man-Woman-Society, which aimed at breaking down sexual stereotypes. (Another of the founders, Hedy d'Ancona, became Minister of Public Welfare, Health and Culture in 1989.) Other groups to emerge included the Work Group 2000 and the left-wing Dolle Mina or Mad Mina (see p.105), named after Wilhelmina Drucker (see p.105). Mainly represented by students, the Dolle Mina became internationally renowned for their promotion of abortion. In 1969 they stormed a Gynaecologists' Congress with '*Baas in eigen Buik*' (Boss of Our Own Bellies) written across their tummies – the first of many outrageous attempts to change the government's abortion policies. On a more local level they protested against the lack of public loos for women in Amsterdam by tying up the urinals with pink ribbons, waving banners proclaiming that 'women had the right to pee', and baring their bums to pee into the canals, watched by the forewarned international media.

The government eventually responded with women's health centres, rape crisis centres, therapy groups and abortion on the national health. Divorce laws changed, allowing consenting partners to split after one year; they established a committee on the status of women and funded the *Nederlandse Vrouwen Raad* (The Netherlands Council of Women) which today has over one million members. The government also tackled controversial issues like prostitution and, most importantly, funded feminist studies in universities and schools. Meanwhile feminism itself became less active, but more visible in the setting up of feminist cafés, shops and educational projects.

The Netherlands is sometimes seen as a feminist country with few feminists. Scholars struggle to understand why women fail to take advantage of the favourable feminist environment. Women make up around 35% of the work force which is among the lowest in Western Europe. Certainly most women do work before marriage, but they tend to leave after having children. Husbands usually prefer their wives not to work, and the social welfare system pays single women, whether unmarried, divorced or widowed, to bring up their children.

Today more women go on to further education and it is hoped that this will be reflected in the work force. Feminist issues have gone far beyond equal rights; equal pay has been achieved in most areas and women's participation in politics ranks among the highest in Western Europe. Yet Dutch women fail to represent such egalitarian attitudes fully, partly because statistics obviously do not take into account the difference between urban and rural areas. Don't expect to see the streets of Amsterdam full of Dutch housewives wearing traditional costume, tending to the two kids and rushing home to feed the husband. Most women in Amsterdam are surprised by the statistical assessment of their situation. Some will even tell you they don't know of anyone who does not work and you only have to look around you to notice women working in high and low positions throughout the city. Many women with children take part-time work which is not included in the statistics.

WOMEN'S ORGANISATIONS IN AMSTERDAM

IIAV (Women's Archive)
Obiplein 4, 109 4 RB, Amsterdam, tel. 624 4268 (due to change.)
The International Archives of Women's and Lesbian Movement holds extensive collections of books, photographs, periodicals and cuttings. Mainly in Dutch but the staff are helpful and will provide material in English where possible.

Het Vrouwenhuis (The Women's House)
Nieuwe Herengracht 95, IE, tel. 625 2066 (nr the Botanical Garden). Open Mon–Fri; info 11 a.m.–4 p.m.; bar 7–midnight after classes. Closed July and August.
There are a number of Women's Houses throughout the Netherlands, organising events like International Woman's Day on March 8, festivities, exhibitions, workshops, courses and support groups for women. The café is a good place to meet people. It is not specifically a lesbian organisation and welcomes all women. A number of women's organisations run from the same building including:

STAV tel. 620 2066. Help group for women unable to work.
ZAMI, tel. 639 3138. Assistance for Black Migrant Women.
Vrouwen en de Bijstand, tel. 624 6666. Women needing advice on Social Security.

Amazone
Singel, 72, tel. 627 9000.
Cultural organisation for courses and exhibitions concerning women (about to relocate).

SVBK (Society for women artists)
Entrepodok 66, tel. 626 6589.
Organisation for women artists with a library and archive.

STEW
Weesperzijde 4, OE, tel. 665 5016. Open Mon–Thurs 1 p.m.–5 p.m.
Information on businesses run by women in the Netherlands.

Women's International Network
PO Box 15692, 1001 ND, Amsterdam, tel. 679 9951. Membership f150 is open to professional women, over 25 and employed for over 5 years. English spoken at meetings, lectures and outings.
A good idea for women wishing to make contact with other businesswomen.

Rechthulp for Vrouwen
Willemstraat 24 b, tel. 624 03 23. Open Mon 1.30 p.m.–4.30 p.m. Tues–Fri 9.30–12.30 & 1.30–4.30.
Legal aid for women.

Vrouwen Bellen Vrouwen (Women Call Women)
Tel. 625 0105. Open Tues & Thurs 9.30 a.m.–12.30 p.m. 7.30 p.m.–10.30 p.m.

> *Wed 7.30–10.30 p.m. and Fri 9 a.m.–noon.*
> Helpline for women wanting advice and support.
>
> **Zwarte Vrouwentelefoon (Black women's helpline)**
> *tel. 085 42 4713.*

Lesbian and Gay Amsterdam

Often referred to as the gay capital of Europe, Amsterdam has few exclusively lesbian haunts while the network of male clubs, hotels, bars and shops is unsurpassed anywhere in Europe. Some gay clubs have a women's night once a week and the women's cafés are popular lesbian haunts. The arrival of the exotic erotic **Clit Club** for women was something of a breakthrough, but customers were saddened by a change of policy (since abandoned) to allow men in after 1 a.m. to swell the numbers. That said, there is lots going on for the lesbian community if you can find out what is on and where it is happening; the venues and times seem to change from month to month. Your best bet is to ring the **Gay and Lesbian Switchboard** (tel. 623 6565) for the latest reliable information. One thing is certain: lesbians can happily live in Amsterdam without having to hide their sexual identity; couples can hug, hold hands and kiss in public without causing any raised eyebrows and if you wish you can even have your relationship formally registered at the Town Hall. The city is an Associate Member of the ILGA (International Lesbian and Gay Association) and the current city council supports the full emancipation of gay people.

Gay Amsterdam; a brief history

Gay and lesbian Amsterdammers haven't always had it easy. A wave of Dutch sodomy trials in the Calvinist eighteenth century caught the attention of journalists in Britain and America. Gay men had to live in a clandestine world of meeting places, code signs and nicknames. In Amsterdam they developed a series of pet names for one another like 'Janey with the shiny arse', 'English trotter' and 'Oh so Jolly Jenny'. Out of the 46 Amsterdam men arrested in the first wave of persecutions in 1730, five were executed by garrotte (a method usually only used for women) in their main cruising area, Dam Square. The death penalty was not used in the city for sodomy after 1765 – they were usually imprisoned or exiled.

Women were also prosecuted but mainly for transvestism – it was some time before anyone made a link between female relationships and sex. Female transvestites were tried in Amsterdam throughout the seventeenth and eighteenth centuries. Many women took to cross dressing to work as sailors and soldiers (see p.205), sometimes to secure better jobs. The Amsterdam teenager, Martigen Jans, left her job in a silk throwing mill to become a sailor; as David Jans she later returned to her old job and was given a higher salary and immediate promotion. Other women dressed as men in order to live with other women. Maria van Antwerpen was tried in 1769 for transvestism and for unlawfully marrying her lover – about twenty years later she was tried again for transvestism and 'seducing and debauching a young girl'. Perhaps the best known Amsterdam transvestite was Claartje who worked as a stable boy and coach-man. Her biography, published after her death in 1743, was very popular and tells of a happy ending, alive and married to a rich gent. Only in the 1790s were women arrested for 'dirty caresses of one another'. Thus was lesbian love formally recognised. Most con-victed transvestites and lesbians (Jolly Judys and Merry Marys) were sentenced to a short stay in a correction house. Elizabeth Wiebes was the only lesbian to be executed, sentenced for killing her girlfriend's lover in 1792.

People convicted for sodomy and tribadism (used to describe sex between women from the Greek *Tribein* meaning to rub) were almost always from poor families. More wealthy educated gays and lesbians could usually afford bribes and lawyers to prevent the case ever coming to court. The new breed of 'educated ladies' to emerge in the eighteenth century frequently lived together, but were seldom suspected of anything untoward. Their writings are among the first to express lesbian love. Maria Bavinck wrote to her friend the writer Aagje Deken: 'You first showed me how to love; inspired by passion just as strong I yield myself to you – my soul and all my senses.' Aagje Deken, with her friend Elisabeth Wolff, wrote *Sara Burgerhart*, perhaps the Netherlands' first novel, as an exchange of letters in which love, passion and morality between women are all explored.

Attitudes loosened up in the nineteenth century, when the 1811 Penal Code restricted punishable offences to the seduction of minors and violation of public decency, but even so public morality was strictly controlled. The designers of Amsterdam's urinals were instructed to consider public morality – hence the S shaped urinals in the city – though the lack of space and open base at knee level still failed to deter gay courtings. Police were instructed to make thorough checks of parks and loos every day, but it wasn't until 1894 that two women were discovered making love in the park, the evidence in this case being the first concerning women since the introduction of the Penal Code.

The increased emancipation of women at the end of the nine-teenth century greatly improved the lesbian's lot. Amsterdam had a number of women-only clubs and societies, such as rambling associations, fencing clubs, reading circles, wrestling clubs and cycling schools. At the same time gay men and women welcomed the ideas of a 'third sex' being considered by doctors and psychiatrists under the influence of the Berlin sexologist Magnus Hirschfeld. Unfortunately biological explanations also implied the possibility of a cure and many people volunteered themselves for labotomy, castration or implantation of sex glands in an attempt to change their behaviour. However, Hirschfeld's explanation also gave homosexuals a case for recognition as 'natural' and homosexuality at last became an issue for open debate.

It did not work to their advantage. The twentieth century has seen a long struggle for gay people in the Netherlands, beginning with the infamous article 248b in which the age of consent for sex between two partners was raised from 16 to 21. The level of arrests for unlawful relationships among gays rose steadily and gay people once again had to meet privately. Women were advised not to hold hands or show even normal levels of friendship in public. Hopes of reconciliation were dashed by the Nazi persecution of homosexuals, but their courage and resistance during the Second World War brought homosexuals increased public support and respect, though it was short-lived. Life as a lesbian was lonely; it is not surprising that almost all the lesbian literature to come out of Holland in the first half of the twentieth century is concerned with sadness and isolation. In the same vein as Radclyffe Hall's *Well of Loneliness* Marie Louise Doudart de la Gree published *Woe to the Solitary* and Anna Blaman (pseudonym of Johanna Vrugt) brought out *Lonely Adventure*.

The beginnings of gay emancipation came with the foundation of the Shakespeare Club 1946, rechristened **COC** in 1949, a social club where gays were allowed to meet under the watchful eye of the vice squad. Women's involvement in the club remained minimal until the 1960s when Holland became a Mecca for liberated people from around the world. Gays and lesbians flocked to Amsterdam to be part of a sexual revolution where anything went. Homosexuality was discussed openly in the media and the arts worked together to get rid of the taboo of love between the same sex. The explicit descriptions of lesbian love and sex in *The Horrors of the North* by Andreas Burnier (pseudonym of Catharina Dessaur) provoked a series of debates among academics, the clergy and politicians about gay and lesbian love.

In 1971, the founders of COC were rewarded with the repeal of Article 248b and COC was formally and legally recognised by the authorities two years later. Today gay life in Amsterdam has never looked better and some of the wealthiest citizens own gay clubs and bars in the city.

Women and the COC have not always seen eye to eye; in the 60s a group of lesbian feminists formed a splinter group called

Purple September, protesting against male domination of COC and their tolerance of heterolesbians. For a while their slogan 'Lovely Lesbians' was splattered around the city's walls and monuments. Meanwhile another group, the **Lesbian Nation**, promoted a militant and political approach to the cause. Eventually lesbians opened cafés, bookshops, businesses, and publishing houses together and the *Lesbisch Prachtboek* (*What Lesbians Love*), published in 1978, became the national lesbian handbook.

Helped by support from the town mayor and the city council, Amsterdam's gay community is thriving; the number of gay residents increases each year. Meanwhile lesbians continue to strive for their own clubs and venues in the city, though at present they have to make do sharing with the boys.

USEFUL ADDRESSES

Gay and Lesbian Switchboard
tel. 623 6565

COC

Rozenstraat 14, IW, tel. 623 1192. Open Daily 10 a.m.–10 p.m.
Information, café and women's disco, Sat 10 p.m.–3 a.m. Youth club atmosphere is great for newcomers to the city.

Schorer Stichting

P.C. Hooftstraat 5, tel. 662 4206. Open Mon–Fri 9 a.m.–5.30 p.m.
Gay and lesbian sexual counselling and AIDS information.

Sjalhomo

tel. 023 312318. Ring Evenings only.
Organises cultural and social activities for Jewish gays and lesbians.
The University of Amsterdam offers courses in gay and lesbian studies at *Oude Hoogstraat 24, tel. 525 2217.*

Lesbian Archives
Open Mon–Fri 1 p.m.–5 p.m. or by appointment for a.m. or Tuesday evenings. Readings, lectures and cultural activities on the first Sunday of the month 4 p.m.–6 p.m. *Eerste Helmerstraat 17, tel. 618 5879.*

Gay and Lesbian Archives

Homodok, O.Z. Achterburgwal 185, tel. 525 2601. Open Wed, Fri 2 p.m.–5 p.m. or by appointment.

Gay and Lesbian Bookshops

Vrolijk Boekhandel, Paleistraatt 135, tel. 623 5140. Open Mon 11 a.m.–6 p.m., Tues, Wed & Fri 10 a.m.–6 p.m., Thurs 10 a.m.–9 p.m., Sat 10 a.m.–5 p.m.

Working in the Netherlands

All EC nationals have the right to live and work in the Netherlands without a work permit. UK nationals are entitled to the same rights as Dutch nationals in terms of pay, working conditions, access to housing, training, social security and trade union membership. Families and immediate dependants may join you and enjoy similar rights.

If you are thinking of moving to the Netherlands from the UK, information and, occasionally, jobs are available from the **Employment Service Overseas Placing Unit** in the UK (tel. 0742 596191). There is not much work to be had, but use any contacts you can, read the Saturday listings in *De Telegraaf, het Algemeen Dagblad* and *De Volkskrant*, contact the local job centre, **Arbeidsbureau** (known as AB) and private employment agencies (*Uitzendbureaus*) like **Manpower, BBB, ASB** and **Randstad.** Consult the telephone directory for your nearest office.

Any UK national with a full passport can go to the Netherlands for three months to look for work. If you receive unemployment benefit in the UK you may be able to continue receiving it for up to three months while you look for work there. To stay on you will probably be asked to provide a contract from an employer.

Warning: living in the Netherlands is not cheap and accommodation is very difficult to find. Also moving to a different country means coping with a new culture, strange language and making new friends. Many foreigners find work difficult to secure because they are up against Dutch nationals who usually speak two or three languages.

USEFUL ADDRESSES

The Employment Service Overseas Placing Unit, c/o Rockingham House, 123 West Street, Sheffield, S1 4ER UK, tel. 1742 596191.

Centraal Bureau voor de Arbeidsvoorziening, Visseringlaan 26, Postbus 5814 2280 HV Rijswijk (2–H), tel. 070 3130911 for a list of regional employment offices.

Project Bureau 'Bolwerk', Dorpen 22, 1741 EE Schagen, tel. 02242 17057 for information on seasonal work.

Central Office of the Employment Service, Bureau IABS, PO Box 437, 2280 Rijkswijk, tel. 070 3130228. Take applications for short term (six weeks minimum) employment over the summer.

Department of Social Security, Overseas Branch, Newcastle upon Tyne, NE98 1YX, tel. 091 213 5000, will give you details on social security payments for migrant workers.

Studying in Amsterdam

Dutch schools are all state run and comprise of primary schools, secondary schools, special schools, institutes of higher education and institutes of international education with a few outlets for adult education such as Open School and Open University.

PRACTICALITIES

Amsterdam's 65,000 university students make up 8% of the city's population. The city has two universities, the University of Amsterdam (UVA) and the Free University (VU), established as a Christian University in 1878. It also has twenty HBO's Institutes for Higher Education which train people for specific professions such as teaching, social work, accounting and journalism. You will see UVA buildings all over the city, marked with bright red placards by the door. Women are well represented at the University making up just over 50% and a thriving Women's Studies Department has been boosted by the compulsory inclusion of Women's Studies into the national curriculum.

For people who want to study in Amsterdam the UVA offer international courses, taught in English, for undergraduates and postgraduates. Many foreign students take advantage of the Erasmus Project to encourage international exchange and the UVA Summer University courses are very popular for people wanting to take a short course. If you want to learn Dutch, a number of language schools offer courses that are not too expensive.

EDUCATION INFORMATION

UVA, University of Amsterdam, Administration, Maagdenhuis, Spui, C, tel. 525 9111.

UVA (Women's Studies), Institut Belle van Zuylen, O.Z. Achterburgwal 185, 1012 DK, tel. 525 2119.

ASVA (main Students Union), Spinhuissteeg 1, tel. 622 5771 for information and help. Also a very useful accommodation agency, tel, 623 8052. Open August Mon–Fri 10.30 a.m.–4.30 p.m., Sept–June 12.30–4.30 p.m.

VU, Vrije Universiteit, De Boelelaan 1105, OS, tel. 548 9222

Amsterdam Summer University, Felix Meritis Building, Keizersgracht 324, IW, tel. 620 1225.

Foreign Student Service, Oranje Nassaulaan 5, 1075 AH, tel. 671 5915 for information on studying in the NL and help once you are there.

Student Information Helpline, tel. 525 4307 (English spoken)

The following language schools run Dutch language courses: **British Language Training Centre**, Keizersgracht 389, 1016 RJ, tel. 622 3634 **VU Dept Applied Linguistics**, De Boelelaan 1105, Room 9A21, tel. 548 4968 *Volksuniversiteit Amsterdam*, Herenmarkt 93, 1013, tel. 626 1626.

Women with Disabilities

Since the Netherlands is one of the few countries to adopt raised insignia on their banknotes for the partially sighted, one would expect the national consciousness towards disabled people to be good. Unfortunately wheelchair users will find this is not so – new public buildings are still going up with no facilities for disabled people whatsoever.

People with mobility problems will find Amsterdam a nightmare with cobbled streets, steep stairs, narrow doorways, few facilities on public transport and a meagre range of hotels and restaurants to choose from. If you use a battery operated wheelchair you may even find some humped-backed bridges too steep to cross. One of the worst problems is the lack of public loos for wheelchair users which can make every day a case of careful planning.

Don't let this put you off, there are many ways of getting to the city and enjoying it provided you do your research before you go. Many of the museums and galleries are accessible and have lifts and loos available and if you go in the summer you will find plenty of street entertainment, café seating outside and live performances of dance, theatre, film and music in the open air theatre of Vondelpark. People are always willing to help (once asked) if you need assistance.

Getting there is straightforward enough as Schipol airport and trains and ferries are all equipped for disabled people, but once in Amsterdam you will have problems with public transport – no trams, a metro that will only take you to the outer boroughs and a specialist taxi service that needs booking a couple of days in advance. It would be advisable to go with a company offering holidays specifically tailored to your needs (see below) or, if you can't go with an able-bodied companion, think about employing the services of a helper through the Holiday Care Service (see below). It may even be possible to organise an exchange through Mobility International Nederland (see below).

Whatever your disability if you are thinking of travelling to Amsterdam you should contact the **SGOA** (**Stichting Gehandicapten Overleg Amsterdam**), tel. 638 3838, a network set up to help travellers in the city. They represent a number of organisations and can give advice on a number of issues; for instance they can advise wheelchair users on public loos and hotels, diabetics on where to go for extra insulin and put those with AIDS in touch with Aids support groups.

Holiday companies and Holiday Care
Carefree Holidays (64 Florence Rd, Abington, Northampton NN1 4NA, tel. 0604 34301). Coach tours in adapted vehicles for elderly and disabled people. Nursing care can also be provided. **Thomson Holidays** (Greater London House, Hampstead Rd, London NW1 7SD, tel. 071 387 9321). Special Holiday feature in their City Breaks brochure. **Travelscene** (11 St Ann's Road, Harrow, Middlesex HA1 1AS, tel 081 427 4445). Offer holidays for people with disabilities.

Holiday Care Service (2 Old Bank Chambers, Station Rd, Horley, Surrey RH6 9HW, tel 0293 774535). Will give general advice to travellers with disabilities and their carers, organise holidays and (sometimes) financial assistance. They can also provide holiday helpers if you have no one to travel with, but you will be asked to pay their way.

Exchange visits

Mobility International Nederland (Postbus, 165, 6560 AD Groesbeek, tel. 8891 71744, Wed only 9a.m.–5p.m.). Assists individuals and groups and organises exchanges.

Public transport in Amsterdam

Schipol Airport has good facilities for disabled people with normal arm function and the IHD International support services run an assistance service at the airport. Rail users should contact the info line 30 331 253 for details of accessibility and assistance available – both are usually good. Metro is theoretically user friendly for handicapped people, but it is unlikely to take you where you want. The only station you might use at Waterlooplein does not have a lift. Trams are difficult, usually impossible for people with mobility problems, but the following lines have a few trains accessible in theory to wheelchair users; 1, 2, 5, 6, 10, 16, 24. Taxis can only take wheelchairs if they are folded so if you need to travel in your wheelchair you have to use the car service for wheelchair users, tel 613 4134. They need to be booked a couple of days in advance and cost slightly more than the standard taxis at around f2.80 per kilometre.

Hotels and Restaurants

The SGOA will send you a list of hotels and restaurants accessible to wheelchair users. Most of the hotels are modern and in the upper price bracket and beware, quite a way from the centre. It would be best to choose somewhere in the historic centre like the expensive *Krasnapolsky* (see p.236) or the cheaper *Ibis* in the rather noisy position on Stationsplein. Alternatively, if you wish to visit the museums and galleries take a hotel in the Museum Quarter like the delightful, reasonably priced *Aalders* (see p.243) which is a stone's throw from the Van Gogh Museum.

Restaurants suggested tend to be similarly upmarket and often attached to the big hotels. If this is not what you want, in summer you will find you can eat outside which would give you a much broader choice, including brown bars and designer cafés.

Toilets

The SGOA also issue a list of the meagre collection of loos for handicapped users. Listed below are the ones open to the public which are not attached to the major museums and galleries.

Centraal Station, first track on the west side of Platform 2A. Take lift. In the day time get the key from lavatory attendant. Night time get key from railroad police next door to the lavatory. **C & A Damrak**. Enter store from passage between Nieuwendijk and Damrak and take lift to the basement. **T'Nieuwe Café** (Dam Square). Open 9 a.m. – 5 p.m.; take lift to basement. **University Library** (Singel 425). Open 9.30 a.m.–midnight Mon–Fri; take lift to second floor.

V & D department store, by Munt/Kalverstraat; lift to fourth floor and ask restaurant cashier for key. **New City Hall** (Amstel 1). On every storey opposite Rooms 1310, 2310, 3310, 4310 and 5310. Open 24 hours. **Jewish Historical Museum** (Nieuwe Amstelstraat 3). Open 11 a.m.–5 p.m.; take lift to basement.

The following places have toilets for visitors only: the Maritime Museum, Amsterdam Historical Museum, Allard Pierson Museum, Theater de Brakke Grond, Muziektheater, Public Library on Prinsengracht 587 (you can get in here without being noticed), Artis Zoo, Rijksmuseum, Van Gogh Museum, Stedelijk Museum and Concertegebouw.

Directory

Amsterdam has its own Yellow Pages in English for tourists to be found in hotels, hostels, the VVV and all over town. It is Yellow, has Visitor Guide marked clearly at the top and lists most of the things you will need giving a few entries for each. Shops, restaurants and service industries are well covered. (The Visitors Guide is also usually included in the Dutch Yellow Pages, the *Gouden Gids*.) If you are calling from outside the city use the area code 020 before the number given.

AIDS
AIDS Helpline Freephone 06 022 2220, see p.34.

AIRLINE OFFICES
British Airways, Stadhouderskade 4, OS (tel. 601 5413); **KLM,** Museumplein, IS (tel. 474 7747); **British Midland**, Ticket desk Schipol (tel. 604 1459, Freephone info 06 022 2426); **TWA**, Singel 540, C (626 2277).

AIRPORTS
Schipol inquiries tel. 601 9111.

AMBULANCE
tel. 0611.

BABYSITTING
Babyzitcentrale Babyhome, Chassestraat 97 (tel. 616 1119). Employs only women; **Oppascentrale Kriterion**, 2E Rozendwarsstraat (tel. 624 5848). Uses men and women. For more details see p.308.

BIKE HIRE
See p.60.

BUS/TRAM/METRO
Tel. 551 4911 for information.

CAR BREAKDOWN

ANWB Royal Dutch Touring Club, Museumplein 5 (tel. 673 0844). 24-hour emergency line, freephone 06 0888. They will assist free if you are a member of a foreign motoring organisation. If not, you can join them for f90. Always check the method of payment when calling for assistance as they don't always take credit cards or cheques.

CAR HIRE

Europcar, Overtoom 51–53, OW (tel. 618 4595); **Avis,** Nassaukade 380 (tel. 683 6061); **Adam's Rent a car,** Nassaukade 344 (tel. 685 0111); **Budget,** Overtoom 121, OW (tel. 612 6066); **Hertz,** Overtoom 85 OW (tel. 612 2441).

CAR PARKS

De Bijenkorf, Beursplein, Damrak, C. Open Mon–Sat 8 a.m.–midnight, fl.25 first half hour, then f2.50 for subsequent half hours; **Europarking,** Marnixstraat 250, IW (tel. 623 6694). Open Mon–Thurs 6.30 a.m.–12.30 a.m., Fri–Sat 6.30 a.m.–1.30 a.m, Sun 7 a.m.–12.30 a.m. **Museumplein,** uncovered (tel. 671 6418); open daily 8 a.m.–8 p.m. f3 per hour. Free Sunday; **Prinsengracht** 540–542 IS (tel. 625 9852) Open Mon–Fri 7.30 a.m.– 4.30 p.m., Sat 3 p.m.–5.30 a.m. Sun 6 p.m.–4.30 a.m. f3 per hour.

CASUALTY DEPARTMENTS

Onze Lieve Vrouwe Gasthuis, 1E Oosterparkstraat 179 (tel. 599 9111) is the nearest to the city centre; see p.36.

CHEMISTS

24-hour opening information, tel. 664 2111. See p.36.

CHURCH

Catholic, St John and St Ursula, Begijnhof 30, C (tel. 622 1918) and Papegaai, Kalverstraat 58 (tel. 623 1889); **Christian Scientist,** Richard Wagnerstraat 32, OS (tel. 622 7438); **Dutch Reformed,** Westerkerk, Prinsengracht 281 (tel. 624 7766); **English Episcopal,** Groenburgwal 42, C (tel. 624 8877); **English Reformed church,** Begijnhof 48, C (tel. 624 9665); **Jewish,** Liberal Jewish Community, Jacob Soetendorpstraat 8, OS (tel. 642 3562); **Muslim,** Thaiba, Kraaiennest 125, OS tel. 698 2526); **Quaker,** Vossiusstraat 20, OS (tel. 679 4238); **Russian Orthodox,** Utrechtsedwarstraat 5a (tel. 622 5385).

CONTRACEPTION

See p.33.

CRÈCHES AND PLAYGROUPS

Crèche facilities for foreigners are non-existent in Amsterdam, but try the babysitting firms for daycare. See above and p.308.

CLAMPING

Tel. 523 3115. A note on your windscreen will tell you where to pay the fine – cost at least f120, or f250 if over 24 hours. Take cash and passport. No credit cards.

DENTAL CARE

Central Medical Service for referral to dentists, tel. 664 2111.

DISABLED

SGOA, Keizersgracht 523, 1017 (tel. 638 3838) for general information on provisions for disabled people in Amsterdam. See p.46.

DOCTORS

Central Medical Service for referral to doctors, tel. 664 2111. See p.36.

DRY CLEANERS

Cleaning Shop Express, Huidenstraat 22, IW (tel. 623 1219). Open Mon–Fri 8.30 a.m.–6 p.m. Sat 8.30 a.m.–1 p.m.; **Clean Center**, Ferdinand Bolstraat 7–9 (tel. 662 7167).

ELECTRICITY

Voltage is 220 AC which is compatible with the UK; American visitors will need a transformer. Wall sockets take two-pronged plugs.

EMBASSIES AND CONSULATES

American Consulate General, Museumplein 19, OS (tel. 664 5661) Mon–Fri 1.30–5.15 p.m.; **British Consulate General**, Koningslaan 44, OS (tel. 676 4343) Mon–Fri 9 a.m.–noon, 2–3.30 p.m. **Australian Embassy**, Carnegielaan 4, 2517-KH Den Haag (tel. 070 310 8200) Mon–Thur 9 a.m.–12.30 p.m, 1.15 p.m.–5.15 p.m, Fri 9 a.m–12.30 p.m. **Canadian Embassy**, Sophialaan 7, 2514 JP, Den Haag (tel. 070 361 4111). Mon–Fri 9 a.m.–1 p.m, 2–5.30 p.m. **Eire Embassy**, Dr Kuyperstraat 9, 2514 BA, Den Haag (tel. 070 63 0993), Mon–Fri 10 a.m.–12.30 p.m., 2.30–5 p.m., **New Zealand Embassy**, Mauritskade 25, 2514 HD, Den Haag (tel. 070 346 9324) Mon–Thurs 9 a.m.–12.30 p.m. 1.30–5.30 p.m. Friday 9 a.m.–5.30 p.m.

EMERGENCY SERVICES

For Police, Ambulance and Fire call 0611.

FAXING

See p.320.

FEMINIST ORGANISATIONS

See p.40.

FINDING A FLAT

Try the daily *De Telegraaf* and *De Volkskrant* for 'rented accommodation offered' (*woonruimte te huur aangeboden*). You may have more luck in the free weekly *Via Via*, but be prepared to start ringing early. Most flats go by word of mouth so ask everyone you meet. If you are prepared to pay through the nose try some of the agencies: **Inter Agency Holland**, Weteringschans 53 (tel. 624 84 44); **GIS Appartments**, Keizersgracht 33 (tel. 625 0071), **IDA Housing**, Den Texstraat 30 (tel. 624 8301).

FINDING A JOB

It is not easy if you don't speak Dutch. *De Volkskrant* has a good section on Saturday and the *uitzendburo* (employment agency) may be able to help. Ask around friends, in bars and cafés for casual work. If planning to move from the UK it is worth trying the international employment agency, see p.45.

HITCH HIKING

The Lift Centre, N.Z. Voorburgwal 256 (tel. 622 4342) for introductions to drivers and hikers.

HELPLINES

Alcoholics Anonymous, tel. 686 5142, 24-hour helpline; **Crisis Helpline**, tel. 616 1666, Mon–Thurs 9 a.m.–3 a.m., Fri–Sun 24 hours, counselling helpline similar to the Samaritans (English usually spoken); **Drug abuse**, tel. 570 2325, Mon–Fri 9 a.m.–5.30 p.m. (see p.000); **AIDS helpline**, tel. 06 022 2220; **Weather**, tel. 003.

LAUNDERETTES
Clean Brothers, Jacob van Lennepkade 179, OW (tel. 618 3637). Open Mon–Fri 8 a.m.–8 p.m. but closes Wed 6 p.m., Sat 9 a.m.–5 p.m. For self-service, service washes and dry cleaning.

LEFT LUGGAGE
Lockers at Centraal Station and a manned left luggage counter at Schipol Airport, daily 7 a.m.–10.45 p.m.

LEGAL HELP
Legal Advice Line, tel. 548 2611, Mon–Thurs 9 a.m.–5 p.m., Fri 9 a.m.–1 p.m., run by student lawyers for general advice;
Legal Advice Centre (*Bureau voor Rechtshulp*) Spuistraat 10, C (tel 626 4477), Mon 1 p.m.–4 p.m, Tues–Fri 9 a.m.–noon;
Rechthulp voor Vrouwen, Willemstraat 24b (tel. 624 0323), legal aid for women, Mon 1.30 p.m.–4.30 p.m., Tues–Fri 9.30 a.m.–12.30 p.m. & 1.30 a.m.–4.30 p.m.

LESBIAN ORGANISATIONS
See p.44.

LIBRARIES
Centrale Bibliotheek, Prinsengracht 587, IW (tel. 523 0900), Mon 1p.m.–9 p.m. Tues–Fri 10 a.m.–9 p.m., Sat 10 a.m.–5 p.m., includes children's library; **IIAV,** Women's Archive, Keizersgracht 10, CN (tel. 624 4268), Mon–Fri 10 a.m.–4 p.m., Thurs until 8.45 p.m.; **British Council Library** Keizersgracht 343, IW (tel. 622 3644), Mon–Fri 10 a.m.–4.30 p.m.; **American Institute** Plantage Muiderstraat 12, OE (tel. 525 4380), Mon, Wed & Fri 10 a.m.–4 p.m.; **De Graaf Stichting,** (**archive of prostitution**) Westermarkt 4 (tel. 624 7149). For gay and lesbian research centres, see p.44.

LOCKSMITHS
Amsterdam Security Center, Prinsengracht 1097, IS (tel. 671 6316) for car and house.

LOST PROPERTY
Centraal Station, NS lost property information, Stationsplein 15 (tel. 557 8544) for items lost on a train or station; **GVB** head office, Prins Hendrikade 108–114 (tel. 551 4911) for items lost on a bus, tram or metro; **Police Lost Property,** Waterlooplein 11, C (tel. 559 8005) for items lost in the city. Anything found is transferred here having gone through the local station, so wait a couple of days before trying or go to the local police station.

MOSQUITOES
Be warned, Amsterdam is seething with them in summer. Take repellent with you as it is difficult to find, and antihistamine cream if you react badly to being bitten.

PETS
To bring in cats and dogs requires a rabies certificate. Vets (*dierenartsen*) and kennels (*dierenpensions*) are listed in the Yellow Pages. **Dierenambulance Stichting Central,** Hoogte Kadijk 61, (tel. 626 1058; 24-hour service, tel. 6262 2121). Ambulance service for animals cost f25 whether it is your animal or not.

PETROL STATIONS (24-HOUR)
Sarphatistraat 225; Spaarndammerdijk 218; Marnixstraat 250.

PHOTOCOPYING
See p.320.

POLICE
Emergency tel. 0611. See p.27 for individual stations.

SWIMMING POOLS AND SPORTS CENTRES
See p.291.

QUEUING
Supermarkets, delicatessens, banks, clinics and many public institutions have a ticketing system where you take a ticket and wait your turn. It is advisable not to step over the boundary mark on the floor until it's your turn.

TIPPING
It is customary, though not strictly necessary, to round up restaurant and bar bills to the nearest guilder though people never expect more than f5. Taxi drivers expect 10%.

TOILETS AND BABY-CHANGING FACILITIES
Public toilets in Amsterdam are few and far between, so make the most of conveniences in museums, galleries and restaurants. If you need somewhere in a hurry use the nearest bar where quite often you will be asked to pay, whether or not you are a patron. Bar toilets are quite often dirty, damp, smelly and incredibly small, so avoid them if possible. There is no such thing as a free pee in Amsterdam; even the large department stores like Bijenkorf and Hema will charge you upwards of 30c for the privilege and if you go in with a child don't be surprised if they ask you how many used the loo and charge you both. Baby-changing facilities in the Netherlands mean a changing mat, a bucket and another 30c. You will find them at Bijenkorf, Dam Square, Hema Stores all over town and Central Station, plus a few of the department stores. Wheelchair users will find the lack of facilities in the city very frustrating and you will probably have to plan your day around them. 'T Nieuwe Café on Dam Square is the only café to advertise facilities for the disabled. For a list of toilets and how to reach them see p.49.

TRAIN INFORMATION
Centraal Station Information Desk, Stationsplein 13 (tel. 069292), Mon–Fri 5.15–10 p.m. weekends 9 a.m.–8 p.m.

TRAVEL AGENTS
NBBS, Dam 17, C (tel. 620 5071); Travel Express, Rokin 38, C (tel. 626 4434).

WINDSCREEN REPLACEMENT
If your car is broken into it is cheapest to go to a garage to have your window replaced. Consult the Yellow Pages for a full list.

Orientation

It shouldn't take long to find your feet in Amsterdam. First impressions may be of graffiti, dope dealers and accommodation touts but, unlike many cities, its gentler side is never far away and once you have got your bearings you can pick and choose how to tackle it. Using the Arrival and Getting around section you should be able to reach your hotel unflustered and ready to take on the city. We have chosen not to recommend hotels in the Red Light District because, although it is safe and sociable, first impressions can be unnerving: instead our recommendations are in safe, attractive and often quiet locations, all in or within walking distance of the centre and well placed for restaurants, clubs and sightseeing.

Once you have arrived, take a stroll in the neighbourhood around your hotel with a map to get your bearings, stopping for a drink along the way. Don't rush off to the nearest gallery but take some time to work out what you want to do. Take a boat trip around the canals, wander across the historic centre to the flea market on Waterlooplein or saunter into the fashionable shops along P.C. Hooftstraat. Hire a bicycle and explore the Grachten Gordle, visit a canal house or wander around Vondelpark and have dinner in one of the restaurants on Spuistraat.

If you only have a weekend it's best to plan a few visits around opening times, but allowing plenty of scope for a change of plan. If you are in the city for longer it is well worth taking at least one excursion to get a taste of the open pastures, bulb fields, beaches and typical little towns within easy reach by train. If travelling with children it is essential to plan something specifically for them – even the most tolerant kids can easily tire of boat rides and pancakes.

It is very tempting to tackle each area as a separate unit but don't. The divisions in this book, though historic and so thematic, should not be taken too literally. The historic centre lies within the natural crescent of the Singel; to the west are the Grachten Gordle and the Jordaan; to the east you find what remains of the old Jewish quarter; southwards is the museum quarter and De Pijp; and remnants of Amsterdam's maritime past run from west to east along the harbour to the north. They all make up the compact centre of the sprawling city, where everything is within easy walking distance. To really enjoy Amsterdam make sure you visit more than one area each day – mix the galleries with a stroll around the Jordaan, take in the Maritime Museum before collapsing for a live jazz session in the historic centre, visit a canal house, socialise in Leidseplein and crash out in Vondelpark. By night sip gin with smart stockbrokers in Dam Square, eat with the locals in the Jordaan, gawp at the prostitutes in the Red Light District and go clubbing with tourists in Rembrandtsplein.

HIT LIST

For weekenders Buy armfuls of flowers for your hotel room at the flower market (p.134); brunch at Lucky Mothers (p.269); take a canal boat trip or hire a pedalo (p.59); rummage at Waterlooplein flea market (p.184); enjoy some grandeur at the Van Loon Museum (p.137); climb the Westorren (p.123); pay your respects at the Anne Frank House or see the church in the attic at the Amstelkring (p.93); don't miss the Sunday afternoon jazz at De Engelbewaarder (p.258); and watch a good film in the eccentric surroundings of the Tuschinski (p.133).

For art lovers The biggest museum is the Rijksmuseum (p.151); the most popular is the Van Gogh Museum (p.160); the most controversial is the Stedelijk (p.163); and the most intimate is the Six Collection (p.130). For buying art and antiques check out the Spiegel quarter (p.139).

For specialists Secret codes, papers and pistols at the Resistance Museum (p.177); venture backstage at the Musiektheatre (p.185); study Rembrandt's etchings in the Rembrandthuis (p.186); and watch old movies at the Film Museum (p.169).

For photographers Walk around the Western Isles (p.208); take in wacky architecture in the New South (p.174); and snap the locals at the Albert Cuyp Market (p.173).

For children Stand in a soap bubble at the NINT (p.309); cook your own dinner at the Kinderkook Café (p.313); scrub the deck at the Maritime Museum (p.201); watch a Tibetan puppet show at the Tropenmuseum (p.198); and meet giant alligators at the ARTIS zoo (p.197).

Excursions For Dutch ceramic tiles go to the Rijksmuseum Huis Lambert van Meerten in Delft; for art go to the Mauritshuis in the Hague or spend a day in the Kroller Muller Museum; for children go to De Efteling theme park and for a quaint Dutch town go to Gouda. Alternatively, spend a day at the beach, take an old tram to Amsterdam Bos or experience tulip mania at the Keukenhof.

Opening Times

Museums Opening times for museums and galleries vary and seem to frequently change. In the current economic climate a number of the smaller museums are having to close their doors or cut down on opening hours, so check first either at the hotel reception or by phone. All times given in this book were correct in late 1993. Most galleries open quite late at 10 a.m. or 11 a.m. and close around 5 p.m. which means the clearance bells sound about 4.45 p.m. A lot of galleries are closed on Monday and they are often full of schoolchildren after noon on Wednesdays as most primary schools have the afternoon off. Tickets are reasonably priced – usually between f5 and f10 – but if you intend to visit a few places it is well worth buying the **Annual Museum Card** (*Museumjaarkaart*) which costs f40 for adults and f25 for under 18s and pensioners. The ticket offers free or reduced fees at over 400 museums throughout the Netherlands. They can be bought from any participating museum plus VVV offices and the AUB Uitburo (see p.13). Remember to take a passport photo with you. You will find the museums seriously overcrowded on National Museum Weekend which takes place around the second weekend of April when admission to galleries and museums is free or reduced.

Shops, restaurants and bars In general shops open Mon 1 p.m. –6 p.m., Tues, Wed & Fri 9 a.m.–6 p.m., Thurs 9 a.m.–9 p.m., Sat 9 a.m.–5 p.m., closed Sun. Some stay open late (see p.255). As lunch is not a main meal in the Netherlands few restaurants open for lunch but many brown cafés and designer bars serve lunch from noon–2 p.m.. Restaurants are open in the evening from 5 p.m.–11 p.m. but some close as early as 9 p.m. Some close Sun & Mon. Bars tend to open after 10 a.m. and close Sun–Thurs around 1 a.m., staying open later, until 2 a.m. on Fri & Sat nights.

Arrival

Amsterdam's airport at **Schipol**, eight miles south west of the city, is one of Europe's busiest. It also has a reputation for being one of the most efficient, clean and clearly signed. By far the easiest way into the city is by train; weekend packages usually include a train ticket. Follow signs to the station (trolleys can be taken all the way to the platform) and jump on the next train to Centraal Station. Trains leave daily at fifteen-minute intervals between 4 a.m. and midnight; then hourly 12.45–3.45a.m. – journey-time around twenty minutes. Tickets cost f5 single and f8 return for adults, f1 for under twelves with adult, free for under fours. No credit cards. Don't be tempted to get off at any stations on the way; wait for Central Station. The KLM bus service is also open to anyone and leaves the main exit of the airport, half-hourly between 6.30 a.m. and 3 p.m. and at 5 p.m. daily. Tickets f15. It is only worth taking this option if you are staying at one of the hotels en route: Golden Tulip Barbizon (Leidseplein), Pulitzer (Westermarkt/Keizersgracht), Kraspnapolsky (Dam Square), Holiday Inn and Sonesta (N.Z. Voorburgwal), Barbizon Palace (Zeedijk). Schipol is the one place in Amsterdam where taxi drivers are obliged to wear a tie and jacket – you will find a taxi rank at the airport's main exit. The journey will cost around f60, though it is best to arrange a price before you leave just in case you get stuck in a traffic jam.

AIRPORT INFORMATION
Schipol Airport inquiries tel. 601 0966.
Schipol Airport Rail Service tel. 06 9292
KLM Bus Service tel. 649 1393/5651
Car Hire see p.50.

Arriving by train and bus
Whether you arrive in Amsterdam by plane, train or bus you are likely to enter the city through **Central Station**. The station itself is well lit, well staffed and has two good cafés, public loos with attendant, baby-changing facilities and a police station. As with all crowded places it is also a favourite spot for pickpockets, conmen and dodgy-looking types so keep your hand on your bags and money and look

purposeful. Make sure to leave the station by the main entrance to Stationsplein, following the signs to the **VVV Tourist Information**. If you leave out of the back you will find yourself in one of the prime soliciting spots for Amsterdam's prostitutes. If you need accommodation or information go to the VVV Tourist Office in the white pavilion situated alongside the water across Stationsplein. If you want to ring hotels and hostels yourself there are pay phones just outside the station. Be warned: accommodation touts work day and night in Stationsplein. If you are approached by anybody claiming that all the city's hotels are full or too expensive don't believe them or take their offer of a cheap alternative. These men can be quite unnerving, tapping on the windows as you phone the hostels, pushing you aside as you try to walk ahead and generally hassling you, but they can always be told to '*Rot op*' (get lost). Much of the city centre is within walking distance from the station but if you are heavily laden, tired or feel uncomfortable make the most of Amsterdam's excellent public transport system or pick up a taxi from the taxi rank out at the front. Buy tram and bus tickets from the **GVB Municipal Transport Authority** at Stationsplein 15, C (tel. 551 4911), by the entrance to the metro. If it is closed pay the driver as you board.

Arriving by Car

If you intend to drive to Amsterdam be prepared for **parking difficulties,** a maze of one-way systems, thousands of pedestrians and cyclists and a break-in. Buy a good map of the city like the *Hallwag* and work out your parking priorities beforehand. Parking meters in the centre are hard to find during the day, expensive and usually limited to two hours. Car parks are always expensive and the 'Park and Ride' parks mean long journeys into town. If you want free parking on the street the best area is the upmarket residential area south of Museumplein, but be prepared to find your window taken out in the morning. Don't park your car on the streets with a radio in it – foreign cars are prime targets for local drug addicts. (For car parks see p.50.)

Getting Around

The best way to see Amsterdam is **on foot**. The city is compact, safe and easily negotiable providing you have a good map and a reasonable sense of direction. Use the **trams** for quick trips from A to B, but bear in mind that they are difficult with pushchairs, impossible in wheelchairs and not that easy to board in a hurry if you are elderly. **Buses** are slower than trams, but reach areas where the trams don't go and run a good night service. The canal boats are best seen as entertainment rather than transport, but you may enjoy taking to the water for a change. The **Museum Boat** is one of the easiest and most pleasant ways of combining the sights with a canal trip. Of course Amsterdammers will tell you the only way to travel in the city is by **bicycle** – given that it is cheap, flexible, demands a little puff and a lot of wit, they are probably right.

Buses and Trams

Trams hurtle around the city at quite a pace which is great if you are on them and downright dangerous when you are not. Motorists, pedestrians and cyclists are advised to give way to trams and always listen out for the warning bells. Tram services run from 6 a.m. Mon–Fri, 6.30 a.m. Sat and 7.30 a.m. Sun with a special **night bus** service taking over after midnight. Yellow signs at the tram and bus stops mark the name of the stop and list the destinations. There are usually maps and diagrams of the routes in the shelters and on board, but if you are not sure ask the driver (virtually all speak English). It is better to buy your ticket in advance (see below) but if you have trouble and are in a hurry board at the front and pay the driver (this is more expensive than the strip cards) – try to avoid doing this in rush hour. To get on or off the tram press the yellow button next to the doors at the front, middle or back of the vehicle. Stops should be announced, but keep an eye out and if you are unsure ask a fellow passenger for help. As you get off remember that many tram stops are in the middle of the road, so don't get run over by the traffic scooting around the sides between the tram and the pavement.

Buses run the same way as trams with the same kind of stops, ticketing and efficiency. Night buses are numbered from '71' to '77' with '73' and '76' running through the city centre. Night bus stops are marked with a black square with the bus number on it. Night buses run from 1 a.m.–5.30 a.m. weekdays and from 1 a.m.–6.30 a.m. at weekends.

Metro

The underground or metro is mainly used by commuters who live in the suburbs. Trains run from 6 a.m. to around 12.30 a.m. weekdays and start at 6.30 a.m. on Saturday and 7.30 a.m. Sunday. All three lines terminate at Central Station, but don't be tempted to use it when you first arrive in town. Before you know it you will be miles out of the centre, so stick to trams and buses.

Tickets for buses, trams and the Metro   The ticketing system for public transport is initially confusing even though the same ticket strips are valid on buses, trams and metro. Buy a strip of tickets known as *strippenkaart* from the **GVB Municipal Transport Authority** office on Stationsplein, Amstel Station or the mobile unit on Leidseplein which appears from time to time. Some tourist shops and tobacconists also stock them. Tickets cost f2.75 for two units, f10.25 for 15 and f29 for 45 units. Children under four travel free, but there is no reduction for the elderly or unemployed.

The confusing part is working out how many strips to stamp. The city is divided into five zones: *Noord* (North), *West, Centrum, Oost* (East) and *Zuid* (South). Most of the places you will be visiting are in *Centrum*. For travel in a single zone stamp two strips, i.e. the journey costs f2.75. Stamp three for two zones, four for three zones and so on. Stamping boxes are usually **yellow boxes** in the back of the trams, at the entrance to the metro, and the driver stamps them by hand on the buses. Once stamped, you can use the ticket for an hour before restamping, but you are unlikely to be on any tram that long.

One strip can be used for more than one person providing you stamp the appropriate number of strips. However confusing it may seem, stamp the ticket because whatever your intentions ticket inspectors can and do impose hefty fines on the spot for people travelling without stamped tickets or with no ticket at all. People may boast that they have enjoyed free transport in Amsterdam for months, but a f100 fine makes it an expensive risk. A **day ticket** (*dagkaarten*) is a cheaper option offering unlimited travel for f11 for one day, f13.60 for two days and f16.80 for three, with each additional day costing f3.60. Kids aged four to eleven get them cheap at f6.80 for two days, f8.40 for three days and f1.60 a day thereafter. **Season tickets** (*sterabonnement*) can be bought for a week, month or year for f13.50, f46 and f460 respectively. Buy them at the GVB and you will need a passport and a photograph.

Taxis

Taxis can be picked up from a taxi rank or by phone to the **Central Taxi Office** (tel. 677 7777). You cannot hail a taxi. While taxi drivers are always pleasant and usually honest some tourists report being ripped off. Just in case, check the meter is blank before you start and ask the driver for an estimate before you set out. As ever most speak English. They will always be expensive, costing around f2.60 per kilometre by day and f3.25 by night. The chances are you will get stuck behind unloading lorries and cyclists and by the time you have tipped the driver even short journeys cost a lot. If you feel you have been ripped off ask for a receipt and refer it to the Central Taxi Office.

Canal bus, water taxis and canal bikes

The **canal bus** is a daily service running half hourly from the Rijksmuseum to Centraal Station between 10 a.m–8 p.m., and stopping at Leidseplein, Leidsestraat, Keizersgracht and Westerkerk (Anne Frank House). It is quite expensive at f12.50 for a day ticket, f8 for under twelves or f20 for a two-day pass (f17.50 for under twelves), but it is picturesque and you don't have to put up with a commentary as you do on the canal boat trips. The **Museum Boat** is a more useful means of getting around, stopping within easy walk of all the major sights in a round trip and venturing across the harbour to the Maritime Museum and eastwards to the zoo; it works out a little more expensive than the canal bus. The **water taxis** are seldom used to get from A to B, but are usually rented out to groups for sightseeing trips and parties. An eight-person boat costs f90 for half-an-hour and f2 per minute. If you have a lot of friends, a 35-person boat will set you back f195 for half-an-hour, then f300 per hour. If you have lots of time, good weather and plenty of energy try hiring a canal bike (pedalo for two or four people) for f18.50 per hour for two or f27.50 for four. Don't worry if you haven't got the energy for a round trip because the hire company has five moorings around the city – Leidseplein, Rijksmuseum, Westerkerk on Prinsengracht, Keizersgracht near Leidsestraat and Centraal Station, where you can abandon your craft when you run out of steam.

Cycle Hire

Before you think of hiring a bicycle remember you will be riding on the right hand side of the road and that trams, motorists and other cyclists will not know you are a tourist and will expect you to ride confidently but cautiously.

The tram lines frequently bring tourists tumbling to the ground. If you get your front wheel caught in the tracks there is no way out which is both humiliating and highly dangerous. That said, biking in Amsterdam is the best and only way to really enjoy the city. There are plenty of bike hire firms offering good daily rates around f12 (see below) and if you are planning to stay for a while it may be worth buying your own. Don't be tempted to buy an ultra cheap one from a guy in the street – it will undoubtedly be stolen. On the other hand don't buy an ultra expensive one from a smart bike shop either since it will certainly be pinched. An old roadworthy bike should cost around f150 and it is worth buying a strong lock to hold onto it. The hire firms usually have a few for sale (see below for details).

Trains

If you are going to spend a few days exploring the countryside, beaches, bulb fields and surrounding towns and cities the best way is by train. Rail services are frequent, reliable and relatively inexpensive. You can also get direct trains to many destinations across Europe, though remember to reserve seats for international destinations at least seven days in advance through the reservations office in Central Station. Timetables are displayed at the station and are easy to understand.

TRANSPORT INFORMATION

GVB Municipal Transport Authority (for tickets and information), Stationsplein 15, C (tel. 551 4911). Open Mon–Fri 8 a.m.–10.30 p.m., Sat 9 a.m.–10.30 p.m.

Centraal Station Information Desk Stationsplein 13a (tel. 069292). Open Mon–Fri 5.15 a.m.–10 p.m., Sat–Sun 9 a.m.–8 p.m. Reservations office Mon–Fri 8 a.m.–8 p.m., Sat–Sun 9 a.m.–5 p.m. Credit cards Master Card/Visa.

Central Taxi Office, tel. 677 7777
Taxi service for wheelchair users, tel. 613 4134 to book in advance.

Taxi Ranks are situated in most main squares: Rembrandtsplein, Leidseplein, Nieuwmarkt, Dam Square, Central Station.

Water Taxi Centrale, Stationsplein 8, C (tel. 622 2181). Open daily 9 a.m.–1 a.m.

Museum Boat, Stationsplein 8 (tel. 622 2181). Open 10 a.m.–5 p.m. every 30 mins in summer and 45 mins in winter. Seven pick-up points: Central Station, Anne Frank House, Leidseplein, Museumplein, Herengracht (nr flower market), Opera House, Maritime Museum. Look for *Lovers* sign. Day ticket f19 adults, children under 13 and OAPs f15.

Canal Bus, Neuweukeizersgracht 8, IE (tel. 623 9886). Open Mon–Fri 9 a.m.–5 p.m.

Bicycle Hire: The Bulldog, O.Z. Voorburgwal 126, C (tel. 624 8248). Open May–Sept daily 10 a.m.–6.30 p.m. (in Red Light District, short walk from the station). f200 deposit and passport needed; no credit cards.

Take a Bike, Centraal Station, Stationsplein 6 (tel. 624 8391). Open daily 6 a.m.–10 p.m. Need f200 deposit. No credit cards. **Rent a Bike**, Pieter Jacobsdwarsstraat 11 (tel. 625 5029). Open 9 a.m.–6 p.m. f50 deposit and passport; major credit cards accepted.

Tours

One of the best ways to get your bearings in the city is to take a trip around the canals or join an organised tour, either on foot or by bike. You will probably find a mountain of leaflets advertising tours in your hotel reception. If not, look in bars, cafés and bookshops or take one of those listed below.

Walking Tours

Many companies run walking tours and in summer fill up quickly with coachloads of pre-booked tourists. Numbers need not always be to your disadvantage, particularly if you choose to visit the Red Light District – walking tours around this notorious area are especially popular with single women.

Amsterdam Travel and Tours

Evening walking tours with a guide through the Red Light District last two hours and cost f25. Three-hourly historic city tours on Saturday and Sunday mornings cost f27. All tours are led by an

English-speaking guide. Book in advance because at present tours only run over the summer. *Dam 10 tel. 627 6236 Open 10 a.m.–6 p.m. See also Yellow Bike Tours (below).*

Water

It may not be quite your style to join a boat full of fellow tourists for a trip around the canals, but it is well worth it. Numerous trips are available from candlelit cruises and romantic dinners to straightforward sightseeing trips. If taking children, remember that most trips last at least an hour (no loos on board) and it is best not to take kids liable to be seasick. You don't need to book for daily round trips but it is advisable for evening, lunch and dinner cruises. An alternative and cheaper way to see the city from the water is by Canal Bus or Museum Boat (see p.59).

Holland International One of the biggest companies offering daily cruises every 15 minutes between 9 a.m. and 6 p.m. lasting 1½ hours and a candlelit night cruise every night at 9.30 p.m. Day trips cost f11 for adults and f7 for children; night trips f42.50 and f25, cheese and wine included. They also offer luncheon and dinner cruises which work out very expensive at f52.50 and f145 respectively. All the other companies offer similar trips for similar prices. *Depart opposite Central Station, tel. 622 7788.*

Lovers Despite its tacky name the round city tours are quite good, leaving every 15 minutes for one hour. Candlelit tours run between April and October, every evening at 9.30, lasting two hours. Prices vary, as do the tours, but they are among the cheapest. *Depart opposite Central Station, tel. 622 2181.*

The Best of Holland Round trips, one hour, 1½ hour, depart every 30 minutes from 9 a.m.–6 p.m. daily. Night cruise 9 p.m. daily. *Depart opposite Central Station, tel. 623 1539.*

Rondvaarten From mid March to October round trips, one hour, leaving every thirty minutes from 9 a.m.–10 p.m. October–February every thirty minutes 10 a.m.–4 p.m. Good for evening round trips and not quite as 'touristy' as the rest. No credit cards. *Depart opposite Rokin 125, nr Spui, tel. 623 3810.*

Bike Tours If you have the energy bike tours are good fun and take you out of the city centre at a reasonably sedate pace. Prices include the hire of the bike. If you are more interested in cycling into the countryside on your own the VVV provides excellent cycling maps with routes, cycle lanes and watering holes.

Yellow Bike Guided Tours All tours are led by English-speaking guides and operate daily. City tours leave at 9.30 a.m. and 1 p.m. every day from N.Z. Kolk 20, opposite the booking office and last three hours (stops included) f29. Country tours are well worth the f42.50 for fresh air, 30 km of spectacular views and little villages with trips to a windmill, cheese farm and a clog factory; they leave every day at 9 a.m. and noon and last 6½ hours. Meet outside the VVV office on Central Station for coach journey to starting point at Marken. All tours operate March 30–October 31. A city walking tour also leaves daily 9.45 a.m. from N.Z. Kolk 29, lasting 1¾ hours for f15. Tickets also sold at the VVV and Canal Bike moorings. *N.Z. Voorburgwal 66, tel. 620 69 40.*

Ena's Bike Tour For a seven hour ride across Amsterdam city and beyond, a row or swim across a lake and a visit to a windmill and cheese farm join the Amsterdam Tour. *Leaves 10 a.m. from Amstel Station, Julianaplein, June–Sept. Cost f40. Information from PO Box 2807, 2601 CV Delft, tel. 692 5384.*

Specialist Tours

Mee in Mokum Tours, limited to eight people, are run by elderly Amsterdam residents who enjoy the chance to show visitors an intimate side of the city. Leave Tues, Fri and Sun 11 a.m. from outside the Historical Museum. To guarantee an English-speaking guide, book at least a week in advance. Cost f4. Tours for individuals can also be arranged. *Information from Hartenstraat 18, tel. 625 1390.*

Archivise A fairly new company offering tailor made architectural tours around the city's monuments, many normally closed to tourists. Booking essential. *Information from PO Box 14603, 1001 LC, tel. 625 8908, Tues–Thurs 9.30 a.m.–noon.*

Helicopters It is always interesting to see a city from above. If you feel inclined helicopters can be chartered for between 10 and 25 passengers from KLM. *Prices start at f4.605 per hour. KLM Helicopter Tours, PO Box 7700, 3337 ZL Schipol East, tel. 649 2041, Mon–Fri 9 a.m.–5 p.m.*

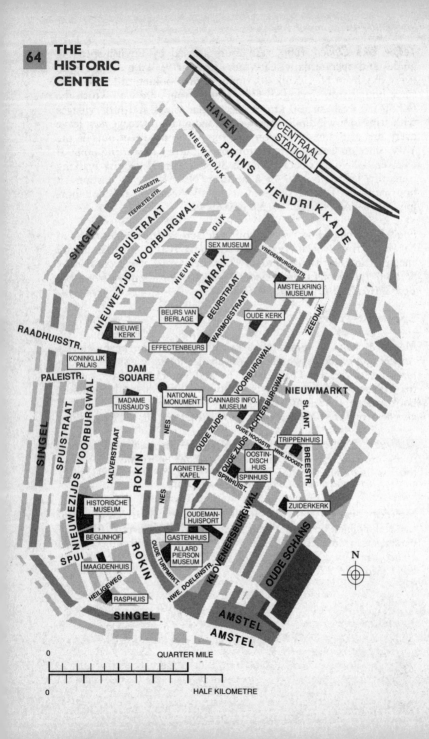

CENTRAAL STATION

HAVEN

PRINS HENDRIKKADE

SINGEL

KOGGESTR.

TEERKETELSTR.

SPUISTRAAT

NIEUWEZIJDS VOORBURGWAL

NIEUWENDIJK

DIJK

NIEUWEN-

SEX MUSEUM

DAMRAK

VREDENBURGERSTR.

AMSTELKRING MUSEUM

Beurstraat

Beerstraat

ZEEDIJK

RAADHUISSTR.

BEURS VAN BERLAGE

WARMOESTRAAT

OUDE KERK

NIEUWE KERK

EFFECTENBEURS

KONINKLIJK PALAIS

PALEISTR.

DAM SQUARE

VOORBURGWAL

NIEUWMARKT

SINGEL

SPUISTRAAT

NIEUWEZIJDS VOORBURGWAL

MADAME TUSSAUD'S

NATIONAL MONUMENT

CANNABIS INFO. MUSEUM

ACHTERBURGWAL

St. ANT.

KALVERSTRAAT

NES

OUDE ZIJDS

OUDE HOOGSTR.

NWE. HOOGSTR.

BREESTR.

TRIPPENHUIS

ROKIN

AGNIETEN-KAPEL

OUDE ZIJDS

OOSTIN-DISCH HUIS

SPINHUIS

SPINHUIST.

HISTORISCHE MUSEUM

NES

ZUIDERKERK

BEGIJNHOF

OUDEMAN-HUISPORT

SPUI

ROKIN

GASTENHUIS

OUDE TURFMRKT.

ALLARD PIERSON MUSEUM

KLOVENIERSBURGWAL

OUDE SCHANS

MAAGDENHUIS

HEILIGEWEG

RASPHUIS

NWE. DOELENSTR.

N

SINGEL

AMSTEL

AMSTEL

0   QUARTER MILE

0   HALF KILOMETRE

THE HISTORIC CENTRE

Amsterdam's historic centre is a city in itself, bounded by the huge meander of the River Singel and centred on the old harbour, now obscured by the flamboyant neo-Gothic Central Station. Trams and bicycles hurtle away from the station and pedestrians pour down Damrak past neon lights, burger bars and the busy Stock Exchange to the department stores on Dam Square. A few streets away residents chat in foodstores, delicatessens, bakeries and florists, and art galleries compete with garish sex shops, leather bars and prostitutes for passing trade in one of Europe's best known red light districts. Further south, as the red lights fade in the distance, bicycles rattle along cobbled streets, cafés spill out onto the pavements, crowds gather for live jazz, dance and mime, and students lounge on the steps of gabled houses, once the homes of wealthy merchants and now the lecture halls and residences of the city's university.

City life is attractive, appealing and impulsive. Few people have difficulty joining in the social life, but the city's history is a more challenging voyage of discovery and exploration. Amsterdam has lost many of her historic monuments to fires, religious disturbances and redevelopment. Most of the medieval city was razed to the ground in the great fire of 1472, the mass of convents, monasteries and churches were purged in the sixteenth century during the Reformation and the old adminstrative centre around Dam Square was cleared to make way for the illustrious Town Hall (now Royal Palace) in the Golden Age. The most significant change was the construction of the station across the old harbour and the later filling in of the canals to make way for motorised traffic. As if this wasn't enough, city planners condemned a number of old buildings to make way for the metro in the 1980s. Despite all this, the activities of the inhabitants have changed little since medieval times; business continues around Dam Square, prostitutes work the streets and alleys hounded by well-meaning Christians, sailors drink in dingy brown bars and foreign travellers drop in for fun.

The area from Centraal Station to Dam Square is one of big department stores, large hotels, burger bars and banks, tied by a series of tramlines and a forbidding causeway. You will probably return here again and again, but usually on your way to somewhere else. It is the only place in Amsterdam where you are guaranteed to be hassled by dope dealers, pickpockets and cheap accommodation touts. You will also witness some of the best (and the worst) buskers in town.

Sex, smut and sin are only part of the attraction of the Red Light District. It is a lively area of gabled canal houses, cobbled streets, dark alleys and humped-backed bridges riddled with cafés, restaurants, offbeat shops and far out clubs. To be on the streets with prowling men is intimidating, challenging and at times frightening; to peer at prostitutes explicitly flaunting themselves from windows is fascinating, exciting and embarrassing, but it is too blatant to be threatening. On the edge of the Red Light District you find the city at its most intimate; children play alongside treelined canals, dogs send ducks flapping into the water and old people gossip on wooden benches. The melodious peel of carillon bells competes with the whirr of concrete mixers and the banging of workmen in dilapidated houses.

Spui (pronounced like 'spout' without the t) is an area for socialising, shopping and snoozing. A constant stream of people pour down the pedestrianised shopping street of Kalverstraat each day. By night they cram into the restaurants and bars along Spuistraat or eat *al fresco* along the pavements. The little Beginhof garden tucked behind the busy square is the only patch of greenery in Amsterdam's lively historic centre and the neighbouring Historical Museum is the best place to delve into the city's fascinating and complex history.

A City in the Making   Even the Romans refrained from settling in the waterlogged tidal flats of Northern Holland. Pliny got as far as Leiden in AD 50, but went no further. At that time much of the area which now makes up Amsterdam would have been partially underwater, fit for frogs, fish and fowl but little else. The story goes that three men and a dog (never mind the women) sailed down the Rhine and set up home on a man-made hillock and set about draining the surrounding land. Archaeologists confirm that people, probably peasants, were building dykes and dams in the Amstelland or 'waterland' of Northern Holland in the eleventh century. Despite the appalling boggy conditions they secured themselves a patch of land around the Amstel River by diking the riverbanks and joining them to a dam across the river. The modern streets of Zeedijk, Warmoestraat, the Dam, Nieuwendijk and Harlemmerdijk follow the line of Amsterdam's oldest sea defences.

No sooner had the peasants secured some stable ground than the aristocracy moved in. A belligerent man named Gijsbrecht built a castle on the dam itself and consolidated his hold on the surrounding land, only to be faced by another chap, Floris V, Count of Holland trying to stake his claim. In a bid to win popular support Floris granted toll privileges to the people living in the province of Amstelle Dam in 1275 – the first reference to the people living here. Gijsbrecht had him murdered, but failed to win his prize and the whole area was confiscated by the Bishops of Utrecht and given to the Counts of Holland. Since that day Amsterdam has remained part of the province of Northern Holland.

Amsterdam owed her ensuing prosperity to beer. The city was one of two toll points for imported beer in the fourteenth century; beer drinking was a national obsession (mainly because water was poisonous) and Amsterdam's trade in beer (and no doubt the brew itself) went from strength to strength. The economy was also boosted by a new trend in curing herring which allowed ships to stay out to sea for much longer and thus profits increased. As trade prospered, the city grew and merchants ventured further afield to find essential goods like wood, grain, furs, iron ore and cloth. A fierce trade war with the Hanseatic League, Europe's most powerful trading power, ended in victory for Amsterdam and opened trade routes throughout Europe to the city's merchants. It also opened the city gates to the European people and power struggles. None was felt more strongly in the Netherlands than the Reformation.

Catholicism challenged: Amsterdam and the Reformation

Like most of Europe, fifteenth-century Holland was firmly in the grip of the Roman Catholic Church. The centre of Amsterdam was riddled with monasteries and convents: chants and prayers were heard all day. One street was crammed so full of Christian establishments that it adopted the name 'Praying without end'. The *Amsterdam Miracle*, the story of an indestructible communion wafer with healing powers (see p.107), had lucratively elevated the city to Pilgrimage status and Christians poured in from all over the continent. Catholicism remained effectively unchallenged in the city until the sixteenth century when it became caught up in the wave of alternative religious ideas raging through Northern Europe known as the Reformation.

It began when an Augustinian monk, Martin Luther pinned up his 95 theses on a church door in Wittenburg, challenging the universal authority and corrupt practices of the Roman Catholic Church. Europe was ripe for revolution; economic, social and political pressures, the spread of literacy, the translation of the Bible into the vernacular and the development of printing turned one man's thoughts into everyone's concern. Theologians everywhere became braver and more audible. In Rotterdam Erasmus flaunted ideas of Man the creator rather than Man the sinner; in Geneva the philosopher John Calvin spoke of separating the State from the Church.

As Dutch merchants brought news of the religious fervour in Northern Europe to Amsterdam the citizens were slow to react. Many of those who did were tried for heresy though the tolerant city fathers in Amsterdam failed to carry out many of the sentences. The first to rock the boat were a group of Anabaptists from Germany who staged a naked demonstration of their prelapsarian innocence in Dam Square and occupied the Town Hall in 1535. They hoped to found a New Jerusalem in their 'chosen city'. An inebriated civic guard finally managed to control the uprising. The participants were sentenced to an horrific death, 'The chest is to be opened while they are still alive, the heart removed and thrust into their faces, whereupon they are to be beheaded and quartered. Their heads are to be mounted on stakes at the town gates, and their parts to be hung outside the gates.' Clearly the city fathers could tolerate a degree of heresy, but any threat to their civic position was totally unacceptable.

It was the Calvinist preachers who caught the imagination of the Dutch. Many came from Geneva to the Netherlands, the only safe haven outside Switzerland and Germany where they were tolerated and rarely challenged. Protestantism provided the Dutch with a focus of opposition to Spanish domination and the rule of Philip of Spain, to whom they were subject. Even Philip's sister, Margaret of Parma, whom he had sent to Amsterdam to keep peace was persuaded to show Protestant sympathies by the city regents.

In 1566 religious discontent in Amsterdam erupted into an iconoclastic fury. Calvinist sympathisers rampaged through the streets, smashing church windows, pulling statues from their pedestals and vandalising any religious monument. A group of women successfully defended the Heilige Stede, site of the Amsterdam Miracle (see p.107) but elsewhere little was saved. Philip of Spain was outraged and sent the Duke of Alva to restore order. His brutal regime earned the city the name of 'Murderam'. The Calvinist Prince William of Orange led a popular challenge against the Duke's rule starting the Eighty Years War between Dutch Protestants and Spain.

Amsterdam sided with Spain until it looked as if William was going to win the war. In 1578 Amsterdam simply swapped sides. The Catholic City Council was removed and a new Protestant city government appointed. The city converted from Catholic to Protestant in an agreement quaintly termed 'The Alteration'. From this point on, Catholics were obliged to worship in secret, convents were closed, churches were whitewashed and stripped of any decor that might distract the congregation and the emphasis of the service shifted from the sacraments, celebrated at the altar at the end of the church, to the sermon delivered from a central pulpit. You will notice throughout the city, Protestant churches are arranged around a central pulpit. Altars, if they remain, are no longer used. The Reformation stripped Amsterdam's churches of their heritage; chalices, sculptures, religious painting and priestly vestments are a rare sight. (If you are interested in Christianity in the Netherlands it is worth making the trip to the Museum of Christianity at the Convent of St Catharine, Utrecht, see p.229.)

A year after the Alteration the seven Protestant provinces of the Low Countries united in opposition to Philip II in the Union of Utrecht. The resulting Republic of Seven United Provinces were represented by a national council known as the States General which met in the Hague (still the political seat of the Netherlands) and each province elected its own *stadhouder* to command the army and navy and appoint local regents and governors. William of Orange was an obvious choice in the province of Holland. Although the provinces could elect separate *stadhouders*, in practice they tended to elect the same one and by 1641 the power of the House of Orange was sufficiently well established for a later William to marry Princess Mary of England.

WOMEN AND THE REFORMATION

Many women supported the Reformers despite Martin Luther's apparent disresepct for their sex. A statement in 1531 reveals Luther's thoughts on the matter. 'Women ought to stay at home; the way they were created indicates this, for they have broad hips and a wide fundament to sit upon, keep house and bear children.' For women, the emphasis of Luther's teachings was on the family and their position within it.

Many Dutch women's lives were changed and challenged by the Reformation. Former convents, which for years had represented the hub of intellectual life among women, were disbanded and nuns were encouraged to marry. Luther himself married a former nun. Sex within marriage was encouraged by the Reformers who recognised a woman's 'needs of the flesh'. While marriage was encouraged Luther also recognised the possibility of divorce on the grounds of adultery and impotence. His *Praise for a Pious Wife* would have given both husbands and wives food for thought: 'A pious God fearing wife is a rare treasure, more noble than a pearl. Her husband relies on her and trusts her in every respect. She gives him joy and makes him happy, does not distress him, shows loving kindness to him all through his life, and never gives him pain. She handles flax and wool, likes work to her hands; she benefits the house and resembles the merchant's ship which brings many goods from far away countries. She rises early, feeds her servants and gives her maids what is their due. She likes working and caring for what concerns her and does not busy herself with what is not her concern. She girds her loins and stretches her arms, works with energy in the house. She notices what is convenient and prevents damage. Her light is not extinguished at night. She puts her hand to the distaff and her fingers grip the spindle; she works with pleasure and diligence. She holds her hands over the poor and needy.'

While Luther's message to women was clear, he inadvertently did much to improve a woman's lot by encouraging literacy among both sexes. Clearly this was intended to enable women to read the Bible, but it also opened up a whole new world. Protestant women in the Netherlands were educated and literate long before their counterparts in Catholic countries. English travellers to Amsterdam in the seventeeth century were amazed at the number of women who ran their own businesses, like Clementia van Vondel (1586–1648) who ran a silk business from Warmoestraat. They were the products of Protestant schools specifically set up to teach them reading, writing and arithmetic along with religion and household management.

The Reformer's educational programme was so successful that by the seventeenth century Amsterdam was the home of many well educated women: the wealthy intellectual sisters Maria and Anna Tesselschade were the talk of the town; the artists Rachel Ruysch and Judith Leyster were successful in a male dominated profession and one independent spirit, Dorothea Bokstel, was advertising her services in the local paper as a dentist.

From Centraal Station to Dam Square

Most travellers get their first glimpse of Amsterdam's spires and waterways from the forecourt of Centraal Station which spans the entire width of the old harbour entrance. Trains carry people from boats, planes and European stations right into the geographical, social and commercial heart of the city.

For centuries most travellers arrived by boat, across the harbour, past the city gallows where bits of criminals were strung out for all to see, and into the moorings along Damrak. The whole harbour would have been full of billowing sails, wooden masts and bronzed sailors. Inns and warehouses bobbed on wooden platforms far out to sea alongside the large ships that couldn't dock in shallower waters. Smaller craft packed with sacks of grain, precious cloth and pungent spices sailed into the city to unload their wares and huge water barges sluggishly pushed their way inwards. Goods were trundled into Dam Square on wooden trolleys to be weighed while wily merchants struck deals with tradesmen and drunken sailors quenched their thirst on the local brew.

Beer still flows freely, but the days of maritime splendour have long gone. The walk from the station to Dam Square is the natural entrance into Amsterdam. The immediate vicinity is more an area to endure than enjoy, but take a look inside De Bijenkorf, the city's most prestigious store, enjoy the cool interior of the Gothic Nieuwe Kerk, meet Michael Jackson at Madame Tussauds, walk across an imaginary world inside the Koninklijk Palais and watch Punch beat up Judy in Dam Square. If you wish to experience the true meaning of Dutch courage, join the stockbrokers over a glass of cool clear *genever* (Dutch gin) at the city's oldest drinking house, De Drie Fleschjes (see p.260).

The towers, spires and glistening gold of P.J. Cuypers vast neo-classical station are an impressive tribute to industrialisation. After much deliberation as to where Amsterdam's station should be built, the site across the harbour seems ingenious, adventurous and tragic in its transformation of an historic site, yet it was well received in the 1880s.

Trains glide into the cast iron hall, porters look anxiously for overloaded punters and businessmen head for the congenial atmosphere in the café on Platform 2. Behind the station prostitutes and rent boys bring traffic to a standstill along the dusty Ruiterkade and the free harbour ferry chugs back and forth across the river Ij. In front of the station international buskers captivate audiences with mime and dance. Expect to encounter Caribbean tin drum quartets competing with classical guitar and the inevitable lone junkie singing to the pigeons. Cyclists, taxis, trams and buses rattle past, bells clanging and lights flashing as pedestrians spread across the road. A few ugly phone boxes and a flowerstall filled with exotic blooms are the only things that stay still on the busy square.

Tired backpackers settle on the pavement and admire the ornate pediment above the main entrance – the central female figure 'Amsterdam' welcomes traders from around the world. Beneath her a tiled centrepiece is crammed with an intriguing display of the city's coats of arms. The single masted ship, known as the Hog was replaced by the crosses of St Andrew in the fifteenth-century. These three crosses, the most familiar arms of Amsterdam, crop up all over the city on bollards, buildings and T-shirts.

The station has always been a sociable place. Young travellers congregate around the tourist office (the white pavilion over the tram lines), friends exchange kisses and greetings under the arches, children cling to their parents, entranced by the street entertainers, and the harmless drunks settle down on benches for a chat and a booze. Unfortunately, the jovial atmosphere is ruined by pickpockets and a number of dodgy characters flogging cheap rooms who spend their days convincing young women that they have arrived in the most dangerous hell hole in Europe (see p.57). Harassment of this kind is not new. At the turn of the century so many girls got lured away by pimps at the station that a group of ladies formed the 'Association for the Interest of Young Girls', to protect female visitors. The 'station ladies' recognisable by their distinctive red, white and black armbands, met the trains and directed lone women to respectable areas and lodging houses before anyone could get to them. There are no station ladies today, but if you can cope with a long wait the tourist office will fix you up with a suitable place to stay.

At first glance Damrak, one of the city's principal tourist thoroughfares, is one of Amsterdam's least attractive streets. For almost its entire length from Centraal Station to Dam Square, its historic buildings are hung with neon lights and national flags, while at street level they house burger joints, *bureaux de change*, amusement arcades and tacky restaurants. Trams hurtle up and down the street and herds of pedestrians swarm along the pavements. Groups of young men down pints of beer and bags of chips while their mates stop for a titter at the Sex Museum. Dope dealers cruise up and down flogging expensive dope to uninformed tourists and pickpockets have a heyday.

Once the ships that sailed into the harbour used to moor along the leafy banks of the Amstel – now Damrak – getting as close as possible to the main commodities markets on Dam Square. Goods were unloaded and taken off to be weighed while captains struck deals with tradesmen hanging around in the square. The small patch of water at the station end is a meagre tribute to its maritime past.

To enjoy Damrak you really need to be there on a sunny morning before the shops open around 10 a.m. To the north the imposing Centraal Station glistens in the distance, trams rattle past ringing their bells at dozy street cleaners and seagulls soar overhead. Cruise boats bob across the wide expanse of water, shattering the reflections of the old houses on the other side. A formidable statue of Gijsbrecht stares down from his plinth on the corner of the sturdy red brick Beurs building and a mass of starlings chatter in the trees behind.

Sex Museum

Damrak 18, tel. 627 7431. Open 10 a.m.–11.30 p.m. daily. Admission f4. Tram 4, 9, 16, 24, 25 to Damrak.

Sex is fun, intriguing and guaranteed to pull in the punters. The Sex Museum, however, is nothing but a pathetic display of mags, sex aids, sexy underwear and sexy images from around the world, tempered by offensive posters. The most memorable exhibits are a couple of ferocious seventeenth-century chastity belts and a six-foot penis.

Amsterdam's Sex Industry

Sex is Amsterdam is in danger of overkill. After a few days in the city you will have seen enough dildos, sex aids and pictures of copulating couples in shop windows to keep the imagination going for years. You may be shocked, embarrassed, surprised, fascinated or simply giggle, but curiously most sex industry products are not nearly as offensive or provocative as many Dutch advertising campaigns – we even witnessed one man so taken with an ice cream advertisement that he was openly masturbating over it at a bus stop while a queue of Dutch women watched on totally unperturbed. This is Amsterdam, where sex can be perverse and blatant but is so commonplace that it fails to be as offensive as one might expect.

Prostitution alone generates an average turnover of one billion guilders a year, making it an important component of the tourist industry (see p.86 for more on prostitution). Amsterdam is also an important centre for the publishing and marketing of pornography, but surprisingly little is actually produced in the Netherlands. Most of the pornographic photos and films are made elsewhere, particularly in the Czech and Slovak Republics and Hungary. The only laws that seem to be enforced by the Dutch vice squads are those against child pornography. They turn a blind eye to anything else passing through the sex shops.

Recent rumours of owners of gay brothels and sex shops being among the city's wealthiest residents are not unfounded; a lot of people make a lot of money out of sex in Amsterdam. The two main companies publishing pornography and manufacturing sex articles are Scala and Everex, both of whom attract frequent media attention linking them to organised crime in the capital. Porn shops and brothels are notorious for money laundering and undercover crime networks.

But not all sex shops in the city are offensive. A few are shedding their sleazy image as a younger generation enter the trade, offering goods for the purchaser's private pleasure that do not exploit others; the city has a number of upmarket leather/S&M shops and straight condom and vibrator shops which bar pornography altogether.

Beurs van Berlage (Former Commodities Exchange)

Beursplein 3.

The raw brick exterior of the former commodities exchange on the east side of the Damrak is a stark contrast to the flashing lights and gabled houses across the road. On a wet day the dampened bricks give a solemn touch to this prison-like building and if the sun is shining the sandstone sculptures on the corners gleam against the red brick walls and it seems noble in its simplicity. Sadly the café at the southern end is temporarily closed. If you want to see the impressive interior you can attend one of the many exhibitions held here or relax in the newly converted concert hall while listening to the resident Netherlands Philharmonic Orchestra.

The Exchange building caused quite a stir when it first went up at the turn of the century. Critics spoke of it as 'melancholy, sombre and unfriendly' and warned that 'This undesirable impression could have been avoided if more account had been taken of our heritage and examples of our noble old Dutch architecture'. Many Amsterdammers felt it was unsuitable as the city's main Commodities Exchange. But the liberal city council had chosen their architect very carefully. Hendrik Petrus Berlage was an idealist and a socialist who believed that the days of capitalism were numbered and it would not be long before the city had no need for an exchange at all. He therefore designed the building hoping that one day it could be used as a town hall. The sculptures outside by Lambertus Zijl depict historical figures and inside the murals by Jan Toorop have more to do with communism than commodities; the three-tiled tableaux represent *Past, Present and Future* as a class struggle, featuring the *Emancipation of Women* and the *Liberation of the Workers* – hardly matters taxing the minds of the commodities brokers.

Berlage's vision proved to be wrong. The Exchange closed not because capitalism was obsolete, but because the building could technically no longer support a modern exchange system. Gradually each exchange moved to its own premises in the city and, ironically, Berlage achieved his dream to use the building as a public space. The building, which apparently disregards centuries of Dutch architectural styles that preceded it became a milestone in Dutch architecture. Its simple brick walls and lack of ornamentation became a hallmark of the Amsterdam School (see p.174), the capital's predominant contribution to modern architecture.

Effectenbeurs (Stock Exchange)

Tours by appointment. Tel. 523 4567. Free admission. Tram 4, 9, 16, 24, 25 to Dam Square.

The city's commercial activity has always centred around Dam Square and even if you don't find stocks and shares particularly exciting you may find a trip around the oldest Stock Exchange in the world quite intriguing.

The East India Company issued the first share in Amsterdam in 1606. Throughout the seventeenth-century the city's money markets were among the most sophisticated in the world. Today, as the recession hits the Netherlands, the Exchange is keen to attract foreign investment and the PR department enjoys any opportunity to sell Dutch business to foreigners. Tourists are treated to a cosy slide show and a chat over coffee to clear up any questions about the workings of a stock exchange. You will be allowed a glance at the suited men peering at screens and clutching telephones on the trading floor before leaving. While the Amsterdam Stock Exchange is proud to be as technologically advanced as New York, London or Tokyo, it has a long way to go with respect to women, who count for less than 2% of the brokers.

*20 N.Z. Voorburgwal, tel. 6230632. Open Mon–Sat 10 a.m.–
6 p.m. Admission, adults f2.50, children f1.25. Short walk from
Centraal Station. Trams 1, 2, 5, 13, 17 to Martelaargracht.*

This may look like any old souvenir shop in one of the most
touristy streets in the city, but the daily demonstrations of clog
making are good fun. A professional man whittles away at blocks of
wood with a variety of hand-made tools and more robust machin-
ery while chicks and guinea fowl peck around his feet and a manky
cockerel provides the music. There is often a small display of
photos, paper cuttings and clogs for enthusiasts. Clogs for sale come
in all shapes, sizes and colours, mounted as roller skates, hanging
off key-rings and turned into flowerpots.

Clogs have been in use for around 600 years. The Dutch took
to wood because it was water resistant, cheap and hard wearing –
just what the farmers needed in the boggy marshlands. They were
all cut by hand until the 1930s when machines took over.
Wellington boots have failed to make traditionalists change their
footwear, but even clog fanatics will agree that most clogs these
days are sold to tourists.

Dam Square

'The public places or squares in Amsterdam are not very handsome.' Such was the view of the eighteenth-century traveller
Thomas Nugent, and twentieth-century Dam Square is no better.
Trams hurtle across the cobbled square while pedestrians cling to
the pavements or stay stranded in the centre. The National
Monument, a blunted little obelisk to the east, is dwarfed by grand
hotels and department stores. At the other end the former Town
Hall (Koninklijk Palais) and the Nieuwe Kerk make a handsome,
if grimy, pair. Dodgy types hang around the cash dispensers on
the corners, dope dealers hassle tourists, foreign men pick up
foreign girls and junkies beg. During the summer groups of children
gather in the centre to see the regular Punch and Judy shows
every Monday, and on Queen's Day, 30 April, the whole square
turns into a fairground, the big wheel soaring way above the rooftops.

It is natural to expect great things to happen in Dam Square
as this is the most prominent square in the city and the point at
which the River Amstel was originally dammed. In the past Dam
Square has witnessed riots, demos, public executions, witch trials
and hippie invasions, but the current mood here seems tame by
comparison.

Executions were festive occasions when everyone turned out to heckle and cheer at hapless criminals, and journalists rushed to take notes on the gory finale. A fairly poignant one appeared in the *Yiddish Chronicle*, in 1748, following the 'tax farmers' riot' against corrupt tax collectors. When the three ringleaders were sentenced to death, one of them, a Jewish woman, captured the hearts of the crowd: 'The drummers began beating their drums ... to prevent people from hearing the woman's screams but she cried out most pitifully "Vengeance, vengeance dear fellow citizens. Help me. You watch me die in this humiliating way but I did not fight for myself, I did it for the whole country, to rid us of the tyranny of the tax farmers, those tormentors who forcibly steal our money and possessions" ... then the spectators saw the pulley move. When she was hoisted out of the window she was still screaming ... and so she hung outside the window, and struggled until she was dead.'

Other women to meet their fate here were alleged witches. The Dutch, though renowned for their leniency towards heretics, were very superstitious of women displaying supernatural tendencies. Most witches were tried according to their weight; if they were too heavy to fly on a broomstick they were thought innocent, but little waifs were sent to the scaffold. The last witch to be tried in Amsterdam was Payns of Purmerend who was burnt at the stake in 1555 having admitted to killing both men and animals in a 'pact with the devil'.

Staged beatings, wife batterings and bottom pinchings still go on in the square every Monday (over the summer) with regular Punch and Judy shows. They started in the seventeenth century when Jan and Katrijn Klaasen brought their puppets to the Dam as a satirical protest against the authorities' conduct of war against England. The message today has been tempered to suit the under tens.

WITCHES

Sorcerers, witches, the devils' handmaidens, over a million people, mainly women but also men were executed for suspected devil worship in the sixteenth century. Talk of human witchcraft had been around for some time: the Babylonians believed in women riding on 'a piece of wood' to meet the devil. Early Christians feared werewolves and magic, but the first person to put it in writing was St Thomas Aquinas who confirmed that Satan had his helpers on Mother Earth, a view seconded by Pope Innocent VIII at the end of the fifteenth century. The fanatical anti-witch craze was started by two Dominican Friars, inquisitors who were employed by the Pope to publish *The Witches Hammer*, a manual on witchcraft, witches and their accomplices. This fired popular imagination, inspired widespread suspicion and fuelled a witch hunt in France,

Germany, Sweden, the Netherlands, Hungary, England and even new America. In the Netherlands trials and executions were frequent, ruthless and usually ended in execution, but, unlike the rest of Europe, the Dutch soon questioned the suspicion and trial of witches and put an end to the trials long before the belief in sorcery was dead.

Anyone could find themselves being dragged to the gallows for witchcraft. If a heavy hailstorm destroyed a harvest, a child died very young, or a cow suddenly gave less milk someone, nearly always women and children, seldom men – was singled out as having given it the evil eye. Even an anonymous note to the burgermaster was enough to lay a charge. Many husbands accused their wives of witchcraft simply to get rid of them, as divorce was not an option.

Once suspicion was raised, the accused was put through a number of trials: the feathers in her pillow were checked to see if they stuck together or formed a fairy ring; a priest put his hands on her head and asked her to cry since real witches cannot shed tears; she was bound and thrown into water – if she sank (and so probably drowned anyway) she was proved innocent, but if she floated it was proof that she was light enough to fly on a broomstick; and she was made to walk on hot coals – if her feet blistered she was innocent because anyone who had a pact with the devil could not burn so easily. The most common trial was by weighing. Suspects were taken to the weighing-house, (every town had one for weighing in goods) where they would be strip-searched for hidden weights. A midwife checked the women and a beadle did the men and then they were put to the test. Unusually light suspects were obviously witches and were burnt at the stake. Weigh masters were reputedly open to bribery so there were many cases of women being recorded as weightless or weighing no more than a fly.

In 1545 Emperor Charles V witnessed a suspected witch being weighed in Polsbroek. The dishonest weigh master weighed her in at 2.5 kilograms which the Emperor found unbelievable so he took her to another weigh house at Oudewater where she weighed in at 50 kilograms and was subsequently acquitted. Charles V then granted Oudewater the privilege to issue certificates throughout his empire to anyone who wanted to be weighed there. If acquitted, the bearer of the certificate could never be tried for witchcraft again. Henceforth, people came from all over Europe to be tried at Oudewater (as tourists still do) and no one has ever been too light. Oudewater was one of the few weighing-houses to judge weight in accordance with the natural proportions of the body.

The last trials to be carried out in the Netherlands were in the 1590s, preceding other European countries by over a century. In 1595 a family of sorcerers were accused of dancing like cats with the devil, turning into werewolves and biting chunks out of the cattle – they were all burnt at the stake in Utrecht. The last convicted witch in the Netherlands was Marigje Arriens, a seventy-year-old herbalist from Schoonhoven who was sent to trial and subsequent death in 1591 by some dissatisfied customers.

Suspicion of witchcraft continued, as did the trials, but no one else was executed. Academics and theologians in the Netherlands began to speak out against the witch trials at home and abroad. The poet, statesman and writer on women's issues, Jacob Cats, stood for the defence at a trial in 1610. He wrote a short verse to commemorate his victory:

'Behold ye! After court had passed sentence thus
All witchcraft from the nation seemed expelled at once!

The woman, for a while by everyone despised
had quiet and blameless rest, by no one criticised.'

Active opponents to the belief in witches in the Netherlands were Gerard Tuining, Abraham Paling and the Amsterdam parson, Balthasar Bekker.

Bekker wrote a four volume book The ensorcelled World in 1692, the outraged response to which resulted in him fleeing to Sweden. People didn't mind him denying the existence of witches, but he also suggested the devil had no power on earth which caused quite a stir. His writings and the weighing-house at Oudewater did much to quell popular fear of witches, but obviously not enough for some – almost two centuries later women were still trying to prove their innocence. A woman in Deldenerbroek volunteered herself for trial by water to prove her innocence. Women could no longer be convicted but this didn't stop accusations from malicious folk.

The National Monument

As flared trousers and long hair come back into fashion a few young hopefuls hang around the white obelisk on Dam Square, awaiting a revival of 60s and 70s Amsterdam. In the 60s, enticed by the relaxed drugs laws, sexual liberation, Provo success (see p.103) and each other, young people from around the world set up home in the waiting halls of Centraal Station, on the steps of the National Monument and in the open spaces in Vondelpark. As a Dam sitter of the 70s said, 'this is where it is all happening', and for a time it was. The perpetual party on Dam Square was the best in the world. Impromptu dancing, smoking, singing and copulating were occasionally dropped for sleeping and putting the world to rights, or tuning to Radio Veronica (the pirate station bobbing around in the North Sea). Even John Lennon and Yoko Ono chose Amsterdam for their famous *Sleep In for World Peace*, but couldn't hack the tarmac so chose the Hilton instead.

Public patience ran out as local offices and hotels found their loos perpetually clogged with Dam sitters and the stench around the monument became unbearable. In 1967 the marines were called in to wash the hippies away. Armed with water cannons they charged down Damrak into the square, hosing the sleepers out of their roosts and out of the city.

The monument itself is a rather disappointing tribute to all those who died in World War II. Oppressed men cower at the feet of Lady Liberation as doves flutter up the white obelisk. A curved wall behind, bearing inscriptions, gives the whole sculpture a urinal quality which even the potted plants can't hide. Designed by J.J.P. Oud, it was paid for by the sale of 400,000 shares which entitled the owners to a share of the Dam. Inside the obelisk are twelve urns, each filled with soil from the battlefields across the provinces and one with soil from Dutch military cemeteries in Indonesia.

Dam Square 20, tel. 622 9949. Open daily 10 a.m.–5.30 p.m. Admission adults f17, children under 15 and senior citizens f12, family tickets for 2 adults and 2 children f46. Tram 4, 9, 14, 16, 24, 25 to Dam Square.

This is the only branch of the popular waxworks museum outside England, but lacks the original's vigour. The display has a strong Dutch flavour with a steady run through the history of Amsterdam. An animated giant, conveniently named Mr Amsterdam, welcomes you to the show. Canals, brothels, painters, merchants and skaters give a taste of the city's history before leaving you to fend for yourself on a mock up of the moon. Back on planet earth you will meet wax politicians, monarchs and pop stars, and be invited to take a seat next to the model of Holland's favourite chat show host, Tineke. The finale is a universal celebration of the twentieth century. A personification of World Peace sits in a revolving Tulip, bobbing to the chorus of Beethoven's Ninth Symphony. Once Chaplin, Bogart, Einstein and Churchill have returned to their slots in the sky, closely followed by a mounted St Nicolaas, you find yourself in the souvenir shop with a long walk down to the street.

MADAME TUSSAUD

Madame Tussaud was born Marie Grosholz, in 1761. She was the daughter of a Strasbourg widow who worked as a maid for the wax modeller and artist, Dr Curtius. It was Curtius who taught the young Marie the art of wax modelling and took her to Paris, where he exhibited at the Palais Royal. Louis XVI's sister Elizabeth was the first to recognise Marie's talent and invited her to become art tutor at Versailles where she stayed for the next nine years. When the Revolution began in 1789 she returned to live with Curtius, where she was employed making death masks of many unfortunate victims of the Guillotine, including Louis XVI and Marie Antoinette. She married in Paris and had two children while trying to run Curtius's exhibition which he had bequeathed to her. In 1802 she left Paris and her husband and son for England, to tour with her exhibition. She never returned to Paris and in 1835 set up a permanent exhibition in Baker Street, London.

Nieuwe Kerk (New Church)

Dam Square. Open Mon–Sat 11 a.m.–4 p.m., Sun 12 noon–2 p.m. Admission varies according to the exhibition on show.

The Nieuwe Kerk is one of Amsterdam's most impressive churches and despite being stripped of its decoration during the Reformation there is still lots to see: the elegant Gothic architecture, huge stained-glass windows, an exuberant pulpit and a fantastic organ. It is also used as a venue for world-class exhibitions which may hide the architecture, but are well worth checking out.

The Nieuwe Kerk was built in the fifteenth century when the Oude Kerk became too small to cope with the number of worshippers trying to use it. As a contemporary put it, the 'spiritual tutelage' of the Oude Kerk was being 'heavily overtaxed'. That the church has survived at all is something of a miracle; it was nearly burnt down in 1421, 1452 and again in 1645. Resilient as ever, it survived the iconoclastic riots of 1566 when Protestant sympathisers went on the rampage against Catholicism (see p.68) and remained standing despite serious subsidence problems over the years. Since its foundation there has been constant rivalry between the Old Church and the new. Each made endless plans to upstage the other. The Nieuwe Kerk lost out when the plans for towers and spires were abandoned, leaving the church with a stump over the crossing, but it has definitely become pre-eminent in twentieth-century Amsterdam. After extensive restoration the church is now a lively social centre with a bookshop and café, yet maintains its ecclesiastical role, having been promoted to national status as the inaugural church of the Netherlands. The last monarch to be crowned here was Queen Beatrix in 1980.

Inside, the church is a massive but elegant building; soaring columns are set against white walls, light pours through the tall windows and a sweeping ambulatory invites you to take a stroll round the building. It lacks the height of the great French Gothic cathedrals, but in Amsterdam, where foundations were soft and soggy, it was important to spread the weight over a broad base. You can't fail to notice the flamboyant Gothic pulpit designed by Albert Jansz Vinckenbrink in 1645, radiating from a pillar like an exotic hat – there is certainly no need for kids to snooze through the sermon here. The pulpit tells its own story. Around the rostrum the Virtues, personified by women, would have been clearly recognisable to the lay public. Fortitude leans on her pillar, Faith clutches her Bible, Charity looks after a couple of children, a blindfolded Justice displays her impartiality and Prudence holds a mirror in her hand and a snake in the other. The snake derives from Matthew (10:16) 'Be ye wise (*prudentes*) as serpents'. The mirror signifies that a wise person is able to see her true self. Once you have worked them out, there is plenty more to see; the pulpit is riddled with biblical references and stories, saints and evangelists are carved in fascinating detail. The screen around the pulpit is common in Protestant churches. It prevented the people, their children and their dogs from disturbing the priest, and also designates a certain liturgical area.

When Catholicism was replaced by Protestantism (see p.68)

the whole emphasis of the service itself changed from the celebration of mass held at the altar to the sermon being delivered from the pulpit. In the Nieuwe Kerk the redundant altar space is now taken up with the tomb of one of the Netherlands' most celebrated naval heroes, Michiel de Ruyter. He ran off to sea as a cabin boy and eventually made it to the rank of Admiral. His most daring exploit, in 1667, was to sail up the Medway and set fire to the English Fleet. He eventually died of wounds fighting the French at Syracuse in Italy. It seems fitting that such a powerful man should have ended up on the altar of Amsterdam's prestigious church like an offering to the Gods. Behind his effigy, in the carved backdrop, Fame blows her trumpet over a stormy sea complete with ships, marine life and beautifully carved shells.

The Organ   If you get the chance to hear an organ concert in the Nieuwe Kerk you are in for a treat. The wonderful instrument, designed in 1655 by Roelof Barentsz Duyschot, sounds as good as it looks. The pipes are supported by a magnificent arrangement of columns, pilasters and pillars and frivolous sculptural details by Artus Quellijn. A musical mayhem of cherubs crowd the marble base; cymbals are clashed, pipes blown and drums beaten; faces gleam with sheer delight at static noise, instruments decked with garlands of flowers smother the pilasters and parrots peck at plump delicacies on the cornice. The festive charm continues upwards where three winged women carry the city Alms. Above, the muses of lyric poetry and musical harmony, Euterpe and Harmonia lean heavily on their globe – a bold attempt to represent spherical harmony.

If you find the shutters closed you will see how the painter, thought to be Gerrit van Bronchorst, uses the curve of the shutters to enhance the perspective of the columns and stairs, themselves a platform for the happy gang of dancers and players. Bronchorst obviously spotted this work as a good opportunity to advertise his services as a painter, so he decided to include a self-portrait hanging out of the left-hand window.

The Windows   The stained-glass windows are a good way of genning up on the Dutch royal family who have been crowned here since the nineteenth century. The Netherlands has had female sovereigns for over a century since Wilhelmina succeeded to the throne in 1898, her mother Emma reigning in her place during Wilhelmina's minority. The two stained-glass windows, just before the north transept, were presented to Queen Wilhelmina by the City of Amsterdam to mark her fortieth year on the throne. In the top left-hand window, Queen Wilhelmina stands with her mother beside her. To the right there is a gathering of royal women: Emma the Queen mother, Princess Juliana and the baby Princess Beatrix. Juliana took over from her mother Wilhelmina after spending the war in exile in 1948, and Beatrix took office in 1980. The theme of Dutch nationalism continues in the south transept where an enthroned Queen Wilhelmina receives her constitution from a winged woman.

Koninklijk Palais (The Royal Palace)

Dam Square. Open Wed 1.45 p.m.–4 p.m., Tel 624 8698 ext 217. Admission f5, under 12s f1.50. Tram 4, 9, 14, 16, 24, 25 to Dam Square.

It seems hard to believe that this grimy building was once described as the 'Eighth Wonder of the World' by the astute poet, Constantijn Huygens. If it wasn't for the regular peal of carillon bells from the tower and the constant chatter of little birds from the rooftops one would almost miss the tower and massive block at the end of Dam Square. It opens once a week to hordes of tourists drawn by its grand title of Royal Palace – a misnomer, since it was built in the seventeenth century as the Town Hall, turned into the royal residence during the French Occupation and now lies empty except during state occasions and tourist invasions every Wednesday afternoon.

If you happen to be passing when it is open, brave the crowds and take a look. The rooms are barely furnished and the atmosphere is sterile but there are lots of sumptuous sculptural decorations by Artus van Quellien and an opulent Citizen's Hall for a taste of the Golden Age. Visitors are divided into large groups and guided, usually in Dutch, as quickly as possible around the first floor. As crowds pour in, the groups are disbanded and chaos reigns so get there early and pick up an English leaflet at the ticket desk. A more expensive guide is available inside if you wish to know more about city administration in the seventeenth century.

The Palace was built in the seventeenth century to replace the existing Town Hall, incorporating the administrative and judicial departments of the city government. Travellers marvelled at this monstrous building slap in the middle of Amsterdam. For many it was a symbol of the wealth and power of Amsterdam in the Golden Age comparable to other grand European buildings like the Ducal Palace in Venice. The most noticeable thing about the building is the absence of a grand entrance; instead the front is pierced with seven little arches said to refer to the seven provinces that made up the Dutch Republic following the Treaty of Utrecht (see p.69). Once crammed with eager faces watching the proceedings in the death chamber beyond, nowadays the arched loggia plays host to the city's pigeons. If you are interested in the architecture your best bet is to look at the model of the building in the Amsterdam Historical Museum (see p.108).

City administration in the seventeenth century was highly efficient, well funded and exclusively male. Four burgomasters, representing the most influential men in the city, appointed a sheriff and magistrates and referred issues to the city council for approval. The city's main source of income was taxes levied on property and commodities, as it is now. One of the best known organisations housed here was the Exchange Bank, described by William Temple as the 'greatest treasure, either real or imaginary, that is known anywhere in the world'. Like all banks this was only the case if you had money. Founded in 1609, the Bank changed money, set up deposit accounts, handled direct transfers from one account to another and bought non-current coins and ingots of metal to be deposited in various mints. Owners of overdrawn accounts were fined immediately and those wanting credit facilities had to go to private money lenders. The Bank was internationally renowned.

It remained the Town Hall until King Louis Bonaparte, Napoleon's brother, decided he wanted to live here in 1780. Louis moved in, totally refurbished it, filled it with French imperialist furniture and demolished the weighing-house outside on the Dam to improve his view. The current dynasty prefer their home outside the Hague, so it lies empty and unused. Robbed of its Town Hall the city has only just opened a new one, over a century later, on Waterlooplein.

The interior   An eerie silence fills the cold marble room on the ground floor, known as the **Tribunal**. Prisoners were summoned from cells and torture chambers round the corner to the Tribunal for the sole purpose of hearing their death sentence. Only those who admitted their crime could be sentenced to death, but the means of eeking a confession from them were hardly humane – many would have found the scaffold a welcome relief after a few hours in the torture chamber.

Along the back wall two caryatids cower beneath the ceiling, representing 'oppressed and captive women'. They divide three gruesome classical reliefs representing Mercy, Wisdom and Righteousness. The left-hand panel shows the Greek legislator Zaleucus having his eyes gouged out in an act of mercy to save the sight of his convicted son. In the centre panel a wise King Solomon presides over two brawling women and to the right Brutus condemns his treacherous sons to death in an act of righteousness.

If you make your way upstairs you will arrive in the vast **Citizen's Hall**. If someone would lift the carpets you'd be able to see the entire Eastern and Western hemispheres mapped out on the floor. As it is, you have to make do with parts of it. The idea was that the citizens of Amsterdam had the world at their feet – an idea that was not far from the truth in the seventeenth century. High above, a statue of Atlas staggers under his globe, presiding over all that goes on below.

If you take a closer look at the extravagant array of sculpture in the Hall you will notice that there are a large number of women; look even closer and they all represent something rather than someone. Above the entrance Amsterdam surveys her world, accompanied by Minerva, the goddess of Wisdom, while Strength is depicted as a woman wearing a lion's skin. A seventeenth-century public would have expected statues of women to represent something whereas statues of men were automatically expected to represent an important person. The public anonymity of women made them more suitable for symbolic sculpture. Thus Amsterdam is so often represented by a woman.

Leaving the Hall, in either direction, you can walk around the gallery and admire the delightful sculptural reliefs over the doorways, each one a comment on the proceedings carried out in the room beyond. Above the entrance to the Insurance Office, the Greek poet Arion is saved from the sea by a friendly dolphin and at the door of the Bankruptcy Chamber Icarus plunges to his death, having melted his wax wings flying too close to the sun. Pop your head into the magistrates court and admire the architectural decoration of turtledoves and children, a reference to the many marriages that took place here. Carry on round the gallery, stopping at the door to the Secretariat where silence holds a finger to her lips and a faithful hound guards his dead master in an act of fidelity.

For a good view of Dam Square and some impressive paintings, take a look at the **City Council Chamber**, the council boardroom. The decorative scheme is aptly concerned with advice. A large painting of *Moses Selecting Seventy Elders* covers the west wall. The rays of light beaming from his head come from a misinterpretation of the word *cornutum* (horned), used in the Vulgate. Artists had used them to define Moses since the Middle Ages. The eighteenth-century artist, Jacob De Wit, is responsible for the fine *grisailles* work (painted sculpture) over the doors. Wit was so accomplished that in Amsterdam such work is referred to as 'Witjes'.

THE RED LIGHT DISTRICT

Amsterdam's Red Light District, known locally as the 'Walletjes' (little walls) is by turns intimate and intimidating, compulsive and repulsive. It is centred on the **Oude Kerk**, bordered by Warmoestraat, the oldest street in the city, and stretches across two canals, O.Z. Voorburgwal and O.Z. Auchterburgwal. Here, day and night, prostitutes flaunt themselves from windows, under dim red lights. Lacy underwear and teeth gleam in ultra violet, whips, chains and bunches of dried flowers hang on the walls and the covers are neatly turned back on the little beds behind. A seething mass of men and tittering tourists pours down narrow alleys and parades up and down the canals while the city's drug dealers dart in and out of unmarked doors. Neon lights declare 'Free Sex', 'Foreign Girls' and 'Group Extravaganzas' and shop windows brim with dildos, pornographic mags and sado-masochistic gear. Noisy tourists booze in brash pubs, old men sip cool genever in ancient drinking houses and a marijuana-mellowed youth peer through the psychedelic windows of hip coffeeshops.

There is a gentler side to the area, one of little cafés where children spoon the cream off frothy hot chocolate, where housewives gossip over steaming soup and groups of men play cards in the corner. It is a sociable neighbourhood, where residents share their lives with the prostitutes regardless of what goes on behind the curtains; restaurants, galleries, arts centres, clubs and a local market give it an intimate quality of its own. To the south of Damstraat and Oude Hoogstraat the sex industry comes to an abrupt halt and you can enjoy the atmosphere without being intimidated by skulking men.

The Red Light District is one of Amsterdam's main tourist attractions. In fact the most common problem in the area is tourists taking photos of prostitutes. Be warned, they do not like it. Remember they are people with emotions, pride and a career. Photographers are likely to have their cameras ripped off them, the film taken out and thrown into the canal.

We would not recommend that you stay in the heart of the Red Light District because, although not dangerous, it can be unnerving at times. The street which runs along the northern edge, the Zeedijk, is a prime area for hard drug dealers so unless you need drugs it is best to avoid it especially if alone. You are unlikely to come to any harm but the atmosphere is somewhat daunting. The basic rules are to avoid eye contact with anyone and dress sensibly and you will be left alone. If you feel frightened, threatened or just uneasy head for a crowded street or a busy café. Remember the area only makes up a very small part of a large city and you can be in a highly respectable and safe place in a matter of minutes. If you don't want to go through it, go round it. If you are travelling alone try and join someone else staying at your hotel or take one of the organised tours on offer. (see p.61). That said, anyone who has been in the city for more than a week will assure you that it's neither unnerving nor unpleasant to walk through alone, day or night.

For centuries the prostitutes have lived and worked on Amsterdam's 'old side'. The area has also always had a large Christian community, represented today by Christian groups offering free haircuts, manicures and coffee to lonely prostitutes, and in the past by a number of local convents and monasteries. Chapels, cloisters and refectories have mostly disappeared, but their presence is remembered by street names and buildings like the Agnietenkapel and the cloister of the Eleven Thousand Virgins. After the Reformation many of these buildings were taken over by charitable institutions and have since been commandeered by the university. If you wander southwards from the Red Light District you will come across a number of clues to the city's past, among them the Women's Prison (*Spinhuis*), the Almshouses (*Oudmanshuis*) and the old City Hospital (*Gastenhuis*).

PROSTITUTION

Sex is business for as long as there is a business in sex. Over 5000 women work as prostitutes in Amsterdam with over 2000 working daily. The number of clients is less easy to ascertain – some women see ten a day and some perhaps a couple.

Even among the great ports of Europe Amsterdam has long been renowned for prostitution. For centuries the municipal government has debated how best to accept that it is part of society. They have penalised it, ignored it, tolerated it, supported it, controlled it and still the debate goes on.

By the fifteenth century the port of Amsterdam was, as it is now, the centre of a huge prostitution business. Popular songs recalled the goings on in brothels, bath houses and music halls and travellers wrote reams about the city's apparent decadence. In 1478 the authorities tried to organise it by demanding that all prostitutes live with the servants of the sheriff or bailiffs in either the Pilsteeg or the adjoining Halsteeg (now Damstraat), thereby containing prostitution within a couple of streets. Disobedient whores were ceremoniously paraded home, accompanied by a drum and flutes.

At the end of the sixteenth century the Protestant patriciate had a go at banning prostitution. Offenders occasionally found themselves banned from whore houses and taverns, but the punishment was mild and ineffectual. In fact it was the clients who were of more interest to the authorities than the women involved. Adultery was so serious a crime that husbands caught with prostitutes were only too happy to hand out vast sums of money to avoid prosecution. Local judiciary officials made their fortunes by receiving bribes from adulterers.

By the seventeenth century toleration was the norm. In the words of William Carr, consul of Amsterdam: 'There are tolerated in the city of Amsterdam, amongst other abuses, at least 50 music houses where lewd persons of both sexes meet and practise their villainies. There is also a place called the long seller, a tolerated exchange or public meeting house for the whores and the rogues to rendezvous in and make their filthy bargains'. Writing for an English audience, he goes on to qualify why sex should be tolerated in this way: 'I have heard ... that when the East India Fleets come home, the seamen are so mad for women that if they do not have such houses to bait in, they would force the very citizens' wives and daughters.'

So who were these women? Many were single childless women from the lower classes who were rarely entitled to state help or care and found it hard to find jobs. Single men in this situation joined the navy, army or the East India Company, all of which commanded great respect. For women the only realistic option was prostitution. There were, of course, women who actually wanted to make a career of prostitution and went on to own and run their own brothels. Most of the 'vice houses' were in fact run by women, few of whom were ever convicted for their work. Trijn Nages was an exception when she appeared before the magistrates in 1677, described as 'forty years old and a whore hostess'. There are numerous descriptions of seventeenth-century whore houses. Portraits of girls were hung on the doors of their rooms so clients could take their pick. There was endless haggling over prices and prettiness, but this was all part of the game. However, urban prostitution such as this had become the object of embryonic organisation and once again we find the police sergeants were given the privilege of managing these brothels in specific areas of town. Prostitutes who were unlucky enough to end up in the *Spinhuis* (women's prison) were ruthlessly exploited by hypocritical governors who took large sums of money in return for the sexual services of women in their care.

Famous nineteenth-century brothels like *De Pijl* (The Arrow) in the Pilsteeg and *De Fontein* (The Fountain) in Nieuwmarkt are just names today. By 1900 the area for soliciting had moved well into Dam Square and Kalverstraat where 'nice' women were seldom seen, as whores and punters paraded the street from morning to night. The notoriously chic brothel 'Maison Weinthal' finally closed its doors in 1920. Today in the Red Light District, known locally as the *Walletijies* sex is sold as it has been for hundreds of years. Apart from the neon lights, exotic sex shops and glamorous posters it looks as though little has changed over the years. For the prostitutes, however, life is changing fast.

Prostitutes' Rights

At last these women have taken hold of their profession. In 1985 the 'Rode Draad' or Red Thread was founded – the first prostitutes' union to have gained an international reputation and to have given its members a political voice. The first International Whores Congress, held in Utrecht and Amsterdam in 1985, gained world-wide support. As a result the International Committee for Prostitutes' Rights (IPCR) was founded. The Red Thread promoted international interest in fighting for the rights of prostitutes throughout the world.

Victims or businesswomen? Feminists continue to debate the issue, but the prostitutes have won the support of some who hastily created the support group, Pink Thread, as a link between them. Prostitution in Amsterdam has become a complex mix of working women who need social recognition, professional status, and self-respect and support until this can be achieved.

Women who work in clubs and private houses endure the employee/employer relationship with the club owner. Brothels have been illegal but tolerated since 1911 and until brothels can be formally legalised prostitutes have no rights concerning working conditions and pay. At present brothel owners take around 50% of women's earnings and often a lot more. The City Council continue to delay their final decision regarding the lifting of this 'brothel ban' despite constant pressure from the Red Thread to decriminalise Amsterdam's brothels. Window prostitutes are effectively self-employed. They are entitled to their earnings, but have to pay exorbitant rents for their room. Most have to work shifts so that overheads can be shared. Street prostitutes are a more vulnerable group who have few overheads, but earn less. In the world of prostitution ambitious girls work themselves 'off' the street. Unfortunately many street prostitutes are addicts; their business is for immediate cash for drugs rather than for eventual promotion and they are more tempted to practise unsafe sex and subsequently exploited by clients.

At least half of the 5000 prostitutes working in Amsterdam are foreigners and many are from Latin America, Africa, the Philippines and Thailand. More recently, young boys from Eastern Europe have joined the work force. The influx of foreigners has seriously changed the nature of prostitution in Amsterdam and the social balance among the prostitutes. Many women from these areas have worked as prostitutes in their home country and choose to work in Western Europe to increase their income. Some are the innocent victims of trafficking, brought into the country as mail order brides, domestic helps and go go girls and forced into prostitution against their will. Many are victims of sexual and racial abuse and are locked in a constant battle to overcome language barriers and cultural differences.

Victims or not, all prostitutes suffer the stress of living life as a social outcast. They work long hours (often ten hours a day) at anti-social times, suffer health problems, threats of violence and have no rights. The Red Thread continues to fight for legal and other reforms concerning human rights, working conditions, health care, social services, taxes and social prejudice. Their slogan reads 'We never had rights. Never. We have a lot of catching up to do.'

Warmoestraat

A few paces from the grand entrance of the Hotel Krasnapolsky on Dam Square is the oldest, seediest and often liveliest of Amsterdam's streets, Warmoestraat. The Dam Square end is often dingy and desolate, apart from a lone junkie tripping along the pavement or a suited businessman returning at a pace from the brothels beyond. Further on, flower shops, galleries, restaurants and cafés jostle for a position among the leather bars, sex shops, brothels and the police station. Mothers take their kids out to buy bread, gay men strut into the leather shops for gear, pimps check on their charges while an off duty prostitute chats over a *cappuccino* with her grandmother.

Tourists tend to head for the noisy smoking bars, stopping at the **Condomerie** on the way.

Warmoestraat started as a row of wattle and daub cottages, but by the sixteenth century it was popular with wealthy merchants and bankers. Most of the locals left when the Spanish Duke of Alva was put up here during a last attempt by the Spanish to control the Dutch in 1574, but it wasn't long before they were back. The poet Vondel ran his hosiery business from No. 101, just a few doors away from his sister's hosiery shop. Like many seventeenth-century women, Clementia van den Vondel worked in her husband's shop and ran it after his death. Mozart senior is reputed to have sold tickets for his son's concerts in the pubs here and Karl Marx chose to write from one of the inns.

Today the street is as lively as ever, packed with a number of really excellent restaurants, good clubs for live music, galleries and the famous condom shop.

THE CONDOMERIE

Condomerie Het Gylden Vlies (The Golden Fleece), Warmoestraat 141, must be one of the world's best advocators of safe sex. Run by two women, it's a welcome relief from the many sordid sex shops further down the street. The owner, Marijke Vee, spends her days discussing the pros and cons of the little 'rubber' with condom users from all over the world.

It's a highly professional set-up where condoms come in every conceivable shape, size, colour, flavour and texture. They offer a wide selection of 'user friendly' packaging, from boiled sweets to designer pens. Friendly staff are on hand to give advice on the many brands (no femidoms yet) available and their use. The best thing about the shop is that no one looks embarrassed. One warning though: the so called 'fantasy range' are not recommended for safe sex.

Next door to the Condomerie, hiding behind a mass of structural scaffolding, is the offbeat **Gallery 139**. The building was originally squatted by a group of art lovers who decided that Amsterdam needed a venue where new artists could show their work without having to fight for space and recognition at the better-known galleries. The huge whitewashed walls provide artists with a perfect (though cold and dirty) space to display their work. Sculpture reaches into the rafters and large canvasses occupy the vacant white spaces. Often the work on show is pretty dire, but you may be lucky enough to stumble across a gem. If you don't like what you see you can join the arty crowd at the gallery bar for a coffee.

Moving on down Warmoestraat you may meet a group of nuns, 'the sisters of Warmoestraat', running daily errands from one of the city's few remaining convents at No. 159. Few nuns live here today, but they offer board and lodging to local women and children who need help. If you want to look inside, join the nuns for daily prayer – the times are shown on the door.

Beyond a concentration of shops selling dildos, dirty mags and SM gear, a little further down the street is one of Amsterdam's best coffee and tea shops, Geels and Co., and some of the city's most popular restaurants. (See Eating and Drinking p.247.) Before long the street runs into the rough Zeedijk, renowned as a hot spot for hard drug dealers and full of rather seedy-looking types, both day and night. Like so many places in Amsterdam Zeedijk may seem worse than it is. Unless you are looking for drugs it is best not to engage in conversation with anyone along here, but you are unlikely to be approached if you walk purposefully. Despite this it is inevitably daunting and you may prefer to avoid it altogether.

BET VAN BEEREN, QUEEN OF THE ZEEDIJK (1902–1967)

The leather-clad lesbian biker first came into the pubic eye in 1927 when she opened a café, *Het Mandje* (The Little Basket), in the most dangerous street in the city, the Zeedijk (No.63). Everyone was welcome but, following her example, it was particularly popular with the gay community.

The Red Light District was already known as a good area for 'tolerant' pubs and cafés. In a quarter which depended on whores, sailors and exotic foreigners, café owners were generally fairly tolerant of homosexuals. Many Amsterdammers recall the strong personality and gutsy life of this extraordinary woman. Customers were kept in line, kissing was not allowed and dancing was only permitted on certain public holidays in keeping with the city ruling. Bet made sure that everyone joined in when the Salvation Army dropped in for a sing song and no one could leave without buying their latest literature. On Queen's Day, Bet's customers apparently spilled out onto the street and the dancing went on way into the early hours. It was also the only day in the year when transvestites were allowed to walk the streets. The law stated that on no other day should gay couples wear clothes belonging 'to the sex to which they do not belong'. Women got around this all year round by simply sewing up the flies on their trousers.

During the Second World War the Zeedijk was forbidden ground for the German army. Bet sheltered both weapons and people from the enemy; the Jewish writer, Hermine Heijermans, was among the many she helped. After her death in 1967, Bet lay in state surrounded by the many souvenirs she had gathered from her customers over the years, among them postcards, photographs and hundreds of dolls. The café was run by her sister for a while, but closed after a few years. It is sadly not open today but has been turned into a city monument. The brown neon light still hangs outside and a brightly painted basket of flowers acts as the gablestone. Photos of Bet, her bike and her friends fill the window and, up above, the upstairs window is crammed with dolls and memorabilia.

Oude Kerk (Old Church)

Church open Fri–Sat 1 p.m.–4 p.m. Admission f3. Tower open 1 June–15 Sept, Mon 2 p.m.–5 p.m., Tues–Wed 11 a.m.–2 p.m. Admission f3. Tram 4, 9, 16, 24, 25 to Dam Square.

Slap in the middle of the Red Light District is Amsterdam's oldest church. The interior is pretty bleak, but the views from the tower of the city and the church itself are a substantial reward for the climb.

You will probably end up circling the church trying to find the entrance which is hidden between the limpet houses on the south side. Take this chance to look at the lovely eighteenth-century tower which in fact encases its thirteenth-century predecessor. Oude Kerksplein, the square in which it stands, has been a prime venue for prostitution for centuries so expect to hear the heavy tapping of windows and to see lots of sexily dressed women touting for business. This is Amsterdam at its most bizarre; children attend classes at the vicar's house against the church, prostitutes flaunt flesh from the windows opposite and old ladies gossip on the benches in between.

There has been a church on this site since the thirteenth century which was repeatedly extended and rebuilt over the next 300 years. The original basilica was dismantled in favour of a larger structure with choir, aisles and, later, transepts. Side chapels started to appear as patrons (usually guilds) had money to spend, and the church continued to expand despite the presence of the nearby Nieuwe Kerk. Houses were added to the exterior in the seventeenth and eighteenth centuries. This arrangement was not unusual. Many churches built an outer layer of housing to house the clergymen and boost their income when times were hard. Today many are offices.

The church suffered iconoclastic vandalism in the sixteenth century, appalling bouts of restoration in the eighteenth century, near collapse in the nineteenth and a total rehaul in the twentieth. It was finally restored to its present shape from 1955 to 1971.

In years gone by the Oude Kerk was a hive of activity. Inside, merchants clinched deals, peddlers set up their stalls, beggars and travellers sheltered from the elements, pilgrims filed in to say a prayer and locals dropped in to celebrate mass. In 1566, when Amsterdam Calvinists got wind of the unchallenged iconoclastic riots in Antwerp, they gathered up friends and free spirits, headed for the Oude Kerk and smashed everything in sight while the *Schutters* (Burgher Guard) looked on in terror. The excitement was too much for the young Lange Weyn who hurled her shoe at a picture of the Virgin Mary. She was subsequently bundled into a tub and thrown off the Dam to drown in the canal. The Calvinist outrage was temporarily quashed until William of Orange and his men arrived, in 1578, to expel the Catholic magistrates and clergy from the city and declare Amsterdam a 'Calvinist' city in the so-called 'Alteration' (see p.68). They cleared the Oude Kerk of its motley band of resident parishioners, confiscated any remaining idols and dropped St Nicolaas as the church's dedicated saint. Since then it has been known as the 'Old Church' or Oude Kerk.

It is difficult to imagine such excitement these days. The church is usually empty, very cold and completely consumes the audiences that gather here for concerts and services. Little decoration survived the Protestant outrage save some faded vault paintings and the misericords in the choir. The delightful fifteenth-century misericords (small ledges for tired priests to prop their bums on) are carved with a grisly band of fiends and beasts alluding to some long-forgotten Dutch proverbs.

Nearby the Elizabeth Gaven chapel, named after its founder,

has a delightful monument to Vice-Admiral Abraham van der Hulst by Artus de Witt (1666). A number of constipated looking cherubs hold up a baroque extravaganza of swirling seas and ships. As you wander round the church you trample over the graves of the famous and the unknown. A number of interesting women – all of whom lived in the area – were buried here, Rembrandt's first wife, Saskia van Uylenburg (d. 1642), Joost Vondel's sister Clementia van den Vondel, the poets Lucretia van Marken (1721–1789) and Betje Wolff, and the intellectual poet and musician Maria Tesselschade Visscher (see below), to name just a few. On your way out you pass the Bridal Chamber. Countless couples have taken the plunge here, undeterred by the inscription above the door that reads 'T'is Heast Getrout, dat Lange Rout' (Marry in Haste, Mourn at Leisure).

MARIA TESSELSCHADE VISSCHER (1594–1649)

The night Maria Visscher was born her father, the wealthy merchant and writer Roemer Visscher, was swimming for his life off the north coast of Holland having run aground on the island of Texel. He marked his survival by burdening his daughter with the additional name of Tesselschade or Texel harm – a name to live up to. She never looked back and became one of Amsterdam's most celebrated intellectuals of the seventeenth century.

Maria and her sister Anna grew up in Amsterdam and were educated by their father at their home in Gelderskade. They received a thorough grounding in the arts and literature and also learned to fence and swim. Roemer Visscher's urge to educate his children had no bounds; he even dug a canal around his country house for their swimming lessons. Their father's involvement with other writers and artists brought them in touch with the Muiderkring (Muiden circle), a society of writers formed around the poet P.C. Hooft. They often attended the regular meetings that took place at the family home and were finally accepted as members. Despite glowing reports from fellow members, the sisters were never included in the portraits of the Muiderkring, indicating a certain amount of sexual discrimination among intellectuals.

Maria was an extraordinarily talented musician and artist. She played the lute, viola and harpsichord, and had a beautiful singing voice and was an accomplished painter, engraver and intellectual. Respected by some of Europe's greatest intellectuals of the time, she did not take kindly to criticism. When Rene Descartes (also living in Amsterdam) found her reading the Bible in Hebrew he was quick to point out that he felt she was wasting her time on such a trivial and meaningless pursuit. Maria was livid, sent him on his way and told him not to return, claiming that 'God has dismissed this profane man from my heart'. Descartes was only one among many admirers. She was courted by the most respected men in Amsterdam: Vondel, Bredero, Hooft and Huygens. Men seemed totally undeterred by her lopsided looks following the loss of an eye to a blacksmith's anvil, and she ended up marrying a sea captain from Alkmaar. After his premature death she returned to Amsterdam where she assumed her role as the city's leading Renaissance woman. Her home became one of the foremost literary Salons in the city and her talents continued to impress the locals. Her wealth had obviously established her eminent social position, but it was her intellect that maintained it. Somaizes Dictionnaire des Précieuses acknowledges the sharpness of her wit, listing her as 'Satira'.

Oudezijds Voorburgwal 40, tel. 624 6604. Open Mon–Sat 10 a.m.
–5 p.m., Sun 1 p.m.–5 p.m. Admission f3.50, f2.50 under 14s. Tram
4, 9, 16, 24, 25 to Dam Square.

This little canal house in the Red Light District is one of
Amsterdam's most compact museums. A maze of simply furnished
living rooms, bedrooms and lethally steep stairways leads up to the
attic where you suddenly find yourself in a galleried Catholic
church. It is the last surviving clandestine church in Amsterdam
where Catholics could worship in secret following the Alteration
(the changeover from Catholic to a Protestant City Council, see
p.68).

The museum is clearly marked by a red flag of Amsterdam
hanging over the door. The front of the house is shown as a domestic interior with all artefacts clearly labelled in English and Dutch.
The back is given over to exhibits relating to Catholicism. A short
English guide is available at the front desk. As the stairs are narrow
and steep it is a good idea to follow the marked route, starting in
the front room from where the original owners ran a sock shop. Jan
Hartman and his wife developed the site in 1663. They ran the shop
from downstairs, lived upstairs and let out rooms in the two buildings behind. They converted the two top storeys of the canal house
and the attic of all three buildings into the church.

Upstairs the *Sael* is one of the few rooms to keep its seventeenth-century character. A huge fireplace carrying the family coat
of arms (the hart for Hartman and the compass for his wife) dominates the room, as if designed for a palace rather than a tiny house.
The size of the room hardly justifies the grandeur or the size of the
architectural fittings, or the furniture that fills it, but it alludes to
wealth. The huge oak and walnut cupboard was a symbol of success, ambition, wealth and comfort and the dream of every Dutch
housewife. Whether this was because it reflected having space to
accommodate it or things to fill it is uncertain, but the obsession
was universal. The wall cupboard is in fact a cupboard bed, a space-
saving device whereby the bed came down at night and slotted back
into the wall by day. There is another one in the little room overlooking the canal upstairs. Space was so important that the Dutch
even had to compromise in the way they slept. As you will see in the
priest's room, beds were much shorter than standard beds today. In
addition, families would sleep together, adults in a near-sitting position, propped up on a pile of pillows. The little stools on the floor
are foot warmers. Hot coals smouldered underneath sending warm
air through the holes above.

Upstairs is the gloriously lit Catholic church, suffused with the scents of musty books and polished wood. A couple of neo-classical statues of Sts Peter and Paul stand behind the back pew, while out of the window red lights glint in the canal. Within the altar is a revolving pulpit and the altar reredos is in fact made up of three paintings by Jacob de Wit which were alternated according to the Christian calendar. In the gallery, beside the organ is a small case of chalices and reliquaries. Past the altar takes you back into the old house, where the priest lived alongside the confessional and the sacristy. The stairs lead down to the original entrance to the church in the little side street.

Cannabis Info Museum

O.Z. Achterburgwal 150, tel. 623 5961. Open daily 11 a.m.– 10 p.m. Admission f6. Tram 4, 9, 14, 16, 24, 25 to Dam Square.

This is the only museum of its kind in Europe. Exhibits cover the growing and use of marijuana and trace the history of the weed over the centuries. Occupying a single room, with a grow room at the back, it doesn't take long to see it all, peruse the books and information leaflets, and buy a packet of seeds. The shop next door will sell you equipment to cultivate them.

The police have gradually depleted the number of exhibits over the past few years, forcing the museum to close down for a while. It has recently re-opened, having to make do with fake hash and marijuana, which seems rather silly given that you only have to pop into a café to see the real thing. They are, however, allowed to house the plants so you can at least see it in its vegetative state. Hardened dope smokers will hanker after the beautiful pipes and hubble bubbles from around the world while interested newcomers to the subject can find out more about the trade and the habit. A number of interesting videos (all in English) explain the medicinal use of cannabis in the 1990s; for instance, it relieves some side effects of chemotherapy and features in the treament of glaucoma and multiple sclerosis.

Nieuwmarkt

Don't be put off when people tell you this is the seediest square in town. Nieuwmarkt is one of the few squares where you are likely to meet the locals; schoolchildren, prostitutes, housewives, drunks and drug dealers queue in the local supermarket, drop into the bank or chat over a mountain of fresh Dutch cheese at the daily market. Dogs chase pigeons across the brick-paved square, students doze on the Gaudiesque public benches and drivers smoke Gitanes in the taxi rank.

On weekdays regulars are greeted with smiles and free slices of cheese at the little market, cute kids are rewarded with candies and chocolates and housewives stock up with organic vegetables, freshly baked bread and corn-fed chicken. Opposite, a tank full of eels await their fate at the fishmongers while aproned ladies carve fine white slithers off fresh Turbot, Halibut and Cod. The aroma of fresh herbs and spices bursts out of the ancient lotion and potion shop, Hooey & Co., a little further down. On the opposite side of the square Chinese men fold crisp white linen in the laundry, Chinese women busy themselves in the Chinese supermarket and their children play on the streets – a few shops and restaurants in the adjoining streets make up Amsterdam's tiny Chinatown. On Sundays, in summer, a lively antique market sprawls across the square while on public holidays it turns into a fair ground or sometimes hosts a visiting circus.

In the middle, the medieval city gate of **St Antoniespoort** looks like something out of Euro Disney.

Built in 1488, St Antoniespoort was once the main city gate on the east side. It was a popular place for executions and would usually have had the remnants of various criminals swinging from its walls as a warning to others. When the city expanded in the seventeenth century it was used as the weighing-house or '*Waag*' as it is often referred to today. All goods had to be weighed here on arrival to make sure no traders were being cheated. Smugglers got round the law by entering the city under the Waag along the sewers. A number of guilds also had their offices here, including the Surgeons', whose activities inspired Rembrandt in his research for the famous painting, *The Anatomy lesson of Professor Tulp*. For a long time the building served as the Jewish Historical Museum as it stands on the edge of the Jewish Quarter which runs off down St Antoniebreestraat. In recent years it has been covered with scaffolding while developers decide whether it is destined to be a TV studio or a restaurant.

The history of the square itself over the past twenty years is one of destruction and despair. Many of the old houses were torn down to make way for the **metro** (see box) and it became a hot spot for drug dealers and addicts. Unsavoury types still hang around, but there is enough space to avoid them and members of the police are never far away; a prefab floating police station floats on the canal and ruins the view. Like most such places, it is more daunting at night.

METRO MANIA: AMSTERDAMMERS V CITY COUNCIL

Few Council decisions have been so violently opposed as the plans to build a metro. The original plan in 1968 was to build a four-line subway network through Nieuwmarkt to the newly constructed city suburb of Bijlmermeer at an estimated cost of f250 million. By 1973, the cost had risen to f1500 million for a single line and the city was up in arms. Two neighbourhood action groups, the *Difficult Amsterdammers* and the *Safe Traffic* group, staged a protest exhibition on Leidesplein to give the people the real subway story, estimating the true costs of the project: the loss of housing, their heritage and the inevitable rise in cost of other public services. No one really wanted a metro in the first place. Nor did they want the beehive complex in Beejilmermeer, intended to house 100,000 people.

Peter Hakkenberg, a *kabouter* (see p.103) serving on the Municipal Council, summed up the real reasons behind the project: 'The subway is not being built for social purposes; it is an economic and prestige question since Rotterdam has a subway. This is a status symbol for a city that prides itself on being the "gateway for European tourism and an international money centre".' His attitude was shared by the majority of the city's population but it did not deter the Council from continuing with the project. On 25 March, 1975 there were violent demonstrations when the police tried to clear the first houses in Nieuwmarkt for demolition. The police rammed the doors with armoured vehicles and threw teargas through the windows to disperse angry and frightened residents from their homes. Violent confrontations continued for the next three years when the City Council managed to calm residents by agreeing to renovate other areas of the city. The metro finally opened in 1980. As the locals predicted, the upheaval of their city was a waste of time – few people have reason to use it.

Trippenhuis (The Trip House)

Kloveniersburgwal 29. (Not open to the public.)

Just down the canal from Nieuwmarkt, the massive neo-classical house with canon-shaped chimneys and martial-shaped decorations was an appropriate home for two wealthy arms dealers in the seventeenth century. The Trip brothers, together with another Dutchman, De Geer, controlled almost all Europe's arms supply in the seventeenth century – a good time to be into arms when almost everyone except the Dutch was at war in Europe. At the time, Kloveniersburgwal was an upmarket address so the hugely extravagant decoration would not have looked as out of place or as grubby as it does today. Their coachman complained that he would be happy with a house the size of their front door so the canny brothers saw to his request. If you look across the canal you will see his house, at No. 26, which measures a paltry seven feet wide.

Oude Hoogstraat 24. (Not open to the public.)

Like so many of the historical buildings in the old centre, the head-quarters of the Dutch East India Company has been taken over by the university. Graffiti-covered brick and a mountain of disregarded bikes does little justice to the formidable building attributed to Hendrick de Keyser. The inner courtyard is a lively mass of sandstone against red brick. The elaborate ensemble of scrolls and volutes on the entrance façade and the free-standing balustrade on the top are typical of Keyser at his most exuberant. In the seventeenth century sailors would have poured in here to join the crews of the hundreds of ships setting sail around the world for the East India Company, known as the VOC (*Vereinigde Oostindische Compagnie*). The only women to get signed on had to trick their employers into thinking they were male. A surprising number of transvestite sailors were discovered on VOC ships and many more probably went undetected (see p.205).

Agnietenkapel

O.Z. Voorburgwal 231, tel. 525 3341. Open Mon–Fri 9 a.m. –5 p.m. Ring bell.

The last remaining part of the Convent of St Agnes, which operated between 1397 and 1585, has been part of the university since its foundation as the Atheneum Illustre in 1632. Exhibitions relating to the university are shown when someone feels like organising one. You may like to drop in to see Amsterdam's oldest lecture hall upstairs – the doorman will show you the way.

The lecture hall, known as the *Grote Gerhoorzal*, is where many great seventeenth-century lecturers like Vossius and Barlaeus made their debut lectures. Rows of folding seats and little wooden bookrests evoke silence and studiousness. Above, a wooden ceiling is studded with Renaissance motifs and the walls are lined with portraits of celebrated academics, Vondel, Hooft, Descartes, Erasmus, Luther and Calvin, to name a few. Even Thomas More gets wall space.

On leaving the Agnietenkapel, across the pedestrian bridge is the Bank van Lening, at O.Z. Voorburgwal 300. Nicknamed 'Old John', the bank has offered a respectable alternative to professional moneylenders since 1614. (Interest rates are fixed according to your ability to repay the loan.) The poet Vondel worked out his final years here, bankrupted by his son. On the arches a few paces down the adjoining alley, his inscriptions advise the rich to hurry by since there is no business for them inside.

Gastenhuis (Former City Hospital)

The little corner where the canals meet at the end of Oude Zijds Achterburgwal is usually a mass of bicycles and students hurrying to lectures, chatting outside the mensa or socialising in the middle of the street. On the corner, at No. 249, the step-gabled house, known as the 'House on Three Canals' is the only one to afford such a position in the entire city. Opposite a rather grand gateway, reputedly copied from a design by Michelangelo, marks the former entrance to the City Hospital or *Gastenhuis*. You get a good view of the original building from the university mensa which is tacked onto the side. The building itself and the splendid gateway say something of the past sophistication of Amsterdam's social services which intrigued travellers from around the world (their present system is fairly impressive, too).

When Amsterdam's merchants were enjoying excessive wealth in the seventeenth century the citizens did not forget their poor. Huge fund-raising projects were launched by the municipal government to raise money for social services.

Taxes were imposed on imported grain and de luxe funerals (one way of getting to the rich), and locals organised charity auctions, banquets and lotteries. By 1700, the city supported over 20,000 people in lodgings throughout the city. Even the lodgings were worthy of comment, as William Carr put it, 'They looked more like palaces than lodgings for poor people'.

Oudemanshuispoort (Old Man's House Gate) and the Book Market

Oude Zijds Achterburgwal 120.

Along what was once called Amsterdam's velvet canal, owing to the wealthy merchants who lived on it, you may notice a constant stream of young academics passing under a grubby little arch. Take a closer look and you will see that the pediment decoration is a pair of little round glasses, reminiscent of the ones that Brits used to get on the National Health and John Lennon had to pay for. They refer to neither – in fact they allude to the old people's home that used to be here in the eighteenth century. If you follow the students, you will find yourself in a dingy passage crammed with second-hand bookstalls. Stall owners huddle over cups of coffee and book catalogues, dogs doze at their feet and would-be-buyers peruse faded volumes. If nothing takes your fancy take a break in the elegant courtyard of the almshouse, surrounded by a magnificent rose garden. The almshouse or *Oudemanshuis* was built here in 1754 on the site of a former convent for elderly Amsterdammers with no dependants. The head count in 1765 was 115 women to 51 men, suggesting that the old women of Amsterdam were a hardy bunch compared to their menfolk. If you leave from the other end of the book market, a very grand arch leads onto Kloveniersburwal, sporting a relief of a dramatic young woman bestowing her cornucopia on a couple of old people. You are now in the area where the feminist Rosa Manus lived while she pursued her mission to gain suffrage for Dutch women.

ROSA MANUS (1881–1942)

Rosa first came in touch with Amsterdam's feminist community when she went along with her classmates to dance at a convention for the Women's Suffrage Association in 1908. Living on the edge of the Jewish Quarter in Amsterdam, she had a sheltered Jewish upbringing and was constantly at odds with her over-protective father. When she decided to join the Women's Suffrage Association (VVVK, see p.38) there was mayhem at home, but she persevered to become one of Holland's most active feminists. She was a close friend of Aletta Jacobs (see p.149) and worked with Johanna Naber at the International Woman's Suffrage Alliance (IWSA) as a special adviser. Her organisational skills were formidable. She mounted an exhibition on 'The Work and Strife of Dutch women 1812–1913' with Mia Boissevain and long after suffrage was won, in 1919, she went on to organise exhibitions and conferences to expose the needs of women to the nation. Queen Wilhelmena awarded her the public honour of Order of Orange Nassau in recognition of her service to society.

Rosa had spoken openly about the atrocities of anti-Semitism for many years. She instigated and presided over the Amsterdam Women's Volunteer Corps, devoted to the care of refugees and victims of Nazi oppression, which was sponsored by the Dutch government. When the Germans occupied Amsterdam they dissolved the Corps and destroyed the archive which Rosa had built up. In 1941 she was arrested and deported, to die a year later in Ravensbruck concentration camp. Mourned by feminists in Europe and America, the American Carrie Catt summed up her achievements in a lettter: 'Rosa was a little Dutch girl, dancing with other boys and girls in Dutch costume for the entertainment of the delegates of the Amsterdam Convention of 1908. At that time she scarcely knew what we were about. She grew into a dependable worker in the women's movement and, curiously enough, was the first of us to suffer and die for our cause.' Sadly Rosa's personal papers and belongings were destroyed in the war so there is very little written evidence of the important work she did for the Dutch Women's Movement, other than the recollections of her colleagues. She is one of Amsterdam's most important women, yet she is invariably omitted from the history books.

Oude Zijds Achterburgwal/Spinhuissteeg.

It's heartening that Amsterdam's former women's prison should now be an **Institute for Women's Studies** (see p.46). Students chat in the little courtyard, read the papers and discuss women's issues in the refectory, almost oblivious to the building's grisly past.

The Spinhuis, founded in 1597 and rebuilt in 1643, was a mysterious set up – a cross between a charitable institution and a secure prison for hardened criminals. Above the entrance (in *Spinhuissteeg*) there is a grim relief of women being thrashed with a cat-o-nine tails. The inscription above reads 'My hand is punishment but my intentions are loving.' It was more of a correction house than a prison and, as the name might suggest, most women were subjected to manual labour, spinning flax and knotting fishing nets until they were seen fit to return to society. There was a curious mix of inmates; beggars, prostitutes and thieves mingled with young girls, confined at their parents request – sending one's kids to the Spinhuis for a few weeks was considered to be a reasonable way to deal with difficult daughters in the seventeenth century. Many foreigners wrote about the 'secret place' in the Spinhuis where the inmates were not allowed visitors, lessons or work. Great speculation went on as to who was kept in the secret place, but it seems likely that they were the daughters serving time at their parents' will. One traveller speculated that the girls in hiding were 'little venuses too beautiful to be seen by anybody.' Other inmates were always available for anyone to see – visitors could pay a small entrance fee to come and ogle at them, and if they slipped a few coins to the governor they could stay the night with the prostitute of their choice. One traveller found it to be 'built with such splendour that one would consider it to be an inn for princesses rather than a home for such detestable and ugly maidens'.

In the eighteenth-century, the Spinhuis assumed the role of a working prison as many of the less dangerous inmates were sent to the New Workhouse in the east of the city. The Workhouse, initiated as an education institute for tramps and beggars, was a revolutionary concept in Europe. A large number of women entered as volunteers – for many poor women it was a means to an education and a better life. In the nineteenth century the prison system changed in Holland and many light offenders ended up working in the colonies.

If you are looking for the entrance to the Institute, walk around the Spinhuis to the courtyard in the unpronounceable (try it!) *Elfduizendmaagdenklooster* (Cloister of the Eleven Thousand

Virgins). The name does not refer to the women at the Spinhuis, but recalls the even earlier convent of St Ursula that was on this site. The legendary St Ursula was the daughter of a British Christian King (fourth century), who managed to delay her marriage to a pagan prince to travel instead. She supposedly took with her 11,000 cruise companions. They ended up being bludgeoned to death in Cologne by heathen Huns after Ursula refused to marry their chief. The citizens of Cologne built a church in her honour. Her cult was particularly popular in the Rhineland, Northern France and the Low Countries.

Zuiderkerk (South Church)

Tower open from 1 June – 15 Oct, Wed–Sat 2–4 p.m. Church open Mon–Fri 12.30 p.m.–4 p.m., tel. 622 2692.

The best views of Hendrick de Keyser's splendid spire, embellished with freestanding columns and topped with an onion dome, are from the bridge where Staalstraat crosses Groenburgwal. Constructed between 1603 and 1614, it was the first Protestant church to be built in Amsterdam. During the war it was turned into a temporary mortuary for the area. Today it is a centre for urban development and renewal and as such it is only visited by people who are fascinated by the city's planning projects or looking for ancient buildings needing renovation. They do however stage interesting architectural exhibitions on a highly imaginative raised platform which runs around the interior. A cluster of seventeenth-century tombstones are all that remains of its ecclesiastical past. If you want a good view of this side of Amsterdam and have the energy, it is well worth a hike up the tower.

The church is a survivor of the 1980s metro demolition and redevelopment of the area. Outside, children practise wheelies on their bicycles in the concrete courtyard while their Mums hang washing out to dry from their homes in the Zuiderkerhof. This pentagonal complex around the church is an imaginative piece of community housing, designed by Hagenbeek in 1983–4. Even so, one can't help wondering what was there before.

AROUND SPUI

The main roads running down the west side of the Historic Centre converge at Spui, a large square bordered by the medieval cloister of the *Begijnhof*, the arid red-brick university administration building and some of the trendiest cafés in town. The narrow alleys and surrounding streets are crammed with huge department stores, cut-price bookshops and exclusive galleries. It is a great area in which to stay: right in the middle of the city and only a short walk to all the major sights. If you are wondering where to eat on your first night in Amsterdam, the concentration of cafés on Spuistraat is always brimming with locals.

By day an army of shoppers push their way down Kalverstraat, stopping to watch mime artists and puppeteers before being caught up again in the swell. Tourists enjoy the city's past at the **Historical Museum** while families tuck into pancakes and fizzy pop in the David and Goliath Café down below. Old ladies tend to their little gardens in the Begijnhof while businessmen and women stroll through on their way to work.

Life on the Spui has not always been as calm as it is today. In the 1960s crowds frequently gathered around the seemingly harmless little bronze statue, *Het Lieverge*, at the southern end to watch the pyromaniac demonstrations given by the anti-smoking campaigner, Robert Grootveld, to take part in the anti-establishment demonstrations of the Provos and in support of students wanting more control over their university. The central position of the square in the city has always made it a prime venue for gatherings – today you will find it at the hub of the city's social life.

The Lieverdje statue (Little Darling)

The bronze statue of a pubescent boy, head cocked and skinny arms propped on his hips, donated to the city by the Hunter cigarette company, is one of Amsterdam's most significant monuments. In 1965, every Saturday night, weather permitting, crowds would gather around the statue to watch the magic happenings of the anti-smoking campaigner and magician Robert Jaspar Grootveld. Grootveld performed various Pyromaniac tricks over and around the little boy, conducted communal sing-songs of the coughing song ('Ugghe, Ugghe, Uggh') and warned of the forthcoming revolt of the addicted consumer. Much of his mystical forecasts ring true in the 90s as the ozone layer thins, and addicts mount lawsuits against cigarette companies, but at the time he was seen by most of his fans as a nutty entertainer and self-proclaimed exorcisist of spirits.

'The problem of smoke is a magical problem: the cigarette comes from Mother Earth. The plant is being picked, fermented and rolled in the body of a cigarette. Then Holy Fire enters: smoke ascends. That is magic; every young kid in the streets, making a bonfire, will be able to tell you that. Ascending smoke has a magical power. Didn't age-old cultures know of smoke sacrifices? This is now our sacrifice: publicity pillars with posters for cigarettes are this society's totem poles. The entire world is our jungle – ask our astronaut who sees the earth from outer space. But there is a development of smoke over our heads, which is going to engulf and destroy us.'

Grootveld taunted the police by plastering the letter K (for Kancer) all over cigarette advertisements in the city and filling cigarette machines with fake marijuana cigarettes in Day Glo packets. He paid for it by spending a couple of months in prison, but paved the way for other anti-establishment groups like the Provos. Looking for a ready-made audience with anarchistic tendencies the Provos chose Lieverdje as a prime venue for 'happenings'.

PROVOS AND KABOUTERS

In the 60s Amsterdam became the centre of an anarchist revolt which spawned imitators throughout Europe and fuelled the fashion for pop, poetry and pot in Britain and America. The keynote of the Provo movement was provocation. The bespectacled bearded theoretician Roel van Duyn decided to launch the first edition of *Provo* among crowds watching one of Grootveld's happenings at the Lieverdje in 1965, further copies were distributed with the morning papers. Five hundred leaflets were distributed encouraging people to join the bandwagon against authoritarianism with hints at how to '*provocate*'. The police seized most of them because they included an (ineffective) bomb recipe and initiated a vigorous campaign against the forthcoming marriage of Princess Beatrix and former Nazi Claus von Amsberg. Their plans included laughing gas in the organ, hidden recordings of machine guns, and lion manure on the procession route to frighten away the horses. None of these actually came to fruition on the day, but television all over the world captured the scenes of Provos throwing smoke bombs and subsequently being beaten up by the police. Provos could not have hoped for better publicity. *De Telegraaf* reported 'Provo terror' and the media throughout the world reported rebellion in Amsterdam.

When there was nothing as dramatic as a royal wedding to react to, Provos staged outrageous 'happenings' around the city to maintain public interest; the painter Fred Wessels staged an 'ice happening' in his Jordaan home, throwing open all the windows in the middle of winter while a few women skated around a *pretend* ice rink in their clogs; Marijke Koger, 'the hippest chick in town', stripped off seven layers of clothing to reveal her completely painted body beneath; Dr Bart Hughes drilled a hole in his head, calling it 'his third eye' and claiming he had reached the state of a permanent high, which he demonstrated frequently by dancing through the streets with a mannequin. Meanwhile Robert Grootveld, the anti-smoking campaigner, was pulling his best stunt ever, dressing up as a woman and dropping acetone on the floor of tobacco shops destroying the taste of every cigarette in the store. He attempted to appease angry shopkeepers by saying 'I am a fanatical social worker'. From the start, the police were unable to deal with the situation and their often heavy-handed reaction to frivolous theatrical happenings only motivated more Amsterdammers to support the Provos. One provo young woman, Koosje Koster was arrested for handing out raisins to the public in the Spui – she spent 28 days behind bars for 'disturbing public order'. It was clearly a moment of misjudgement and panic on the part of a police officer.

Provos were essentially non-violent. Their motives were laid down in the *White Plans* for a cleaner, kinder and safer city. White Bicycles were proposed for public use, free for anyone who wanted to use them, and everyone was encouraged to take their bikes for a free painting at the Spui. The police confiscated most bikes on the pretext that they might be stolen, so provos retaliated by painting police bikes. 'White Chickens' (slang for policemen) suggested that all police officers should become social workers armed with food, matches and contraceptives; 'White Wives' was a plan that encouraged free contraception and abortion for all; 'White Housing' recommended the restoration and occupancy of condemned properties; and 'White Chimneys' proposed that there should be compulsory smokeless zones in the city. One of the most intriguing proposals was the 'White Corpse', intended to dramatise traffic accidents – murderous drivers should be made to dig an outline of the body into the tarmac on the spot where the victim was mown down and fill it with white mortar.

There were very few people who actually called themselves Provos; Van Duyn surrounded himself with immediate supporters such as Luud Schimmelpennick, Rob Stohle, Robert Grootveld and Irene van Weetering. The student Irene was made Provo leader only a week after joining, mainly because she was unknown and the big names were being harassed by the police, but it was a good choice. Her position as a Provo met with strong disapproval from a number of people who felt she was acting irresponsibly for a mother of two. Other women found it was great to have an understanding ear at the heart of a movement led by men.

Provos had hundreds of supporters. To quote from *Provo*: 'What is the Provotariat? Provos, beatniks, pleiners, nozems, teddy boys, rockers, blousons, noirs, hooligans, mangupi, students, artists, misfits, anarchists, ban the bombers ... Those who don't want a career and who lead irregular lives; those who come from the asphalt jungles of London, Paris, Amsterdam, New York, Moscow, Tokyo, Berlin, Milan, Warsaw and who feel ill-adapted to this society ... PROVO despairs of the coming of Revolution and anarchy. Nevertheless it puts faith in anarchism; for PROVO anarchism is the only admissible social concept. It is PROVO's ideological weapon against the authoritarian forces which oppose us.' Support reached its zenith when Van Duyn was elected to the City Council in 1966.

Lacking a conventional organisation, the movement began to disintegrate and wound up in 1968, but it helped to spawn a tradition of anarchistic movements in Holland which included the student seizure of the Maagdenhuis (see p.105), the sexual revolution, drug culture, a psychedelic sub-culture, a host of imaginative movements and the creation of the *kabouter* movement under ex-Provo Van Duyn. In 1970, a number of Amsterdammers woke up to find gnomes at the bottom of their garden, the trademark of the new organisation known as the kabouters (meaning gnomes). Kabouters set up an Orange Free State proposing non-authoritarian crèches and schools, flower gardens on the roofs of cars, 'non poisonous' food shops, non-profit making small industries, bedtime stories for the elderly – an ideal world. The Premier called it a 'whiff of perfume amid the stale smell of cabbages in our politics'. The public response was sensational, within six months of its foundation the Orange Free State won 11% of the vote and six places on the municipal council. As it became clear that ideal worlds were difficult to realise, the Free State's popularity withered away and it was disbanded in 1971.

The Maagdenhuis (Maiden's House)

Spui 21. Tram 1, 2, 5 to Spui.

The busy administrative centre of the university was once the home of 250 virgins. It was founded in the sixteenth century as a Roman

Catholic orphanage by two well-meaning ladies, Aaltje Foppens and Marijte Spiegel, who felt children should be given the opportunity to experience a religious upbringing. Rules were tight; anyone caught singing rude songs was banned from the home, given six weeks 'on the block' or imprisoned.

This was nothing compared to the events of 1969 when the Maagdenhuis, by then the central university building, was at the heart of a student revolt. Outraged students occupied the building, demanded democracy within the administration, and refused to budge. It was during this occupation that the most influential woman's lib group 'Dolle Mina' was born (see p.39). While the men held meetings, painted banners and contacted the local radio station, the women found themselves preparing food and cleaning out the loos. When they were finally evicted by the police the women received lighter sentences than their male colleagues for their protest was seen as less serious than the men. The women named their group after the pacifist and feminist Wilhelmina Drucker who had lived just round the corner from the Maagdenhuis. While the men continued to protest against the rise in tuition fees, the Dolle Minas spent the 70s standing outside the marriage bureau at the Town Hall shouting 'Faith forever, but who will clean the sink', setting up abortion clinics and fighting for female liberation (see p.39).

WILHELMINA DRUCKER (1847–1925)

Wilhelmina grew up with her grandmother, mother and sister in a little house on Heligteweg. The illegitimate daughter of a single mother, she was unimpressed by marriage which she described as an 'indelicate form of living together'. From an early age she joined her mother at Social Democrat meetings and became so involved in the fight for equal rights that in 1889 she founded the Liberal Woman's Association Vrije Vrouwen Vereniging for women of any class, creed or colour. She was also involved in the fight for women's suffrage, but left the Association for Women's Vote Vereeniging Voor Vronweskiesreecht in 1916 because she felt it was not radical enough. She was an ardent pacifist and in effect a socialist, but she deliberately didn't join the Social Democratic party in order to maintain her independence. She was a popular speaker at De Dagaraad, the society for free thinkers, and founded the magazine for free speech, *Evolutie* (Evolution) with Dora Haver.

The Rasphuis (Men's Prison)

Heligteweg 19.

You may wonder why there is an ornate classical gateway with men cowering beneath the Maid of Amsterdam whose hand is raised (someone stole the whip) to scold them, in the middle of this small shopping street behind the Maagdenhuis. The Rasphuis or Rasp

House is the male equivalent to the women's prison, the Spinhuis. Inmates were forced to rasp wood daily until the powder was fine enough to be used in dye. Visitors were allowed in to gawp at the prisoners as this helped to plump up the regents' coffers – light entertainment was always laid on; lazy prisoners were branded, beaten with a bull's penis or made to pump themselves out of a tub of water racing against the constant flow that filled it.

Allard Pierson Museum

Oude Turfmarkt 127, tel. 5252556. Open Tues–Fri 10 a.m.–5 p.m., weekends and public holidays 1 p.m.–5 p.m. Admission f5 students and OAP f3.50, under 12s free. Tram 4, 9, 14, 16, 24, 25 to Spui. Tram 4, 9, 14, 16, 24 to Muntplein.

The university's extensive archaeological collection is impressive, entertaining and nicely displayed in its grand neo-classical home, which once belonged to the Nederlandsche Bank. It lies along the banks of the Singel, along the 'Old Peat market'. Peat was one of the city's few home grown businesses in medieval times to be managed by the municipal council. While hearty men were employed to cut the turf many women found employment as 'fillers' who controlled the quality and quantity of the peat. Inside, young lads peer through the glass at rows of mummified corpses while their peers take in fragments of daily life from the ancient world. There is some very fine Roman jewellery and a reproduction chariot familiar to Ben Hur fans. It is really a specialist collection, but attracts surprising numbers of tourists wanting a change from boats, clogs and tulips. Collections include Coptic, Etruscan, Egyptian, Roman and Greek. Audio-guides are available at the ticket desk in the main hall and a free information sheet comes with the admission ticket. If you are interested in Dutch archaeology you should visit the national collection in Leiden which is a short train journey away (see p.227).

Statue of Queen Wilhelmina

Opposite Rokin 112.

Obscured by flags and advertisements for canal boat trips is a rather elegant bronze by Theresia van de Pant of Queen Wilhelmina, mounted on a prancing steed. Queen Wilhelmina (1880–1962) was one of Holland's most popular monarchs. She ascended to the throne at the age of eighteen after the regency of her mother, Queen Emma. Amsterdammers clubbed together to pay for a gilded coach for her inauguration which has since been used for the opening of

Parliament each September. She made it her duty to spend regular periods in Amsterdam, where she could walk the streets, sail on the canals and meet the people. On one occasion her anxious body-guards beseeched her not to visit the Jordaan for fear of angry locals hurling flowerpots at her. Wilhelmina insisted and they threw flowers instead. She appeared to have let her people down when she fled to England during the Second World War, but her frequent radio messages gave the people hope and inspiration. In honour of Dutch resistance to the Nazis she granted the city a motto for its coat of arms: 'Heroic, Resolute, Merciful'. She played a fairly passive role in the Women's Suffrage Movement, despite being constantly called upon for assistance. However her housewifely appearance and down-to-earth nature meant that women found her approachable, even if she didn't achieve much for them. The royal family has had its scandals, like the marriage of Beatrix to an ex-Nazi, but they have not yet fallen victims to a glamourising press. Wilhelmina's granddaughter, the present Queen Beatrix is as popular as ever. The official celebration of the Queen's birthday is a still a national holiday and a national party. The celebrations are not exactly reverent. In Amsterdam while Queen Beatrix waves to the crowds from the canal, drunken youths play 'throw the bean bag at the Queen's fanny' in Vondelpark, kids hurl rotten tomatoes at the cardboard cut-outs of their monarch in the Jordaan and hundreds of crowned Queen lookalikes greet one another on the streets and in bars.

Kalverstraat

Kalverstraat, one of the foremost shopping streets, shoots off Dam Square towards Spui, taking with it a steady stream of shoppers, tourists, pickpockets and buskers. It is good for high street fashion, department stores and familiar European shops, but lacks charm. Clogs, windmills and smiling dolls in traditional costume compete with Dutch designer watches in the souvenir shops. Ex-pats stock up with undies at Marks & Spencer and Amsterdam trendies check out the latest fashion at Sissy Boy. There are a number of good bookshops and department stores for essentials (see Shopping p.292).

Amid all the commotion it's difficult to notice much, but take a look at De Pappegaai, a small Catholic church which takes its name from the grimy old parrot sitting on the Gothic porch. A few centuries ago Kalverstraat witnessed one of the most important events in the city's history, the Amsterdam Miracle.

THE AMSTERDAM MIRACLE

One fine night, in March 1345, an old man lay dying in his house just off Kalverstraat. The priest was summoned to give the last rites, including communion. According to legend the man spewed up the host (wafer) and the nurse threw it onto the fire. The next day, the maid found the wafer intact in the grate so it was removed and saved in a wooden chest. The patient survived to see the effect of the miracle. A chapel was built on the site and consecrated a couple of years later. The vomited host apparently survived more flames when the chapel was consumed by fire, confirming its miraculous qualities. Pilgrims poured into the city to pay homage to the indigestible, fire-resistant wafer and Amsterdam made a packet as one of Europe's pilgrimage centres.

Miracles were fairly common in the Middle Ages and the competition between pilgrimage centres was rife. It is not surprising that the holy wafer soon developed miraculous healing powers as well as being able to move between churches overnight, so that everyone could get a look. One of those healed by the blessed wafer was the Emperor of Austria, Maximilian I. He was so honoured by the healing, and the military support that he was receiving from Amsterdammers in his fight for control of the Low countries, that he granted the city the right to use his royal insignia (the golden crown) in its coat of arms.

If you happen to be in Amsterdam on the Sunday closest to 15 March, you may witness a silent procession, the *Stille Omgang*, moving slowly through the streets in commemoration of the miracle. Local Catholics follow the route that pilgrims have used for centuries known as the Holy Way or *Heligeweg*.

Amsterdam Historische Museum (Amsterdam Historical Museum)

Kalverstraat 92, tel. 523 1870. Open Mon–Fri 10 a.m.–5 p.m., weekends 11 a.m.–5 p.m. Admission adults f5, children and OAPs f2.50, under 6s free.

The former city orphanage is now a lively complex in the heart of the city and home to the Amsterdam Historical Museum. Families and friends eat al fresco outside the excellent restaurant while the best of the city's buskers take turns in the other courtyard. The museum itself is entertaining, informative and fun, and not dull as its name might suggest. Maps, models, paintings, furniture, music and lots more trace the economic and social history of Amsterdam.

The Building The city orphanage, known as the *Burgerweeshuis*, moved to this building, a former convent, in 1580. Most of the children who ended up here seemed to be from wealthy families and by 1850 over 500 children lived here. If you enter through the grand, lopsided entrance on Kalverstraat you will find yourself in the boys' courtyard – the wooden lockers have been left along the wall, there are no smelly socks but a few things on display in the open ones.

The courtyard is usually full of people tucking into pancakes, crab sandwiches and apple pie from the David and Goliath Café in the loggia. The bizarre wooden models of the giant and his assassin, Goliath and David, were rescued from the Amsterdam Pleasure Gardens where the animated figures entertained their seventeenth-century audience. For live entertainment today you will have to go to the girls' courtyard, where the show depends on the quality of the busker but they are often very good.

The girls at the orphanage lived, worked and played separately from the boys. Strict rules required the girls to be sober and serene even playing with dolls was forbidden in case it encouraged sensuousness. They were probably very pleased to reach the age of twenty when they were allowed to leave with a good trousseau and a golden handshake of three guilders. For a glimpse at past life in the orphanage take a look at the **Regent's Chamber** and the **Van Speyk Room** on the ground floor of the museum. The boardroom is littered with portraits of the governors, including a fine painting by Jacob Becker of 'The Board of Regentesses' who were responsible for the girls. Next door there are some delightful portraits of the children wearing their distinctive red, white and black uniforms and floppy white caps, and an abundance of works relating to one of the orphanage's most famous inmates, Jan Carel van Speyck, who grew up to command the Dutch Fleet.

The Collections   A history of miracles, maritime victories and mercenary achievements offer good scope for entertainment. The collection of maps, models, paintings and artefacts are arranged chronologically, concentrating on certain themes relating to each era so it is easy to pick and choose what you want to see. Allow a couple of hours to enjoy everything and pick up the red guide (in English), available at the ticket desk, which backs up the collection with a potted history of Amsterdam.

An old shoe, a misshapen pot and a model timber house hint at the city's murky beginnings while flashing lights make out its progressive expansion on a large map. Music, paintings, sculpture and the odd spinning wheel outline the activities of the fourteenth and fifteenth centuries, when Amsterdam was already an active commercial and religious centre. The earliest surviving *Map of Amsterdam* by Cornelis Anthonisz, in Room 4, is for many the pride of the collection. The city in 1538 is recognisably Amsterdam and the birds-eye view includes numerous artistic details; convents, churches, ships, trees are all mapped out along the wide canals and little streets.

Amsterdam's unrivalled commerce in the seventeenth century and the social implications of success are celebrated from Room 6. For a good cross-section of society take a look at Adriaan van

Nieulandt's *Procession of the Lepers* showing the city's sick turning out for their annual day of freedom when they were allowed to leave their asylums to collect alms. Rich noblemen dig in their pockets for loose change while others turn away as they ride past in their carriages; crowds gather around to buy lottery tickets, women shop and gossip while a pathetic group of helpless lepers limp through the middle. Also in Room 6 is a model of the Town Hall (now the Royal Palace) on Dam Square, a picture of the *Town Hall Under Construction* by Johannes Lingelbach and a delightful oil by Gerrit Adraensz of the finished Town Hall with Far-Eastern merchants trading in the foreground. The next couple of rooms are almost entirely devoted to trade, commodities, banking and business. Don't miss the exquisite model merchant ship half way up the stairs (Room 7).

Most Amsterdammers seem to have had a good time in the seventeenth and eighteenth centuries; even the poor did quite well, being set up in charitable institutions. Silver goblets, spice boxes, salt cellars and trick cups show that the Dutch knew how to throw a good party and a gory painting by Jacob Hercules of the *Shop of a Surgeon* shows the strange medicinal practices of the time. The master of the house gently performs the common cure of blood letting while his wife sews and children play in the foreground.

It would be a shame to pass by without trying your hand at the carillon bells in Room 10, but you may find a young enthusiast has beaten you to it. If music is your thing, check out the musical instruments in Rooms 14 and 15 which is also the best place for good furniture, clocks and a look at Amsterdam's foremost means of transport in the eighteenth century – the sled. Carriages proved too noisy and cumbersome over the humped-backed bridges and cobbled streets, so a Frenchman devised an alternative carriage on runners which could glide around the city relatively quietly save the panting and puffing of two energetic youths, hired to run alongside and smear grease on the runners at regular intervals. The English traveller, Thomas Nugent, was unconvinced, calling them a 'heavy unpleasant carriage, fit for none but old women'.

The paintings in the museum are more informative than magnificent, but the small collection in Room 13 is worth seeing, if only to take a look at one of the few surviving paintings by one of Holland's most eminent seventeenth-century women artists, Rachel Ruysch. You may like to take in one of the temporary exhibitions or the display of nineteenth-century manufacturing industries upstairs in the attic before you leave, but don't miss the Dolls' House (Room 16) which is a perfect reconstruction of a narrow canal house, complete with kitchen and cupboard beds.

RACHEL RUYSCH (1664–1750)

Rachel Ruysch was among the greatest Dutch flower painters in the second half of the seventeenth century. She was the first woman in Holland to achieve international recognition as an artist in her lifetime and to have maintained a reputation long after her death.

Ruysch was born in Amsterdam to distinguished parents; her father was an eminent professor of botany and anatomy and her mother was the daughter of the architect, Pieter Post. At an early age, her father organised her apprenticeship to the well-known still life painter, Willem van Aelst. Choosing her subject matter posed little problem as the family had a large collection of shells, fossils, plants, minerals and reference books. It was her acute accuracy and great sense of colour that earned her international recognition; flower and fruit pictures were riddled with gleaming beetles, crinkled caterpillars, translucent butterflies and little reptiles. Her enthusiasm for zoology and botany is very obvious. Many of her paintings were even accompanied by a detailed catalogue of all the species represented. Interestingly, although many flower paintings can be read as *vanitas* – a comment on the brevity of human life – Rachel Ruysch seemed less concerned with this than the immediate beauty of the object.

She was professionally active for some years before she married the portrait painter, Juriaan Pool, in 1693. The couple were both elected members of the Guild of Painters at the Hague, in 1701, and twice summoned to the German Courts, where they spent eight years (1708–1716) as court painters to the Elector Palatine in Dusseldorf, Johann Wilhelm von Pfaiz. Rachel was a formidable woman; she continued to paint into her eighties and raised a family of ten children. She included her age alongside her signature on later works to impress the buyers.

Civic Guards Gallery

Adjoining the Amsterdam Historical Museum.

The Begijn ditch (*Begijnensloot*), once a sewer separating the sexes at the orphanage, has been covered and enclosed as a street gallery. Glass doors glide open for anyone wishing to take a look at the portraits of the **Civic Guard** while wandering home from the shops.

The Civic Guard provided the cities of the Netherlands with an armed civilian force. Members supplied their own weapons and armour. The headquarters, where many of these portraits are staged, naturally became a social centre for the wealthy members. The pictures are a wonderful display of men. Beautifully painted faces are set off against silks, satins, lace and velvet. Natty hats and neatly healed shoes belie the strength of their weapons.

Tram 1, 2, 5 to Spui.

Tucked away behind Kalverstraat and Spui is the tranquil little complex of tiny gabled houses, a church and a garden, built for a community of lay sisters in the fourteenth century. It is a welcome piece of greenery in the middle of the city and a good place to sit if you need a break from the shops.

A group of lay sisters the Begijns first set up home here in 1346, with a few houses nestling around the church in the centre. As their numbers increased more houses were built to complete the circle. The last Begijns to live here died in 1976, but the houses are still lived in by elderly women, who sit by open windows or tend tiny but exquisite gardens. If you take a look through the lace curtains you may catch a glimpse of the impressive timber frame running inside some of the houses. The central lawn was once used for hanging out bleached linen to dry, but today serves little purpose other than to control pedestrians who file around it, trying to 'keep off the grass'. The wooden house opposite the church door is one of the oldest surviving houses in the city. Most of the wooden houses were demolished after brick and stone became compulsory building materials to lessen the risk of fire.

A graceful bronze of a Begijn nun in flowing robes and floppy hat seems to glide across the grass beside the church in memory of the sisters who worked and lived here. A small plaque on the garden wall near the church marks the grave of one sister, Cornelia Arens, who chose to be buried in the gutter as a penance for her family's refusal to declare their allegiance to the Catholic Church. Cynical feminists claim that she actually chose to be buried here, under a public footpath, because she had spent her life being 'walked over'.

Each year a bunch of flowers is laid on her grave to commemorate her death on 2 May, 1654.

The Begijns worshipped in the medieval church in the centre until the Alteration (the switch from Catholicism to Protestantism in 1578, see p.68) when it was used as a warehouse. It was reopened in 1607 when the Dutch Reformed Church granted the building to English and Presbyterian settlers fleeing discrimination in England at the time. Large groups of ex-pats still gather here every Sunday at 10.30 a.m. for worship, as it is now the English Reformed Church. In order to catch a glimpse of the interior you will have to join them or attend one of the evening concerts frequently held here. The inside has been heavily restored and there is little of note apart from a stained-glass window in the chancel, commemorating the departure of the Pilgrim Fathers (many of whom were in the congregation), to America and some pulpit panels designed by a very young and stylistically unrecognisable Piet Mondrian.

When the Begijns were ousted from their main church in 1578, they did not have to look far for an alternative place to worship; they just converted a couple of houses into a clandestine Catholic church where they could celebrate mass in secret. Nos. 29–30, just across from their former church, were remodelled in the seventeenth century – the door is usually left open for private prayer and contemplation. The cool interior is dominated by an imposing gallery which was probably necessary for a congregation of over 300 people. The reredos behind the high altar shows scenes of the Amsterdam Miracle, a theme which is reiterated throughout the chapel in painting and stained glass. A rather dingy mural of the Silent Procession (an annual march in honour of the Miracle) occupies the north wall. In comparison, an enchanting 'Nativity' by Nicolas Moiaert, to the right of the altar, exudes a captivating light. The most impressive artworks in the chapel are the more recently executed stained-glass windows by Gisele van Waterschoot van der Gracht (1950s); a magical mix of rich blues, greens and purple dance across the chapel as the sun streams in.

THE BEGIJNS

The Begijns were no ordinary order of nuns. They were a group of Catholic women who organised themselves into a lay sisterhood where they could live a simple life without the ties of an organised religious order, but with the security of communal living, the freedom to work and the opportunity to leave should they wish. It was also, of course, a socially acceptable way to escape marriage.

The Middle Ages offered little respite for women who wished to remain single, unless they wanted to become nuns. Girls married at thirteen and widows tended to remarry, so unmarried women were unusual. In Amsterdam, lower-class women often turned to prostitution, some took to cross-dressing to secure work usually reserved for the boys, and for the more aristocratic ladies monastic life proved to be the easiest and most respectful option. But life within the religious orders was not all that easy for women. As the numbers of women joining the orders escalated during the twelfth century, their male counterparts took extensive precautionary steps to curb the authority of women in the orders. The Cistercians were notorious for sexual discrimination – in Holland there were 32 convents and 14 monasteries when the Abbots decided to restrict the power of the Abbesses. Sexual discrimination in the Church was a serious concern. Innocent III raised the issue in 1138 and it was debated by successive Popes, but without result. Many nuns were prepared to tolerate the situation, but the Begijns devised the ultimate escape from the commitments of secular and religious life and miraculously suffered few heretical allegations.

They were the first group to set up an association of women loosely bound by the desire to lead a religious life. Tradition holds that their name 'Begijn' is a contraction of the heretical sect, the Albigensians. This derivation, whatever truth it held, was soon forgotten; as the great English chronicler Matthew Paris recalled, 'No one knows why they are called Begijns, nor how they began'. Their organisation and name was more probably based on an association of women set up by the priest of Liege, Lambert le Begue.

Groups of Begijns gathered throughout the Netherlands. As in Amsterdam, they chose to live in 'a city within a city' but not a convent. The movement had no allegiance to male-dominated religious movements, it had no rule, no saintly founder, no patrons, no papal authority, no official organisation and promised no benefits. Any vows taken (usually obedience and chastity) were chosen by the participant and reversible. They did benefit from some wealthy benefactors, but generally speaking these women came from all backgrounds and were essentially self-sufficient. They did not beg; instead they worked, usually in hospitals or doing handwork, such as embroidery or weaving. They were indebted to no one and succeeded through their passiveness. Unlike the other orders, they even survived the Alteration. Their church was closed and they had to conform to the laws on discrete worship but they were not disbanded. The locals saw them as a group of independent, well-meaning women who chose to lead a religious life.

It is not surprising that the Begijns had enemies. Priests lost parishioners, fathers lost daughters, men lost prospective wives. It hurt most because these women were not lost to a life of poverty, prayer and chastity as true nuns, but to a life with freedom of choice. Groups of Begijns settled in many cities throughout the Netherlands. The movement spread through Germany, France and Switzerland, but each group varied enormously. Some were eventually integrated with established orders, others were swept up by mystic movements which did their reputation no good. By 1400, most of the women joining up came from poorer backgrounds and the Begijnhofs took on the role of religious almshouses. However, the looseness of their organisation meant that Begijn communities all over the Netherlands survived the religious upheavals of the following centuries. The last Begijn in Amsterdam, Sister Antonia died in 1971.

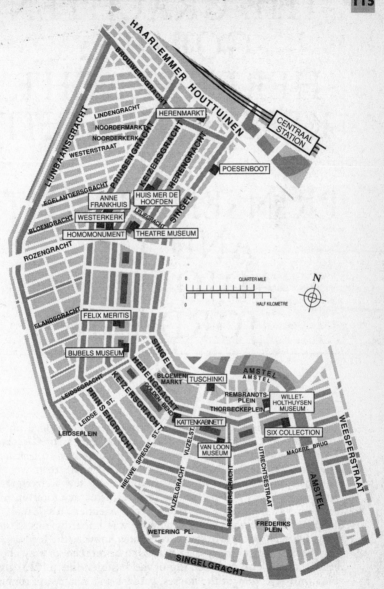

HAARLEMMER HOUTTUINEN

BROUWERSGRACHT

LIJNBAANSGRACHT

LINDENGRACHT

NOORDERMARKT

NOORDERKERK

WESTERSTRAAT

PRINSENGRACHT

KEIZERSGRACHT

HERENGRACHT

SINGEL

HERENMARKT

CENTRAAL STATION

POESENBOOT

EGELANTIERSGRACHT

ANNE FRANKHUIS

HUIS MER DE HOOFDEN

BLOEMGRACHT

WESTERKERK

HOMOMONUMENT

THEATRE MUSEUM

LELIEGRACHT

ROZENGRACHT

QUARTER MILE

0

0

HALF KILOMETRE

N

ELANDSGRACHT

FELIX MERITIS

BIJBELS MUSEUM

SINGEL

LEIDSEGRACHT

PRINSENGRACHT

KEIZERSGRACHT

HERENGRACHT

GOLDEN BEND

BLOEMEN MARKT

TUSCHINKI

AMSTEL

AMSTEL

REMBRANDTS-PLEIN

WILLET-HOLTHUYSEN MUSEUM

THORBECKEPLEIN

LEIDSE ST.

KATTENKABINETT

LEIDSEPLEIN

NIEUWE SPIEGEL ST.

VIJZELST.

SIX COLLECTION

VAN LOON MUSEUM

MAGERE BRUG

WEESPERSTRAAT

VIJZELGRACHT

REGULIERSGRACHT

UTRECHTSESTRAAT

AMSTEL

WETERING PL.

FREDERIKS PLEIN

SINGELGRACHT

THE GRACHTEN GORDLE: HERENGRACHT, KEIZERSGRACHT AND PRINSENGRACHT; AND THE ADJOINING JORDAAN

City expansion in the seventeenth century literally wrapped up old Amsterdam in a band of concentric canals known as the Grachten Gordle – the canal girdle. Successful merchants moved to neat little gabled houses on the **Prinsengracht** (Prince's Canal), their wealthy colleagues moved into sizeable dwellings on the **Keizersgracht** (Emperor's Canal) and the simply loaded aristocracy took up residency in vast mansions on **Herengracht** (Gentleman's Canal). A damp meadow alongside Prinsengracht was hurriedly turned into living quarters for the working classes, now know as the **Jordaan**.

The best way to enjoy the canals is to be on them or way above them. A quick look from the top of the westoren (see p. 123) gives you a birds-eye view of the houses, gardens and waterways running between them. Down below, canal boats ferry people along the canals at regular intervals. If you are feeling particularly adventurous hire a pedalo, pack a picnic and pedal off into the unknown.

Murky green waters lap along the red brick walls picking up reflected glimpses of the gabled houses on either side; houseboats make good buffers and the ducks get in the way.

At street level, cars scoot up and down looking for a parking space. Couriers drop off paper packages to banks and offices and fluttering leaves race solitary pedestrians to the end of the street. The relative calm is broken intermittently by the bustle of shoppers, checking out the intriguing shops and watering holes along the narrow streets which run at right angles to the main canals. At times the canals, particularly to the west, seem deserted, largely because the impressive houses have been turned into offices, hotels and university departments. However, the little streets that cross them are full of intriguing shops, cosy cafés and upmarket restaurants for anyone tired of looking at houses.

You will find more to do at the eastern end of the canals; step inside a magnificent seventeenth-century canal house at the **Van Loon,** enjoy the collection of paintings at the **Six Collection**. Ogle at priceless antiques in the **Spiegel Quarter,** watch fire eaters on Leidseplein and wear dark glasses for a rave at the Melkweg. As the evening wears on, join the teeny boppers, transvestites and go go girls around Rembrandtsplein.

For a contrast, head for the Jordaan where narrow streets are lined with tiny houses and houseboats cling to ivy-covered quays. Wisteria hangs off crumbling walls and caged birds sing from open windows. Music wafts down still canals and kids play in the streets. Rummage through boxes of second-hand clothes, search for bargains in Looiersstraat antiques market before relaxing in a friendly bar with a glass of wine and stuffed *ciabatta*.

The Golden Age The seventeenth century was a good time to be Dutch; England, France and Germany were caught up in their own wars and recessions. The Northern Netherlands had extricated themselves from Spanish rule in 1581 and formed themselves into the United Provinces. The Spanish occupation of Antwerp left Amsterdam as the master of the unrivalled Dutch fleets. Trade was already booming when the incorporation of the Dutch East India Company, in 1602, sent it through the roof. Dutch fleets dominated the oceans for the next fifty years. Foreigners flocked to Amsterdam to take part in the city's economic prosperity, political peace and immensely exciting cultural activity. Persecuted refugees headed to Amsterdam for security, work and money. Portuguese Jews flocked to the city bringing with them news of Far-Eastern trade routes, Protestant merchants left Antwerp for Amsterdam and the city's population exploded to almost 200,000 by the middle of the century. The city took on huge building projects: the town hall, the great canal extension, churches, spires and stately homes. Municipal almshouses housed the poor, orphanages took the unwanted and prisons offered lenient respite for the wicked.

The nation's wealth fuelled a Golden Age of cultural enlightenment. Architecture burgeoned under the municipal architect Hendrick de Keyser (1565–1621) who embellished the city with frivolously decorated Renaissance palaces, centrally planned Protestant churches, flamboyant spires and august classical façades. After his death, the short tempered Jacob van Camden was persuaded to create the 'Eighth Wonder of The World' with the neo-classical Town Hall (now Koninklijk Palais) on Dam Square. Philip Vingboons (1614–78) designed more classical canal houses to impress the aristocracy.

The arts flourished. The Golden Age produced great poets like Gerbrand Bredero, Joost van den Vondel and Pieter Cornelisz Hooft. Rembrandt, Vermeer and Hals were among just a few of the great Dutch artists to emerge in the seventeenth century. The art market soared as the new bourgeoisie sought to possess anything they could get their hands on. Stately canal houses, country mansions, family portraits, porcelain, oriental rugs and even tulips were essential status symbols for any reasonably wealthy merchant.

Women did well out of all of this. Education of middle-class women was encouraged, as was the training of women in business. Literacy was all the rage and seemingly highly attainable. Jacob Cats must have been pleasantly surprised when 50,000 women chose to buy his guides to womanhood (p. 139). Women were no longer painted as dumpy obedient wives but free spirits, engaged in reading, writing and playing music. Suzanna van Lee was the first actress to appear on stage in 1655. Everyone had had enough of boys taking female leads. Women were making their mark.

While many women tried their hand at painting, some made a living from it. Still life artists like Clara Peeters and Maria Sibylla Merian worked alongside the better-known Judith Leyster and Rachel Ruysch, who turned into something of a celebrity (see p. 110). For some, like the poet Anna Maria Schurmann (1607–1678) and the Tesselschade Visscher sisters (p. 92), painting was just one of the many talents in which they were allowed to succeed.

THE WESTERN SECTION OF THE GRACHTEN GORDLE: FROM BROUWERSGRACHT TO LEIDSEGRACHT

The area around Westerkerk is always full of tourists, mainly because it's near Amsterdam's most visited canal house, the **Anne Frank House**. The rest of the western section of the Grachten Gordle is a great place to gen up on Dutch architecture, compare gables, sketch the odd view and peer in on bored office workers. It is best not to slog off down one canal at a time as they are longer than you think; the entire length of Prinsengracht is two miles, but start at Brouwersgracht on the Herengracht side and zig zag your way over to the Westerkerk and you'll get a taste of what there is to see. If you are not keen on walking, the canal-boat trips take in the major sights – those who really want to delve into Dutch architecture could join a guided tour (see p. 63).

Apart from the Singel which was once the city's defensive moat the three canals, Herengracht, Keizersgracht and Prinsengracht were part of the city's famous seventeenth-century expansion scheme, started in 1613, to house the growing population. These were intersected at right angles by smaller canals and bridged by a number of smaller shopping streets which nowadays serve the same purpose. Most of the richer merchants lived in six or seven-storey houses on the Herengracht. The less wealthy tended to have lower houses on the other canals and Prinsengracht was earmarked as the canal for workshops, warehouses, churches, shops and artisans' houses. The plan by Frans Oetgens and Hendrick Staets disregarded the natural line of ditches and pastures and divided the land on a mathematical basis. Plots were narrow and deep because tax was paid according to the width of the canal frontage which resulted in the rows of tall, narrow, brick houses that we see today. No provision was made for the public gardens or parks that were so popular in Paris at the time.

The limitations of the site left architects little scope for innovative designs and structural systems over the years. Instead they turned their attentions to decoration, using white sandstone to enliven plain brick walls and window castings. As the Dutch Renaissance style gave way to neo-classicism, pilasters and pediments gave buildings a more refined touch. By the eighteenth century façades were embellished in imperial Louis XVI style. At street level most of the façades are very plain and best viewed across the canal. The character of individual buildings relies almost entirely on their gables. It is this gabled skyline which turns lines of plain red brick into rows of charming, exquisite and endearing houses.

Hendrick de Keyser used the step gable, a stepped triangle which could be 'iced' with intricate decoration. Philip Vingboons rocked the boat when he introduced the neck gable, a rectangle standing in the centre, as if on shoulders, which was good for plonking pediments on or hanging sculptural drapery down the side. Decorative possibilities were endless; you will come across dolphins and horses, swags and urns, pillars and balustrades, lots of froth and not a single satellite dish. The warehouses, dominated by large semi-circular doors (now windows) down the centre, are usually topped with an upturned funnel, technically known as a spout gable.

With this in mind, you will find the area a rich patchwork of Dutch architectural styles: the Renaissance Barlotti House, the sober neo-classical façade of the Theatre Museum and Gerrit van Arkel's flamboyant Art Nouveau house at Keizersgracht 174 are among the many interesting buildings to see.

Brouwersgracht

This is the place for a pre-dinner drink on a summer's evening. Classical music wafts across the water from the smart warehouse conversions on the far side and cafés sit on the water's edge. Young executives relax on the decks of their houseboats after a hard day's work and elderly Jordaaners gulp beer in the dark brown bars. It is a colourful area with brightly painted boats, shutters and bicycles, humped-backed bridges, grassy verges and views down the grandest of Amsterdam's canals. Running across the top of the Grachten Gordle, it links the harbour with the grand residential canals and the once heavily populated working-class Jordaan area. It is this that has always given Brouwersgracht its unique mixture and community spirit.

This has always been a popular area, its trades and inhabitants creating a folkloric eccentricity. It was once a bawdy area of brothels, beer, fish and seamen. In the seventeenth century the canal literally ran along the edge of the harbour. Bickering fishwives haggled with customers over the latest trawl retrieved by their husbands at the Singel end. Further west along the canal, great flat boats delivered fresh water to the 24 breweries along the banks whose brew was served in dingy drinking houses. Local girls and rich merchants made assignations in the bars or went outside for polite conversation in the leafy square of the Herenmarkt. In the last century a herd of donkeys was driven here for milking every morning. (Apparently donkey's milk tastes like mother's milk.) There is little eccentricity these days, but plenty to see all the same.

Herenmarkt

Flesh has been sold here for centuries. A busy meat market was built on the site in 1615 and leased to the West India Company (renowned for their hand in the slave trade) in 1623. At the turn of the century, this windswept square was popularly known as the *hoerenmarkt* where ladies flaunted bits of flesh and gentlemen paid for more. You will probably find it full of trendy kids playing basketball and mothers watching their toddlers kicking sand in the playground.

The formal brick building behind was once the headquarters of the West India Company which was founded on the back of the East India Company but was not nearly as successful. It was particularly active in the slave trade, but lost most of its funds waging war against the Portuguese and Spanish. The Company's main claim to fame was in the discovery and administration of New Amsterdam, unfortunately it let it go to the British who renamed it New York. In the inner courtyard there is a statue of the first Dutch governor of New Amsterdam, Pieter Stuyvestant. The house was largely reconstructed in 1826, as an orphanage, and was used more recently as the main marriage bureau in Amsterdam which is now somewhere in the vast Stadhuis on Waterlooplein.

CANALS: CONSTRUCTION, CLEANLINESS AND DROWNINGS

Canal design is not just a matter of enlarging ditches and filling them with water. Water has to be carefully directed to avoid stagnant ponds and floods. The original city grew up along the banks of the Amstel with a couple of canals being built in the fifteenth century along with Singel and Kloveniersburgwal following around the city walls. In 1607, as part of the great city expansion scheme, four men, Henrik Staets, Frans Oetgens, Lucas Stink and Daniel Stalpaert, were commissioned to design a canal network to enable the trade – and the city – to expand. The unlikely foursome – master carpenter, ex-mayor, surveyor and architect – came up with the plan we see today. The width of the main canals allowed large barges to be brought right into the city, drawn by horses and men from the tow path. The most ingenious planning involved the locks, which could be closed to prevent flooding at high tide and opened to flush the canals with clean water. This system of cleaning the canals worked moderately well, but obviously as the city expanded it was not powerful enough to clear the urban sewage from the canals. In 1765, new proposals to improve water circulation met with strong opposition – 30,000 domestic maids petitioned against the clean-up for fear of losing their jobs. They felt that a reduction in the vile overflow from the canals into the streets and houses would lose them their cleaning work. As it happened, the old system was in operation until 1876 when the harbour was dammed to stop it silting up. The subsequent stagnation of the canals led to serious outbreaks of disease and city officials struggled to solve the problem, eventually building sluice gates across the dam. Since 1932, when the great *Afsluitdijk* (dike) was built across the Zuider Zee, Amsterdam has not been flushed with tidal waters. The canals are now flushed mechanically with the fresh water of the IJsselmeer.

Every night, between 7 p.m. and 8.30 p.m., 15 sluice gates in the city centre are closed (mostly by hand). Once shut, the city's pumping station on the artificial island of Zeeburg starts pumping around 700 million litres of fresh water into the canals. Old water is flushed out through a couple of gates left open. The best place from which to watch this process is on the banks of the river Amstel, opposite the Carre Theatre near the Magere bridge.

You are unlikely to come across a body in the canal or lose your life in one. Amsterdam's canals claim on average 52 lives a year and most of these are drunks who topple in while having a pee. The occasional murder victim ends up being tossed in, but the water police are so efficient you are very unlikely to see any gory remains. Accidental dippings are more frequent but not recommended as the water is pretty disgusting; it is relatively shallow (three metres deep) should you find yourself in it. Very occasionally, careless drivers reverse too far and fall over the edge, but the police fish out the drivers and their cars with unbelievable speed, using specially designed inflatable bags.

Opposite Singel 40. Open daily 1 p.m.–3 p.m. Donations welcome. Tram 1, 2, 5, 13, 17 to Martlaarsgracht.

Just off Brouwersgracht Henriette van Weelde, known as the mother of 250 cats, is usually to be seen chatting to her charges or propping up her feet on a small radiator in the anteroom. She proudly presents her boat full of neglected moggies to passers by, as if they were pedigree Persians.

The boat is essentially a home for elderly cats whiling away their final years. Cats sprawl across the deck, cats huddle in cane chairs and cats curl into plastic washing-up bowls. Hungry pussies exercise their teeth on a pile of dead day-old chicks thrown in the corner and others lick matted fur in a post-prandial clean up. Everyone is strikingly content and, given the number and nature of the inhabitants, the air is surprisingly sweet.

Theatre Museum

Herengracht 168, tel. 6235104. Open Tues–Sun 11 a.m.–5 p.m. Admission f5, students, OAPs and children 4–9 f3, under 4s free. Tram 13, 14, 17 to Westerkerk.

A little way down Herengracht the Netherlands Theatre Institute regularly draws on its collection of costumes, props, posters and sound effects for temporary exhibitions on Dutch theatre, dance, mime and film. Most people drop in for a quick look at the lavish interior, a quicker look at the exhibits and a long coffee in the café. If this is not enough, you can create a storm with thunder and lightning machines in a downstairs room.

The interior is riddled with elaborate plasterwork and a richly carved sweeping staircase, but more impressive are the painted canvases by Jacob de Wit and Isaac de Moucheron in the front rooms. The walls are covered with scenes from the life of Jephthah, the Israelite judge who sacrificed his daughter in fulfilment of a vow.

Ironically, the Theatre Museum is more famous for its exterior than for its exhibits. Philip Vingboons gave it this sober sandstone façade with pedimented step gable when renovating it for the founder of the West India Company, Michel Pauw. Next door, Nos. 170–2, also part of the Theatre Museum, is one of Herengracht's best-known houses, the Renaissance **Bartolotti House**. Designed by Hendrick de Keyser, the two houses are linked by a flamboyant stepped gable covered in plasterwork, balustrades, vases, squiggles and lines. It seems absurd until you see the rather dull roof that it is meant to hide.

Keizersgracht 123 (Headquarters of the Council for the Protection of Historic Buildings).

Over on Keizersgracht the impressive Dutch Renaissance façade with its huge stepped gable covered in balustrades, obelisks, niches and curved pediment is almost as noteworthy as the legend that surrounds the seven sculptured heads that decorate the front. The story goes that seven burglars broke into the house. The first six lost their heads to the maid who was armed with an axe, but she fell in love with the seventh and married him instead. Bizarrely the thieves, or at least their heads, are commemorated as Apollo, Ceres, Mars, Pallas Athene, Bacchus and Diana.

Westerkerk (West Church)

Tower open April-Sept Mon–Sat 10 a.m.–4 p.m. Admission fl.50. Tram 13, 14, 17 to Westerkerk.

Trams, cars and bikes pound along the south side of Westermarkt, leaving pedestrians no choice but to shelter beneath the imposing red brick walls of Westerkerk. This huge building was perhaps Henrick de Keyser's grandest. It was built to serve the wealthy bourgeoisie living in the smart new development along the Grachten Gordle. Lesser mortals were obliged to worship on the wrong side of the canal in another church, the Noorderkerk (North Church).

From the outside the church looks more like a huge town hall with clear windows and classical decoration. Even the famous spire sports a bulbous tribute to the state in the form of a gaudily painted crown of Maximillian of Austria. The 85m-high tower itself is the highest in Amsterdam and offers brilliant views of the seventeenth-century canal grid for those who have a head for heights.

The interior is bright, whitewashed and imposing. Built for Protestant worship, everything focuses on the canopied pulpit in the centre. If you arrive after a service you find elegantly dressed ladies sipping fresh coffee while their children run amok in the box pews intended for the glitterati. Most visitors spend their time in a fruitless search for the unmarked grave of Rembrandt who is buried here somewhere with his son Titus. Others merely titter at the voluptuous Queen of Sheba depicted on the organ shutters.

Outside, at the east end of the church, stands a frail bronze statue of Anne Frank, by the Dutch sculptor Mari Andriessen, where people lay wreaths as a sign of respect or deck her out in a Heineken T-shirt and baseball hat.

If you head to the leafy area behind the Westerkerk on the Keizersgracht you are quite likely to find yourself sitting or standing on one of the three pink granite triangles that make up the Homo-Monument. Karin Daan's impressive sculpture was unveiled in 1987 as a tribute to men and women who have been persecuted because of their homosexuality and is a monument to the gay and lesbian movement in their struggle against oppression. The Homo-Monument has three dimensions: a warning from the past, confrontation and recognition in the present and an inspiration for the future.

The pink triangle, the sign that homosexuals wore in Nazi concentration camps, is a universally acknowledged symbol of homosexuality. The placing of the triangles is particularly important. The 'memorial triangle' is set in the ground and points in the direction of the Anne Frank House, the centre for the struggle against fascism, anti-semitism and racism. On it a large inscription, taken from a poem by Jacob Israal de Haan, reads: 'Such an unlimited longing for friendship'. The present is represented by a stepped triangle on the water's edge, usually strewn with flowers as a tribute to AIDS victims. The 'podium' triangle points in the direction of the headquarters of COC, the centre for gay and lesbian liberation in the Netherlands (see p. 44).

It is a bold statement, supported financially by the Dutch government, the Town Council and numerous gay and lesbian organisations. Its situation beside the most prestigious church in the city is enlightened and encouraging and it has become a monument recognised by gays and lesbians all over the world. A busy taxi rank running through the middle spoils the view of the monument, but enhances its symbolic integration.

Anne Frankhuis (Anne Frank House)

Prinsengracht 263, tel. 626 45 33. Open Mon–Sat 9 a.m.–5 p.m., Sun & holidays 10 a.m.–5 p.m. 1 Jun–1 Sept weekdays 9 a.m.–7 p.m. Closed 25 Dec, 1 Jan and Yom Kippur. Entrance fee 7f, 10–17s f3.50, under 10s free; no museum cards. Tram 13, 14, 17 to Westerkerk.

A stone's throw from Westerkerk, this tiny canal house is one of Amsterdam's most popular sights. Get there early or prepare yourself for a long wait. Six hundred thousand people every year file up the steep narrow stairs for a look at the tiny annexe where the Frank family and their friends spent two years avoiding Nazi persecution during the Second World War, until their discovery and deportation in August 1944.

The family moved to the annexe after Anne's 16-year-old sister Margot received deportation orders from the German *Sicherheitsdienst* (Security Service) in July 1942. Otto Frank ran his spice and herb business from the building and had been preparing the annexe for some months. The windows were already blacked out to protect the herbs in storage so neighbours would not have been aware of any change. Inside, the entrance was hidden by a hinged bookcase. The family were joined by his business colleague, Mr Van Daen, his wife and teenage son Peter. They were later joined by a rather dour dentist known as Dussell. The eight inmates were supported by the four office workers who brought them food and clothing.

Models of the rooms, reconstructed with the help of Anne's father after the war, hint at the real appearance of Anne's 'beautiful secret annexe'. The posters, postcards and photos of movie stars strewn across the bedroom wall are the only connection with the little teenager whose diary brought the families' experience to the homes of people all over the world. An exhibition about the Jews, Anne and her diary in the attic room is perhaps more interesting than the annexe itself.

Visitors have flocked to the annexe since the initial publication of the diary in 1947. The **Anne Frank Stichting** was founded in 1957 when the house at No. 263 was threatened with demolition. They completely restored the house and later bought the house next door. The organisation now employs over eighty staff, disseminating information and exhibitions on anti-semitism, racism and discrimination.

ANNE FRANK (1930–1945)

Anne Frank, daughter of German Jewish immigrants living in Amsterdam, was given a diary for her thirteenth birthday, 12 June 1942. Three weeks later her family went into hiding to avoid the Nazi occupying forces. Her account of the next two years won her posthumous international fame and realised her ambition: 'My greatest wish is to become a journalist some day and later on a famous writer ... I want to publish a book entitled *Het Achterhuis* (Dutch title of her book) after the war. Whether I shall succeed or not, I cannot say, but my diary will be a great help.'

Anne's diary – a small contribution from a pubescent girl – is a significant historical and literary work. It has been translated into over fifty languages and more than thirteen million copies have been sold. She is an important Jewish martyr representing the thousands of Jews who died at the hands of the Nazis in the Second World War.

The Frank family moved to Amsterdam in 1933 to escape Nazi oppression in Germany. When the Germans occupied the Netherlands in 1941 she was forced to go to a Jewish School where 'stylish' Anne was the envy of her classmates. As the persecution of the Jews in the Netherlands increased, the whole family were forced into hiding in the back rooms of the tiny canal house on Prinsengracht. It was here that she recorded the extraordinary events of the following years in her diary. Writing to her imaginary friend Kitty, Anne lucidly reveals her hopes and fears, her relationship with her family and friends, her emerging sexuality and her passions. Crammed into the tiny annexe, she was seen by her seven companions as, in her own words, 'boy crazy, flirt, know-all, reader of love stories'. The only thing she managed to keep to herself were her periods which she welcomed as 'that secret within me'. Her optimism never failed her: 'I know what I want, I have a goal, an opinion, I have religion and love.'

She was aware of the historical importance of her writings, having listened to the Dutch government minister, Bolkestein, reporting on Radio Oranje in May 1944: 'History cannot be written on the basis of documents alone ... what we really need are ordinary documents – a diary, letters'. She was prompted by this to edit the diary. It was at this point that she invented fictional names for the inhabitants and helpers in the annexe.

Anne's powerful account of her life in hiding reveals the fear, faith, courage and optimism held by many Jews living in the city at the time. Seen through the eyes of a teenager, it carries a poignant message.

The family were finally discovered and deported. The diary was miraculously saved by one of the office workers, referred to in its pages as 'Miep', before the house was cleared by the Germans. She only handed the diary over once it was confirmed that Anne and her sister Margot had died of typhoid in Bergen Belsen concentration camp, shortly after deportation. Anne's father was the only survivor of the family. In publishing her diary he fulfilled his daughter's greatest ambition, 'to go on living, even after my death'.

RACISM

The Netherlands is renowned for its tolerant reputation and liberal policies towards minorities and immigrants, but there is still a significant amount of racism that is most evident in employment and housing discrimination. To date the country has not been significantly affected by the extreme racism and xenophobia currently sweeping through Europe, but many fear that the nation's 'hidden' racism could ignite in the future.

Immigrants and their children make up about 4% of the population. In the 1950s and 60s huge numbers of Moroccans and Turks were recruited as 'guests' to labour for Holland's rapid industrial growth. The government expected them to leave and made no attempt to integrate them. A large number managed to stay and they now make up the largest immigrant community. Natives of the former Dutch colonies such as Surinam and Indonesia have been better integrated, but their situation is by no means satisfactory.

The Dutch government prohibits 'discrimination on the grounds of religion, way of life, political view, race, sex or any other grounds', but this is not reflected in Dutch society. An estimated 40% of the minorities are currently unemployed, partly due to unfair hiring practices and discrimination by employment agencies.

Racism at street level is difficult to define. Traditionally dressed Muslim women have learnt to expect racist abuse while other women of colour report nothing at all. Anti-semitic slogans are not uncommon but they are usually painted over in a matter of days. While the 80s saw an increase in racial violence, this is becoming less common.

The strict 'pillarisation' of Dutch society begins in childhood, when children attend different schools according to their religion which does little to enhance the integration of minority groups. Another appalling case of racism, which affects every child, is in the seemingly harmless tradition of St Nicolaas Day on 5 December; the Dutch Santa is accompanied by a black slave known as Schwartz Pete and shops are full of caricatures of this stereotyped black male.

The political status of minorities is more complex. They are represented in local government and in parliament, but have to face an extreme right racist party, the Centrum Democrats or C.D. that has a fair amount of support and one member in parliament. According to the C.D. housing shortages, unemployment, crime, education, environmental degradation, drug abuse, V.D. and 'feelings of alienation' would all be solved with the deportation of foreigners. Fortunately, on a national level the C.D. is fairly isolated, but they issue mountains of propaganda and have an active youth faction, 'The Young Guezen'.

For the time being racism does not flourish in the Netherlands. However the strengthening of the European Community and the inevitable spread of ideas from less open societies is beginning to pose a real threat to the future of racial tolerance in the Netherlands.

Felix Meritis Building (Shaffy Theatre)

Keizersgracht 324. Tel. 626 2321. Café open Tues–Fri noon–1 a.m., Sat 5 p.m.–2 a.m. Tram 1, 2, 5 to Leidestraat.

Three blocks down from Westerkerk is the Shaffy Theatre. The palladian façade seems fitting for an intellectual meeting place that was once the cultural centre of Amsterdam. The building is best seen from the opposite side of the canal; four huge columns support a pediment inscribed with Felix Meritis (Happiness Through Achievement), the motto of the fellowship who commissioned the building as an arts and scientific centre.

When Napoleon made his grand entry into Amsterdam he was brought here for a great reception. The little man had only got his foot through the door when he complained that it stank of tobacco smoke and left in a sulk.

Women were not allowed to join as members, but were admitted as listeners. The day after opening in 1778 there was a rerun of the solemn proceedings for about 400 women who felt they had been hard done by. The first woman allowed to speak in the building was Elise van Calcar with a lecture on education in 1860.

High society lost its verve and the building at the end of the nineteenth century and it later became used as the headquarters of the Communist Party. The Shaffy Theatre moved here in 1970 and continues to run a programme of modern Dutch theatre and dance. The lively café downstairs is a good place for mixing with students from the Amsterdam Summer University which also operates out of the building.

Herengracht 366. Tel. 624 2436. Open Tues–Sat 10 a.m.–5 p.m. Admission f3. Tram 1, 2, 5 to Singer.

The pale sandstone façade with its garlands and pedimented windows is barely visible beneath a thick layer of city grime. A disproportionately large neck gable competes with its neighbour to reach the sky; itself a hallmark of the well-known architect, Philip Vingboons. The reverend Leendert Schouten opened the Bijbels Museum in 1860 to show his personal collection of **Bibles** and biblical objects. The interior of the house is lost to showcases, thin dividing walls and makeshift rooms, but if you are interested in the history of the Dutch Bible this is the place for you. You might like to join the security camera in the top room for a look at an intriguing model of Solomon's Temple.

THE EASTERN SECTION OF THE GRACHTEN GORDLE: FROM LEIDSEGRACHT TO THE AMSTEL

This is the area where you can sample a little of everything. Start with cream cheese and salmon bagels at Lucky Mothers, take a walk along the windswept Amstel, look at architecture on the grand canals and enjoy views of receding bridges and wide waterways. Step inside a stately home, go to the movies in an Art Deco cinema or bury your nose in tulips at the flower market. Check out the galleries in Kerkstraat, empty your wallet on exquisite antiques in Nieuwe Spiegelstraat and have your pockets emptied on Leisdsestraat. For an evening meal take your pick from the many restaurants in Utrechtsestraat. Sip cocktails or drink beer on Leidseplein and dance the night away on Rembrandtsplein.

Intended originally as a residential area for the rich it is a great place to be based in. Tourism is essentially confined to a few streets and squares and the area as a whole maintains its dignity as the most prestigious section of the Grachten Gordle. It started in 1668 as part of the second phase of the seventeenth-century city expansion. By the 1660s the plots on the new canals in the west were selling like hot cakes and the city decided to continue the Herengracht, Keizersgracht and Prinsengracht around the city over the River Amstel and up the river Ij. In the small area between Leidsegracht and the Amstel some of Amsterdam's most distinguished houses were constructed. The most impressive lie on the '**Golden Bend**', a stretch of the Herengracht which runs between Leidsestraat to Vijzelstraat. Canal boats chug around the main canals by day and night while their commentators point out imposing façades and curly gables in monotonous tones. Walkers and photographers enjoy the charm of **Reguliersgracht**, one of the few cross canals to escape being filled in and used as a thoroughfare.

If you enjoy eating chips, watching buskers, drinking, dancing, hanging out and socialising, then there is no need to look further than Rembrandtsplein and Leidseplein. If you enjoy sleeping, it's a good idea to find a hotel round the corner.

Rembrandtsplein

Tram 4, 9, 14 to Rembrandtsplein.

The best way to enjoy Rembrandtsplein is to head up the stairs at No. 17 to De Kroon Café, find a seat on the balcony and people watch. This lively square competes with Leidseplein as the hub of café life and as a magnet for tourists. Suited businessmen and women mix with pop stars and politicians in the smart Schiller Hotel, leather-clad boys strut off down Reguliersdwarsstraat for more of the same, well-dressed Dutch youth hang out in De Kroon while tourists sit ten deep on the pavement below, dipping chips into globs of mayonnaise.

By night the tempo increases as rock competes with house music in neighbouring bars. Hunky bouncers hang around closed doors while barely clad punters push past into clubs, bikers size up the talent and lager-filled tourists burst into song. Discos and clubs throb well into the early hours when clubbers stagger across the street to sleep it off under the rhododendron bushes.

The square is seldom quiet. The huge statue of Rembrandt in the centre is the only static element. People, trams, road sweepers, pigeons, police, taxis are always on the move. The square is guaranteed to meet almost every demand a tourist might have – telephones, trams, tram tickets, excursion tickets, taxis, money, food, drink, people, entertainment, clubs and discos. With these come the inevitable drawbacks of noise, pickpockets, weirdos, fumbling men and no peace.

Thorbeckeplein

Clinging to the south western edge of Rembrandtsplein this small rectangular square is named after the liberal statesman and thrice prime minister, Johan Rudolf Thorbecke, whose statue looks over the Herengracht at the far end. The forlorn bandstand in the centre lies empty while neon lights glint and flash on either side, offering more private entertainment. The square is really an extension of its larger neighbour, but it does have a small art market on Saturday mornings which makes a change from the people who sell beaded bracelets, home-made earrings and hair extensions here during the week.

THE GRACHTEN GORDLE

Amstel 218, tel. (Rijksmuseum) 673 2121. Open for guided tours Mon, Wed, Fri 10–11 a.m. on presentation of an invitation card previously obtained from the Rijksmuseum information desk (passport must be shown to get ticket). Admission free. No photography or note taking. Tram 4, 9, 14 to Rembrandtsplein.

The Six family extend a warm welcome to anyone who goes to the trouble to get an invitation to view their delightful home and exquisite collection of furniture, paintings and family treasures. They do not welcome those who turn up without going through the Rijksmuseum. Enter through the servants' entrance into the semi-basement and a well-informed student will give you an entertaining tour of the first floor. The rest of the house is still inhabited by the family.

The Six family came to Amsterdam as Huguenot refugees in the seventeenth century, bringing their cloth business with them. Jan Six married a Dutch aristocrat and the family have been producing generations of 'Jans' ever since. Catch up on the family history in the garden room and if you can tear yourself away from looking into the garden, don't miss the lovely *View of Buurkerk in Utrecht* by Pieter Saenredam, one of his impressive church interiors where the chandelier hangs in space to focus the perspective.

The Six family lived in various houses over the centuries and moved from the Herengracht to the present house on the Amstel in 1914. When they moved here, not only did they bring their belongings but a large part of the previous house as well, including doors, wall hangings and fixtures, cornices and light fittings. By chance they also found a rather grand painting rolled up in the attic. Not only did they decide to hang it, but they built a room for it. Paulus Potter's painting of Diederik Tulp astride his horse now dominates this small room at the centre of the building.

Jan Six's marriage in 1655 to Margetha the daughter of Amsterdam's most famous anatomist, Dr Nicolaas Tulp (depicted in Rembrandt's *Anatomy Lesson*) was a wise move both financially and socially. It also accounts for a number of paintings of the Tulp family hanging around the house. One which pays particular attention to their special status is the jolly family group by Nicolaas Elias (1653). The children play an early form of golf while mother Tulp sits on the bank. Behind them stands the Tulp carriage with the family crest emblazoned on the back. The painting was done when it was forbidden for most people to have carriages in Amsterdam because of the noise and the damage to bridges – only the elite were allowed to ride in wheeled carriages. On leaving the room there is a rather unsettling nineteenth-century portrait of a dead child by the popular

Amsterdam artist, Therese Schwartze. Members of the family who died young were often commemorated in posthumous portraits, lain on a bed and decked in roses. It is not as sinister as a death mask, but a serene semblance of the child.

Two Rembrandts in the front room are the pride of the collection. *Anna Wijmer* is dressed up in her Sunday best and poses formally for the great master. Her face is clearly painted expressing few signs of her true character. The painting of *Jan Six*, painted ten years later by the same artist is lively, spontaneous and surprisingly informal. Nothing is clearly defined but as a whole the picture works perfectly through the casual slapping on of paint, of dabs and swishes. If you stand back from it it becomes evident that the same palette is used throughout. All the colour used in his clothing can be picked up in his face and vice versa. They say that Rembrandt painted this picture of his friend Jan Six for nothing. While it may have been seen as a part payment for money borrowed, the relaxed nature of the picture suggests it was an appreciation of one friend by another.

The tour continues in the dining room then you end peering into a huge glass cabinet in the hall stuffed with exquisite, intriguing and eccentric family belongings: shrivelled remains of Rembrandt's paints, tiny tea sets, valuable glass and family trinkets. If you are not shown it, ask to see the Jack in a cup, an ingenious vessel designed to announce a pregnancy. Women kept their bump well hidden under layers of clothes until it was to be made public and then the pregnancy cup was brought out. The woman drank, the guests watched and up jumped Jack.

Before leaving you will be handed a large swan's feather and asked to sign your name which makes you feel that you really have gone back in time.

THERESE SCHWARTZE (1851–1918)

Therese was the daughter of an Amsterdam portrait painter, Goerg Schwartze, from whom she learned the rudiments of painting as a child. After her father's death she spent a year training in Munich under Gabriel Max and Lenbach before returning to the family house on the Prinsengracht. She continued to paint with the help of her father's friends, including the painter Josef Israels. She tried Paris a couple of times before she finally settled there in 1884 and subsequently began to establish a reputation as a portrait painter. She also made some genre and still life paintings, working in oil, watercolour and pastel. She exhibited throughout Europe, including a one-woman show in Amsterdam in 1890. Both she and her sculptor sister, Georgina, exhibited in the Paris Exposition of 1900.

In Amsterdam, Therese was popular among the aristocracy and royal family. When painting Queen Wilhelmina at the palace Therese is reputed to have complained about the poor light and insisted that the Queen should move to her studio on the

Prinsengracht which, of course, she did. Therese was also employed as the royal art teacher.

She married at 55 to Anton van Duyl but continued to work as an artist inspiring many other women to do the same. Her house (she owned three adjoining canal houses) was used for regular meetings of the Amsterdam Joffers (see p. 135), a group of women painters in the city who regarded themselves as professional artists. Therese was highly successful and became very wealthy, leaving over a million guilders on her death.

Magere Brug (Skinny Bridge)

Outside the Six Collection large boats chug up the wide Amstel River, dogs bark from huge barges and seagulls dive for scraps. A little way down is the Magere Bridge. This narrow white bridge is a replica of the original which was reputedly built in the seventeenth century by two elderly sisters named Mager (meaning skinny) who lived on opposite sides of the Amstel. They couldn't be bothered to walk all the way round via the Munttoren bridge so they built their own and gave themselves a direct route to one another. There was an uproar when the City Council discussed demolishing the rotten frame in 1929 and the bridge was saved by a single vote.

Across the Amstel the long dark brick building is the Amstelhof, a seventeenth-century almshouse which is still used for the old and infirm. A little further down the Carré Theatre with its frieze of jesters and clowns was built as a circus for Oscar Carré in 1887. Nowadays the only time you can see a circus there is over Christmas; for the rest of the year it hosts international musicals, most of which seem to be by Andrew Lloyd Webber. Way down the river in the distance the palatial Amstel Hotel hogs the east bank. The hotel was made famous by a massage doctor, Johan G. Mezger, who moved there three years after it opened in 1870. Patients visited his surgery from all over Europe and the hotel continued to attract classy clients even after his death. Isadora Duncan, Orson Wells, Yehudi Menuhin, Gladstone and Queen Elizabeth II are among the many famous visitors to have stayed here. In the 1890s the hotel was the talk of the town when it installed electricity and opened its own light factory. Guests still enjoy the private boat, the Rolls Royce and the splendid views across the Amstel.

Willet-Holthuysen Museum

Herengracht 605, tel. 523 1822. Open Mon–Fri 10 a.m.–5 p.m., weekends 11 a.m.–5 p.m. Admission adults f5, 6–16s f2.50, under 6s free. Tram 4, 9, 14 to Rembrandtsplein.

It used to be said that the quietest place in Amsterdam was the Willet-Holthuysen Museum. The jokes about the lack of visitors have ceased since the public realised it provided their only chance to step inside one of the grand merchant houses on Amsterdam's most prestigious canal, the Herengracht. Today it serves as a showcase of period rooms. Lush sitting rooms, an elegant dining room, immaculate kitchen and formal displays of glass, silver and artefacts are livened up with headless mannequins and the constant ticking of clocks.

Over the centuries Amsterdam's glitterati wined, dined and danced here. The last residents were the art collector, Abraham Willet and his wife Sandrina Louisa Holthuysen. She died in 1895, riddled with cancer and surrounded by cats. She left the house and its contents to the city in her will with the proviso that it would be opened to the public and known as the Willet-Holthuysen Museum.

The layout of the house is typical of Amsterdam's grandest residences, the so-called double canal house. It is set symmetrically around the central doorway instead of the usual one-sided arrangement. Anyone who could afford a symmetrical house with a double-sided stoop (stairs to the front door) was effectively buying two houses. Visitors enter through the small door under the stoop which leads into the servants' quarters and the storerooms. You will be directed to a small video room for a 15-minute introduction to the house, after which you are free to wander accompanied by bored caretakers.

Before you go upstairs take a look at the eighteenth-century kitchen with a strangely tiled tableau showing the landing of British and Russian troops at Bergen in 1799. The next floor was primarily used as a reception area. The best china is out, the furniture is highly polished, the ballroom is ready, yet it is hard to imagine the frivolous masked balls, banquets and courtships that took place here. If you like glass take a look at Abraham Willet's collection upstairs; animals dance round hefty beakers and bible stories are illustrated on little Dutch glasses.

The garden is usually open to visitors and affords a good view of the attractive back of the house. If you don't like traipsing around stately homes you can always look at the garden from the rather seedy Amstelstraat just off Rembrandtsplein.

Tuschinki Cinema

26 Reguliersbreestraat. Tel. 626 2633, open 12.15–10 p.m. daily, tours: July–Aug 10.30 a.m. Mon and Sun; admission f7.50. Tram 4, 9, 14 to Rembrandtsplein.

Never turn down a date at the Tuschinki. Whatever is showing the exuberant Art Deco cinema is entertainment in itself. If you follow the trams out of Rembrandtsplein you can't miss the wild exterior; alligators guard the little bronze doors, flag poles shoot out of the side and the cupolas on top look like something off a DC10. Lavish architecture continues into the lobby and the screen to see is No. 1, the main cinema. If you really want to make the most of it buy balcony tickets, sit back and enjoy the wickedly sumptuous interior with its Persian carpets, Art Deco fittings and fixtures, thousands of electric lights, stained glass and more. You could be sitting in a film set.

The lavish cinema was the dream of Abraham Tuschinki, a Jewish émigré from Poland who stopped off in the Netherlands on his way to the States. He opened his first cinema in a disused church in Rotterdam in 1911, forgot about moving on to America and opened the Tuschinki in Amsterdam instead, in 1921 – the public have enjoyed his fantastically kitsch creation ever since.

Munttoren

At the end of Reguliersbreestraat there is a meeting of streets, canals, tramlines and traffic and a frivolous clock tower known as the Munttoren. The heavy polygonal base dates back to the time when it was attached to the fifteenth-century defence gates of Regulierspoort. The name Munttoren refers back to the seventeenth century when it was used as a temporary mint, and the onion shaped orb on the top dates back to the time when Hendrick de Keyser was brought in to turn it into a landmark.

As a landmark it is exceptionally useful. Over the bridge to the north is the old centre; follow the road south and you come to the Herengracht, Keizersgracht and the Prinsengracht. The wide street Rokin takes you to Dam Square and in the opposite direction follows the Amstel to the Stopera. Behind the tower on the other side of the canal you come to the famous flower market.

Bloemenmarkt (Flower market)

Amsterdam's famous floating flower market can be magical on a cold winter's morning and hell on a hot summer's day. The stalls are actually shops enclosed under overhead tarpaulin and so full of flowers, bulbs, pots and trinkets that it comes as a surprise to find they are afloat.

Luscious fresh flowers are stuffed into buckets and sold in bunches of fifty. There can't be many markets where lilies and orchids are as common as tulips and daffodils. As the day wears on more sightseers converge on the narrow street and cafés put out chairs and tables to add to the congestion. Tempers rise as flowers get trampled on and people hold up the traffic to take a photo. By the end of the day wilting blooms are sold off at bargain prices and hot, sticky stallholders go home for a bath.

However you respond to it, you cannot fail to enjoy the smell and the colours; scarlet tulips are set against salmon pink roses, deep blue irises mingle with purple violets and rich emerald ferns compete with earthy olive foliage. Unsurprisingly, the market is a hit with artists and phtographers from all over the world. The street itself was a popular location for artists' studios at the turn of the century. Coba Ritsema took a studio at No. 512 which was used by fellow women artists, the Amsterdam 'Joffers'.

AMSTERDAM JOFFERS

The best-known European woman artist of the nineteenth century, the Frenchwoman, Rosa Bonheur described her fellow female artists as 'sisters of the palette'. She was referring to women who painted as a profession as well as a hobby. 'Look at their self-portraits' she instructed 'proudly identified by the tools of their trade, dressed in work clothes instead of fine feathers.'

Inspired by the success of Therese Schwartze (see p. 000) a group of Amsterdam women took up painting seriously and became 'sisters of the palette'. The eight women were known as the Amsterdam Joffers loosely translated as the 'misses'. They caused a furore, not because of their art which took the form of inoffensive portraits and still lives but because of their gender. Women, particularly married women, as two of them were, had seldom worked as professonal artists. Coba Ritsema (1876–1961), the best known, was described by the weekly *Haagse Post* as 'one of the very few Dutch bohemians'. Coba Surie and Ans van de Berg, called Ans and Co because they lived together for 36 years, mainly produced still lives with flowers. Ans was the only joffer who didn't have an art school background. Jo Bauer Stumff let the side down when she gave up painting and destroyed everything because she felt she should spend more time looking after her husband. She did however resume her work after his death.

Although their fame was confined to the Netherlands they encouraged other women to study painting and to make a living from their art. Therese Schwartze's nieces Lizzy and Theresia Ansingh, were among several women who followed their example.

TULIP MANIA

The Dutch brought this little cliché upon themselves nearly 400 years ago.

Tulips were first seen by Dutch diplomats in Turkey and were brought back to Holland via Vienna around 1600. The aristocracy were hooked immediately, but it took some time to capture the imagination of the nation. When a Leiden botanist discovered ways of changing the shape, colours and colour variations of the bloom, tulip cultivation became a national obsession. By 1636 'Everyone, rich and poor, began to grow the new Turkish flower in their windows and courtyards'. Even the Delft potters cashed in on the trend, doing a roaring trade in blue and white pyramids and pagodas to exhibit the blooms.

Horticulturists continued to breed exotic species and popularity pushed prices to ridiculous heights. Irregular blooms of the flamed or striped variety were the most precious. (It was only in the last century that botanists discovered that these were in fact the result of a virus.) Single bulbs fetched as much as f3,000, a small fortune given that the average annual salary was f150. Fierce rivalry and madness gripped the nation, as bulbs were swapped for houses and great banquets were held in honour of such transactions.

The intriguing aspect of all this was that the trade was only in bulbs, not tulips. Huge sums of money were paid for something they had never seen. Buyers leafed through the trade catalogues, known as tulip books, and relied totally on artists' impressions of their potential purchase. Once the builb did bloom proud owners were keen to record it – some employed artists to paint them as they would their wives or daughters. The wonderful still life paintings of the period were as much a comment on status as a pretty piece of wall decoration.

Tulip mania spread and soaring prices fuelled investment further. Sales took place by contract, and gradually more and more middlemen came between the grower and the eventual purchaser. Prices rose and at the end of the day they all wanted a cut of the profits. Effectively, they bought on credit with money they never had with no intention of acquiring the product but with every intention of selling on to another dealer. However, the bubble eventually had to burst; in February 1637 prices plummeted and the magistrates had to rescue growers from inevitable bankruptcy. Many great people lost their fortunes and their reputations to the tulip, including the landscape artist Jan van Goyen who spent years repaying debts for unsold bulbs.

In retrospect, the absurd prices, the speculation, the stories of rags to riches and vice versa are highly entertaining. Artists and writers have enjoyed it ever since. As for the tulips, the market and prices were stabilised the following year and serious tulip cultivation remains fiercely competitive and highly lucrative to this day.

The Golden Bend

The most upmarket address in Amsterdam would place you somewhere on the Herengracht between Vijzelstraat and Liedsestraat, on the stretch called the Golden Bend. Most of the large sandstone houses are double fronted with a central stoop, topped with balustrades and statues. The street was named not so much for its houses as for the wealthy people who lived there, several of them rich spinsters. The mayor's house at No. 446 eventually fell into the hands of Alida Johanna de Graeff whose painter didn't think much of her. Decorators recently uncovered some plinths in the house inscribed: 'Anno 1740. Jan Venerius worked here and declares by his heart that he never met a more stingy person in his life.' Three sisters lived in No. 450 and after their death the building became a Reading Museum for women which was active from 1900 to 1920. The vast library was used by over 1100 members; educated women gathered here to listen to readings and to engage in enlightened conversation.

Kattenkabinett (Cat Cabinet)

Herengracht 497, tel. 626 5378. Open Tues–Sun noon–5 p.m. Entrance 5f. Tram 16, 24, 25 to Herengracht.

When the big ginger tom, John Pierpont Morgan, died in 1984 his owner decided to open a museum to his memory. Six years later the museum opened with an exhibition of cat pictures by Sal Meijer and a live performance of the song 'Memory', sung by Pia Douwes (and not a violin in sight). The permanent exhibition of works of art on a cat theme is relatively small, but has a pleasant mixture of entertaining, intellectual and sickly sweet depictions of cats. There are also a number of interesting works by contemporary Dutch women artists.

A leaflet available in the entrance hall will explain every painting in the building and usually the artists' motives as well. Don't miss Sonja Dwingers simple watercolour sketches. Etchings by Rembrandt and Picasso add a touch of class, as does the rather splendid case of Japanese netsuke, small figures carved in ivory and other precious material. Louis Wain enthusiasts will be glad to see a cartoon of cats clinging to a merry-go-round. Exhibitions are generally inspired and if you like cats and a quick glance at a canal house you won't be disappointed.

Van Loon Museum

Keizersgracht 672, tel. 6245255. Open Mon 10 a.m.–6 p.m., Sun 1 p.m.–5 p.m. Admission 3f.

Few canal houses maintain their original character as well as the Van Loon. Behind the simple façade is a beautifully restored lush eighteenth-century interior. Richly furnished rooms are decorated with a wealth of family portraits and mementoes and despite the stately decor, there is an informal atmosphere.

The Van Loon family are relative newcomers at No. 672. The house was given to Willem Van Loon and Thora Edegius as a wedding present in 1884. Many of the family pictures hanging here go back to the seventeenth century, the Golden Age when the Van Loons ranked among the five most prestigious families in Amsterdam. They helped to set up the East India Company and they maintained their wealth and power throughout the seventeenth and eighteenth centuries. While they did well in business there is no doubt that intermarriage with wealthy families seems to have been the key to their success. The house was used briefly to shelter the homeless following the war and has not been lived in, in its entirety, since. Like so many stately homes, democracy and the economy has sent the aristocracy to live in their attics and forced them to open their doors to the public.

Musicians occasionally play in the marble hallway, but don't be distracted from the jovial painting *The Wedding of Willem van Loon and Margaretha Bos* by Jan Miense Molenaer (1637). The couple sit just left of centre, surrounded by the entire Van Loon generation alive at the time. The rather stiff lady dressed in black is not about to hurl her lemon at the couple; the fruit would have been known to contemporaries as a symbolic reference to her recently deceased brother. Other symbols include the washing of glasses on the left which refers to the bride's chastity. It is rather confusing given that the bride is hanging on to a small child. The child is in fact Willem Van Loon's by his first marriage.

Looking into the formal garden from the little room at the end, you will see a neo-classical temple. This is not the summerhouse that it might seem, but the former stables and coachhouse. The first floor windows were painted out to stop the coachman and his family spying on their employers.

The bright little room overlooking the garden would have been primarily a ladies room where they would sip tea, chat over embroidery and chuckle over their latest discovery in the popular women's handbooks by Jacob Cats.

While the ladies were busy sewing in the garden room next door the men puffed and sniffed in the smoking room. Snuff taking and smoking was almost universal among men, but only lower-class women indulged. Non-smoking women found it so unpleasant that many insisted that their husbands confine their smoke to a special room. Some even put an 'anti-smoking clause' in their marriage contract. There is another interesting work by Molenaer in this room entitled *The Four Ages or the Five Senses*. This unique idea of combining a family portrait with the senses is highly entertaining. He combines childhood with touch and taste, courtship with smell, parenthood with hearing (don't miss the wonderful allusion to making music together) and old age with sight.

The rooms at the front of the house are where more formal entertaining took place. The Dutch have always been keen on their food. Families would tuck into four huge meals a day, starting with breakfast at around 6 a.m., lunch at noon, tea at 4 p.m. and dinner around 8 p.m. so maybe they did find a use for the 240-piece service of Amstel china shown in the dining room. The more sober drawing room was primarily for meeting people. It was here that Thora van Loon-Edigius entertained her society friends. As the *dame du palais*, (a superior lady in waiting) to Queen Wilhelmina she knew them all.

The luxurious decoration continues upstairs in the bedrooms. The small room at the top of the stairs is decorated by large painted canvases of classical scenes. Big canvases, produced in painting factories were popular in the eighteenth century and usually used in the downstairs rooms. It is worth popping into the main bedroom for a glimpse at a number of family portraits, including a portrait of Hendrick van Loon junior painted by Therese Schwartze in 1890.

JACOB CATS: THE MAESTRO OF DOMESTICITY IN SEVENTEENTH-CENTURY AMSTERDAM

It may be a far cry from *Mrs Beeton*, *The Joy of Sex* and *Women's Pleasure*, but Dutch women have been well informed for years. By 1655, an estimated 50,000 copies of Jacob Cats's *The Wise Cook* or *Careful Householder* were in circulation in the Netherlands. Intended as a handbook for the contemporary family, as a guide to life it was almost as popular as the Bible. Although Cats was a traditionalist, his books do reflect the more liberal attitude to women emerging at the beginning of the seventeenth century.

'A young woman should show the virgin virtues; she should wait patiently until God brings her a partner. He should be approved by her parents, but of her own choosing. Forced marriages are wrong because love is free. Within marriage both men and women should be virtuous; the woman should submit to her husband whose duty it is to instruct her. Men should obey the law and women their husbands.'

For a more raunchy read, women looked at *Marriage*, published in 1625. This is really directed at the unmarried woman, presumably a virgin, who wants to know all those things about which one just cannot ask. Written in the form of a series of dialogues between an older lady and curious young woman, it was seen as an ingenious means of enlightenment by the younger generation.

Cats's advice wasn't superseded for over a hundred years when the first women's journal went on sale. A tutor, Justus van Effen, launched *De Hollandsche Spectator*, a weekly magazine crammed with moralistic essays, reputedly less sympathetic than those of Jacob Cats.

The Spiegel Quarter

There is something very intimate about the Spiegel Quarter, the centre of Amsterdam's antique business. Antique shops run the entire length of **Nieuwe Spiegelstraat** and down the neighbouring **Kerkstraat**. Its proximity to the Rijksmuseum ensures a steady flow of art enthusiasts and tourists. This is where museum curators rub shoulders with the riff raff in search of something new. There are few bargains but numerous good buys. Windows gleam with polished silver, elegantly cut glass and precious gems. Courteous ladies entertain well heeled clients while the gentlemen load blanketed French cabinets into anonymous lorries. Modern art galleries compete with outrageous window displays and extortionate prices.

Whether you are buying or not, Nieuwe Spiegelstraat is a nice walk and the gallery owners are generally friendly and always well informed. When tired of rummaging through piles of prints in junk shops for a misplaced Rembrandt etching, pop into Erik Kappers (No. 32); he is sure to have plenty. If you have a particular passion for Dutch glass or Delft tiles take a look in Frides Lameris (No. 55). Try Elisabeth den Bieman de Haas (No. 44) for good modern art and a taste of the contemporary scene. For the macabre, Thom and Lenny Nelis, just round the corner on Kiezersgracht 541, have a gruesome collection of medical instruments.

The ICA (No. 10) serves a good cup of tea and Françoise, on Kerkstraat 176, makes the best applecake in town.

Leidseplein

Tram 1, 2, 5, 6, 7, 10 to Leidseplein.

Amsterdam's highest concentration of cafés, restaurants and tourists are around Leidseplein. The square itself is carved in two by a busy tramline. One side is entirely given over to chairs and tables where the youth of the world drink beer, play cards and chat under strings of fairground lights. Bikers drive their classic Harley Davidsons at snail's pace around the square and local lads ogle at foreign girls. On the other side, fire eaters and puppeteers entertain hordes of tourists among discarded Coke cans and scrunched-up burger cartons. Women plait coloured ribbons and beads into schoolgirls' hair and cartoonists ridicule their subjects.

The streets converging on Leidseplein are given over to tourists. Leidsestraat is the place to change your money, wait at the tourist board, book your flight home, send a fax and buy your tampons. The maze of streets to the east are packed with restaurants and cafés. Neon lights and signboards are as dense as the smell of chips, steak and popcorn. Lager-filled boys bleat silly songs and smiling women flog little red roses morning, day and night.

Dress code is all important in Leidseplein. Liberty dresses are still in fashion at the exuberant but elegant Café Americain. If you want to hang out in the square, then dark glasses are obligatory and it is best to adopt the 'Albert Cuyp' look – uncoordinated, carefully chosen grunge topped with an embroidered waistcoat (named after the trendy people who frequent the Albert Cuyp's market). Round the corner at the Palladium Café sophisticates touch up in the ladies' loo before sipping vodka out front.

In the 60s Leidseplein was the stomping ground of the *Pleiners* (modelled on the English Mods). The Rocker equivalent, known as the *Dijkers*, hung out around Nieuwendijk. In the 60s and 70s hippies swayed to guitar music, adjusted their headbands and welcomed the impromptu concerts by the 'Choir of Beautifully Disturbed Women', despite the fact that none of the thirty-strong choir sang in unison or in tune. More serious music and space cakes are available today, as they were then at the **Melkweg** just around the corner. While the hippie element has gone, this converted dairy is one of the city's prime art centres (see p. 288).

For most of the year the square services junk tourism; in winter the square is quintessentially Dutch. Tables and chairs are replaced by a public skating rink. Parents peer through steamed-up windows while their children practise their antics on the ice under the lights.

THE JORDAAN

This maze of narrow streets, picturesque canals and tiny bridges, designer shops, cafés and restaurants is one of Amsterdam's most popular quarters. As in so many working-class areas, the real Jordaaners are gradually being edged out by artists, students, musicians and money, but the spirit of the place is very much alive. The Jordaan is full of surprises; picturesque little *Hofjes* (see p. 142), ancient gable stones and a number of worthwhile street markets. It is best to wander through the area at leisure – following a map can be a nightmare because the streets are so short that you are constantly looking for directions. Use the soaring tower of the Westerkerk as a landmark and explore. A map is however useful for guiding you home when you have had enough. The tourist board (VVV) publishes a good *Walk through the Jordaan* if you feel that you need some guidance.

While the rich merchants built themselves palatial dwellings in the Herengracht, Keizersgracht and the Prinsengracht, the marshy area to the west was developed to house the workers and industries that served the city. Jordaan may be a corruption of *jardin* the name given to the area by the French Huguenot refugees who settled here in the seventeenth century. Streets take the names of plants and trees in keeping with this explanation.

Unlike the layout of the waterways, planning here was haphazard; ditches were turned into canals and paths into streets; the plots were tiny and houses minuscule. Small is beautiful and may be quaint to us but earlier generations found it impossible. Poverty has been the hallmark of the Jordaan up to the last fifty years. Women struggled to raise families in cramped and damp conditions and raw sewage ran into stagnant canals, causing frequent cholera epidemics. Men were forced to pawn their belongings to pay weekly bills and not surprisingly rioted at any available opportunity. Jordaaners struggled together. They share worries, friendships, dialect, hobbies and tastes.

By 1900, over 80,000 people lived in the Jordaan area – an average of 10 per house. This caring community looked after the elderly for years, housing them in the hofjes throughout the city, but the need for adequate low-rent housing was immense.

At the turn of the century, inspired by the work of the English housing reformer Octavia Hill in London, a number of Amsterdam women attacked the housing problems in Amsterdam. Helene Mercier set up a building concern called 'Jordaan' to build and manage low-rent housing projects in the area. She also opened 'Our House', a centre for social education where 'shame and irritation about this terrible difference between poverty and wealth can be forgotten for a while'.

Another well-educated woman, Johanna ter Meulen, worked alongside Octavia Hill before setting up the Housing Association, 'Oud Amsterdam'. She, too, managed a housing project in the Jordaan with the help of her lover, Cornelia de Lange.

The twentieth century has seen a significant change in the area. Authentic Jordaaners are dying off or leaving, to be replaced by students, artists and musicians. Houses have been demolished or restored, rebuilt and sold at inflated prices. In the 1970s local action groups pressured the municipal government to save the Jordaan. The area north of the Rozengracht has been designated primarily residential and subsidised low-rent housing has been built. Small industries and businesses continue to the south, but offer little employment to the workers who have stayed in the neighbourhood. To a certain extent, the social balance between workers and intellectuals has been maintained; children still kick footballs up and down the streets, elderly men still prop up the bars, and the lack of hotels pays homage to the success of the pressure groups to save the community from total yuppiedom.

GABLE STONES

Numbering houses was only introduced in the Napoleonic era. Before, the gable stone or gevelstenen, an embedded plaque on the front of a house, giving a pictorial description of the owner's trade or occupation, was the only way of distinguishing addresses. The Jordaan is full of gable stones. Look out for the 'world turned upside down' at Lindengracht 55, where fish swim in the tree and the name 'Hcardnednil' is actually Lindengracht backwards. Others you will spot include pigs and sheep for butchers, loaves of bread, a breast-feeding woman for wet nurses (of which there were many in the area) and a number of milkmaids who usually indicate the tobacco industry in reference to the famous 'Meilkmeisjesburg' pipe from Gouda. To give you some clues, the main industries in the area were the smelly ones – leather tanning, glue making, cloth weaving and dying. If you happen to see a pigeon on the gable stone this refers to the traditional hobby of all Jordaaners; pigeon racing.

HOFJES

The Jordaan was the first area to have purpose-built social housing provided by charitable institutions. These almshouses are scattered all over the neighbourhood.

Most of them are now privately owned and easily recognisable by their long façades and central doorways. They look institutional and are usually marked above the door on a large gable stone set into the wall. Inside, residents enjoy magically peaceful garden courtyards. You may find the central door already open, but if not, the residents rarely complain if you want a quick peep. Such invasion of privacy by nosy tourists seems to be taken for granted. It is best not to make a special effort to visit individual hofjes because the chances are that you will get lost — you'll probably see more by chance than design.

Particularly noteworthy ones include the **Claes Claesz Hofje** or, as the gable stone says, the Ansloshofje in Eerste Eglantiersdwarstraat which contains three inner courtyards, complete with cherry trees and music students from the Sweelinck Music School. Nearby, on Egelantiersgracht 107–114, the St Andrieshofje has a lovely blue and white-tiled passage to the pretty garden courtyard beyond. It was originally managed by a begijn sister, Anna de Magistris, for Catholic widows who had the funds to buy themselves in. From the 1920s it was inhabited by the intriguingly named Auxiliary Sisters of the Souls in Purgatory.

The hofje that seems to attract the most attention is just off the square, in **Karthuizerstraat 89–171**. Originally intended for poor widows when it was built in 1630, it now houses young people, hence the mountain of bikes propped up against the two 'sea monster' water pumps in the middle of the courtyard. There were once a hundred houses here for widows over fifty and unmarried women over sixty. Regulations stipulated that they needn't be poor but should show 'enough modesty' to justify a place.

Hofjes were eventually established all over the city. Once you have seen one you will start to recognise them all over the place, but don't get too blasé about opening closed doors.

Lindengracht

As the Jordaan's principal canal, Lindengracht was the prime location for the popular sport of eel-pulling. An unfortunate eel was smeared with soap and suspended from a rope over the canal, the idea being to grab as much of the creature as possible. This led to much hilarity as men toppled from their boats and the eel gradually fell apart. The game was unpopularly declared illegal on grounds of cruelty in 1886; when a policeman cut the rope in an attempt to break up a meeting, the gamesters in true Jordaan style fought back, igniting the famous Eel Riot of 1886.

The riot was less jovial than it might sound. It was finally quashed by the army after three days, leaving 26 dead and hundreds injured. Afterwards an eel sympathiser, Chrisje van der Wouden, was awarded an annual gratuity of 200 guilders for hiding a policeman under her skirts to avoid the raging crowd.

Today the wide space, created by filling in the canal, is used as a car park, but the street maintains its atmosphere as cafés and restaurants encroach beyond the pavements, and on Saturdays locals shop in the lively street market for their weekend fodder.

Known as the Herengracht of the Jordaan, this is one of the prettiest canals in the city. Large pot plants keep cars off the sidewalks and houseboats rock gently against the quay. Children throw stones from the humped-backed bridges while their mothers pretend not to notice.

A row of rather beautiful step gabled houses, Nos. 87–91 by Hendrick de Keyser, known as the 'three Hendricks' seem superior for the Jordaan. Their original names are indicated by gablestones; the townsman, the countryman and the seaman. These houses were not, however, as luxurious as it might seem. Locals report impossibly steep staircases and a maze of tiny rooms.

Just across the canal, Anthony Perkins murdered a couple of women in the showers at the Hotel Onna for his little-known sequel to *Psycho*, *Twice a Woman*. The proprietor will be only too pleased to show you the pictures of the film you never saw. Other guest appearances here include visits from the Queen on Queen's Day; in recent years she has sailed up Bloemgracht to wave to the merry masses drinking in her honour.

Noorderkerk (North Church)

Tram 13, 14, 17 to Westerkerk.

Until recently huge congregations of Bonders, members of a Calvinist sect, gathered here on Sundays to be welcomed by their preacher kitted out in mid-nineteenth-century dress. The spectacle is temporarily halted as the church is undergoing a massive restoration programme, due to finish in 1998.

The unimpressive, squat church was one of Hendrick de Keyser's last and least successful. His style is easily recognised in the ludicrous balustraded gables. The rather humble appearance is in keeping with his commission to produce a church for the working-class population of the Jordaan.

Noordermarkt

The best time to visit this large windswept square is on a Monday morning. The market is a local affair, but takes up the entire square and the length of the adjoining Westerstraat. Housewives check out the fruit, veg and fat wedges of local cheese, bargain-hunters try out cane chairs, parents rock their babies in antique cradles and dilapidated prams, designers pick through bundles of lace, buttons and discarded fabric, transvestites try on peroxide wigs and everyone checks out the second-hand clothes.

It is something of a junk exchange. People buy, friends gossip, children munch at honeyed waffles and Peruvian pipers provide the music. Meanwhile the cafés and bars around the square churn out coffees and hot chocolates by the dozen. By lunch time everyone is packing up to go home and the square is restored to its former function as children's playground and dog walk.

Take time to look at the incredibly touching bronze group standing near the entrance to the church, inscribed *Eenheid de Sterkste Keten* (The strongest chains are those of Unity). The three bound figures commemorate the 1934 Jordaan Riots against proposals to reduce dole money during the Depression.

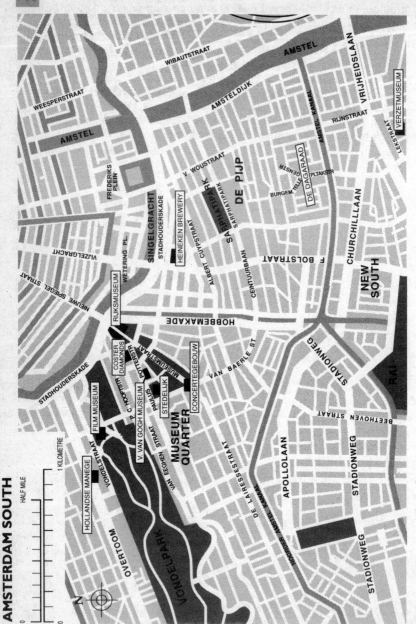

AMSTERDAM SOUTH

HALF MILE

1 KILOMETRE

WEESPERSTRAAT

AMSTEL

FREDERIKS PLEIN

VIJZELGRACHT

NIEUWE SPIEGEL STRAAT

STADHOUDERSKADE

HOLLANDSE MANEGE

VONDELSTRAAT

OVERTOOM

VONDELPARK

FILM MUSEUM

P. C. HOOFTSTR

V. VAN GOGH MUSEUM

VAN EEGHEN STRAAT

PAULUS

STEDELIJK

MUSEUMSTRAAT

POTTERSTR

COSTER DIAMONDS

RIJKSMUSEUM

WETERING PL.

SINGELGRACHT

STADHOUDERSKADE

HEINEKEN BREWERY

V. WOUSTRAAT

SARPHATIPARK

ALBERT CUYPSTRAAT

CEINTUURBAAN

HOBBEMAKADE

MUSEUM QUARTER

CONCERTGEBOUW

VAN BAERLE ST

DE LAIRESSESTRAAT

APOLLOLAAN

NOORDER AMSTEL KANAAL

WIBAUTSTRAAT

AMSTEL

AMSTELDIJK

DE PIJP

F BOLSTRAAT

NEW SOUTH

STADIONWEG

BEETHOVEN STRAAT

STADIONWEG

STADIONWEG

STADIONWEG

RAI

CHURCHILLLAAN

AMSTEL KANAAL

DE DAGERAAD

BURGEM. TELLEGENSTR

PLTAKSTR

RIJNSTRAAT

LEKSTRAAT

VERZETMUSEUM

VRIJHEIDSLAAN

AMSTERDAM SOUTH: THE MUSEUM QUARTER, 'DE PIJP' AND THE NEW SOUTH

The nineteenth-century residential area of Amsterdam South is surprisingly unspoilt by the concentration of museums at its core. Beyond the unimpressive tourist-ridden Museumplein to the west are one of Amsterdam's most upmarket residential areas, the city's smartest shopping streets and the delightful Vondelpark. Wide tree-lined avenues and large four-storey buildings are disappointingly average after the sparkling canals and dainty little gabled houses in the centre, but the sense of community here is tangible. The area around Vondelpark is particularly pleasant. Local restaurants fill with families and friends, shoppers are welcomed by name and anyone can walk the streets safely at night. If you wish to avoid Amsterdam's sex industry completely this is a good area to stay in – quiet, safe, friendly and still within walking distance of the centre.

A little further south, community charm gives way to wealth and the residents hide behind iron bars and security systems. By contrast, in the east the lively 'De Pijp' area's village atmosphere is best experienced in the throbbing market at Albert Cuypstraat. Beyond the market it becomes a maze of narrow streets and community housing where curtains twitch and children play. You eventually find yourself at the heart of the New South, where the eccentric 1920s architecture of the Amsterdam School turns municipal housing into something akin to an adventure playground.

The Museum Quarter has enough to entertain you for days:

Amsterdam's main museums are conveniently strung out around Museumplein and while you couldn't possibly do them all in one day at least they are easy to locate. There is a profusion of Dutch art at the **Rijksmuseum**, the world's greatest collection of works by one man at the **Van Gogh Museum**, and something up to date and usually provocative at the **Stedelijk**. You may also enjoy an evening concert at the **Concertegebouw**. Beyond the boundaries of Museumplein join shoppers in the delis and designer shops of **P.C. Hooftstraat**, reminisce over silent movies in the **Film Museum** and relax among the easy-going crowd in **Vondelpark**.

Save 'De Pijp' for a morning away from culture. You are bound to find something both cheap and authentic at the market and it will be the closest you come to feeling what it is like to live in Amsterdam. The fascinating **Resistance Museum** is well worth the tram ride to the New South but this area is only really worth a visit if you have a keen interest in town planning, 1920s architecture or if there is something good on at the **RAI Exhibition Centre**.

From Chaos to Contraception: Nineteenth-Century Amsterdam

Amsterdam was late to join the Industrial Revolution. French occupation had left the Dutch penniless and despondent. Louis Napoleon left the city in 1813, having established Amsterdam as the capital of the United Netherlands, home of the monarchy and seat of the government. Unfortunately the Napoleonic wars had strangled Dutch trade, appointed London as centre of the money markets and allowed the British to control the Dutch colonies.

A disinterested city fell into despair. The government returned to the Hague, the River Ij became unnavigable to big ships, the Stock Exchange building fell down and the population mushroomed. A stagnant city of crumbling canal houses, squalid slums and disease-infested canals needed help. With the opening of the North Sea Canal Amsterdam gained a quick route to the sea, the Suez Canal provided a short route to the East and the burgeoning European railway system opened another door. At last Amsterdam had ways to recover and led by the entrepreneur, Dr Samuel Sarphati, it did. His vast glass and steel Palace of Industry (modelled on Crystal Palace) went up on Frederiksplein and encouraged the population to take interest. By the 1880s the city was caught in a massive wave of industrialisation and expansion.

New housing was built haphazardly around the former city walls. The working classes were crammed into areas like 'De Pijp' while the middle classes secured mansions and villas in the area around Vondelpark and the Rijksmuseum. The arts blossomed and once again Amsterdam became a city of international standing. At the same time, the population continued to increase and with it the squalor; poor families suddenly became everyone's concern.

The world's first birth control clinic was opened in Amsterdam in 1882 by the pioneering doctor, Aletta Jacobs. This major event, heralding the introduction of a safe and legal method of contraception, and the Housing Act of 1901, were largely responsible for improving conditions for the city's working class.

ALETTA JACOBS (1851–1929)

Holland's first woman doctor, the celebrated feminist and birth control campaigner, Aletta Jacobs, is one of the country's best-known women.

At nineteen, Aletta was determined to follow in her father's footsteps and study medicine. 'Seized with the horror of the idea of having to dedicate her entire life to housework', she fantasised about fleeing home dressed up as a boy. As a woman she was barred from medical school, but managed to qualify as an apprentice dispenser before writing to the Dutch Prime Minister, Thorbecke, requesting permission to attend university. Permission was granted for one year only, but she was allowed to complete the course and amidst violent opposition from her male colleagues, became the first woman to qualify as a doctor in the Netherlands.

At first, she worked for her father and then started her own clinic working with poor families in Amsterdam. It was not long before she was running a free surgery and courses in child care, hygiene and health for the poor, sponsored by the Trades Union Council. While taking these courses she realised it was crucial to provide women with a safe and effective form of contraception.

In 1880 there was no reliable method of contraception in use in Holland. Her investigations led her to Flensburg where a 'safe' method using a *pessarium*, (confusingly the Dutch for a diaphragm), the original **Dutch Cap** was being investigated by a Dr Mesinga. In 1882, she opened the first birth control clinic in the world in Amsterdam, offering 'advice for patients who wished to avoid pregnancy for medical, economic or ethical reasons'. She carefully documented every case to avoid false claims of harm to patients from hostile doctors.

At the same time she was hard at work campaigning for women's rights in many areas; the fight for suffrage, shorter working hours, safety at work, sex education, the abolition of regulated prostitution, penal reform and reform of the marriage laws. She initiated the Association for Women's Suffrage in 1894 (Amsterdam) and was instrumental in the foundation of similar organisations in Berlin and Washington DC. In protest against the legal status of women (married women had no legal independence from their husbands in Holland until 1956) Aletta lived with her partner, the journalist Carel Gerritsen for several years until they married to have children. Their only child died after only one day and her husband died in 1905.

Aletta never tired of the struggle for the emancipation of women. She toured the globe with the American feminist Carrie Chapman Catt in an attempt to reach women all over the world. During the First World War she led the Women's Peace Movement with Jane Addams and once women's suffrage was achieved in Holland, in 1919, she continued to work for the International Alliance of Women, primarily concerned for women in Asia.

Aletta's achievements were numerous but her most significant one was in birth control. Largely thanks to her, by 1927 large families in Holland were unusual, and scientific birth control was widely used throughout the country except in orthodox religious circles. By now it was known in England and America as the 'Dutch Method'.

letta wrote; 'actual experience has shown that 45 years of birth control work has brought about the good results that I expected when I began my work'. Her work for women's rights were no less significant. The ceremonial unveiling of a memorial plaque on the wall of her house prompted her to sum up her achievements in a letter to Carrie Chapman Catt, shortly before her death: 'Here in Holland we now have activated in each city a large group of women interested in our work and convinced they have to continue it if they don't want to lose the freedom we have already won for them. Young, intelligent women have put a stone on the house Tesselschaderstraat in Amsterdam … in which is engraved I lived and worked there, so coming generations won't forget what I did for them.'

THE MUSEUM QUARTER

Trams and bicycles came to Amsterdam in the 1880s, around the same time as the area south of the Singelgracht, now the Museum Quarter, was being developed. A steady flow of educated middle-class citizens left the stinking canals of the overcrowded inner city for the elegant four-storey houses and exotic villas being built to the south. The State provided them with a national art museum (the Rijksmuseum) for Sunday afternoon jaunts, but it was the residents themselves who were ultimately responsible for creating the refined area it is today. Locals clubbed together to create a graceful park, a concert hall, and a riding school.

Roads were built to accommodate sparkling new motor cars and trams. Even the plan of the Rijksmuseum was determined by a central causeway for city traffic. Bike lanes were an after-thought – in 1880 it was cyclists not motorists who had to watch themselves. Women cyclists were obliged to attend special schools to learn the art of elegant cycling. Today traffic thunders slap through the middle of Museumplein and main roads carve up the Museum Quarter in various directions.

The Rijksmuseum is Amsterdam's biggest and best art gallery and consequently the most popular. People come from all over the world to see the richly painted Rembrandts, to admire the crisp details of the still life artists and to chuckle at the bawdy genre scenes unique to Dutch art. Just across the square a constant stream of people pays homage to the extraordinary artist, Vincent Van Gogh, while next door at the Stedelijk a sophisticated audience takes in the latest trends in contemporary art. If you are visiting the galleries it is well worth taking the courage to escape the confines of the litter-strewn coach park of Museumplein to explore the surrounding area. P.C. Hooftstraat has some of the smartest shops in Amsterdam and the wide open spaces, winding lakes and festive crowd in Vondelpark can breathe new life into you after a few hours slogging around a gallery.

Stadhouderskade 42, tel. 673 2121. Open Tues–Sat 10 a.m.–5 p.m., Sun and public holidays 1 p.m.–5 p.m. Closed Mon (except on public holidays). Admission Adults f10; 6–18 f5; over 65 f5. Disabled Access (ask at door for help). Tram 2, 5, 6, 7, 10 to Rijkmuseum.

The Rijksmuseum is the largest national museum in the Netherlands, but don't be put off by size. The vast collection of over 5000 paintings, 30,000 sculptures and pieces of applied art, 17,000 historical objects and 3000 works of Asiatic art are conveniently divided into manageable collections, well displayed and explained. Unlike most national museums the Rijksmuseum collections in the main part concentrate on Dutch art and Dutch history, so this is your chance to come to terms with Dutch culture without being bombarded by themes and images from around the world.

Tickets are sold, at present, in the shabby little portakabin sitting on the tarmac just outside the front entrance on Stadhouderskade. Once inside, you are likely to find yourself queuing for the cloakroom where friendly but frustrated staff look after coats, bags and umbrellas. Toilets and telephones are in the basement and there is a disappointing café for weak coffee and more queues on the westside ground floor.

The main reception hall on the first floor has a souvenir shop at either end, a few comfortable chairs and an information desk in the centre. It is a good idea to plan what you want to see, using the free ground plan available either here or in the ticket office. The most popular collection consists of Dutch paintings from the fifteenth to the seventeenth century. You could easily spend the whole morning here, if not a whole day. Ask at the desk about guided tours as they can often alleviate the pressure of deciding where to go and what to see. If time is limited and you are looking for highlights, check out one of the free *Viewfinders*. These direct you to about twelve pictures with a theme in mind and are both entertaining and informative, lasting about half an hour. The museum also runs regular introductory films and slide shows to help you understand Dutch art, but with so much to see you might prefer to look at the real thing. (If you are hoping to go to visit the **Six Collection**, see p. 130, remember to pick up a ticket here by showing your passport.)

The Building From afar, the Rijksmuseum looks more like an asylum than a national gallery of art. The vast red brick building is pierced through the middle by a wide arched passageway, topped with steep roofs and surrounded by a kilometre of cast-iron railings. On closer inspection it is alive with elaborate decoration. Tiled tableaux give a potted history of Dutch art, drainpipes turn into gargoyles, rooftops are iced with intricate ironwork and sculptured stonemasons wield their tools in the rafters. Below, the grounds are divided into period gardens, dotted with bits of old Dutch sculpture and architectural fragments that didn't end up incorporated in the building itself.

After much discussion and two competitions, PJH Cuypers (of Centraal Station fame) was chosen to provide the nation with a national art gallery. For a building that was intended to be quintessentially Dutch, the jurors and the city were appalled at the result. By chance Cuypers had been allowed to modify his original plan, scrapping the Dutch Renaissance and adding Gothic windows, rib vaults and fantastic decoration. To the Dutch, Gothic meant medieval Catholicism. As it happened the architect, the project co-ordinator, the government adviser and the master decorator were all Roman Catholics. Catholicism was still a very sensitive subject in Holland, a predominantly Protestant nation. Protestant jurors failed to anticipate a Catholic conspiracy until the final touches were being made to the neo-Gothic outcome. King William V, after whom the building was to be named, refused to set foot in the 'monastery'. Critics bemoaned that 'for two million guilders we have obtained the most dreadful building imaginable'. Cuypers was obviously little moved. He had a tiled tableau made for his own house depicting an architect, a craftsman and their critic with the inscription 'What does it matter anyway?'.

While the critics sounded off about the building's monstrous appearance, it seems that they weren't too happy with its functioning either. The Gallery of Honour, designed for Rembrandt's *Night Watch*, was thought to be badly lit. Another room was built, but the light found to be no better and the painting returned to its original destination. Meanwhile private donations to the gallery increased and it was not long before it was being extended. The Drucker wing was added in 1913 to house the nineteenth-century collection and enlarged again in 1919. Building work at the Rijksmuseum continues today and optimists predict that the new-look Rijksmuseum will be fully operational by 1995.

Fifteenth to Seventeenth-century Painting The seventeenth-century Dutch paintings, by far the most important collection in the Rijksmuseum, are preceded by a small collection of earlier works. While these are themselves a pale imitation of early Renaissance works in Italy and Flanders, they display the attention to minute detail and use of rich colour that became a hallmark of Dutch art. It is a good idea to start here, if only to join the general flow of people and to get your eye ready for the great works to come.

Dutch seventeenth-century art is unique, varied and captivating.

While the megastars of mainstream Europe were providing Baroque blockbusters for popes and princes the Dutch were looking for more homely decoration: portraits of the family, brightly coloured flower paintings, local landscapes, domestic interiors and bawdy scenes of everyday life. Painters reproduced everyday life with a unique and unprecedented intimacy, providing us with a complete pictorial record of their culture and, in particular, the role of women within it. Such typical scenes are commonly known as 'genre'.

While the diversity of subject matter is entertaining it also says much about art of the seventeenth century. Dutch artists were specialists who chose one type of painting and stuck to it. The Northern Netherlands produced few great masters who had either the will or ability to transcend their narrow field. Among them, Rembrandt crossed all the boundaries, painting magnificent portraits, dramatic history paintings and intimate genre scenes. Frans Hals and Vermeer broke away from the rules within their fields of portraiture and genre respectively, adding their own interpretation to an already well founded theme. Unlike most art galleries the art here was mostly painted as domestic decoration. There were no cardinal or princely patrons wanting monumental tributes for their cathedrals, churches and palaces. Artists worked for everyone and it was mainly the middle classes who kept them in business. Even a large group portrait like the *Night Watch* was painted as a group commission. However knowledgeable you are about art Dutch painting is easily comprehensible and highly entertaining.

Madonnas, Maidens and Martyrs Make the most of the religious paintings in the first few rooms because the religious art soon dries up. Someone else was obviously impressed by the *Madonna Surrounded by Four Saints* when they named the unknown artist 'The Master of the Virgin among Virgins'. The heavy architectural background does little to accommodate the paper-thin women who sit centre stage, contemplating the skinny baby who wriggles in his mother's arms. The 'Dutch' Madonna wears a fur-lined cape to keep out the cold. The saints, Catherine, Barbara, Ursula and Cecilia all have contemporary hairstyles and headdresses and shimmer in vivid silks. Next door a rather complacent St Lucy has a dagger thrust into her throat in *The Martyrdom of St Lucy* by the Master of the Fildor Deposition. St Lucy's big mistake was giving away her riches in gratitude for the miraculous healing of her mother. Her fiancé had her tied to a team of oxen and sent to a brothel, but she could not be moved. She was put through a number of tortures before finally giving in. The picture includes a series of episodes from her life dotted across the landscape, broken up by rocky crags like a strip cartoon. In contrast, Jan van Scorel's plump *Mary Magdalena* (Room 205) represents one of the few local artists to aspire to the High Renaissance. Her round tanned face, full body and sideways glance are a far cry from the skinny, pale-faced Madonnas and saints in previous rooms. Even the landscape with its rocky crags and shady tree have an Italian feel. Dutch artists travelled Europe, saw the great Italian Renaissance works and even had Karel van Mander's handbook on painting based on Italian principle, but they generally chose to absorb and use rather than imitate the great masters.

Flower Painting   There are usually a cluster of enthusiasts in Room 206, testing their botanical knowledge and bemoaning the fact that there aren't very many flower paintings in the Rijksmuseum. The painters of these exquisite little flower arrangements, set against dark backgrounds, were among the highest paid artists in the seventeenth century. Painting was seldom done from the bloom itself – instead the artists painstakingly copied from drawing books, which explains the bizarre cocktail of plants all flowering together in the large *Flower Piece* by Jan Breugal I. Each plant is intricately painted and evenly lit, again indicating that this display was not painted from life. A closer look will reveal a host of creepy crawlies moving in the foliage. Flower painting, as in all still life painting, had its own iconographical attributes, namely shells and insects. The former were included because they ranked with flowers among prized possessions. The function of insects is much debated; butterflies like flowers display human vanity and luxury. Other insects, such as caterpillars which eat flowers and spiders which are predators, bring to mind the eventual corruption of all living things, including ourselves. The iconography is better defined in other forms of still life where certain objects have specific meanings.

Portraiture: The Boy in Girl's Clothing, the Regentess and the Bride   The only art-form that never goes out of fashion is portraiture. By 1600 Dutch artists were churning out portraits in their thousands. Children – dead and alive – were copiously copied for the family album and, confusingly for future generations, little boys always wore girls' clothing. Jacob Willemsz Delff's *Portrait of a Little Boy* (Room 206) is no exception; dressed in a long black dress, his pink cheeks burn against a frilly white collar. As the devil reputedly goes for little boys, the Dutch thought it was best to pretend they were girls so all boys under the age of six or seven were dressed in female attire. Group portraits were equally popular and usually destined for a dining room wall. A striking example is *Three Regentesses and the House Mistress of the Asylum* by Werner van den Valckert (Room 207), in which the shiny nosed, well dressed ladies count their money while a dog licks the sores of one of their charges behind. On the opposite wall, Frans Hals' *Marriage Portrait* *of Isaac Massa and Beatrix van der Laen* is a welcome break from the formal rows of pompous faces elsewhere in the room. Hals places the couple outside, the bride leaning on her husband, who lounges against a tree trunk, and her wedding ring (on her forefinger) coming between them for all to see. Only Hals could capture their familiarity so successfully. If you follow the crowds to Room 211, you will come across the most intimate form of portraiture, Rembrandt's *Self-Portrait*. At 23 he was no stunner yet mysteriously attractive. Who else would paint themselves in semi-shade with unkempt hair? Though self-portraits were rare, Rembrandt painted many as an exercise in skill.

Images of Women While the Rijksmuseum has a number of works by women, unfortunately few merit the hanging space. Tucked away in Room 213, *The Serenade*, a somewhat kitsch painting by Judith Leyster does little justice to this important artist but shows close resemblance both in brushwork and attitude to her mentor Frans Hals.

JUDITH LEYSTER (1609–1660)

Judith Leyster hit the headlines in 1893 when embarrassed curators at the Louvre, Paris, mistakenly bought one of her paintings believing it to be the work of her tutor, Frans Hals. Up to this point she had received little publicity as an artist. However her precocious talent had earned her a mention in a book on her home town of Haarlem, by Samuel Ampzing in 1628, and a further mention in a book by Theodore Shrevel, in 1648, who called her 'a leading star in art' – an obvious pun on her surname which means lodestar in Dutch.

She was brought up in Haarlem where her father worked as a brewer. It is most unusual to find a woman artist who was not the daughter of another painter. This did not prevent her from mixing with Haarlem's great painters, in particular, Frans Hals. By 1633 she was a member of the Haarlem Guild of Painters and a couple of years later three male pupils were attending her studio. That same year she successfully sued Hals for enticing one of them away to join his own studio. Her style shows the influence of painters working in both Haarlem and Utrecht, where she lived for a year. The Haarlem painters were renowned for their small landscapes and genre scenes. Utrecht had a large Catholic population and painters were strongly influenced by the dramatically lit work of the Italian artist, Caravaggio. Their strong use of light and shade, known as *chiaroscuro*, earned them the title 'Caravaggisti'.

Judith Leyster's work declined in quantity and quality after her marriage to fellow artist Jan Molenaar in 1636, despite their move to the cultural centre of Amsterdam. Her husband's work also declined, suggesting that they were both perhaps suffering the stresses of raising three children, as well as enjoying married life in the big city. Both artists had shared a studio as students of Hals and for a while their styles were similar, not surprising given that they were using the same models, props and paints. Although Judith painted portraits, still lives and flower paintings, she was primarily a genre painter. It was here that she was able to use her gender to our advantage. Throughout the sixteenth and seventeenth centuries painters had enjoyed showing men seducing women, demanding sex, paying for sex or imposing themselves on women who clearly hadn't invited them. Judith Leyster was one of the first artists to represent less submissive women, often going about their daily household chores. Men tend to appear ignored while the women carry on with what they are doing. Leyster was one of the first to convey a respect for women, their work and their social situation, a theme which continued in the second half of the seventeenth century under artists like Metsu and Vermeer.

Scenes of everyday life naturally included women, especially scenes in the home. The interpretation of women by different artists varied considerably. When you have made your way through rooms of brothel scenes, dancing peasants and windswept landscapes, take a break in Room 219 to contemplate Jan Steen's *Morning Toilet*. Steen was a popular humorist and the laughs were usually at the expense of women. He moralised more than most Dutch genre painters, alluding to old proverbs, aphorisms, emblems, literature and the theatre. This seemingly innocent little picture, bearing a moral and erotic message, is alive with them. The skull, lute and music book on the floor are conventional symbols of vanity while the erotic content is less blatant but just as strong. An open jewel box refers to the saying 'Neither does one buy pearls in the dark, nor does one look for love at night'. All these symbols would have been enough for the audience to understand that the girl is a prostitute, shown putting on her stocking or *kous* in Dutch. The stocking is another reference to the sexual content of the picture, kous being used as slang for 'vagina'. Meanwhile her dog, itself a symbol of fidelity, lies fast asleep on the bed. The rather quaint title was given to the picture in the nineteenth century to obscure its true meaning.

Room 221 is usually packed, but it is worth waiting for a gap for Vermeer's works were painted to be seen from a distance. If there is one painting you should really see in the Rijksmuseum it is Vermeer's *Milkmaid*. This woman, a maid, is taken seriously by the artist. Hard at work with her sleeves rolled up she pauses, not to rest her feet on the foot warmer or to stare out of the window, but to pour the milk. A subtle light reflects off the white walls, catching the rich crust on the bread, and is absorbed by her shabby gold bodice and thick blue skirt. Vermeer's respect for his subject and understanding of her femininity is expressed through a very simple act – pouring the milk. He captures her character, her thoughtfulness, her purpose and her gracefulness. Her stance, expression, movement and serenity is exquisitely female.

Rembrandt's Night Watch At the far end of the **Gallery of Honour** is the museum's most famous painting, Rembrandt's *Night*

Watch. Few paintings have endured as much. Rembrandt's revolutionary group portrait of *The Company of Captain Frans Cocq and Lieutenant Willem van Ruytenburch* was painted in 1642. In the eighteenth century the edges were hacked off to accommodate it in a new hanging space; in the nineteenth century the Rijksmuseum was designed around it and it acquired the misnomer *Night Watch* when curators mistook grime for night. A lunatic attacked it with a knife in 1911, it spent the 1940s in a bunker and suffered an acid attack in 1975.

It is not surprising that it has commanded such attention. When the militia men of Kloveniersdoelen commissioned the portrait to hang in their banqueting hall, alongside other portraits of the Civic Guard, they could not have envisaged what Rembrandt would make of it. The artist had had enough of the traditional pompous, posed portraits of merry gentlemen so he turned on the action. The handsome Captain in frilly collar and bold red sash instructs the rather camp lieutenant to command his men to march. The couple are highlighted by a glint of light from the right which continues, not to highlight the other members of the Guard, as one might expect, but to the rather plump little redhead, dressed in gold with a dead chicken strung around her waist. The prominent claws allude to the militia's coat of arms. Around her the neatly bearded, spruce young militiamen prepare their weapons. A random shot is fired, a fearful dog cowers under a rolling drum and a little boy runs off in excitement.

A shield behind lists the eighteen militiamen who paid to be included in the painting. Their prominence in the picture is directly related to the sum that each forked out which averaged out at f100 each. Two figures were lost when the picture was trimmed but the rest are clearly incorporated in the composition. Only the drummer was portrayed for free, having been hired by the group. Rembrandt included another fifteen characters as extras, most of whom remain anonymous, obscured by hats, cloaks and bayonets.

Sculpture and Applied Art This vast collection of sculpture, ceramics, glass, china, furniture, costume, tapestry, jewellery and silver is unimaginatively spread over three floors in the west wing and labelled almost entirely in Dutch. The ground plan will help if you are looking for something in particular; for a taste of what there is start on the top floor and work your way down.

The medieval collection offers an entertaining mix, ranging from elegant Limoges enamels to heavy Dutch polychrome virgins with tight little breasts and nipped-in waists. Don't miss the chinless *St Ursula* in Room 246. The matronly saint, with pursed lips and rosy cheeks embraces a group band of portly faced maidens. For more serious stuff take on the enormous collection of Delftware

(Rooms 255-7), the blue and white ceramics to which Delft gave its name in the seventeenth century. Trace the history of its success and if you emerge pop downstairs for a look at the two eighteenth-century dolls' houses. These large houses were in fact not so much toys as collectors' items and would have been decorated and furnished by the lady of the house. Wade your way through sterile period rooms, enjoy the opulent furniture, tapestries and trinkets and drop in on one of the best Meissen collections in the world, in Rooms 170-1. If you have any energy left it would be a shame to miss some stunning pieces of Parisian Art Nouveau jewellery in the basement (Room 35).

Dutch History Collection   If you are interested in sailors and men in uniform, take a look at the Dutch history section on the ground floor which celebrates Dutch achievements from the Middle Ages to the Second World War. Ironically, the labelling in English is more informative than in any other area of the museum, but the exhibits are somewhat tedious. Paintings of ships, sailors, conquests and the colonies are interspersed with models of ships, canons, firearms, medals and memorabilia.

For a concise history of the geographical, political and religious background to the Netherlands it is worth popping into Room 101 to see the excellent explanatory wall posters. Enjoy the dramatic painting of the first major naval victory by the Dutch fleet by Hendrik Cornelisz Vroom, *The explosion of the Spanish flagship during the Battle of Gibraltar 27 April 1607*. Mutilated Spaniards are hurled into the sky in a shower of legs, arms and heads as their blessed Virgin topples into the sea.

Other Collections   The museum runs regular exhibitions of prints, drawings and watercolours in the **Rijkspretenkabinet** which is near the café and much more fun. With over a million works on paper to choose from exhibitions are well worth seeing.

The Asiatic collection, European paintings and eighteenth- and nineteenth-century Dutch paintings will not be on show until 1995 while they revamp the Drucker Wing. However, works from the collections are occasionally shown in other parts of the museum. Ask at the information desk for details.

The lavish **Asiatic collection** is the result of a 300-year-old treasure hunt by Dutch fleets: Japanese textiles, Javanese sculpture, devotional works from China and Japan and lots more. The **foreign paintings** collection is small and often overlooked but includes works by Rubens, Van Dyck and Veronese. The **Dutch eighteenth and nineteenth-century collection** is not as extensive or appealing as the seventeenth, but is a useful link if you intend to visit the Van Gogh museum at some time. There are works by Cornelis Troost,

Jan Ekels, Josef Israels and the well-known Amsterdam artist, G.H. Breitner, whose impressionistic views of Amsterdam are reproduced on café walls all over the city.

Museumplein

Museumplein comes into its own for mass demonstrations and on Queen's Day, when it turns into a fairground. For the rest of the year young men practise their basketball, motorists scream down the runway in the middle and tourists trek across it from one museum to the next. City cleaners are perpetually employed, clearing up litter around the children's play area and souvenir tents or scrubbing graffiti off benches and sculpture. Flanked by the Rijksmuseum and the Concertegebouw at either end and Coster Diamonds, the Van Gogh Museum and the Stedelijk down one side, there is little chance of avoiding it. Oddly, none of the galleries opens onto the square which makes the vast open space in the centre somewhat redundant.

Various sculptural works break up the patches of worn turf. Some have official approval, and were probably commissioned by the City Council, but other pieces have found themselves a permanent place on the square without official permission: Miletic's tall white *Peace Rocket* commemorates the anti-cruise demo here in 1981 and the angry forest of clenched fists across the street from the Van Gogh Museum is a more recent anonymous protest against something, but the staff at the Van Gogh have no notion of what. Locals will tell you it is against the clogging up of the street and square during the Van Gogh Exhibition in 1990.

If looking for somewhere to sit, your best bet is the Stedelijk sculpture garden at the Concertegebouw end, where you may find a patch of grass or a bench and probably a harmless snoozing drunk to keep you company. A five-minute walk would take you to the more salubrious Vondelpark (see p. 168).

Women of Ravensbruck Memorial

Half way across the square, behind the Van Gogh museum, teams of schoolchildren regularly polish the vertical steel slabs that make up the *Vrouwen van Ravensbruck* memorial, placed here in 1975 to commemorate the 92,000 women who died in concentration camps during the Second World War. The text translates 'For those women who until the bitter end refused to accept fascism.' The sculpture was built with an integral sound box which let out a monotonous thud day and night to alert people to its existence. Neither this nor the flickering light around it has been in operation for some time.

2–4 Paulus Potterstraat, tel. 676 22 22. Open Daily 9 a.m.–5 p.m. for guided tours. Admission free. Tram 2, 3, 5, 12, 16 to Museumplein.

Middle-aged gents and smart ladies in uniform suits introduce you to the diamond business. Dirty diamond polishers work behind glass, on show, like monkeys at the zoo, while you are quickly ushered into rooms of gleaming diamonds, gleaming teeth and a mouthful of hard sell. A large number of people seem to feel obliged to flash credit cards and crisp notes, but if you are not there to buy no one really cares.

The message is that diamonds are forever, wherever. As long as they have 57 facets and no colour they are the best you can get. Coster pride themselves on being the polishers of the famous 'Koh-i-Noor', the huge Indian diamond that ended up in the crown of the English Queen Mother. The British apparently acquired the diamond in 1849, but didn't like the finish so Queen Victoria employed the Amsterdam diamond polisher, Voorsanger, to improve it. A tacky replica of the crown and the diamond are displayed in the foyer.

If you seriously want to buy diamonds shop around. Prices and quality vary considerably, a visit to a polishing factory will at least show you what to look for. That said, prices in Amsterdam will be considerably less than other major European cities. For more information on the diamond industry in Amsterdam, see p. 195.

Rijksmuseum Vincent Van Gogh

Paulus Potterstraat 7, tel. 570 52 00. Open Tues–Sat 10 a.m.–5 p.m., Sun & public holidays 1 p.m.–5 p.m. Closed Mon and New Year's Day. Push chairs provided. Admission f10 adults; f5 under 17s; and f5 for OAPs. Tram 2, 3, 5, 12, 16 to Museumplein.

Visiting the Van Gogh Museum can be an emotional experience, in spite of its clinical modernist architecture. Rows of paintings set chronologically on plain walls trace the life of an extraordinary artist. The workings of his head, heart and soul are exposed, making the experience intellectually, emotionally and spiritually exhausting. The lack of seats doesn't help but don't be put off – it is the greatest collection of works by one artist you are ever likely to see.

The museum, opened in 1973, was built as a permanent home for the collection of paintings, drawings, graphic art by Vincent Van Gogh, plus his archive and works by his contemporaries previously owned by Vincent's brother, Theo. Over 200 paintings and 500 drawings are displayed on rotation, more or less chronologically. A large number of the less impressive works have ended up in a show case – the study area – on the second floor, next door to a small exhibition on drawings. The building was designed by the Dutch architect, Gerrit Rietveld, who died before the project was realised and so never saw the sterile pile of concrete, brick and glass he left behind. Tickets are sold through a window on the partially sheltered entrance platform, queues are often long and the wait can be wet and cold. Once in, you are obliged to dump coats and bags in the cloakroom (another queue) before you are released into the inner hallway which stretches to the top of the building. A staircase links the galleries around it.

Plan to spend at least two hours – preferably much longer – allowing yourself a break in the restaurant or the excellent museum shop. Better still, take a couple of hours out and picnic in Vondelpark before coming back for a second go. Frequent exhibitions are held at the museum; it is not advisable to combine both, so head for one or the other. A guided tour on headphones is available, but listening to visitors' comments along the way can be just as intriguing.

The ground floor starts with a taste of the pictures Van Gogh grew up with. A very sentimental *Consoling Christ* by Anj Scheffer seems totally out of place until you learn that Van Gogh had a copy of it on his wall for many years when he was debating whether or not to go into the church. A well-fed *Peasant Family at Table*, idealised by the Hague artist, Josef Israels, offers a glimpse of what his Dutch contemporaries were up to. Moving on, you will find yourself in a room full of French Impressionist works. These are the painters who influenced Van Gogh when he joined Theo, his art dealer brother in Paris. Light and colour are freed from form in Monet's *Tulip Field* where a clash of colour rips across the canvas. Notice how light is atomised in the *pointeliste* style of Van Gogh's friend, Emile Bernard, in *Two Breton Women in a Meadow* and the mood and spirit created by colour alone in Gauguin's *Women by the Riverside, Tahiti*.

If you head upstairs the first thing you come to is a group of grimy peasants whom Van Gogh encountered while staying with his parents in Neunen in 1883–85. Prior to this Van Gogh's life had been a struggle, largely due to the fact that he couldn't make up his mind what to do; he flitted between England, France and the Netherlands, tried his hand as a teacher, preacher and art dealer, attended art school, shacked up with a pregnant prostitute (Sian) and ended up back home painting peasants. He was determined to depict them in a true light but they were not happy when they saw themselves as themselves with deeply worn faces, partially lit by poor light, with years of labour, poverty and cold damp weather behind them.

Van Gogh's life and painting brightened up considerably once he got to Paris in 1886 and met the Impressionists. In a letter to their mother, Theo says of his brother, 'You wouldn't recognise Vincent, he has changed so much ... He is making tremendous strides with his work, and the proof of it is he is beginning to achieve success.' This is the man portrayed in *Self-Portrait as a Painter* (1888). Here Van Gogh has gained the self-confidence to paint himself as a painter, armed with a handful of paintbrushes and a palette laden with vivid orange, reds, blues and greens. He exudes colour. Red lips and eyes enhance the thick red beard and cropped hair. He has started to work in *pointeliste* style, building up quick dabs of contrasting paint showing that it is not necessary to use real colours to paint realistically. While he enjoyed the company of artists and copiously studied many of the works being sold through the family business, he seldom went to galleries. Instead he leafed through the reviews and articles in art magazines to keep in touch with the European art scene. He also built up a collection of Japanese *ukiyo-e* prints which he copied in the *Japonaiserie* of 1887, as a prelude to developing his own oriental style.

Vincent left Paris for Arles in 1888 to get out of the city. By now he was receiving regular financial handouts from his brother Theo, hoping one day to pay him back through the sale of his art. He was in constant contact by letter with his brother: he wrote of his bedroom, 'The floor is of red tiles, the wood of the bed and the chairs are the yellow of fresh butter, the sheets and pillows very light greenish-citroen. The coverlet scarlet. The window green. The toilet table orange, the basin blue. The doors lilac ... Portraits on the walls, and a mirror and a towel.' The palette remains the same in his visual interpretation, *The Bedroom, Arles*. It was here that Van Gogh was joined by Gauguin. Their friendship ended in a tempestuous argument in which Van Gogh cut off part of his ear to prove a point. Gauguin left in disgust.

Eyes light up when *Sunflowers* comes into view. It was 1987 when a similar picture sold at Christies for £24,750,000, which precipitated a year of stupendous prices being paid for Van Gogh flower pieces, culminating in a record £27,450,000 for *Irises* a few months later. *Sunflowers* is far more than a traditional Dutch flower painting. The dying flowers and drooping heads bring to mind the inevitable transition from life to death, a theme with which Van Gogh experimented until his own untimely death. *The Sower* is clearly a celebration of life. The huge round yellow sun dominates the picture, forming a halo over the sower, the giver of live. Way across the room, *The Reaper* is equally positive but, this time, on the subject of death. Fields of sun-ripened corn flow towards the destruction of the reaper's blade. The reaper, a jolly peasant, cuts with a flourish.

There is something hypnotic about *Branches of an Almond Tree in Blossom*, painted after Van Gogh voluntarily admitted himself to the asylum in St Remy. It makes little difference how you look at it; from any angle your eye is led through the branches into the eggshell-blue sky beyond in search of a non-existent horizon. *Roots and Tree Trunks* round the corner has the opposite effect, allowing no way in. The more you try, the more you are shunned by a tangle of roots and branches. Finally the deeply sinister *Crows in a Wheatfield* marks the sombre climax of the inevitable rollercoaster of the artist's life. Shortly after completing the picture Van Gogh shot himself and died two days later, aged 38, with Theo at his bedside.

Stedelijk Museum

Paulus Potterstraat 13, tel. 573 2911. Open Tues–Sat 11 a.m.–5 p.m., Sun 1 p.m.–5 p.m. Closed Mon. Admission f7.50, 7–17s and OAPs F3.75, under 7s free. Tram 2, 3, 5, 12 to Van Baerlestraat.

The wonderful thing about the Stedelijk is that you never know what to expect. The Museum is Amsterdam's foremost venue for contemporary art exhibitions which are seldom conventional, usually controversial and never dull. During the summer months you can expect to find a good selection of modern art 'classics' selected from the permanent collection. The museum also offers an extensive range of lectures, concerts, guided tours, films and courses. Ring or ask at the reception desk for details. In the summer the museum produces a paper (partly in English) with a programme of events, available at the information desk on the ground floor and the extensive bookshop on the second floor.

The red brick neo-Gothic building with a fussy skyline of gables and pinnacles says little of the museum's avant-garde image. The glass addition behind, reminiscent of a school gym, was a 1950s attempt to entice people inside for more. It will shortly be displaced by a massive extension intended to house the permanent collection of modern art, sculpture, prints, drawings, photos, video, applied art, industrial design and posters due to open in 1997.

The Beginnings The rich old lady responsible for the Stedelijk was the eccentric dowager, Sophia Augusta de Bruyn. During her lifetime she amassed a huge collection of antiques, coins, jewellery, watches, trinkets and curios, apparently at the expense of her wardrobe. On her death she gave her collection to the City of Amsterdam which then had the task of finding somewhere to put it. At the same time, the Society for the Information of a Public Collection of Contemporary Art (popularly known as the 'Society with long name') was growing out of its space at the Rijksmuseum.

Eventually, the Society and the City combined forces and built a museum to house the lot. The Suasso Museum, as it was originally called, started out as a showroom for contemporary Dutch and French art, a dowager's hoard and a few period rooms. In the 1970s, the last of de Bruyn's collection went to be placed elsewhere and the museum was devoted exclusively to showing modern art.

Exhibitions From the start, the Stedelijk held exhibitions of modern art. The poet and art critic Guillaume Apollinaire remarked that Amsterdam was the only place where modern art was shown in a museum – he was referring to the showing of works by Braque, Picasso and Cezanne in 1911–12 at the Stedelijk, whose progressive attitude continues. In 1949, under the imaginative directorship of Willem Sandberg, the Stedelijk put on an exhibition of the COBRA group amid violent protests from the public and the press. COBRA was a group of artists from Copenhagen, Brussels and Amsterdam whose 'childlike' unpremeditated paintings spoke out against the apathy and convention of post-war art. They disbanded after only three years in 1951, but the museum has collected works by COBRA artists ever since, especially by Dutch members Karel Appel, Constant and Corneille. Karel Appel's *The Appelbar*, (a small room decorated with vibrant birds, fish and children, which was once the museum café) is one of the few permanent fixtures in the museum today.

Frequently exhibition design at the museum has been as innovative as the show itself. In 1954, the public could view the interior design exhibition *Wonen & Wonen* ('*Living and Living*') from a wooden platform erected outside the building, from which they could see everything through the windows. Amsterdammers have grown accustomed to the Stedelijk's surprises. A recent exhibition of provocative (some say pornographic) works by Jeff Koons caused lots of publicity but little emotion; crowds poured in to see kitsch ceramics, sculptures and photos of Koons, the ex-stockbroker, hard at it with his porn queen/politician wife, Ilona Staller. Exhibitions continue to shock, educate and entertain. As well as the main exhibitions, there are always a number of smaller displays around the museum, set up by its different departments. Photographic displays – usually in a small gallery half way up the marble staircase – are bound to leave you with a memorable image to take home, whether it be a posing superstar by Annie Leibovitz or a greased penis by Robert Mapplethorpe.

Permanent Collections Works from the permanent collections are used in exhibitions, brought out to fill empty walls in between shows and shown *en masse* during the summer. When the museum first opened the 'Society with a long name' brought with them a collection of nineteenth-century French art, including works by Camille Corot, Gustave Courbet and Charles Daubigny, with a number of works by Dutch artists from the Hague School (Anton Mauve, Josef Israels) and the Amsterdam Impressionists, such as Isaac Israels, Willem Witsen and G.H. Breitner. Breitner's atmospheric views of industrial Amsterdam are paced by drayhorses and servant girls in white aprons, heads down against the Dutch climate; he is known to have worked from his own photographs. The Society's conservative attitude – they turned down a portrait from Jan Toorop as a gift in 1909 – led to a major rift between them and the director C.W. Baard. As a result, he was given his own exhibition space and acquired many important loans from private collections. In time many of these ended up as gifts or acquisitions and the collection was enriched with works by Manet, Toulouse Lautrec, Degas, Chagall, Picasso and Van Gogh. The museum managed to hang on to a few Van Goghs, including *La Bercleuse*, a portrait of Madame Roulin, a well-endowed postman's wife dressed in deep emerald green with a mound of orange hair set against a floral green and pink background.

The high point of the collection are numerous works by the Russian artist, Kazimir Malevich, and by the Dutch De Stijl artists Piat Mondrian, Bart van de Leck, Theo van Doesburg, and the furniture designer and architect Gerrit Rietveld. Together they offer a comprehensive insight into the genesis of abstract art. It is possible to follow Malevich from his impressionist works, through a cubist period into his experiments with the abstract. *De Stijl* was not an 'ism' or homogenous group, but more a design school like the Bauhaus, organised and promoted by Theo van Doesburg who published the first copy of the magazine *De Stijl* in 1917. The basic principle behind De Stijl was to reduce art to a minimum, using primary colours of red, yellow and blue, non-colours of black, white and grey and straight lines and right angles. Untempered by emotion or individualism, they hoped their work could be accessible to everyone through an equilibrium of both form and colour.

Expect to find Dutch art well represented, whether it be in the pure lines of De Stijl or the robust realist pictures by Charley Toorop (one of the few women artists to find hanging space here). The collection as a whole offers an excellent overview of art since 1850. Highlights at the summer show might include a large brightly coloured paper cut-out, *The Parakeet and the Mermaid* by Henri Matisse, Anselm Kieffer's huge lead plaque with dead grasses wilting behind glass, movingly remembering *The Women of the Revolution* and an extended neon signature by Bruce Nauman, entitled *My Name as Though it were Written on the Surface of the Moon.*

CHARLEY TOOROP (1891–1955)

The only daughter of the symbolist painter Jan Toorop, Annie Toorop – known as Charley – was destined to be a violinist or a singer, but took up painting instead. While taking lessons from her father she met Mondrian and Jan Sluijters and was a frequent visitor to the Kunstkring exhibitions at the Stedelijk, where she saw works by Cezanne, Picasso, Braque and Kandinsky, among others. She admired Van Gogh's 'deep, grim love of reality' through which she developed her own expressive realism. She frequently entertained friends at her house, designed by Rietveld, and was fascinated by people. She painted with expressive realism, often showing social overtones; prostitutes, peasants and lunatics were depicted in their raw and sombre state. Like Van Gogh, she recorded the worn faces of the miners' wives in Borinage in Belgium. She also did numerous portraits of her family and friends and herself, accurately recording the gradual ageing of her own face.

Stedelijk Sculpture Garden

A somewhat dishevelled area behind the museum makes a small and unimpressive sculpture garden. Children clamber on the sculptures, drunks rest beneath them and a few people pace in between. You can't miss the rusting sheets of metal entitled *Sight Point* by Richard Serra, which would be impressive if it was displayed elsewhere. The garden seems set for demolition once the Stedelijk's new extension gets under way.

Concertegebouw

Concertgebouwplein 2–6, tel. 671 8345. Box office open Mon–Sat 10 a.m.–5 p.m. Lunchtime concerts, Wed 12.30 p.m. (get there at noon). Tram 2, 3, 5, 12 to Van Baerlestraat.

The august neo-classical building that dominates the southern end of Museumplein is known to music lovers throughout the Netherlands for its divine acoustics and excellent resident orchestra, the Royal Concertgebouw Orchestra. Many young musicians have made their debut performances in the *Kleine Zaal* (Small Hall) and internationally renowned orchestras and ensembles have commanded full audiences in the *Grote Zaal* (Great Hall). Drop in for a lunchtime concert and glimpse of the interior, or make an evening of it.

The Concertgebouw was founded in 1888 by Willem Kes who encouraged a group of residents to put up the cash for a substantial concert hall, where seating should be in rows instead of the usual tables with waiter service. They chose as their architect the versatile, cheap and popular A. van Gendt, renowned for his ability to work in any style to secure a commission. Despite having no knowledge of music he managed to produce one of the most acoustically sound concert halls in the world. He cribbed the design of the halls from the oval room at the Felix Meritis house (see p. 127), and miraculously it worked. The dull exterior is livened up with a few muses, busts of composers, a gleaming harp and the impressive extension added by Pi de Bruiyn in 1988. In 1983 the building came near to collapse when the supporting wooden piles fell victim to dry rot. Gala concerts and the odd superstar appearance raised the funds to replace the piles with concrete supports and bring the building up to date. The construction of the glass and steel casing on the east side caused a rumble until people realised the advantages of cafés and public meeting areas for which it was built. It is not only well integrated with the old building, but actually allows you to see it which is more than can be said for most extensions.

When the Concertegebouw opened they appointed a young conductor, Willem Mengelberg, to do what he could with the flagging reputation of Dutch music. He stayed with them until 1954 when he was dismissed for his Nazi sympathies. The reputation of the orchestra continued to strengthen under subsequent conductors, in particular Bernard Haitnink from 1963–1988. The present baton holder is the Italian Riccardo Chailly, their first foreign conductor.

The halls are rarely rented out for functions these days, but this was a popular choice for women's groups in the past. In 1908, 6000 women turned up for the Congress for Women's Suffrage and a further 2000 gathered here for a protest meeting, in 1936, against the Proposal of Rome – a Catholic declaration of no paid work for married women. More recently, in 1986, the hall opened its doors for the launch of the only literary book prize for women in the Netherlands, the Anna Bijns Book Prize. Named after one of Holland's best-known medieval female poets, the prize is intended to promote the 'female voice' in the Netherlands.

Pieter Cornelisz Hooftstraat

'Going down the "P.C." ' in Amsterdam is like saying you are off to Knightsbridge in London. P.C. Hooftstraat is the only street in the city where Porsches, BMWs and convertible Mercedes compete for parking spaces, Armani suits are worn by mannequins and window shoppers alike, and well groomed dogs refrain from pooping on the pavement. Beautifully dressed children spoon cream off their hot chocolate at La Tosca while their mummies compare clothes and price tags.

It is hardly comparable to New York, Paris or London; chic Dutch women tend to shop in Paris anyway. You will however find familiar names like Nicole Farhi, Armani, Katharine Hamnett and Kenzo in Jon and Vera Hartman, beautiful shoes in Stefane Kelian and beautiful people searching for clothes in Azurro. Dutch favourites like Sissy Boy come cheek to cheek with Max Mara,

Mulberry, Benetton and all the others that find their way onto European high streets. In winter the significant lack of fur coats says something of the Dutch attitude to fur. Be warned, don't wear it in Holland. If you tire of silk, suede and cashmere take a look at mountains of Delft porcelain at Focke and Maltzer or treat yourself to chocolates at Oldenbergs, if only to watch the deft folding of boxes and frilling of ribbons.

Despite being named after the famous poet, P.C. Hooft, the street is of little literary significance these days. From 1920–1966, however, there was a women's reading library here which, during the war years, was the only place in the city where readers could borrow books in English. For more poets continue down P.C. Hooftstraat to Vondelpark.

Vondelpark

Tram 1, 2, 3, 5, 6, 12.

Winding avenues of trees, clear lakes and ponds, open lawns and hidden gardens make Vondelpark one of Amsterdam's most popular escapes. Teams of children kick footballs, throw Frisbees and feed scraps to fat goats. Joggers pad around the concrete pathway, avoiding cyclists, prams and pedal cars, and sunbathers search for a quiet patch of grass. There is always lots going on; jugglers, puppeteers, musicians and posers have a captive audience by day and open air theatre, concerts and films keep the people here at night. A couple of tearooms and the splendid Vertigo Café at the Film Museum refresh rumbling stomachs and parched throats and ice cream stalls top up tired kids.

Unlike many inner-city parks Vondelpark is safe, mainly due to the enormous crowds it attracts. On a cold winter's day you may find yourself alone with a handful of joggers, but for the rest of the year the place is teaming with people. The park's only real drawback are the packs of aggressive dogs (Rottweilers, Pit Bulls and Great Danes) and the mess they leave behind. The most direct route to the park is along the narrow strip of greenery that runs from Stadhouderskade, just across the road from Leidseplein. This will take you under the Vondelbridge, a short underpass where people gather to see Amsterdam graffiti experts at work. It is also a popular spot for women's actions against sexual violence, the 'underpass' being an architectural symbol of male planning failing to take account of women's safety. (This however should not deter you from taking this route or visiting the park.) Other entrances are dotted at regular intervals around the park. You can walk the entire length in about half-an-hour, though you are more likely to be distracted by ducks, people, sculpture and the Round Blue Tea House. The latter, a piece

of functionalist architecture designed by H.J. Baanders, looks more
like something you might wear to Ascot than a café in the park.

When Vondelpark opened in 1864 the local newspaper
reported that Amsterdam had 'its own Bois de Boulogne'. It was
paid for by local residents who named it after Holland's best-known
poet and playwright Joost van den Vondel (1582–1674), famous for
the literary classic *Gijsbrecht von Amstel*. His statue, mounted on a
high pedestal, is improved by a recent facelift but hints at the
sombre genius behind lengthy plays and elaborate poems. The laurels
on his head and muses around his feet say little of his impoverished old
age when he was driven to work at the local pawnbrokers, sacked
after ten years for writing poems and died of hypothermia aged 92.

Vondelpark has had a colourful past, but none so bright as the
1970s when Amsterdam became the hippie capital of Europe –
home to over 1500 hippies who seem to have come here firstly for
the space and secondly for the mobile toilets set up in their honour.
Flares, flowers and five-inch platform shoes were all the rage,
money-making went out and love-making came in, guitars and
hubble bubbles were prized possessions and Vondelpark was the
perfect venue for life without timetables or obligations. Sleepers in
the park get moved on today, but for a glimpse of the past you only
have to be here for Queen's Day on April 30th; revellers sing along
to heavy metal, jazz bands and six-year-olds play their violins; second-hand clothing stalls vie with barbecues and face painters for a
position along the path, and rotten eggs get hurled at cardboard
cut-outs of the blessed Queen.

Netherlands Film Museum

*Vondelpark 3, tel. 589 1400. Open for ticket sales Mon–Fri 9
a.m.–11 p.m., weekends 1–11 p.m. Film screenings daily at 4 p.m.,
7 p.m. & 9.30 p.m.; matinees on Wed 2 p.m., weekends 1 p.m. (see
summer brochure for more); summer open air screenings on Sat at
11.30 p.m. are free. Exhibitions open Tues–Sun 1 p.m.–7 p.m.
Admission free. Library Tues–Sat 11 a.m.–5 p.m. Tram 1, 2, 3, 5, 6,
12 to Vondelpark.*

The pavilion nestles just inside Vondelpark beside the Vondelstraat
entrance. Built in 1888 by P.J. & W. Hamer as a resting place for
genteel promenaders, it is now a dynamic venue for film fanatics.
While away hot summer afternoons in the shade of the pavilion,
drink in hand, before settling down to a free open air showing of an
old classic. If the weather is not so good, take advantage of their
excellent programme of ancient movies showing in the sumptuous
Art Deco interior, rescued from Amsterdam's first cinema, the
Cinema Parisien, built in 1910. The Parisien was founded by an

obsessive film distributor, Jean Desmet, who built up the world's most complete archive of the early film industry (now housed in the Film Museum). It was his granddaughter who instigated the removal and relocation of the cinema's lavish interior to save it from demolition.

The museum only really took off in the late 80s under the inspired female director, Hoos Blotcamp. Frequent showings of films from the collection of 30,000 entertain people throughout the year. Silent movies are accompanied by pianists and sometimes explanation, song, dance and variety shows to recreate their original screening. Later films are shown in the pavilion's ornate dining room with Dolby sound coming from all sides. There is a small display on the history of film in the main hall and the library holds an extensive collection of magazines, posters and publicity material. You may catch one of the latest films from *Cinemien*, the feminist film distributors based in Amsterdam.

Hollandse Manege (Riding School)

Vondelstraat 140, tel. 618 0942. Open daily, usually 10 a.m.–12 p.m. Trams 1, 6 to Overtoom.

Just outside Vondelpark is one of Amsterdam's more intriguing and unexpected sights where everyone wears jodhpurs and talks horse, but visitors are welcome and the coffee is cheap. A classical arch frames the entrance and a short cobbled passageway leads to a heavy black door. There is no need to announce your arrival; just go through the door, turn left up the elegant classical staircase and you end up in the café with a balcony overlooking the grand classical interior of the Riding School. A thin layer of sawdust settles on the elegant white plasterwork, complete with classical horses' heads, swags and wreaths as bored horses plod round the arena reflected in old mirrors. It bears little resemblance to the Spanish Riding School in Vienna which reputedly influenced the design by A.L. Gendt, the architect of the Concertegebouw.

The plasterwork continues into the café which, like the arena, is nicely grand and grubby. Parents bide their time with a paper and a drink, waiting for their children to dismount and join them for an ice cream. Gilded mirrors, a marble fireplace, brass chandelier and an old clock allude to something magnificent, but there are no prancing white stallions here, just a multitude of prattling children, a friendly Jack Russell and an experience there for the taking.

VONDELSTRAAT; ORIGINS OF THE SQUATTERS' MOVEMENT

This small street, running beside the Vondelpark in one of Amsterdam's most upmarket areas, hosted one of Amsterdam's most famous squatting events, the 'battle of Amsterdam' in 1980, which marked the first of many and converted an issue into a movement. The acute housing shortage in Amsterdam in the 1960s and 70s, the commercial development of old properties in the city and the development of housing projects outside, complete with an interlinking metro system, led to anger and fear among Amsterdam residents – anger at the subsequent breakdown of a local community life and fear of the heart turning into a business and tourist centre. Many young people saw the advantages and rights of squatting as threefold, to provide housing for themselves, restore old properties destined for demolition and to protect properties from being converted into hotels and offices. In this way they hoped to maintain a residential community in their own city.

At first squatting action was local, but the movement gained momentum following the eviction of three key squats and the national day of squatting on 30 March 1980. Three days after squatters moved into No. 72 Vondelstraat police tanks moved in to evict them. Over a thousand police were involved in the ensuing riot and over fifty people injured. Squatters gained enormous publicity and proved to the city that eviction could be an expensive business and, more importantly, unsuccessful – the squatters moved back a few days later. A mass squat in over two hundred properties throughout the Netherlands was organised in protest at the cost of the coronation of Queen Beatrix on 30 March – money which would have been better spent on housing. In Amsterdam a protest march intended to disrupt the crowning ceremony in Dam Square erupted into a city riot, quelled some hours later by teargas and riot police.

The successes of the 1980s encouraged squatters all over the city. By 1982 around ten thousand people had taken up illegal residency and in many areas boosted local businesses and community life. The surprise eviction of squatters at a smart villa on Jan Luykenstraat called Lucky Luyk sparked off further riots which lasted for three days. Cars were overturned, properties wrecked, a tram burnt and once again national newspapers were splattered with images of water cannons, teargas and armed police. Failing to deter evictions, the Squatters' Movement assumed a political role, offering to work with the City Council in determining the fate of empty buildings. The most famous was Wyers, an old warehouse destined to become a Holiday Inn hotel. Squatters proposed a viable alternative, that it should be converted into a combined cultural residential complex with workspace for studios and small businesses. They were unsuccessful, but gained for themselves an ear from the City Council and clearly defined rights which are still respected today.

'DE PIJP'

The lively 'De Pijp' is the best known of the working-class areas built in the nineteenth century. Locals enjoy their reputation as 'artists and writers', but admit that the colourful nature of the area is largely due to the natural consequences of a working community. The area is tightly packed with community housing and posh apartments, schools, playgrounds, a delightful park, shops, restaurants, a red light area and a daily market in Albert Cuypstraat that draws people from around the city.

For a long time the meadows and canals to the south of Amsterdam were dotted with windmills and sawmills, producing an endless supply of timber for the developing city. Mill owners managed to stave off developers until 1889 when the area was hurriedly built up to house the working classes. Such was their speed that many of the houses collapsed, almost immediately killing a number of new residents, but building continued and the new area was dubbed 'De Pijp' (the Pipe) by the locals. The name probably refers to the long narrow streets that wind through the area, reminiscent of the long clay Gouda pipes, but it was just as likely to have been dreamt up after a few pints of Heineken. No one really knows.

If you are there in September you may be lucky enough to catch the *Kunstroute de Pijp* when local artists (there are some) display their work in cafés, shops and offices. A catalogue with route can be obtained from the VVV (Tourist Office).

Choose a sunny day for tackling this area. Spend a morning in the bustle of the **Albert Cuyp market,** stop for a strong coffee in a café full of ruddy stallholders, haggle over gaudy shirts and cheap shoes, buy a picnic and crash out in **Sarphatipark** just around the corner. Most of the area is residential, but if you want to walk head south to see the eccentric architecture of the **De Dagaraad complex**. For something more absorbing hop on a tram to the Resistance Museum and for the children try the NINT Museum. If you have started the day with the Heineken Brewery forget the haggling and go straight for the picnic.

Heineken Brewery

Stadhouderskade 78, tel. 523 9239. Open Mon–Fri for guided tours at 9.30 a.m. and 11 a.m.; extra tours at 1 p.m. and 2.30 p.m. in June–Oct. Get there half-an-hour in advance as tours are limited to 150 and are almost always sold out. Tour lasts 1 hour. Admission f2 which is donated to charity. Tram 6, 7, 10, 16, 24, 25 to Weteringplein.

For most people the real attraction of the Heineken tour is the free beer at the end, a jolly sing song and a chance to be 'one of the boys' in the first brewery built for the production of Heineken beer. The tour itself takes you through fermentation tanks and brewing halls, giving a short video description of the history of Heineken and the brewing of beer. When you have been convinced by multi-screened commercials that only beautiful people drink the beer that 'reaches the parts other beers cannot reach' you can down as much of the stuff as you wish in the reception centre upstairs. Shirts, hats and tankards are sold in their thousands to sozzled punters in the adjoining shop.

The brewery was built in 1867 on what was then the outskirts of Amsterdam. The city grew, Heineken grew and the site was no longer viable so the beer moved to breweries in Den Bosch and Zoeterwoude while the renovated brewery opened as a successful publicity stunt. Highlights of the tour include a walk past the immaculate stables to meet the famous dray horses and the impressive copper tanks in the brew house. If you feel an hour-and-a-half is a long time to walk for a free drink there are plenty of cafés and bars in the vicinity heading south.

Albert Cuyp Market

Mon–Sat 9 a.m.–5 p.m. (usually gets going properly around 10 a.m.). Tram 16, 24, 25 to Albert Cuypstraat or 4 to Frederiksplein.

This is by far the best general market in Amsterdam and the most entertaining. Stallholders shout at the passing crowd, smile at the children and sing along to Bob Marley. Housewives search for flowers and food at knock-down prices while their teenage daughters get lost in piles of bargain clothes. Locals gossip, laugh and gulp down raw herring while tourists gaze in horror. Stalls are laden with whole rounds of local cheeses, vats of gleaming Italian olives, pickled cucumbers and sun-dried chilli peppers. Fish is piled high on polystyrene trays and lobsters pant on mounds of ice. The smell of freshly baked bread mingles with basil, parsley and cut flowers. Lacy lingerie blows in the wind over rails of denim jeans and leather jackets; baseball boots, jelly shoes and leather pumps stand in pairs on upturned boxes.

The crowd intensifies during the day so the best time to be there is mid-morning when the food and the mood of the stallholders is still fresh. Pickpockets make the most of a captive crowd so watch your belongings. Late-afternoon food gets sold off at bargain prices and the salesmen have one last try at flogging their wares before fat Volvo Estates and new Mercedes vans whisk it off to the storerooms.

Sarphatipark

This small park with a narrow lake snaking through the middle rates as one of Amsterdam's most charming. Children and tramps take it in turns to use the playgrounds and dogs and ducks taunt and terrorise one another in the water. Mature trees surround the area and pretty willows bend over the lake. It is used, as was intended, by the local community. People are friendly but not intrusive, it is perfectly safe and no one will disturb you if you fall asleep in the thick grass.

In the middle is a monument to Dr Sarphati, the doctor and philanthropist after whom the park is named. Sarphati was known as the 'founder of modern Amsterdam'. He took it upon himself to see to the development of South-Eastern Amsterdam, both socially and economically, and didn't do too badly; he founded banks, a commercial college, a construction company, the first hygienic bread factory, the Amstel Hotel and an efficient waste disposal programme. A bronze bust of the man himself sits proudly under a splendid sandstone baldachino supported on granite columns and balusters.

THE NEW SOUTH

A revolutionary Housing Act in 1901 and an inspired piece of town planning by H.P. Berlage in 1917 gave Amsterdam its first piece of proper town planning since the Grachten Gordle extension plan in the seventeenth century.

The Act of 1901 authorised the Municipal Council to declare slum dwellings unfit for habitation and obliged them to work out plans for urban growth and development. As well as instigating their own social building projects, the Council also offered financial assistance to housing associations. At the same time the rising number of Social Democrats on the Council gave energy to the quest for good subsidised housing for the poor and pointed the selectors in Berlage's direction.

His elegant design for South Amsterdam aroused international interest and revolutionised town planning for the future. Wide avenues and small connecting streets reflected the canal layout of the old city, but his plan had no clearly defined boundaries, no obvious centre and provided for both the poor and the wealthy thus accounting for further expansion and the inter-relationships necessary within a working community. The plan provided detached family houses for the wealthy and large four-storey apartment blocks for the less well off. Blocks were generally set around courtyards and squares to provide room for gardens and playgrounds. A didactic Berlage believed in socially educating people through his architecture. Window sills would be high to avoid gossiping and kitchens too small to eat in, encouraging the use of the dining room. He died before his plan could be implemented, but his work was taken up by the lively architects of the Amsterdam School: P.L. Kramer, M. De Klerk and J.M. van der Mey.

There is no mistaking the style of the **Amsterdam School** or 'brick pleasure' as they referred to it. Using concrete beneath a brick surface they created tucks, folds and rolls of red brick. Decoration spread to frames, doors, stained glass, letter boxes, iron work and interiors. Unlike traditional Dutch architecture, surfaces run the length of a street with no obvious division from one house to the next; roofs and balconies get caught in the general sway of brick-work. Unusually shaped windows, carved doors and subtle patterning with different coloured brick liven monotonous walls. High chimneys and whimsical corner decorations give a vertical thrust to otherwise horizontal planes.

The School's interest in aesthetics was not confined to houses alone; bridges, lampposts and railings were decorated with simple sculpture, intricate Art Nouveau metalwork, obelisks and oriental squirls. Chunky plain sculpture pops up all over the area, on bridges, in squares and incorporated into the buildings themselves. The municipal sculptor, Hildo Krop (1884–1970) seems to have spent most of his working life carving square people with square limbs, sitting on square plinths, occasionally accompanied by equally formal and forbidding animals and accessories. Perhaps Krop's mind was on other things. It was recently revealed that he was more involved elsewhere working for the Soviet K.G.B.

If you are interested in De Klerk and Kramer's tenement housing take a look at the *De Dagaraad* complex in P.L. Takstraat and the adjoining Therese Schwartzeplein. For an abundance of De Krop and De Klerk grandeur head west to the area around Apollolaen and Olympiaplein.

De Dagaraad Public Housing: P.L. Takstraat, H. Ronnerplein and T. Schwartzeplein

Tram 4 to Lutmastraat, or short walk from Sarphatipark.

This is the best place to see the architecture of the Amsterdam School. Start at P.L. Takstraat where you will quickly understand the meaning of 'apron architecture', the popular nickname for the tucks, folds and pleats that distinguish the work of M. De Klerk and P.L. Kramer from other architects.

The project was designed for the housing association De Dagaraad (the Dawn) between 1918–1923. On either side of the street the houses are reflected. Sculptural brick walls stream from one end to the other, wrapping themselves around chimneys and stairways like vacuum packing. The horizontal is emphasised by streamlined window panes and a roof full of gently undulating waves. They end up in the swirl of the corner block before shooting off into the crescent of Burgermeester Tellegenstraat. The only traditional touch are the hoists which stand out like stick insects on the smooth wall. The use of deep red brick at ground level define the doorways against the bright orange brick of the complex.

Just around the corner in either direction you will find the complementary squares of Henriette Ronnerplein and Therese Schwartzeplein. Set around a grassy square, these barn-like houses with tall chimneys look like fat insects, probably because of the peculiar arrangement of windows which diminish in size from the ground floor up. The top floor affords two tiny windows set far apart, leaving a vast expanse of brick wall between and presumably allowing little light inside. Reptilian roof tiles fold off the roof down the sides of the building into a 'bucket' balcony which links one house with the next. On closer inspection you will find eccentric letterboxes and decorated doors.

Around Apollolaan

There is little reason to see the western section of the New South unless, of course, you wish to pay homage to the Hilton hotel where John Lennon and Yoko Ono staged their famous 'Bed in' for world peace in 1969. You may of course be staying in the area, in which case you can enjoy one of Amsterdam's most prestigious residential areas where wide streets are lined with hotels, banks and mansion blocks. Swish cars purr out of private drives and classy mansions hide behind iron gates and security systems. Residents and wealthy foreigners peruse the upmarket shops in Beethovenstraat, elegantly dressed old ladies walk little dogs on the grassy verges and off-duty businessmen entertain their escorts.

Streets are named after Gods, composers, artists and musicians, taking on an Olympic theme towards the Olympic stadium (under demolition orders) where the games were held in 1928. There is one street that breaks the rule, Gerrit van der Veenstraat – a sound reminder of the atrocities of Nazi persecution in the Second World War when the area was a Jewish ghetto. Gerrit van der Veen was one of the city's best known resistance fighters. Traces of Jewish history are still evident; an expressionist brick synagogue dominates Jacob Obrechtplein and a sculpture commemorates the shooting of 29 people at the intersection of Beethovenstraat and Apollolaan. You can find out more at the Dutch Resistance Museum which occupies another synagogue on the other side of the New South.

YOKO AND JOHN

The curvilinear concrete block of the Hilton hotel seems an unlikely choice for a week in bed with your lover. Clad only in a vast double sheet, the couple entertained a procession of the world's press and telephoned its baffled leaders with messages of world peace. The event became an icon of the age. Yoko collaborated with the conversion of the room into a 'honeymoon suite', tastefully decorated with the words from *All You Need is Love, Imagine,* and *The Ballad of John and Yoko,* which was written in bed, and equipped with Beatles memorabilia. You can rent the room at a price, but it is doubtful that Richard Nixon or Ho Chi Minh will return your calls.

Lekstraat 63, tel. 644 9797. Open Tues–Fri 10 a.m.–5 p.m.; week-ends 1 p.m.–5 p.m. Closed Mon. Admission f3.50, under 16s f1.75. Tram 4, 12, 25 to Victorieplein.

An absorbing display of photos, film clips, secret papers, false ID cards, guns, grenades and makeshift secret equipment traces the history of the Dutch Resistance movement from 1940 to 1945. It is worth buying the detailed English catalogue to guide you round the maze of temporary stands and exhibits which fill the former Jewish Synagogue.

The museum is run by former members of the Dutch Resistance – people who actively or passively, armed or unarmed, protested against the measures taken by the German occupying forces in the Second World War. About 25,000 people chose active, illegal resistance in the Netherlands. Many more supported their actions, while others preferred to collaborate with the enemy. All of them tried to continue living a normal life at the same time and the message of the museum is 'Peace Not War'.

Photos and films capture the dismay of the Dutch people at the bombing of Rotterdam in 1940 and their despair when they heard that Queen Wilhelmena and the entire Dutch government had fled to England. Their fate was in their own hands and not surprisingly the Dutch were quick to oppose the restrictions imposed by the occupying forces. Men, women and children were active in printing and distributing information, hiding persecuted individuals and in fighting the enemy. A strong Resistance network was shattered in 1942 by the uncanny intervention of the Dutch secret services in London and the British secret services, M16 and SOE, in the *Englandspiel*. One of the first agents to be sent from England was captured by the Germans and forced to continue his radio contact with Britain under supervision. After that many arms drops and agents from Britain fell straight into enemy hands. Many underground networks were exposed with over four hundred Resistance workers being arrested. Naturally the Brits were suspicious of the Dutch Resistance after this and it was some time before arms were sent over again. *Englandspiel* had been a major setback to the Resistance movement which took over a year to gain momentum again. More and more people were forced into hiding as the war intensified: Jews, students, ex-members of the armed forces, those wishing to avoid *Arbeitseinsatz* (working for the Germans) and the Resistance workers themselves. By 1944 there were about 300,000 people in hiding in the Netherlands, dependent on others for food, money and shelter. They owed their lives to the many brave Resistance workers remembered in this museum.

HEROINES AND HOUSEWIVES: WOMEN OF THE DUTCH RESISTANCE

The 'Woman with the Red Hair', Hannie Schaft, is undoubtedly the best-known woman Resistance worker commemorated in a nerve-racking film by Theun de Vries. The daughter of a Communist family, she was encouraged to join the armed Resistance with her friend Truus Oversteegen. The attractive teenage girls joined the most dangerous and almost exclusively male branches of the Resistance. The two often posed as a couple carrying out important assasinations for their comrades. Hannie was hunted by the Germans for some time before she was finally caught, tortured and shot in the dunes near Haarlem. She became a national heroine. Truus survived the war and became a housewife.

Women were well placed to help the Resistance. Their daily routine as housewives enabled them to walk freely with little chance of being searched and questioned. They used this opportunity to the full, playing a vital role in the dissemination of information. Documents could be concealed in shopping bags or more popularly in maternity corsets, arms could be transported in prams and bicycle baskets, they could pass information under the guise of gossip in the streets or flirt with inquisitive guards if things got tricky.

One of the key roles played by women was in hiding people. Thousands, like Anne Frank's family, relied on others for food, clothing, and money. Anyone in hiding was effectively a non-person, with no identity card and no ration card and women all over the country struggled to feed an extended family living in constant fear of being sprung by a neighbour. Many women worked for the L.O., the national organisation formed to assist people in hiding, to provide addresses, ration cards for distribution, money and if possible work. It was dangerous work – of the 14,000 employees of the L.O., 1100 lost their lives.

Professional women also found a place in the underground movement. Gesina van der Molen was among many women who worked on one of the 1200 clandestine papers being produced in occupied Holland. Her work involved finding adoptive families for the many Jewish children who were smuggled out through the crèche on Plantage Middenlaan (see p. 193). Artists who were banned from working were invaluable in document forgery.

When the war ended hundreds of women were dragged onto the streets by enraged mobs to cries of 'Moffen meiden'. They were hit, spat on and abused, their heads were shaved for everyone to see. These were the women who had had German lovers. Whatever their motives – spies, informers or just victims of innocent love – they were all punished for sharing an affection with the enemy. For many it was a cruel reward for the information they gleaned for the Resistance by prostituting themselves.

RAI Exhibition Centre

Europaplein, tel. 549 1212. Open for enquiries Mon–Fri 9 a.m.–5 p.m. Tram 4, 25 to Europaplein.

Several acres of light functional exhibition halls attract business customers from around the world. A mass of glazed and solid bands are topped by a plane of translucent panelling which disconcertingly changes colour on a fine day. The natural white reflects the blue of the sky if the sun is in the right place. The building went up in 1961 as part of the city's plan to attract foreign business. It was gradually enlarged between 1961 and 1981. Trade exhibitions are not always appealing, but remember this is Amsterdam and 'trade exhibitions' take on a new meaning. RAI hosted the largest ever tattoo exhibition in 1993 and the one that really caught the public's imagination was the Tenth World Congress for Sexology in 1991. Lecture halls filled for enlightening talks on *Groin Flap Phallopasty in the Female, The Perfect Penis, Love and Sexuality in Three Mozart Operas* and lots more. Meanwhile theologians discussed sex and religion, lesbian clergy and priests with AIDS. Don't dismiss the RAI on a wet afternoon – there may well be something worth seeing.

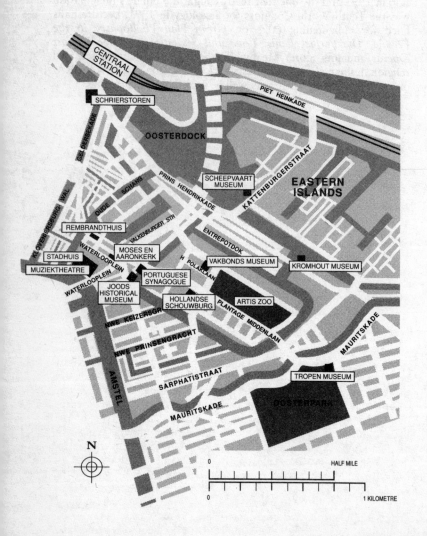

CENTRAAL STATION

SCHRIERSTOREN

PIET HEINKADE

OOSTERDOCK

GELDERSEKADE

PRINS HENDRIKKADE

SCHANS

OUDE

SCHEEPVAART MUSEUM

KATTENBURGERSTRAAT

EASTERN ISLANDS

KL OVENIERSBURG. WAL

REMBRANDTHUIS

VALKENBURGER STR

WATERLOOPLEIN

MOSES EN AARONKERK

ENTREPOTDOK

H. POLAKLAAN

VAKBONDS MUSEUM

KROMHOUT MUSEUM

STADHUIS

MUZIEKTHEATRE

PORTUGUESE SYNAGOGUE

WATERLOOPLEIN

JOODS HISTORICAL MUSEUM

HOLLANDSE SCHOUWBURG

ARTIS ZOO

PLANTAGE MIDDENLAAN

NWE KEIZERSGR

NWE PRINSENGRACHT

MAURITSKADE

AMSTEL

SARPHATISTRAAT

TROPEN MUSEUM

MAURITSKADE

OOSTERPARK

N

0   HALF MILE

0   1 KILOMETRE

AMSTERDAM EAST: THE JEWISH QUARTER AND DOCKLANDS, INCLUDING THE WESTERN ISLANDS

Eastern Amsterdam was never a particularly popular place to live. Jewish immigrants were the first to settle in the waterlogged area in spite of its liability to serious flooding. There was a spurt of activity in the seventeenth century when the city's shipbuilding industry moved into the newly reclaimed Eastern Islands. Meanwhile the canals of the Grachten Gordle were slowly encroaching eastwards over the Amstel towards the grassy recreation area known as the Plantage. At the end of the nineteenth century the Plantage was swallowed up in a major city expansion and Amsterdam has continued to mushroom eastwards ever since. The devastating effects of the war, when almost the entire Jewish Quarter was razed to the ground, left a derelict gap close to the city centre. It is only just coming back to life again since the recent opening of the Stadhuis (Town Hall) and the Musiektheater (Opera House) on Waterlooplein.

Apart from a picturesque little area around St Antonie Sluis and the Rembrandthuis, much of the Jewish Quarter is dominated by vast buildings, wide dual carriageways and deserted car parks. By day, crowds of young people sort through the gracious, groovy and dishevelled goods on sale in the Waterlooplein flea market, striking bargains with cunning stallholders and flaunting their buys from yesterday. A concentration of cafés around the market offers welcome respite to tired punters who gossip over frothy beers, stare blankly into space, wave at passing boats or peruse the theatre listings. By night the area is deserted, daunting and dead unless you happen to be chinking glasses or enjoying the show at the Opera House.

Beyond Waterlooplein traffic thunders past the great Jewish synagogues, through the wide open streets of the Plantage and away into the distance. Excited little faces peer from tram windows on their way to meet leopards, crocodiles and fat pythons at the zoo or heading for an anthropological encounter at the Tropenmuseum.

Towards the harbour, residents and office workers enjoy the calm ambience in the newly renovated warehouses along the wide canals of Amsterdam's docklands, sleepy cats lounge on beautiful houseboats and seagulls dive for scraps in the water. A main road rips along the harbour's edge, obscuring any reasonable views, while down below the magnificent replica ship 'Amsterdam' bobs outside the Maritime Museum. To the west the old dockland area of the Western Islands are among Amsterdam's most magical retreats.

The Jewish Quarter is so close to the city centre that you will probably choose to walk there. A ten-minute walk from Dam Square or five minutes from Rembrandtsplein will take you to Waterlooplein, the Musiektheater or Rembrandtshuis which are the main attractions. It is worth catching a tram to the Zoo, Botanical Gardens and Tropenmuseum since the walk isn't up to much. If you wish to explore on foot what remains of the Jewish Quarter the VVV sells a leaflet, *Jewish Amsterdam*, which follows a circular route around the main sights. Otherwise use the map in this guide. Start at Waterlooplein and visit the sights as they appear in the guide until you have seen enough. The best way to enjoy the docklands is by boat. Most of the canal boat trips take you into the harbour itself and the museum boat goes to the Maritime Museum from where you can explore. Alternatively, hop on a bus along Prins Hendrikkade for a short ride east. The Western Isles are a fifteen-minute walk from Centraal Station.

THE JEWISH QUARTER

Amsterdam never had an area designated specifically for Jews, but the marshy area east of the old centre was favoured by Jewish residents from the sixteenth century mainly because the land was cheap and uninhabited apart from a few charitable institutions which had sprung up here for the same reasons.

Once the city had finally rid itself of the Spanish in 1578 (see p. 68), it became a haven for refugees from many areas of Europe who had been forced to leave for the sake of their religious and political convictions. The Dutch were cautious of these immigrants, but seldom discriminatory compared with other migrant friendly cities. The Jewish population became so well integrated that some Hebrew and Yiddish words have become part of the Amsterdam dialect. Dutch Amsterdammers still call their city 'Mokum' taken from the Yiddish 'Mokum aleph' meaning 'the best city of all'. On parting they often wish each other 'de mazzel', meaning good luck. For a while the Jews were not allowed to own shops so they traded in the streets, spawning such lively markets that they attracted the whole city, forming an important link between Jews and Gentiles from the start. The tradition lives on in the great daily flea markets at Waterlooplein.

The area may have been intriguing and colourful to people who didn't live there. For the residents it was a labyrinth of slums and alleys squashed between the old city and a marshy area known as the 'Plantage', which became a recreation area for city dwellers in the seventeenth century. The Plantage was developed further in the eighteenth century by wealthy Amsterdammers looking for a pleasant site for their country villas (only one survives, at 72 Middenweg). By the end of the nineteenth century the whole area had been absorbed into the city's expansion plan, leaving only two patches of greenery for the Artis Zoo and the Botanical Garden. At the same time Jewish poverty was alleviated to some extent by the development of the diamond industry – one of the few businesses open to them – which enabled many Jews to leave their slums for the more salubrious areas elsewhere in the city.

The area and its people were largely destroyed by the Nazis in the Second World War. Residents were flushed from their homes and sent to concentration camps and what remained of their deserted houses was stripped to provide fuel in the hunger winter of 1944 when the area became a ghost town. While most people were counting their dead after the Liberation, the Jewish community was counting those still alive. In Amsterdam 30,000 Jewish people survived out of a pre-war Jewish community of 130,000.

Squatters were the first to move back into the area in the 1960s, followed by the city planners who took advantage of this derelict space so close to the centre. The metro rumbles beneath a steady stream of traffic and open air car parks and the new Stadhuis and Musiektheater dominate the stark open square of Waterlooplein. Jewish life is documented in the Jewish Historical Museum, remembered in memorial plaques, inscriptions carved into the pavements and commemorative statues. These and a few remaining synagogues, the odd diamond factory and the street names are the only reminders of a once thriving community.

Waterlooplein Flea Market

Mon–Sat 9 a.m.–5 p.m. Tram 9, 14 to Waterlooplein.

The windswept area of Waterlooplein is dominated by one of Amsterdam's most controversial buildings, the combined Stadhuis and Musiektheater known locally as the 'Stopera'; the nickname was coined by the campaigners who fought to 'Stop the Opera' being built. Behind the stark, bland and unimpressive building is the liveliest and largest flea market in the city. Bargain hunters and souvenir shoppers have a heyday, as tightly packed stalls fill the vast windswept square and hordes of shoppers push their way through the narrow alleys between them. Up above, a festive red banner warns newcomers to 'Beware of Pickpockets'.

A dubious assortment of elderly men haggle over gleaming watches and silver snuff-boxes, in huddles around the perimeter, and local down-and-outs try their luck with bundles of old clothes before being moved on by police. The rest of the stallholders who have worked hard for their legal pitch engage in serious hard sell throughout the day. Graffiti artists check out a stall selling paint in aerosol cans, destined for the city's monuments; children scramble onto antique rocking horses; tourists fork out for hand-made clogs, Indonesian jewellery, T-shirts, leggings, baggy trousers and leather jackets; and smokers pour over pot-related paraphernalia. Locals come here for basic essentials: underwear, soap, electrical equipment and a wheelchair for granny. The vast majority of shoppers are bargain-hungry tourists with a touch of 'spring-sale fever'. Best buys are designer hats, exotic theatrical costumes, antiques and second-hand leather.

You may find a bargain, you may be ripped off, but you will undoubtedly enjoy yourself. There is an enormous choice of watering holes to choose from depending on your mood: try Sluyswacht for a light lunch and classical music, the psychedelic Tis Fris for *enchiladas* and Bob Marley, and the Café Dantzig for creamy hot chocolate, a waterfront terrace and trendy people. Once the market has been cleared up, Waterlooplein loses its appeal. An eerie silence fills the square, the stalls turn into padlocked aluminium cases, litter flutters on the red brick and alarming shadows jump out of dark corners as tramps bed down for the night. If you are going to the Opera it is best to approach it from the front not from Waterlooplein.

205 Waterlooplein. Open occasionally for exhibitions and services.

The Jewish Quarter is full of landmarks of which the Moses and Aaron Church is perhaps the most useful. The huge wooden towers, painted to look like sandstone, soar into the sky above the busy flea market on Waterlooplein, providing a useful reference point for those wishing to explore the area. It was originally a clandestine Catholic church. Pop around the back and you will see two gable stones, featuring Moses and Aaron, which once decorated the two housefronts behind which the church was hidden. The neo-classical portico and towers were a nineteenth-century addition.

The Jewish philosopher, Baruch Spinoza, lived in a house on this site in 1632. He was expelled from Amsterdam in 1656 for his secular beliefs and ended up polishing spectacle lenses in the Hague. It was a rash move in the light of his intellectual fame. His work *Ethica*, in which he uses mathematical deduction to justify ethical beliefs, is perhaps the most intriguing study he produced.

The 'Stopera': Musiektheater and Stadhuis (Opera House and Town Hall)

Waterlooplein. City Council, tel. 552 9111; Musiektheater, tel. 625 5455. Guided tours around the Musiektheater, Wed & Sat 4 p.m. Book in advance, f10. Tram 9, 14 to Waterlooplein.

The combined Musiektheater and Stadhuis went up in 1985 amid ferocious battles in Amsterdam. For nearly a century the city had discussed the possibility of creating an Opera House before it was finally erected on the derelict but historic site of Waterlooplein. Locals were appalled at the f300 million being spent on such an elitist building in a city where housing shortages were a major problem.

The building, its decor and its function received widespread criticism. To appreciate the Opera House you really need to be inside, where panoramic views down the Amstel, lush pink carpeting and a starlit auditorium enhance the terrific performances laid on by the Netherlands Opera, the Dutch National Ballet and the many touring companies who grace the stage. From outside the stark red brick building with a distinctive semi-circular mouthful of windows is neither appealing nor exciting. The combined efforts of architects Wilhelm Holzbaur and Cees Dam were unlikely to succeed, given the hostility surrounding the building in the first place, and the Musiektheater, in particular, has had numerous problems: bad acoustics, no purpose-built rehearsal rooms, scenery lifts too small to accommodate tall props and many more.

If you are interested in the theatre and theatre production join one of the guided tours around the Musiektheater where bilingual guides take you behind the scenes to see the artists and technicians at work. If you are lucky rehearsals will be under way in the main auditorium and technicians will be playing around with the ceiling 'sculpture' by Peter Strucken; five hundred lights sunk into the ceiling can be set to twinkle like stars, chase each other like flying saucers or create interchanging patterns to suit the mood of the performance. Behind the scenes, seamstresses put the final touches to elaborate costumes, wig-makers check rows of empty heads of hair, make-up artists experiment with new colours and the rehearsal rooms are alive with flexing limbs and sweaty brows. Stages skim from one hall to the next, supported on special air bearings, scenery shoots up and down from the great tower and there are enough stage assistants hanging around to convince you that it is not magic. To see more book yourself a ticket for the evening performance.

The Musiektheater shares its site with the Town Hall, which accounts for the confusing signs to immigration and passport control when all you need is a theatre ticket. For the theatre enter through the front entrance facing the Amstel. You can't mistake it – there is a bronze violinist pushing his way through the marble floor just inside. The sculpture was installed one night by a phantom sculptor who makes a habit of adorning public places without permission. (His most recent addition to the city, a pair of bronze breasts on Ouderkerksplein, were removed on local request.) The Town Hall (Stadhuis) runs behind, along Waterlooplein, but the two are connected by a covered street running through the middle. In bad weather the route through the Stadhuis is a good shortcut across Waterlooplein and you may have time to look at the three glass columns bubbling with water; two show the water levels at the coastal towns of Vlissingen and Ijmuiden and the third, which stretches way above eye level, marks the level of the floods of Zeeland in 1953. The NAP or Normal Amsterdam Peil (water level) is marked by a brass plaque on the wall down the adjacent circular staircase. Short-term holidaymakers will have little reason to visit the Stadhuis, unless of course you decide to get married in Amsterdam, in which case you can enjoy one of the delightful registry offices where each room is decorated by a different artist.

Rembrandthuis (Rembrandt's House)

Jodenbreestraat 4–6, tel. 624, 9486 Open Mon–Sat 10 a.m.–5 p.m., Sun & public holidays 1 p.m.–5 p.m. Admission f5, 10–15s and OAPs f3.50, under 10s free. Guided tours on request. Tram 9 to Waterlooplein, Metro Nieuwmarkt.

The barely furnished house on Jodenbreestraat is used to display a virtually complete collection of Rembrandt's etchings and a few drawings. A useful introduction to the technique of etching is complemented by a full range of works by the great master, ranging from highly worked biblical scenes to quick sketches of Mr and Mrs Rembrandt. It is worth investing in the small guide (f1.50) which lists the main events and people that influenced his life and work.

The galleried hallway is used as a reception area, bookshop and postcard stall. Beyond this the 245 etchings executed by Rembrandt during his lifetime are displayed on every available wall space around the house. While etchings can become tedious they are an excellent introduction to the artist, his friends and his technique. Start in the small room off the hall where there is a comprehensive display on the etching technique, from waxed copper plate to the black-and-white print of the engraved image. Next door in the **Sydelcaemer** various religious scenes demonstrate the versatility of the medium; impressive crowd scenes fill the foreground of *Christ Presented to the People* and dramatic changes of light and shade are shown in the three different workings of *The Three Crosses*. Enjoy the more down-to-earth rendering of Rembrandt and his friends in the **Actercaemer**, also on the lower floor. There is a wonderful series of the artist pulling silly faces and a touching *Self-portrait with Saskia*. We know Rembrandt and his students used nude models in his studio. Rembrandt's direct approach, catching every lump, bump and pimple was not always popular among his contemporaries, but as the etchings in the **Tussenkamer** show, he worked hard to create real people made of flesh and blood. Upstairs there are some very beautiful landscapes where water ripples, grasses rustle, shadows fall and windmills turn in the wind. Such atmosphere is very difficult to realise in black and white but Rembrandt seems to do it with ease, even catching the different textures of soft moss against rough bark.

There are a few prints for sale at reasonable prices downstairs.

REMBRANDT'S WOMEN

Rembrandt enjoyed the support and companionship of women throughout his life; they included a devoted mother, a passionate wife and a passive lover, who saved him from the agonies of widowhood only to be spurned in favour of another devoted companion who rescued him from total financial ruin.

The son of a Leiden miller and a baker's daughter, Rembrandt van Rijn was the only member of the family of nine children who was encouraged by his parents to attend school and university. They later allowed him to drop out of university in order to study painting under Jacob van Swanenburgh, a local painter who specialised in architectural scenes and pictures of hell. Rembrandt asserted himself immediately and painted neither for the three years they spent together. He was only eighteen when he set up on his own after a short spell in Amsterdam with Pieter Lastman. He used both his parents as models, but especially his mother whose deeply wrinkled face, rounded nose and gaping eyes appear in a number of his early works. His portrayal of the elderly Anna in *Anna Accused by Tobit of Stealing the Kid* in the Rijksmuseum is thought to be modelled on her.

The woman of his life was Saskia van Ulenborch, a coquettish buxom girl who came from a wealthy and respectable family. They met through her cousin, an unconventional art dealer with whom Rembrandt lived in Amsterdam. Rembrandt celebrated their marriage with a drawing of her wearing a large brimmed hat and a proud inscription: 'This is a drawing of my wife, when she was 21-years-old ... 8 June 1633'. Through her Rembrandt was introduced to the patrician class of Amsterdam. Commissions poured in for portraits and Rembrandt became a household name. The artist made the most of his exalted social position and the couple lived extravagantly. They collected art and curiosities (thought to include works by Michelangelo and Raphael), bought a large house on St Antoiniebreestraat and generally enjoyed life. Rembrandt painted himself as an exuberant gentleman decked out in fur, velvet and silk; he depicted his wife in fine clothes or used her as a model for mythological and biblical subjects.

It was a passionate relationship, at times tempestuous but always secure. A delightful little etching in the Rembrandthuis shows them together, she peering over his shoulder while he stares out of the picture, proudly presenting his property. The artist produced scores of paintings in those years, enjoying seemingly endless patronage: sensual portraits, dramatic religious pictures and romantic landscapes packed with mountain ranges, deep valleys, crags and overhanging trees. His art became as flamboyant as his lifestyle. Rembrandt continued to paint Saskia until her tragic and untimely death. Their first three children having died as babies, Saskia died in 1642, leaving their only surviving child, Titus, a babe in arms to the care of his father.

Saskia's death marked the beginning of Rembrandt's financial decline. He had squandered large sums of her money on his extravagant lifestyle and popular taste was changing. He was no longer the only artist worth commissioning in Amsterdam. Soon Rembrandt struck up a relationship with the little plump farm woman whom he had employed to look after Titus, Geertge Dircx. He gave her jewels and treated her as his common-law wife. In retrospect it appears that he spent much of this time outside, perfecting his landscape technique. Whether this is because he needed to escape from home or because it was something he needed to do is unclear, but he certainly did not spend his time sketching or painting his new companion as he had Saskia. He used Geertge as a model, but never made a portrait of her. When she was ousted from the house in 1649 by Rembrandt's new lover, Hendrickje Stoffells, Geertge took Rembrandt to court for breach of promise, using her jewels and their sex life as evidence of commitment. She was awarded an annuity of f200, whereupon vindictive Rembrandt managed to have her arrested and confined in a correction house in Gouda for eleven years. She was rescued by friends after five years, but the story tells us something of Rembrandt's erratic temperament.

Though Rembrandt never married Hendrickje, they lived together for the rest of their lives despite being harassed by the Church. Hendrickje ignored summonses from the Council of the Reformed Church, but finally admitted that she had 'stained herself by fornication with Rembrandt'. She was punished and banned from taking communion, but the stipulation lapsed after the baptism of their daughter Cornelia. Hendrickje came from a humble background; she seems to have demanded little and given everything. She was close to Titus and saw Rembrandt through the financial downfall; the artist was forced to transfer his house to Titus to secure his inheritance and sell all his belongings to pay off his creditors. When the sale failed to raise enough money Titus and Hendrickje formed a business partnership, employing Rembrandt so he could at least save his own earnings by selling works through them. The family ended up living humbly, but happily in the Jordaan. Rembrandt spent the last few months of his life living with his daughter Cornelia, whom he may well have had in mind when he painted the young teenager in one of his last paintings, The Jewish Bride in the Rijksmuseum.

Jewish Historical Museum

Jonas Daniel Meyerplein 2–4, tel. 626 99 45. Open daily 11 a.m.–5 p.m. Admission f9.50, 10–16s f6, under 10s free. Special rates Mon f7, children f3.50. Tram 9, 14; Metro Waterlooplein.

The complex of four synagogues on the edge of the bleak Jonas Daniel Meyerplein opened in 1987 as the new Jewish Historical Museum. An informative display of objects, papers, photographs and paintings provides an insight into the Jewish faith, the history of Jewish people in the Netherlands and the horrors of the Holocaust. There is a good café and an even better bookshop for everything you need to know on the Jewish way of life. Allow yourself a couple of hours to take it all in and save some energy for the temporary exhibitions frequently occupying the last room.

Faith, Persecution and Survival Nearly 80% of Dutch Jews were exterminated during the Second World War. Amsterdam alone lost 100,000 Jews as is evidenced by photographs of Jews being herded, transported and suffering. The mere fact that the museum is located in four disused synagogues is testimony itself to the devastating destruction of the Jewish people under the Nazis. For the Jews left behind in the city and relatives of the persecuted, the museum is an important monument to the suffering of their forefathers and to the strength of the Jewish faith and identity.

Nazi oppression was felt by the whole city of Amsterdam where Jews were an integral part of the community. Locals suddenly found their friends and neighbours being banned from parks, swimming pools and cinemas, and afraid to walk the streets for fear of unprovoked attack. Restrictions increased further; Jews were only allowed to attend special schools, they were not allowed out after dark, they all had to wear the Star of David (roughly-cut yellow cloth stars crudely marked *Jood* for instant recognition). Amsterdammers fought back; photos commemorate the famous February Strike of 1941 in protest against the random arrests of Jews in retaliation for the death of a Dutch national socialist, Koot (see p. 192). The

Germans appointed a Jewish Council to implement the Nazi orders on their own community, although most of the council mistakenly believed that their position was helpful to the community. The work and worries of the Jews employed here are encapsulated in letters, photographs and extracts from the diaries of one of the best documented members, Etty Hillesum. Pictures capture the plight of the Jews as they leave for the transportation camp of Westerbork, the squalid conditions of the camp and the final journey to the extermination camps. Don't miss the colourful series of paintings by Charlotte Salomon called *Life? or Theatre?* a melancholy reflection of her own life as a Jewish woman exile in southern France before she was killed in Auschwitz in 1943.

Jewish Religion, Rituals and Rites

Any Gentile will find the ground floor of the **Great Synagogue** a fascinating trip into another culture. Splendid ceremonial objects are complemented by a wealth of pictures of the feasts themselves. Much of the display concentrates on the greater involvement of women in the modern movements of Judaism, stressing that while rituals exist they are not and need not always be observed. The intriguing *mikveh* is a prime example; women are considered unclean during menstruation so they are obliged to dunk themselves in the *mikveh* – the ritual bath in the synagogue – at the end of their period, after which they are allowed to resume their sex life. Jewish laws and customs like this are explained with quotes from the Bible and explanatory labels.

Remember to take a look at the Synagogue itself with an impressive gallery on three sides, supported on marble columns. Traditionally the congregation would have been segregated; women upstairs and men down below. The Holy Ark dominates the fourth wall from which hangs a very beautiful curtain woven in deep blue wool with silver and gold thread, designed by Jeanette Loeb in 1949.

Jews in Amsterdam

Up in the galleries some delightful paintings and interesting showcases relate the history of Jewish people in Amsterdam. The first Jews to arrive in the city were the Sephardim, a group of wealthy tradesmen from Portugal, most of whom had been converted to Catholicism before they arrived. They were joined by hordes of poor Ashkenazic Jews, fleeing pogroms in Poland and Germany around 1600. The Jewish religion was first practised openly in the capital in 1602, by which time the so-called 'Jewish Nation' was granted considerable freedom in governing itself and judging its own members by Jewish law, as long as this did not conflict with Dutch law. Jews were not required to wear a distinguishing badge, making Holland the only country in Europe where they could retain their religion and enjoy more or less equal rights with the community. Between 1671 and 1752 the Jews built themselves four synagogues at the heart of the Jewish Quarter to accommodate their growing numbers. (The four are now linked in this single museum complex by covered street passages and staircases.) A local scene, *The Vissteeg* by Gerard Staller, captures the once busy fish market on Waterlooplein in the heart of the Jewish Quarter. Just around the gallery you are given an insight into the two trades in which the Jews were most involved; diamonds and textiles. Jews found that they could work in both outside the guild structure which controlled so much of Dutch trade and in this way earn a living without encroaching on Dutch territory and upsetting the locals. Amsterdam was tolerant to Jewish residents and the Jews respected Amsterdammers. Obviously certain sets of Jews were integrated more quickly than others, but by the 1930s Jewish emancipation was more or less complete. It was this that intensified the horror of the Holocaust throughout the city.

ETTY HILLESUM (1914–43)

Etty was a liberated Jewish woman with a healthy appetite for sex, life and philosophy, who kept a diary of her life between 1941 and 1943 when, unlike most Jews in the city, she was allowed to walk freely as an employee of the Jewish Council.

Etty lived with her family in Deventer before enrolling at the University of Amsterdam to study law. She switched to Slavonic languages and was in the throes of studying psychology when she decided to write her diaries. The war was already in full swing. While having a very laid-back affair with her landlord's son, her diaries record her growing infatuation with her mentor, Julius Spier, the founder of psychochirology (the study of palm prints). He became her lover. Etty was Jewish by birth, but practised her own religion: 'I hold a silly, naive or deadly serious dialogue with what is deepest inside me, which for convenience's sake I call God.' She calls on her God for help, guidance, forgiveness and deliverance throughout the diaries. They are intimately concerned with the fate of her family and friends, and paint a vivid picture of Amsterdam under Nazi occupation, so different from that drawn by fellow writers, Anne Frank and Eva Schloss.

In July 1942, as Jews all over Amsterdam fled into hiding, Etty started a job as a typist at the Jewish Council on Nieuwe Keizersgracht. The Nazis used the Council as a go-between among the Nazis and the Jewish people. The Council was under the illusion that it could by negotiation save the Jews from the worst and in this way it was a subtle weapon in the hands of the Nazis. Etty was unsure about taking the job from the start: 'My letter of application to the Jewish Council has upset my cheerful yet deadly serious equilibrium ... Like crowding onto a small piece of wood adrift on an endless ocean after a shipwreck and then saving oneself by pushing others into the water and watching them drown.'

She lasted two weeks there before she voluntarily opted to join her fellow Jews on the train to Westerbork where she stayed for a year, working in the hospital. Owing to her travel permit from the Jewish Council she could return to Amsterdam at will bringing letters from the camp to friends, relatives and resistance groups in the capital and returning with medicines and messages to the trapped Jews. She continued to work at the camp until she, too, was herded on a transportation train to Auschwitz.

Etty boarded the train with the words: 'I have my diaries, my little Bible, my Russian Grammar and Tolstoy with me and God knows what else.' Out of the train window she threw a postcard bearing the message 'we left the camp singing' which was found and posted by farmers, Etty's faith never let her down. She represented one of thousands of persecuted Jews – ordinary people, who found the strength to cope with devastation and inevitable death.

Dokwerker (The Dockworker Monument)

Jonas Daniel Meijerplein.

Once a year crowds gather on this open space beside the hefty Portuguese Synagogue to commemorate the general strike led by the dockworkers against Nazi oppression on 25 February 1941. A bold bronze sculpture by Mari Andriessen captures the defiant nature of Amsterdammers on that day.

Anti-Jewish measures by the Nazis were being gradually but forcefully imposed by 1941. Both Jews and non-Jews living in the Jewish Quarter clubbed together to form protection squads, employing a number of heavyweights from the local boxing clubs to make up the numbers. During a clash between the Germans and one of these protection squads a Dutch Nazi sympathiser named Koot was injured and later died. Germans set up the Jewish Council to restore peace in the disturbance that followed, but they continued to harass the Jewish population. On the 19 February a German patrol was driven out of a Jewish ice-cream parlour and sprayed with ammonia. The German Chief of Police decided to make an example so three days later 425 Jewish men were rounded up on Jonas Daniel Meijerplein, herded into trucks and removed. The next day another round-up took place at a Sunday street market. All of these men died in concentration camps. Word of the round-ups travelled fast and within a few hours the city came to a standstill. Railway and dockworkers were the first to strike, followed by almost the entire city. It was Amsterdam's first anti-pogrom strike, spreading to the surrounding towns and cities.

The next day hundreds were arrested, nine people killed, the mayor was replaced, members of the City Council fired and peace restored. It obviously did little to stop the Nazis, but the enormity of the strike gave people the impetus and confidence to support the growing Resistance Movement.

Portuguese Synagogue

1–3 Mr Visserplein. Open occasionally in summer, but currently undergoing renovation. Ring bell beside the door for entry. Men are obliged to wear skull-caps provided. Tram 9, 14 to Waterlooplein.

The enormous red brick block on the edge of Jonas Daniel Meijerplein, known as the 'Snoga', is the largest synagogue in the world. Built in the seventeenth century for the Sephardic Jews, it is said to have been modelled on a plan of King Solomon's Temple. The size may have something to do with the fact that Jews elsewhere had only been allowed to worship in private and this was a celebration of the freedom and wealth available to them in Amsterdam. Across the main entrance the Hebrew text reads: 'for I shall enter Your house through Your abundant kindness'. The plain austere exterior contrasts with the opulent copper chandeliers and high barrel vault inside.

The famous **Etsh Haim** or 'Tree of Life' library, one of the most important collections of Jewish writings in the world, has been here since the synagogue was built. The Sephardics brought to Amsterdam a wealth of literary, artistic and cultural knowledge which became absorbed into the city's life over the centuries. Amsterdam publishers issued a number of important Hebrew works. The first Hebrew book was published in 1627 and the first Jewish newspaper, *Gazetta de Amsterdam*, in 1678. Even Rembrandt was involved in Jewish publishing ventures; he produced a series of etchings to illustrate *La Piedra Gloriosa* by his friend Rabbi Manasseh ben Israel.

Hollandse Schouwburg (Former Dutch Theatre)

Plantage Middenlaan 24. Tram 9, 14 to Artis.

The Hollandse Schouwburg is the only elegant building in this busy street through the heart of Jewish Amsterdam. In its heyday it was the city's prime venue for showing plays by leading Dutch writers. Herman Heyerman's working-class sitcoms were particular favourites with the audience and the popular actress, Esther de Boer-van Rijk, performed here for many years.

Today the theatre stands as a memorial to the Jews deported under Hitler's brutal regime, it was used as the main deportation centre for the area; terrified families were brought here before being bundled off to Westerbork labour camp. As the writer Mary Dorna recalls, she had used to envy her mother when she left with friends for the theatre but since then 'she had been taken to the Holland Theatre, not to dance and lose the little combs in her hair, because one doesn't dance in the hall of hell'. Across the road from the theatre, at No. 31, hundreds of Jewish children were smuggled out of the crèche to the school at No. 27, and from there to freedom. A bronze plaque commemorates those who made it to safety and those who sheltered them in the crèche.

The crèche has since been demolished, but the theatre was presented to the city at the end of the war as a Jewish memorial. Inside a candle burns in the small chapel erected to those who went through here to their deaths. It is usually open if you want to pay your respects.

Vakbonds Museum (Trade Union Museum)

Henri Polaklaan 9, tel. 624 1166. Open Tues–Fri 11 a.m.–5 p.m., Sun 1–5 p.m. Closed Mon. Admission f5, 13–18, students, OAPs f3, Under 13s free. Tram 9 to Plantage Kerklaan.

The sturdy tower and castellated roof of the Vakbonds Museum seem misplaced in this leafy residential street close to the zoo. Once they have been put in context they appear highly appropriate. Papers, photographs and newspaper cuttings are rather dryly displayed in the oldest trade union building in the Netherlands. Known locally as the 'Castle' the building was designed by H.P. Berlage as the headquarters of the A.N.D.B., the General Dutch Diamond Workers' Union. Despite friendly staff, a couple of informative leaflets in English and lots to see, it is difficult to come to grips with the exhibitions if you don't speak Dutch. However, it is well worth popping in to see the building and interior decoration where architecture, sculpture, murals, light fittings and even hinges are designed as part of an integral whole.

The A.N.D.B.: Holland's First 'Modern' Trade Union

Amsterdam's diamond workers were a tough bunch, employed in a business that was dangerous, financially unpredictable, demanded long hours in appalling conditions and relied totally on the availability of the raw materials from around the world. One of their number, Henri Polak, was inspired by his involvement in the socialist movement to fight for real rights for diamond workers. He believed that the working classes should achieve economic and political power for the successful realisation of a socialist society. He founded the Social Democratic Labour Party in 1894. In the same year he founded the General Dutch Diamond Workers Union A.N.D.B. in the wake of a successfully concluded workers' strike. His Union was essentially a modern organisation; it worked on a centrally planned policy, entailing unconditional discipline of members, professional leaders, good accounting and a strong strike fund. Membership fees were understandably high and discipline ruthless, but it worked. The Union fought to achieve, among other things, reasonable working hours, better working conditions, health care, unemployment and sickness benefit. It soon became the most powerful and wealthiest union in the Netherlands and the first union in the world to achieve an eight hour working day.

Popular attitude to Polak and his Union was varied; the majority of the 10,000 people in the diamond business, many of whom were women, joined, but some, particularly the older members found it restrictive rather than advantageous; one elderly man summed up his feelings: 'The struggle for workers' rights was a very noble, very splendid business – only they didn't know where to draw the line.' Polak's objective was clear-cut; he wanted to educate his members as class-conscious socialists, protected by each other in their chosen line of work. He also wanted to inspire them culturally and the headquarters building was his golden opportunity. The socialist architect Berlage was an obvious choice. From the street the building is a powerful statement: undecorated walls, heavy studded wooden doors, a sturdy brick tower punctuated by an A.N.D.B. emblem and a round diamond window at the top. Inside, a light inner court coated in yellow tiles is warm and welcoming. The panelled boardroom is sincere and secure. The interior murals were completed by a fellow socialist, Rik Roland Holst, who used quotes from poems written by his wife Henriette.

The Union building became a monument to the people who lived and worked in the diamond industry. Henriette Roland Holst summed it up in 1904: 'Men and women sleep without fear. A local guard also wakes over them in the night.'

AMSTERDAM: A CITY OF DIAMONDS

The art of diamond cutting, polishing and setting is a grim and grimy process, at odds with the sparkling final result. For centuries the diamond industry has relied on the availability of cheap labour and lots of it. Diamonds were being cut by the Dutch in Amsterdam as long ago as the sixteenth century, but the business established itself in the hands of Jewish immigrants. It was mainly the poor immigrants from Eastern Europe who turned to diamonds as one of the few trades available to them. Most trades at the time were under guild control which barred immigrant workers, so poor Jewish people had little option than to join the diamond workers. The Jewish Quarter in Amsterdam very quickly became the hub of the diamond industry, a business that has stayed with them to the present day.

In the early days it was a cottage industry, done from home in appalling conditions. The work was time consuming; with the cleaving, sawing, cutting and polishing shared by various members of the family. As families grew so did business. By the eighteenth century it was a big business in Amsterdam, which rocketed when Dutch merchants secured complete control of diamonds coming out of Brazil from 1725 to 1792. By the end of the century much of the cottage industry had been taken over by factories where women were employed to work the polishing machines. When things got tough and the Brazilian trade dried up, the machines were adapted so that they could be driven by horses and the women lost their jobs. By 1800, business hit rock bottom. Amsterdam was no longer a major port and poverty and unemployment were endemic, but the diamond workers continued to pick up what work they could.

Steam-powered polishing factories speeded up the process and many cutters joined forces with traders so that most of the 560 mills were owned jointly by traders and processors. There was never a shortage of workers, despite the appalling working conditions; life expectancy of polishers was 35 and about 50% of the workforce was destined to lose their sight; setters could expect no more than 26 years. They were vulnerable to pulmonary consumption, caused by using their lungs as bellows, and from lead poisoning contracted while soldering. As early as 1865 the diamond workers were campaigning for better conditions.

Tremendous finds in South Africa during the 1870s resulted in a renaissance in Amsterdam's diamond trade and the city itself. Business boomed, factories expanded and many diamond workers made a lot of money. Workers would arrive at work in horse-drawn carriages, light cigars with f10 notes and generally flash their new found wealth. So great were the imports of South African diamonds that even women were encouraged to join the workforce. Costers set up a special school to train women cutters, who generally cut the little diamonds known as 'roses'. Their employers insisted that women were better at the more delicate work, but in retrospect it seems that female workers were simply a source of cheap labour. These were among the first women to join a union with the establishment of the A.N.D.B. (see above). The 'rose cutters' were listed in the Union as Series 7. These women were renowned for their foul language and quick tempers and the title Series 7 was quickly picked up as a term of abuse, used to describe the less 'ladylike' members of the population. Women brokers were less common. Some did exist, but they wre not allowed into the main Diamond Exchange – sexual discrimination was seen as an easy way to ward off competition. Women members were considered from the beginning of the twentieth century and a campaign was launched by a broker's widow, Jannie Roselaar. Female membership was only finally granted in 1952, when the industry needed as many dealers as it could get.

The turbulent nature of the diamond industry continued in the twentieth century. A slump at the turn of the century was followed by years of prosperity until the serious depression of the 1930s. During the Second World War over 2000 Jewish workers were dragged off to German concentration camps, rendering the survival of the business almost impossible. Survivors were quick to revive the industry after the war with the help of foreigners and the government; within four years of the Liberation 100,000 people visited an exhibition at the Diamond Exchange and the Dutch were put back in business. Most of the buildings in the Jewish Quarters are now converted or redundant as business has moved away from the area; the A.N.D.B. headquarters is a museum, the great Exchange in Weesperplein is awaiting conversion into offices, and old mills have either been turned into apartments or demolished. Despite all this, as the posters around town will testify, Amsterdam remains a city of diamonds.

Hortus Botanicus (Botanical Garden)

Plantage Middenlaan 2, tel. 625 8411. Open Mon–Fri 9 a.m.–5 p.m., Sat, Sun & public holidays 11 a.m.–5 p.m. Closed at 4 p.m. Oct–March. Admission f7.5, 5–14s f5.50, OAPs f5.50, under 5s free. Tram 7, 9, 14 to Plantage Kerklaan.

Gone are the days when crowds poured into the pocket-sized botanical garden to stand on the leaves of the giant water lily or sleep overnight in the hope of seeing it flower. These days people go to see the variety of species rather than to ogle at beautiful specimens. Plants are neatly displayed in a little ornamental garden or shut away in humid hothouses. The garden is currently being updated with the addition of an enormous new glasshouse – a temple of sheet glass and aluminium tubing soon to be filled with exotic plants and, the authorities hope, lots of visitors.

The garden has been here since 1682 when it was used as a herb garden for medicinal purposes. Since then it has been considerably enriched by plants brought back from the voyages of the East India Company. In total there are about 6000 species packed into this tiny space. Take a look in the tropical house where carnivorous plants chomp at passing flies or head for the **Palm House** which is gradually being consumed by the oldest and possibly biggest pot plant in the world: the 400-year-old *cycad* (palm fern). Colours are vibrant in the summer; you will find a list of flowers in bloom posted in the **Orangerie**. In winter months there is little to see outside except perhaps a couple of ducks enjoying the ornamental pond.

Once you have explored the specimens, push your way through runaway creepers and enjoy the fragrances of exotic blooms; savour coffee and cake in the Orangerie or peruse the eccentric, traditional and off-beat tomes in the bookshop.

Artis Zoo

Plantage Kerklaan 40, tel. 523 3400. Open daily 9 a.m.–5 p.m.; last planetarium show 4 p.m. Admission to zoo, planetarium, children's farm and Zoological Museum f16; f9 under 10s; under 4s free. No credit cards. Tram 7, 9, 14 Plantage Kerklaan; car park.

Amsterdam's zoo, officially the Natura Artis Magistra (Nature is the teacher of Art), is commonly known as Artis. Whatever the weather, there is plenty to see here, indoors or out. Orangoutangs swing and chatter in the ape house, brilliantly coloured birds preen and squawk in the aviary, huge crocodiles doze in the steamy reptile house, exotic fish cruise in the Aquarium and, if that's not enough, there is a rather splendid dinosaur skeleton in the Zoological Museum and a terrific show in the Planetarium.

Like so many city zoos the Artis has limited space, most of which is given to the animals, so it can get crowded. However the pretty gardens and seemingly healthy-looking creatures make it a very pleasant break from the bustle of the city, despite the high entrance fee. Children can get their hand in at the farmyard where goats, cows and chickens are quite used to the cuddles, curses and edible comforts that come their way. A couple of playgrounds alleviate the congestion around the animals and give parents a chance to sit down and the café serves an abundance of chips and coke throughout the day.

Opened in 1838, this is now the oldest surviving zoo in the Netherlands. (Some of the reptiles look as if they have been there since the beginning.) The area was originally created as a public garden for the locals, dug out by about two hundred city orphans who provided cheap labour at the time. It was a favourite spot for Jewish families enjoying their day of rest on the Sabbath. As they were unable to carry money on the Sabbath, many paid by tab or went back the next day to settle up. Local families still enjoy the zoo, but at a price.

Tropenmuseum

Linnaeusstraat 2, tel. 568 8200. Open Mon–Fri 10 a.m.–5 p.m., weekends and public holidays noon–5 p.m. Admission f7.50; f4 under 18s, f17.40 family CJP card holders; free with Museum Card. Tram 6, 9, 10, 14 to Tropenmuseum

The Tropenmuseum is one of Amsterdam's most entertaining museums and will suit all the family. The museum is concerned with the developing world, its problems and attractions. Wander from one country to the next through colourful reconstructed streets alive with the sounds of beating drums, plaintiff pipes and clucking chickens. Enjoy Oceanic ceremonial boats, African sculpture and Indian textiles or join a music workshop. Regular films and plays are shown in the basement at the **Soterijn Theatre** and kids are further entertained in the adjacent **Tropenmuseum Junior** (see p. 310).

The museum was built in the 1920s to celebrate Dutch colonial achievements and was originally founded as the Colonial Institute – a showroom for the treasures pillaged from the East by travelling Dutchmen. From outside the very grand building with great Renaissance towers and an exotic Gothic roof seems totally out of place in this rather run-down area of town. The decorated capitals and keystones allude to colonial themes, again misplaced by their surroundings and often hidden by graffiti-covered billboards. The grandeur continues inside, but is cleverly disguised by ethnic banners and makeshift shanty-towns. Most of the exotic treasures of the Colonial Institute were cleared when the museum had a change of heart in the 1970s and changed the emphasis from colonial achievements to contemporary life in the developing world.

If you don't get waylaid by one of the captivating temporary exhibitions on the ground floor, head upstairs for a walk around the galleries. Exhibits from Asia and Oceania occupy the first floor while Africa, Latin America and the Middle East take up the second. The wealth of audio-visual material and informative labelling is in Dutch, but this is not really a problem as the main emphasis is on the visual. Menacing masks, frail puppets and handwoven textiles are just a few items that may catch your eye between the nomads' huts, rickshaws and colourful bazaars. It is worth going to the African section just to pore over the irresistible sculpture from the **Tengenenge Artists Community** which includes a touching *Father and Son* by Bernard Matener.

The adjacent **Oosterpark** is a pleasant place to rid yourself of museum fatigue. Fat ducks wait for scraps alongside the winding lake, dogs run wild through clusters of pigeons, veiled Muslim women gently rock their children in prams and pushchairs while local musicians take advantage of the near derelict bandstand in the centre. A small teashop serves ice creams and coffee throughout the day.

AMSTERDAM'S DOCKLANDS

Gone are the days when huge ships lined the harbour and small cargo boats flitted to and fro from ships to store houses along the harbour front. Today we rely on illustrations for an overall picture of the magnificent harbour, packed with merchant ships and guarded by little watch towers. The harbour mouth itself disappeared when Central Station was built across it in 1889 and with it went almost all traces of the port of Amsterdam. The old harbour has gradually been consumed by developers; warehouses are now luxury apartments and offices, and the wide waterways are crammed with seriously large houseboats. The busy modern docks are now way out to the East.

If you are looking for a taste of the city's maritime history the windswept Eastern Islands are your best bet. The replica ship *Amsterdam* rocks proudly on the waves alongside the city's formal arsenal, now the Maritime Museum. Hordes of schoolchildren roam the galleries in search of paintings of battles, sinkings, treasure troves and pirates. Beyond the museum sand swirls as traffic roars down the open highways and a forgotten windmill sits amid 1960s housing and a petrol station. Nearby elderly men restore ancient diesel engines at one of the oldest shipyards, the Kromhout Museum. Just round the corner printers, photographers, designers and businessmen and women have a social lunch alongside the trendy converted warehouses at Entrepodok.

For a more relaxing experience go west to the delightful Western Islands where boat-building has become more of a hobby. Beautiful barges receive daily licks of paint and varnish from dedicated enthusiasts, classical music wafts from the windows of carefully restored warehouses and even the floating police station has a patio garden. Children fill buckets with shells in the sandy playground and chickens peck for crumbs in the urban farmyard. The odd bicycle rattles by or a Porsche purrs off into the distance. Meanwhile chainsaws scream in the sawmill and weather-beaten sailors patch up holed boat bottoms with slicks of tar.

If you decide to visit any of these areas you are quite likely to encounter kerb crawlers on the main roads that run along the harbour edge from Central Station – Prins Hendrikkade, De Ruiterkade, Haarlemmer Houttuinen (see p. 30) – but don'tlet this put you off. Buses run both east and west from Central Station.

Prins Hendrikkade: Remnants of a Maritime Past

Traffic streams across the top of Amsterdam, along the multi-laned Prins Hendrikkade which runs east from Stationsplein. Not a strip to stroll along as if it were a seaside promenade, but you are quite likely to use it on leaving the station or on your way to the Maritime Museum. Also, provided you're not weighed down with backpacks or being hassled by kerb crawlers, a few historical relics are worth a second glance.

A robust brick tower stands guard at No. 95, known as the **Schrierstoren**, or more popularly as the 'Weepers' Tower'. It is one of the original bastions of the Medieval City Wall, built in 1482. This is reputedly the place where sailors' wives, families and friends waved goodbye as their men set out to sea. They had good reason to weep for only one-third of the crew were likely to return and voyages took up to four years. A weather-beaten sixteenth-century stone tablet of a forlorn woman recalls these events. A more recent plaque commemorates the departure of the Englishman, Henry Hudson, who set out from here in search of trade routes to the West, discovering Manhattan on the way and giving his name to the Hudson Bay.

Continue along the street to the bus stop and you will find yourself standing outside the headquarters of the Municipal Transport Authority, also known as the **Scheepvarthuis** (Nos. 108–111). It is not as dull as it may sound. The exuberant building is one of the most impressive examples of the architecture of the Amsterdam School (see p. 174). Strong vertical details run like stripes from top to bottom, the surface of the building is alive with whales, ships, mermaids and pensive busts of well-known mariners and even the iron railings at the base ripple like waves. It was built in 1912 by Johan van der May, with the help of De Klerk and Kramer, and commissioned as the headquarters of seven shipping companies – hence the abundance of marine decoration.

Continue a little further along the street and you cross the wide canal **Oude Schans**, which once served as a moat to the city's defensive wall and became the main entrance to the old shipping quarter.

In the distance the little Sluiswatch (now a café) leans precariously towards the canal. About half way down the **Montelbaanstoren** (tower), complete with Hendrick de Keyser pinnacle, pierces the skyline. It was built in 1512 as a watch tower to protect the fleet, acquired its de Keyser hat in 1606 and now belongs to the Water Authority.

Eastern Islands

Apart from the Maritime Museum and the Kromhout Museum there is little to see in the Eastern Islands. Local residents recall days of extreme poverty when families struggled to survive while ship-building declined at the turn of the century. Despite their proximity to the city, residents are still referred to as islanders.

The area has a turbulent history of rapid growth and steady decline, but for most of the ship-builders poverty was a way of life. Amsterdam was one of the five Admiralties in the Netherlands, founded in 1597 to protect the country's coast, rivers and harbours. They were also responsible for arranging convoys of ships to protect against piracy. The Admiralty had its own dockyards and store-houses scattered all over the city until the mid-seventeenth century when all ship-building moved to the newly reclaimed island of **Kattenburg**. With the reclamation of two further islands – **Wittenburg** and **Oostenburg** – the Eastern Islands, as they were known, became the centre of Amsterdam's ship-building industry. The Admiralty were soon joined by the East India Company VOC who rapidly built shipyards, warehouses and roperies to meet the enormous demands of their fleets. The VOC employed over a thousand workers in the shipyards, making it one of the largest businesses in Europe. Piles of wood would lie in the water for six months until it was sufficiently leached to be used in the construction. Large boats like the *Amsterdam* would take about eighteen months to complete. While the men worked long hours for little pay women stayed at home, running large families in poor conditions.

Scheepvaartmuseum (Maritime Museum)

Kattenburgerplein 1, tel. 5232 222. Open Tues–Sat 10 a.m.–5 p.m., Sun noon–5 p.m. From 15 June–15 Sept open Mon also, 10 a.m.– 5 p.m. Admission f12.50, 6–18s f8, OAPs f10, under 6s free. Bus 22, 28 from Central Station, Museum Boat.

If you have a passion for ships and a soft spot for nautical instruments then this is the place for you. Hundreds of models, maps, paintings and nautical curiosities will tell you more than you probably wish to know about Dutch maritime history. Whether you tackle the main museum or not it's worth sampling the more relaxed and bawdy atmosphere aboard the reconstructed Dutch East Indiaman *Amsterdam* which is included on the same ticket. The best way to get there is aboard the Museum Boat which chugs across the harbour to the main landing stage beneath the bow of the *Amsterdam*.

The sea laps mercilessly around the base of the sturdy square block that was built as the naval arsenal (storehouse) in 1655. Neptune, Amphitrite and various sea deities lounge in the pediments while below there is usually a gathering of super-clean sailors staring out to sea before getting back to work. If you approach from the water you will be asked to go through the building to the main ticket office at the front of the building. Children lounge on redundant cannons or swing on ancient rigging in the central courtyard, unaware of their significance. In the seventeenth century the arsenal would have been jammed with stores of sails, ropes, guns, wagon grease and drinking water. The building was gutted by fire in 1791, but quickly restored and used as an arsenal until 1971, when road and rail transport were considered to be better. Maritime enthusiasts set to work and the museum opened in 1981. Fortunately the exhibits are more appealing than the atrocious labelling so it is a good idea to pick up any leaflets available when you buy your ticket. Special 'Highlights' make the galleries more manageable and comprehensible. Don't expect any guidance or greeting from the gruff guards who hang around the galleries.

Most of the models you see around the museum are contemporary to the ships they imitate. The *Model of a Three-master* in Room 1 is probably the oldest surviving ship model in the world, thought to have been made as a votive ship to be hung in the local church. Sea voyages were highly dangerous and treated with the greatest respect, not least because the world was an unknown quantity; new lands were being discovered, new routes laid but at the end of the day they had very little to lead them. A large *Map of the World* by Joan Blaeu next door gives some indication of what people knew of world geography in 1648, when Dutch Fleets dominated the world's waters. Clearly cartographers relied on seafarers for their information and new discoveries kept them in business. Note here that the north-west coast of Australia is shown, discovered in 1648 by Abel Tasman, who gave his name to Tasmania. Some intriguing illustrations fill vast spaces of unknown territory – don't miss the revelling cannibals in Latin America. In the same room you will find a couple of sixteenth-century travel books. The one to have if you were in the know was by Jan Huyghen van Linschoten, who put the manual together while working in India and the Far East as a Christian agent for the Archbishop. To his personal recollections he added a few navigation tips and maps which proved invaluable to Dutch sailors heading for the Far East. For sailors travelling north to Asia their best bet was to take a copy of Gerrit Jansz de Veer's account of journeys through the area, also shown here.

Continue through the galleries past innumerable paintings of ships in full sail, ships being ravaged by dark storms and ships being blown to pieces by the enemy. Look out for the piece of flesh taken from the mutilated body of the Dutch Lieutenant Jan van Speyck, displayed here in a glass bell jar for all to see. Speyck's claim to fame was the rather rash decision to blow his ship, himself and his crew up to avoid having to surrender to the Belgians. His pride won him the title of national hero (his crew's relatives may have thought otherwise) and someone returned this gory remnant to the city of Amsterdam.

Also worth seeing is the eighteenth-century Planetarium which still shows the position of planets, the sun and stars in relation to one another, provided someone remembers to wind it up each month. Compasses and maps find their place among a mass of weird and wonderful objects.

If you are considering making the journey to the Eastern Islands, be warned that they look nothing like the paintings in Rooms 10 and 11. The busy dockyards, piles of timber, half-built ships, elegant office buildings and general affluence are a far cry from the windswept, deserted docklands of today. The islands were once occupied by the main headquarters and shipyards of the East India Company – it was here that the Russian Tsar Peter the Great was reputed to have studied the art of ship-building. Other displays in the same room are devoted to the Company; printed cargo lists show the extent of their finds in the Far East. After two eight-month journeys the vast ships would return, their crews reduced by the loss of those who emigrated or died, carrying huge quantities of spices, porcelain, precious textiles and lots more. Goods were stored at dock awaiting auction and the ships prepared once again for another trip.

Before trying your hand at the captain's wheel in the *Amsterdam* outside, it is worth taking a look at the industrialisation of the ship-building industry, from Room 18 onwards. The beautiful model of the sleek *Willem Ruys* in Room 23 is proof itself of the perfect designs attainable once boats no longer had to rely on the power of the sail. Children shouldn't miss the impressive royal barge nicknamed the 'golden coach on water' which was last used in the 1960s for the silver wedding anniversary celebrations of Queen Juliana and Prince Bernhard.

There is always a lot of activity on the full-size replica of the *Amsterdam*, one of the vast ships that sailed for the Dutch East India Company in the eighteenth century. Children are generally allowed to run riot; they climb into the tiny bunk-beds, slop cold water around the deck, try the sludgy green peas steaming over the hot coals and steer the boat from the upper deck. A group of grubby deckhands in period costume try to control the ecstatic young hordes while their parents pretend not to notice.

The original *Amsterdam* was abandoned in the mud near Hastings, England, where its hull is still visible today at low tide. With this as their model and countless drawings from the East India Company archives, a team of boat-builders volunteered to work on a replica to be used on special occasions and opened to the public in Amsterdam. The leader of the project, Cees van der Meer, appears as Neptune on the ship's transom (bow).

If you can tolerate flying mops and rowdy children take a walk around the inside; plunge down to the enormous hold which was used to carry building materials, cannons and piles of silver out of Asia, and stuffed with tin, textiles, spices and saltpetre (raw material for gunpowder) on the way home. Upstairs storage chests, hammocks, cannons and chicken coups are crammed into any available space (a crush without the two hundred men who made up the crew). It is hard to imagine the stench of sweat, shit and breath that must have filled the ship. Regular fumigation and sprinklings of vinegar can have done little to alleviate the smell and claustrophobia. While the crew were roughing it the Captain and his mates would have been enjoying the relative comfort of the Great Cabin, complete with porcelain plates, linen napkins and real glasses, comfortable chairs and a pint-sized private lavatory.

These ships were manned by a crew of young men and boys from the lower classes. Many died along the way, unless they were lucky enough to be cured by the unqualified ship's surgeon. Treatment was free unless it was sustained in the service of 'Venus and Mars', a polite way of saying by sex or through a punch-up. On average only 70 of the 200 crew came home. Survivors immediately became worth more for subsequent trips. Meanwhile it was unusual for ships to become wrecked. VOC ships undertook 2800 voyages from the Netherlands to Asia; the *Amsterdam* was among only 2% left wrecked on foreign shores.

THE EAST INDIA COMPANY: LOST WITHOUT WOMEN

No organisation gave Holland more than the Dutch East India Company, set up in 1602 to control Dutch trading and traders in the Orient. For over a century the Dutch had been transporting wares from the East around Europe, but they relied entirely on Portuguese and Spanish merchants to bring back the goods from the Orient in the first place. Philip of Spain put an end to this when he invaded Portugal in 1580, and closed the port of Lisbon to the Dutch. Fortunately the Northern Provinces were inundated with Flemish merchants and, more importantly, Portuguese Jewish refugees who had been kicked out of Antwerp by inquisitioning Spaniards. Extra merchants and inside information on routes to the East meant that the Dutch were in a position to try their hand at trading directly with the Orient.

The first trip was a disaster; half the men died and the venture barely broke even. However, the subsequent voyage was a huge success, yielding a 400% return to its shareholders. East India mania hit the Dutch merchant community and before long fleets were sent from Veere, Middleburgh and Rotterdam. Competition was so fierce that the Dutch fleets came close to destroying the new trade before it had barely started. They finally joined forces in a massive operation which resulted in the establishment of the Dutch East India Company in 1602.

The Company was formed with a capital of six million guilders, of which Amsterdam provided just over half. It was controlled by a team of seventeen directors. Amsterdam was represented by eight of them. This venture was one that involved everyone. Only eighty-four of the original thousand shareholders were bigwigs; the rest were men and women from all walks of life including a hosier, a nanny, soap boilers and seven domestic servants.

The Company went from strength to strength. By 1650 it had over 150 merchant ships protected by 40 battleships manned by 40,000 soldiers. At this stage, it had the monopoly in all lands east of the Cape of Good Hope, as well as unlimited political, judicial and administrative powers in the countries in which it worked. Needless to say, while Amsterdam merchants enjoyed the fruits of the Golden Age, much of the East Indies was open to slavery and exploitation. Men from all over the country joined the VOC fleets. Employment was easy to find with board and lodging thrown in and, for many, a new life at the other end. Scores of young men enrolled for the work at the East India House, but there was never enough so the VOC had literally to 'trade in men' with the local hostel owners. These hard-bitten landladies, known as soul merchants, would take in men, usually foreigners, offering them board and lodging at a reasonable price. After a tipple and a pie they would be asked to sign a slip of paper. Unbeknown to them they were signing on the next ship to the Far East and their landlady had made another sale to the VOC.

Women who wanted to join the VOC were unlucky; it was a men-only concern unless you happened to be married to the Captain. Most women had to make do with waving goodbye to their lovers and friends at the aptly named Weeper's Tower on the Prins Hendrikkade. Other women went to all lengths to join the crews; stowaways were usually found (not surprising given the cramped conditions of the ships) but a number actually made it to the Indies disguised as men. A popular children's rhyme at the time recalls the wily VOC sailor whose disguise was so complete that she 'Pissed through a hornpipe, just as a young man might'.

The women's reasons for leaving Amsterdam were numerous: some joined their husbands, others left them, some ran away from home and the prospect of marriage, some sought reasonable employment and some sought a better life abroad. Those who made it obviously had a great time, much to the disgust of one of their contemporaries, Nicolaas de Graaft, who described them as 'a pack of prison whores, drunken street pigs and thieves who no longer dared remain in Holland'. In a land where white women were esteemed above the natives and in very short supply, life in the Orient must have met all their expectations. There is no doubt they were as corrupt as their male counterparts in these far off lands.

There was only one time when women were welcome in the VOC ships – the homecoming. Apparently randy sailors were so hungry for sex that for two days the ships were anchored offshore and bargeloads of prostitutes were taken to satisfy their needs. Sailors were only allowed to disembark if the captain felt they no longer posed a threat to Amsterdam's female community.

Kromhout Museum

Hoogte Kadijk 147, tel. 627 6777. Open Mon–Fri 10 a.m.–4 p.m. Admission f3.50, 4–18s and OAPs f1.50, under 4s free. Bus 22, 28 to Kadijksplein.

Just along the deserted street of Hoogte Kadijk is one of Amsterdam's oldest private shipyards, now open as the Kromhout Museum.

Ancient engines sit like slugs in the covered yard while elderly boiler-suited men tend to their pistons, pipes and plugs through layers of grease. Lone women are something of a rarity here so don't be surprised if you suddenly find yourself with men explaining the difference between combustion engines and steam engines over a complimentary coffee in the restaurant.

A small display of drawings and photographs trace the history of naval propulsion and in particular the work at the Kromhout shipyard. Boats were being built here as early as 1757. Production moved on to steamships and it was one of the first yards to benefit from a covered awning, a steam slipway and electric lighting. As ships got bigger, the relatively small Kromhout yard started building ships for inland waterways only. Business ceased in 1969 and the shipyard has since been used for repairs and restoration. The masts for the replica ship, the *Amsterdam*, were made here. The Kromhout is one of the few remaining working shipyards of historical and cultural importance, but is only worth visiting if you are fascinated by engines or find yourself in the vicinity with nothing better to do.

If walking through the area you may like to make a detour to the recently renovated Entrepodok district.

ENTREPODOK

Holiday atmosphere pervades the Entrepodok. Locals lounge on the decks of their boats and children play in makeshift gardens behind them. Bicycles rattle over the wooden bridge and glasses chink in the cafés. Across the water faint screeching and squawking comes from the zoo. Meanwhile behind the old warehouse doors printers purr, photocopiers click and telephones ring. Delivery vans stand abandoned with doors flung open, couriers buzz in and out, and salesmen move between the offices.

The renovation of the old warehouses at Entrepodok is one of Amsterdam's most recent dockland developments. The warehouses were so deep that an inner passage was put through the middle of them to bring in light and air. (The passage or street is on the first floor.) At the far end a grand neo-classical arch marks the entrance to what was Amsterdam's customs-free area for goods in transit. Above the doors are the names of innumerable destinations.

WESTERN ISLANDS

Local residents successfully campaigned during the 70s and 80s to stop the Western Islands turning into a concrete jungle of office blocks and community housing, as has befallen so much of Amsterdam's docklands. It remains a residential area punctuated by artists' studios, boat-building yards and small businesses. Seagulls soar overhead, small sail boats bob out to sea and elderly men try their luck with a fishing rod. The Western Islands have a character of their own, far removed from the stuffy streets and raucous sounds of the Jordaan just a few blocks away.

Getting to the Western Islands is no problem provided you have a map. It's about fifteen minutes' walk from Centraal Station. Head west from Centraal Station to the area north of the Jordaan, continue along the touristy Haarlemmerstraat and take the pedestrian underpass on the far side of Korte Prinsengracht. If this is closed or you feel unsure about heading alone into the gloom, go another block and take the wider underpass at Binnenoranjestraat. Either one will take you to Bickersland, the first of the three islands. The area is compact enough to do a pleasant circular walk around the islands with a map to guide you.

The first island you come to, Bickersland, is the least attractive but it's worth stopping to see the exhibition of contemporary sculpture at Zeilmakerstraat 15 the Beeldhouwers Kollektief (Sculptors' Collective). (Open Wed–Fri 10 a.m.–5 p.m., weekends 1 p.m.–5 p.m.) Across on Bickersgracht the sandy streets turn to cobbles and the grassy verges turn to sand riddled with tiny shells and driftwood. At the end of the street hens and pigeons peck in the small urban farmyard. Cross the bridge and you find yourself in the most picturesque island, Realeneiland.

Photographers will find they need an unlimited supply of film in Realeneiland. Gleaming barges reflect in the water, bundles of sail lie heavily against newly varnished decks and ropes tap gently in the wind. Proud owners strut around with dusters and sponges or make polite conversation with their next door neighbours. The neat little seventeenth-century gabled houses along the Zandhoek are as spruce as the boats they overlook. Clean white plasterwork falls like surf over the gables, newly painted doors and window frames gleam against sparkling windows and security alarms warn of opulence. The street was once packed with families of dockworkers. In the nineteenth century the Gildos House at No. 4 was home to eleven families with no less than 36 children; an old lady known as the 'Orange Woman' ran a sweet shop from the cellar at No. 5 and acquired her name for her ceremonial dressing of the orange tree outside. Over a century earlier, a certain Miss Scholten ran a pub from No. 7 which proved to be so lucrative that she bought a further two buildings in the street. It is not unusual to find women in charge of businesses in the docklands – their husbands were hard at work and incomes were so low that families needed extra.

At the end of the street the smart restaurant 'De Gouden Reale' serves some of the best meals in Amsterdam. The building was once the home of Jacob Real after whom the island is named. He made his name smuggling Catholic treasures out of a monastery just before iconoclasts burst in to remove them. The coin in the gable-stone also refers to his name, 'Real' meaning coin. The house has always been known as *De Gouden Reale*, a name that was also used for the title of the well-known novel by the Dutch writer, Jan Men, in which a wily woman, Dolly Griet, runs a pub on the corner of Zandhoek.

Continuing your walk, head for the little white pedestrian bridge that takes you over to the tiny **Prinseneiland**. Facing Bickersland a strong smell of tar and sawn wood from the boat yard mingles with fumes of turpentine and oil paint from the artists' studios across the street. Small wooden boats are trundled along the cobbled streets to the boat yard, workers sing to their radios and gossip over a cigarette in the streets. On the other side of the island flash cars fill the parking lots outside a smart row of converted warehouses and equally smart people hang out of windows to see who's there. It was over this side that the well known artist G. Brietner lived – a perfect spot for inspiration.

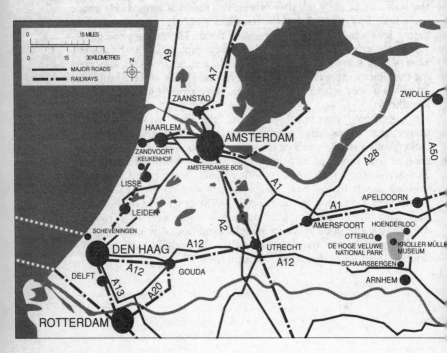

OUT OF THE CENTRE AND GETAWAYS

Amsterdam's geographical position close to the sea, the bulb fields, small sleepy towns and other major cities make day trips fun, not frantic. The efficient train service from Centraal Station makes travelling easy and relatively cheap and short distances mean it is often possible to combine visits to more than one place in a single day.

In the summer Amsterdammers flock to the open spaces and sporting facilities at the Amsterdam Bos or hop on a train for the coast to soak up some sun. Art lovers cannot miss the Mauritshuis in the Hague, not to mention the Frans Hals Museum in Haarlem, while the Kroller Muller Museum and adjoining National Park are well worth the cost of hiring a car. If you are looking for something relaxing head for Gouda or Delft, or a little more taxing, try Utrecht.

The Amsterdam Tourist Board (VVV on Stationsplein) organises and provides details of a number of excursions. These are often the cheapest and easiest way to visit other places, particularly the bulb fields in spring time. The Netherlands Railways also offer special excursion tickets to tie in with seasonal attractions. Most hotels and hostels carry leaflets advertising excursions and will book for you if you wish.

Mondays are not a good day to travel as many museums and shops are closed. If there is something you specifically wish to see it's best to contact the local tourist office (see below) before you go. It also saves time to visit other cities with a map. The Amsterdam tourist office should be able to provide them; otherwise make the local office your first stop when you arrive. Most are signposted from and situated close to the station. For special children's excursions see p.314.

USEFUL ADDRESSES

Tourist Boards

The Hague: Koningin Julianaplein (Centraal Station), tel. 634 03 5051
Gouda: Waagplein 2, tel. 072 114 284
Zandvort: tel. 02507 17947
Delft: Markt 85, tel. 015 126 100
Haarlem: Stationsplein 1, tel. 023 319 059
Leiden: Stationsplein 210, tel. 071 1486 846
Utrecht: Vredenburg 90, tel. 063 403 4085
Kroller Muller Information Centre: tel. 98382 1627

OUT OF THE CENTRE

Amsterdam Bos (Woods)

Take bus 170, 171, 172 from Centraal Station (30 mins) or take an ancient tram from the Tramline Museum. Stop at the main entrance on Van Nijenrodeweg.

If you are planning a day out of Amsterdam with the children or in search of some fresh air for yourself, Amsterdam Bos is a popular retreat.

This vast woodland park was created in the 1930s to alleviate the unemployment problem and provide Amsterdammers with a recreation area close to the city. The park is marked out with specially planned walks, cycle routes and bridle ways. It is huge so the best way to see it is by bike; hire one at the main entrance (tel. 644 5473) and follow the signs to the **Bosmuseum** where you can pick up a free cyclists' map. The Bosmuseum (tel. 643 1414; open 10 a.m.–5 p.m., free admission) has a small display relating to the history of the park and its flora and fauna. Children enjoy the stuffed animals, their spore and photos of poachers being frog-marched out of the bushes. Bird watchers will enjoy the boggy **Botanical Garden** where waders and marsh harriers move among the native Netherlandish plants and you may like to sample delicious creamy cheeses at the **Goat Farm** (open 10 a.m.–6 p.m., closed Tues, admission free). If you go in the spring they sell bottles of milk for feeding the herds of bumptious young kids – the main problem is persuading your children that they have had enough and it's time to go home. They may go once they have seen the nearby **Bison Enclosure** featuring some fine specimens rescued from the Artis Zoo.

The Bos is also good for sport. You may come across an international rowing competition taking place along the flat, straight stretch of water called the **Bosbaan**, or you may catch a national hockey match or some local cricket. Breathless joggers endlessly pad around the training circuits while canoeists pump iron around the waterways. You can hire canoes and pedalos at the **Grote Vijver,** big pond (tel. 645 7831). There are lots of riding schools and a water sports centre if you fancy joining in. There is also a popular nudist area for nude sunbathing if you feel like baring all to the elements.

Small children can finish the day in one of the two paddling pools and then on to the Pancake House where peacocks join you at the tables – adults may prefer to try one of the other two restaurants in the park.

Don't think the Bos has only summer attractions; if you are in Amsterdam in the snow remember there are miles of skating to be enjoyed on the Bos waterways while skiing and tobogganing take over from jogging and cycling.

Tramline Museum

Haarlemmerstation, Amstelveensveg 264, tel. 673 7538. Open April–June, Sept–Oct, Sun only 10.30 a.m.–5.30 p.m., departing every 30 mins. July & Aug departs 10 a.m.; 2.15 p.m. and 3.30 p.m. Tues, Thurs and Sat, and every 30 mins 10.30 a.m.–5.30 p.m. Sun. Take tram 6, 16. Admission f4 adults, f2 under 12s and free under 4s.

This is not really a museum at all but a pleasure ride through Amsterdam Bos in antique electric tram carriages from all over Europe, which appeals to both children and adults.

Aviodome

Schipol Centre, tel. 604 1521. Take the train to Schipol Airport. Open Oct–May Tues–Fri, weekends noon–5 p.m.; May–Sept 10 a.m.–5 p.m. daily. Admission f6, f4 under 12s, free under 4s.

Should you find yourself stranded at the airport or have an aeroplane fanatic as a child the Airport Museum could be a godsend. Over thirty aircraft are on display, some hanging from the ceiling and some waiting for eager children to clamber in. They include a flimsy 1903 Wright Flyer and the Spider, designed by the Dutch aviation pioneer Anthony Fokker. Upstairs in the Space Department you will find the American Mercury Capsule. Aviation fans could spend hours here; children try to but to some people every plane looks like another.

There is also an information centre giving information on the role of Schipol airport and the plans for its future.

Zandvoort

Traffic jams are dreadful so it is best to take the train from Centraal Station for a 31-min journey, cost f12.25 return. Trains leave every half hour and drop you off 2-min walk from the beach.

When the summer heat gets too much join the locals and head for the beach. Amsterdam is surrounded by sandy, tar-free beaches of which the most pleasant and easily accessible is Zandvoort. It can get very crowded but no one seems to mind and the beach is packed with numerous beach clubs: gay, nude, expensive and conventional. If you want to join the bronzing beauties and their trendy set head for *Tijn Akersloot* or if you are more interested in sipping champagne *Riche* sells oysters too. For skinny dipping there is a nude beach to the south; ask for directions.

It may be worth checking on the weather before you go; ask at your hotel or ring the tourist board. An east wind tends to bring shoals of unpleasant jelly fish and if it is cold take a windshield or be prepared to sit on the terraces behind glass.

Keukenhof Bulb Gardens

Nr Lisse, 27km south-west of Amsterdam. Tel. 02521 19034. Open 25 March–25 May, 8 a.m.–6 p.m. daily. Admission f15, f7.50 under 12s and over 65s. If you don't have a car the most economical and efficient way of getting there is taking an excursion, either train and bus from Central Station or bus all the way. Ask VVV for details of annual operators or ask your hotel to arrange it.

Tulip time in the Netherlands is the tourist high season, when hotels ask top prices, restaurants are packed and coachloads of amateur photographers and flower fanatics head for the bulb fields. For a quick glimpse of the brilliant colours take the train from Amsterdam to the Hague and watch the colours flash by. If you want to immerse yourself in the country's finest blooms go to the Keukenhof.

In the fifteenth century this was the kitchen garden of Countess Jacoba van Bieren, renowned for her ability to dispatch four husbands before her own death at the age of 35. In 1949 the garden was taken over by a group of Dutch bulb growers as a showpiece. Over 74 acres you will find nearly 7 million plants, neatly displayed with a tag notifying you of the variety and name of the distributor. The Keukenhof is a particularly good place for elderly and disabled people; wide tarmac paths and closely mown lawns are easy to walk on with only a few gentle slopes along the way. The colours and blooms are spectacular and if you go when the hyacinths are out the smell is almost overpowering. There are plenty of cafés dotted around the grounds and the maze of paths are clearly signposted. Families may prefer to take a picnic, though you will have to eat in the car park or disobey orders to keep off the grass – they may have specially designated picnic areas by now. Children enjoy running around or riding in the kiddy carts provided (pulled by parents) but they get frustrated if you spend too long musing over a single bloom and fed up with not being allowed to pick the flowers or run on the grass.

Some people find the crowds unbearable and the staff dressed in national costume a little too tacky, but if it's plants you have come to see you will undoubtedly enjoy yourself and probably end up forking out for a selection of your favourite bulbs to be sent home.

GOUDA

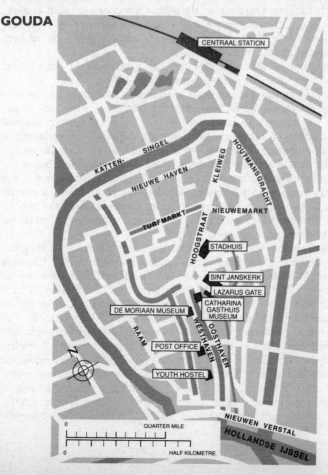

The compact town of Gouda is a good place for an easy day out with plenty to see in and around the beautiful central square, including a spectacular church, imaginative museums, pretty canal walks and some excellent local craft shops for souvenir hunting. Gouda is best known for the huge yellow rounds of cheese consumed throughout the Netherlands and if you go on a Thursday (June–Aug, 9 a.m.–noon) you will catch the spectacular cheese market re-enacted, mainly for the tourists, by ruddy-faced farmers and hardy damsels in traditional costume.

Any other day of the week you are likely to find the square full of wedding guests congratulating a happy couple emerging from the ornate Gothic *Stadhuis*. Couples come from all over the Netherlands to be married in this little town hall, isolated in the centre of the square, with its tiny spires, brightly painted shutters, and jolly carillon. Once a year the square assumes a magical quality, usually during the second week of December, for the Gouda candle festival when the electricity is turned off and every window flickers with candlelight for one night only.

Just beyond the square stands the **Church of St John** (open March–Nov Mon–Sat 9 a.m.–5 p.m., Nov–March 10 a.m.–4 p.m.). Surrounded by tiny gutter canals with small sluice gates and narrow bridges, the church is the longest in the Netherlands and one of the few in the country to have kept its fine sixteenth-century stained glass windows. Most of the windows are the work of the brothers, Dirk and Wouter Crabeth, who worked when Gouda was a Catholic city. Even the Reformers shied away from destroying the beautiful windows when the city turned Protestant at the end of the sixteenth century; instead they continued the project with windows depicting historical rather than religious scenes. During the Second World War the windows were removed and stored safely, to be re-installed once peace resumed.

Next to the southern door of the church through a magnificently sculptured archway is the garden entrance to the **Catarina Hospital Museum** (open Mon–Sat 10 a.m.–5 p.m., Sun noon–5 p.m. Admission f3.50 adults, f2 children under 16, f7.50 family). A curious but entertaining mix of paintings, period interiors, a toy collection, torture chambers and a fine collection of Impressionist and modern art are housed in the fourteenth-century city hospital. Jars, pots and bedpans line the shelves in the tiny dispensary complete with herbs, potions and even a dried alligator, all used for medicinal purposes in medieval times. You will find some reasonable seventeenth-century Dutch art in Room 4, including a still life by one of Holland's foremost female painters, Rachel Ruysch (see p.110). Period rooms are well executed, especially the kitchen complete with cooing turtle dove. The surgeon's room comes complete with amputation saws, hearing aids and a gory picture of an anatomy lesson. Many people come to see the excellent collection of nine-teenth and twentieth-century paintings donated by the painter and collector Paul Arnzentius, which includes works by Daubigny, Redon, Corot, Courbet, Rousseau, Breitner and Toorop, reflecting the collector's interest in the French Barbizon schools and Dutch followers of this style. A small room (18) is kept for the collection of contemporary works with an emphasis on women artists such as Hetty Huisman, Bettie van Haaster and Alice Schorbach. If painting doesn't appeal the cellar holds torture instruments, an execution block, strait-jackets and a lunatic cage.

Not far from the Catarina Hospital at Westhaven 29, is the small **Moriaan Museum** (open Mon–Sat 10 a.m.–5 p.m.; Sun noon–5 p.m. Admission on the same ticket as Catarina Hospital) which has a splendid collection of clay pipes and smoking equip-ment downstairs and exhibits relating to the once flourishing Gouda tobacco industry. Upstairs there is a fine collection of tiles and Art Nouveau ceramics.

If you are looking for something to take home, Gouda is famous for candles and, ironically, the hand-painted blue and white 'Delft' china. The best place to go for china is **Het Tin en Keramiek Huis**, Lange Groenendaal 73 (open Tues–Sat 10 a.m.–5 p.m.) where talented designers paint plates and jugs in the showroom and there are plenty of both Delft style and the more expensive Gouda-style works on sale.

Getting There Fifty-minute train journey from Amsterdam's Centraal Station. Trains average two an hour and the return ticket costs f23.50. Once there it is a 15-min walk to the market square. By car take the A2 and the A12.

DELFT

Delft is a charming city where small gabled town houses line quiet picturesque canals. You can see exquisite Delft tiles at the Lambert van Meerten Museum or buy some at one of the many potteries. There's a good collection of local art at the Prinsenhof and the lovely Nieuwe Kerk, site of the royal mausoleum. State-run museums are all included on one admission ticket, so museum hopping is not an expensive option.

Old ceramic tiles may not appeal to everyone, but the little white tiles, lovingly hand painted since the sixteenth century all over Holland and copied worldwide, captivate both young and old. For a look at a superb collection visit the **Museum Lambert van Meerten**, at Oude Delft 199 (open Tues–Sat 10 a.m.–5 p.m., Sun 1 p.m.–5 p.m. Admission f3.50, children f1.75). The building was built in

1891 for the eccentric industrialist, Lambert van Meerten, who, intending the house to be a museum, incorporated ancient architectural fragments into the building including a Renaissance window and a traditional Dutch cupboard bed in the bedroom. The work almost done, he went bankrupt and committed suicide. Friends donated the house to the state on condition it could be opened as a museum. It was the first museum in the Netherlands to have a female director, Miss Peelen, who succeeded in securing the donation of the collection of tiles from the architect Jan Schouten for which the museum is famous. Sixteenth–nineteenth-century tiles cover the walls – vast landscapes pieced together like jigsaws, voluptuous mermaids, dainty flowers, intricate patterns, exotic birds and animals, and some ludicrous portraits where the medium does little to enhance the beauty of the sitter.

DELFT

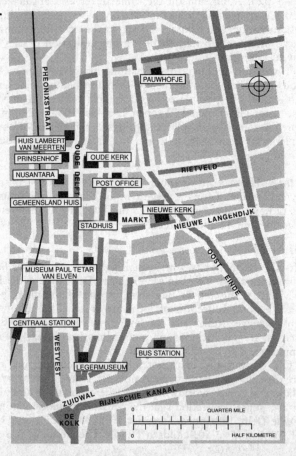

Just down from the Museum Lambert is the **Stedelijk Museum het Prinsenhof**, a pretty fifteenth-century convent which houses the city's collection of paintings. It was here that William of Orange took refuge during the Dutch Revolt against Spain and as the holes in the wall (Room 8) testify it was here that he was assassinated. The museum boasts a collection of good but not great paintings by Delft artists, mainly depicting historical events and members of the city's patrician families; don't miss the delightful sixteenth-century diptych by Jan Mostaert of a very glum Adriaan van den Broucke and his equally glum wife Catarina Vranx. Leaving the Prinsenhof, you may like to pop into the **Volkenkundig Museum Nusantara**, Agathaplein 4 (open Tues–Sat 10 a.m.–5 p.m., Sun 1 a.m.–5 p.m.) which holds a small collection of Indonesian artefacts.

There are two main churches in Delft, the rather sullen **Oude Kerk** (open Mon–Sat April–Sept noon–4 p.m.) with a leaning four-teenth-century tower which boasts the simple grave of the artist Johannes Vermeer, and the exuberant **Nieuwe Kerk** which contains the royal mausoleum under which lie countless Dutch monarchs, including William of Orange and Queen Wilhelmina. The church is a jumble of styles with a soaring fifteenth-century choir, solid four-teenth-century transepts and a nineteenth-century spire. On a sunny day the light pours on to the opulent marble tomb of William of Orange, designed by Hendrick de Keyser and rich in sculptural dec-oration from wailing cherubs to four natty virtues. The effigy itself is beautifully carved. The Prince's feet rest on his loyal dog who is supposed to have pined to death after his master's assassination.

The Nieuwe Kerk dominates the central square as if in competi-tion with Hendrick de Keyser's grand Stadhuis with its golden shells, swirls and painted shutters, at the other end. On Thursdays the square becomes a hive of activity as everyone turns out for the weekly market. The flower market extends down the city's prettiest canal, the Oude Delft, turning it into a photographer's paradise.

The city is full of tourist shops. Beware of paying high prices for poor quality china – you don't want to get home and find your 'authentic piece' was made in Taiwan. The best place for quality Delftware is **De Porceleyne Fles**, at Rotterdamseweg 196 (tel. 015 569214; open Mon–Sat 9 a.m.–5 p.m.) where fine pottery has been produced since the seventeenth century. Prices range from f65 to f3,000 and everything except for a few flawed cheaper pieces from the bargain basket comes with a certificate of authenticity.

Getting There Take the train from Amsterdam's Centraal Station to the Hague (Centraal Station) and change for Delft. Journey takes around an hour. The station is about a 10-min walk from the market square.

KROLLER MULLER MUSEUM AND DE HOGE VELUWE NATIONAL PARK

An unlikely combination of thick forests, open heathland, free bikes for getting around, a wonderful sculpture garden and a fine collection of modern art make this trip well worth the hour's journey from Amsterdam.

The colours in the park are magnificent in autumn as the leaves of huge oak, birch, beech and rowan trees turn, while in summer you will find the heath thick with purple heather and great splashes of red rhododendron bushes bursting from green thickets. The area is roamed by wild boar, roe deer, red deer, curly horned moufflons (sheep) and the occasional kangaroo. An exciting way to see the park is on horseback (ask at the Visitor's Centre) where the dunes offer lengthy gallops. Most people get around on the free white bicycles available at various stations around the park. There are a number of children's bikes, but you may be unlucky so don't rely on it if you are taking the family. Take a picnic, cycle around and stop off when you find a good view and some resident wildlife.

The enormous art collection which has grown around Helene Kroller Muller's bequest is exceptional. In a rather unassuming building that looks more like a school gym than an art gallery you will find numerous works by Van Gogh (the museum has over 300), Braque, Picasso, Leger as well as a number by De Stijl artists. You need to allow at least a couple of hours to do it seriously and allow another hour or two for romping around the sculpture garden. The best thing about the museum is that there is lots of space and not a lot of visitors so you can look at pictures without a constant flow of people pushing you on to the next. Also, the gallery is arranged in a series of smaller rooms so there are no noisy distractions.

Children love the sculpture park. Jean Dubuffet's *Jardin d'Email* is a family favourite where kids can roam across a bumpy white moonscape dissected by thick black lines (the uneven surface is lethal for toddlers). A huge Claes Oldenburg *Trowel* grows out of the ground, Marta Pan's large white *Swan* blows in the wind, boulders hang from the trees and Cornelius Rogge's weird *Tent Project* flaps in the wind. More familiar works by Henry Moore, Barbara Hepworth and Aristide Maillol emerge from the bushes or you may find yourself inside one of Richard Serra's vast rusting installations.

Getting There The easiest way is by car on the A1 to Apeldoorn or the A2 and A12 to Arnhem; there are gates to the park in the villages of Otterlo, Schaarsbergen and Hoenderloo. Alternatively, take a special railway excursion from Centraal Station – times and frequency vary so call for details. From late June to August there is a regular bus service from Arnhem station. Free bicycles for adults and children are available all over the park. For details, phone the Visitor's Centre (98382 1627) or the local Tourist Office (085 420 330). Open 8 a.m.–sundown daily. Admission f7.50 per person, f3.75 6–12s, under 6s free, (no reduction for OAPs), f6 per car, which includes admission to the museum and the sculpture park. Museum and sculpture park open Tues–Sat 10 a.m.–5 p.m., Sun 11 a.m.–5 p.m.; Nov–March opens later at 1 p.m. Sculpture garden April–Nov Tues–Fri 10 a.m.–4.30 p.m., Sun 11 a.m.–4.40 p.m. Closed Mon.

Helene Muller (1869–1937)

Helene Muller was an art lover and heiress to a giant blast furnace corporation. When she married one of her father's employees, Anton Kruller, in 1888, neither of them could have predicted Anton's early inheritance of the business at the age of 27 and its ultimate success. Anton was a brilliant businessman and within a couple of decades he had built the firm into an international concern with interests in shipping, American's corn trade and North African mineral mines. The ensuing fortunes allowed Helene to pursue her greatest passion – collecting art.

She was guided by her mentor, art historian H.P.Bremmer, who not only had the knowledge but contacts with many of the artists working at the turn of the century. Helene said it was Bremmer 'who gave me my first insight into art. He showed me the way to distinguish the wheat from the chaff.' She made her first important purchase in 1909, with three paintings by Van Gogh, and over the following years amassed an enormous collection of contemporary works. By 1921 it was the largest private collection in the country. Often taking Bremmer with her, she travelled to Paris, where she acquired works by Seurat, Signat, Corot, Daumier and others. In the Netherlands she collected hundreds of works by Dutch artists, Van Gogh, Mondrian and the De Stijl group. Bart van der Leck was even offered a job with the family firm as an interior designer. Art dealers had found themselves with a serious and reliable patron.

Art doesn't come cheap. When her husband walked from his office to hers in the same block, he reputedly remarked: 'Here we go from credit to debit.' She was not an easy woman either – some say she was kinder to her horses and dogs than to her numerous servants. Great architects like Berlage and Van der Velde withdrew from vast building projects for her, it seems, out of sheer despair at her demands.

When the family business was hit by economic crisis in the 1930s depression the Krollers' personal property looked seriously in danger of being split up and sold. They saved the de Hoge Veluwe National Park, the buildings and the art collection by setting up a foundation to keep it for the use of the public. The present museum was built as a temporary structure by unemployed workers from Arnhem in 1935 and directed by Helene until her death in 1937.

OUT OF THE CENTRE AND GETAWAYS

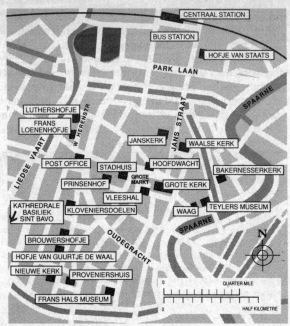

Map labels:
CENTRAAL STATION
BUS STATION
HOFJE VAN STAATS
PARK LAAN
SPAARNE
LUTHERSHOFJE
FRANS LOENENHOFJE
JANS STRAAT
W HERENSTR
JANSKERK
WAALSE KERK
LIEDSE VAART
POST OFFICE
STADHUIS
HOOFDWACHT
BAKERNESSERKERK
PRINSENHOF
GROTE MARKT
GROTE KERK
VLEESHAL
KATHREDRALE BASILIEK SINT BAVO
KLOVENIERSDOELEN
WAAG
TEYLERS MUSEUM
SPAARNE
BROUWERSHOFJE
OUDEGRACHT
HOFJE VAN GUURTJE DE WAAL
NIEUWE KERK
PROVENIERSHUIS
FRANS HALS MUSEUM
N
0   QUARTER MILE
0   HALF KILOMETRE

HAARLEM

Despite its proximity to Amsterdam, Haarlem is a sleepy town with a very pretty centre of cobbled streets, hidden *hofjes* and small shops. The main attractions are the Grote Kerk and central square, the splendid Frans Hals Museum and the quirky Teylers Museum. There is plenty to keep you occupied for the day or you may prefer to combine it with a trip to the beach which is only 11km away.

The small sloping market square is dominated by the vast medieval **Grote Kerk** (Great Church) also known as St Bavos (open Mon–Sat 10 a.m.–4 p.m.; admission f2). The vast whitewashed interior and soaring Gothic columns have been a popular subject for artists for centuries. A beautifully carved choir screen is packed with exotic beasts, a bored monk, bare-breasted women and a religious hypocrite – note the man biting a pillar on the left-hand side. Standing in the nave you have a good view of the magnificent organ made by Christian Muller in the 1730s which stands nearly thirty metres high. Both Handel and the precocious ten-year-old Mozart are said to have played on it. The various chapels skirting the perimeter are clearly marked with their owners' names, from brewers to dog whippers who, callous as they might sound, were responsible for flushing unwanted canines out of the church during services. Before leaving take a quick look at the rather splendid bird's-eye view of seventeenth-century Haarlem.

At the other end of the market square stands the **Stadhuis**. Part of it was the fourteenth-century hunting lodge built for the Count of Holland, but it now incorporates an Italian loggia and a former convent. A more entertaining building is the ornate Renaissance **Vleeshal** (meat market) on the southern side of the square; the intricate stonework, complete with oxen and sheep heads, is complemented by fine metalwork decoration which skims the room like icing on a cake. The whitewashed interior with its marble floor is now used as a temporary exhibition space by the Frans Hals Museum up the road.

Situated in the pretty almshouse or *Oudmannehuis*, the **Frans Hals Museum**, Groot Heiligland 62 (open Mon–Sat 11 a.m.–5 p.m., Sun 1 p.m.–5 p.m. Admission f6.00) is a real treat. The fine collection of paintings, including many important works by Hals himself, cover the walls of the almshouse's small rooms while the courtyard windows afford good views of the ornamental garden beyond. In Room 13 there's a chance to compare the work of Hals with that of his pupil, Judith Leyster (see p.155). Judith's *Portrait of a Woman* wearing a thick white millstone collar is a splendid example of her work. The best place to trace Hal's development as a painter is Room 21 where there are eight large group portraits of the civic guard and the Regents and Regentesses of the almshouse, the last of which was completed when he was eighty. Other fine paintings in the museum include an *Interior of the Grote Church, Haarlem* by Job Berckheyde, an exquisite *Still Life* by Floris Claeszoon van Dijck and some wonderful landscapes by Jan van Goyen, Jacob van Ruisdael and Pieter de Molijn. Don't miss the intriguing *Dutch Proverbs* by Pieter Breugel the younger, where over seventy proverbs are spelt out through the actions of the villagers and their beasts in an imaginery village. (The painting is explained on your entrance ticket.) You will also find a good collection of Haarlem silver, a magnificent eighteenth-century dolls' house and an extensive display of modern Dutch art.

Haarlem is also home of the Netherlands' oldest museum, the **Teyler Museum**, Spaarne 16 (open Tues–Sat 10 a.m.–5 p.m., Sun 1 p.m.–5 p.m. Admission f6.50, under 16, f3.) where there is a fine collection of scientific instruments, fossils and minerals brought together in the eighteenth-century by an eccentric draper and avid collector, Pieter Teyler van der Hulst. The building, with domed entrance hall, rows of polished display cases piled high with bits of bones, stones and inexplicable instruments has a musty charm. The neo-classical oval room is particularly impressive. An unexpected part of the collection is the old master drawings and paintings on display upstairs.

Getting There Take the train from Amsterdam's Centraal Station for the 17-minute journey to Haarlem. The market square is a 15-minute walk from the station.

THE HAGUE

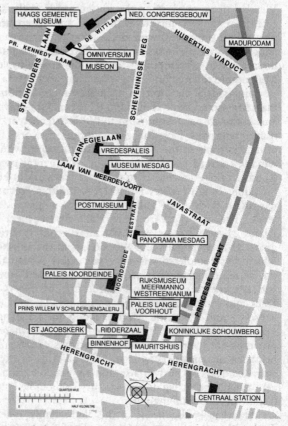

HAAGS GEMEENTE NUSEUM

NED. CONGRESGEBOUW

MADURODAM

OMNIVERSUM

MUSEON

HUBERTUS VIADUCT

PR. KENNEDY LAAN

STADHOUDERS LAAN

D DE WITTLAAN

SCHEVENINGSE WEG

CARNEGIELAAN

VREDESPALEIS

MUSEUM MESDAG

LAAN VAN MEERDEVOORT

POSTMUSEUM

JAVASTRAAT

ZEESTRAAT

PANORAMA MESDAG

PALEIS NOORDEINDE

NOORDEINDE

RIJKSMUSEUM MEERMANNO WESTREENIANUM

PRINS WILLEM V SCHILDERIJENGALERIJ

PALEIS LANGE VOORHOUT

ST JACOBSKERK

RIDDERZAAL

BINNENHOF

MAURITSHUIS

KONINKLIJKE SCHOUWBURG

PRINSESSE GRACHT

HERENGRACHT

HERENGRACHT

CENTRAAL STATION

QUARTER MILE

HALF KILOMETRE

THE HAGUE (DEN HAAG)

While Amsterdam is the capital of the Netherlands, Den Haag or s'Gravenhage is the seat of government and the chosen seat of the present Queen. In stark contrast to Amsterdam the centre is dominated by wide boulevards, stately houses and open squares. Amsterdammers find the atmosphere stuffy, complaining that it is a city full of diplomats, businessmen and politicians, but visitors can find it a welcome contrast to the narrow streets, canals and offbeat nature of the capital. The main attraction is undoubtedly the magical art collection at the Mauritshuis and the government complex at the Binnenhof. There is also a fine collection of modern art at the

Gemeente Museum and children love the model village at Madurodam. If you intend to see everything you will need at least a couple of days, but a trip to the Mauritshuis and a wander around the centre make a very pleasant day out.

Once a vast forest, the Hague was founded by Count William II who built a castle on the present site of the Binnenhof in 1250. The **Binnenhof** is best viewed across the Court Pond or *Hofvijver*, a large fountain-studded lake surrounded by an avenue of trees. From here you can see the amalgam of architectural styles that make up the complex. The tranquil cobbled courtyard is a good place for spotting politicians; it also makes a perfect auditorium for parliamentary protesters. If you are there on the third Tuesday in September you may even see Queen Beatrix arriving in a golden carriage to open parliament. The ceremony takes place in the oldest building, the fourteenth-century Ridderzaal, built as a hunting lodge for the knights of Holland.

Next door to the Binnenhof is the charming seventeenth-century **Mauritshuis** (open Tues–Sat 10 a.m.–5 p.m., Sun 11 a.m.–5 p.m. Admission f7.50, under 17s f4.50, under 6s free), built for a general and now home to the royal collection of paintings – mainly Dutch masters – once owned by William IV and William V. Enter through the side entrance into the basement. Inside the grand yet informal atmosphere makes it the perfect place to see, understand and really enjoy the very best Dutch art; there is a wonderful collection of flower paintings, including works by Bosschaert and Breugel the elder, a stunning *Deposition* by Rogier van der Weyden, refined interiors by Pieter Saenredam, captivating portraits by Hans Holbein, Rembrandt and Frans Hals, bawdy genre scenes by Jan Steen and detailed landscapes by Hendrick Avercamp. The Mauritshuis houses many of Holland's most famous paintings, including Rembrandt's *Anatomy lesson of Dr Tulp* (see p.95). Leave plenty of time for the Vermeers in Room 9. The large *View of Delft* is the only landscape known by this artist and the stunning use of light and shade, subtle colours and vast open sky is magical. Take a long look at the *Girl with the Pearl Earring*. Few artists have achieved such immediacy.

Across the pond from the Mauritshuis you will find the remaining, less impressive, pieces of the royal painting collection in the **Prince William V Gallery** at Buitenhof 35 (open Tues–Sun 11 a.m.–4 p.m.) and next door to the Mauritshuis is the **Rijksmuseum Gevangenpoort** or Prisoner's Gate Museum (open Mon–Fri 10 a.m.–4 p.m., April–Oct also Sun 1 p.m.–4 p.m. Admission f4) for a gory selection of torture instruments.

Further afield is the **Geemente Museum**, Stadhouderslaan 41 (open Tues–Fri 10 a.m.–4 p.m., weekends 1 p.m.–5 p.m. Admission f7, 5–12s and OAPs f6, under 5s free. Tram 10). The long brick building designed by Berlage, surrounded by lily ponds and concrete walkways, houses a fine collection of modern paintings and decorative arts, a unique collection of musical instruments and the national costume collection. The museum is seldom busy so you are likely to find yourself alone in a room full of paintings by Monet, Picasso or Braque. Even the warders admit the only paintings they have to watch are the nudes because men always touch them. However, it is a fine collection with an extensive selection of works by Mondrian and COBRA artists and a stunning *Self-Portrait* by Charley Toorop (see p.166). The musical instrument collection is particularly impressive with exhibits ranging from a fourteenth-century recorder, a beautiful inlaid sixteenth-century Viola da Gamba and a stunning Giovanni Celestini harpsichord. In the costume museum you will find an intriguing mix of clogs, corsets and exuberant costumes from period to punk.

At the other end of the same building is the **Museon**, an imaginative museum of education packed with exhibits relating to genealogy, biology, physics and human rights. If you have children in tow they would probably prefer to see the wacky planetarium, complete with state of the art projections at the **Omniversum**, President Kennedylaan 5 (programmes on the hour Tues–Thurs 11 a.m.– 4 p.m., Fri–Sun 11 a.m.–9 p.m. except 6 p.m., Admission f14). Smaller children would also enjoy a trip to the extensive model village at **Madurodam** (see p.314), a short bus ride away.

If you want to explore the Hague further there are plenty of parks and palaces. Parks are free for everyone to walk in – the locals will tell you they are safe but women walking alone may find the acres of seemingly deserted wooded common land a little unnerving. One of the nicest parks is the **Clingendael** (open dawn to dusk, Bus 18 from Centraal Station) with thickets of rhododendrons, a rosarium and an eighteenth-century Dutch garden. In May and June the delightful Japanese garden is open for people to enjoy the azaleas and cherry blossom. The only palace open to the public is **Vresdespaleis** or Peace Palace, Carnegieplein 1 (guided tours on the hour, Mon–Fri 10 a.m.–3 p.m., Admission f3; tram 4). The first international peace conference was held in 1899 in the Hague, after which it was decided to set up a permanent court of arbitration in the city. The Scottish-born steel magnate, Andrew Carnegie, donated a million pounds for its construction. Various nations have donated fittings, the Danish a fountain and the Japanese wall hangings and the overall effect is of rather brash opulence.

Near the Vresdespaleis is the magnificent **Panorama Mesdeg**, Zeestraat 65b (open Mon–Sat 10 a.m.–5 p.m., Sun noon–5 p.m.). The 120m canvas is one of the few surviving nineteenth-century panoramas in the world and the joint effort of H.W. Mesdag, his wife, Th. de Bock and the Amsterdam Impressionist H.B. Breitner.

Getting There Take the train from Amsterdam Central Station to Den Haag C.S. (Central Spoor). Trains leave four times an hour and the journey takes 50 minutes. Make sure your train is going to the Central Station since the other station, H.S. Hollandse Spoor, is a long way from the centre.

LEIDEN

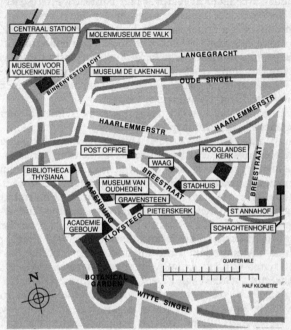

LEIDEN

The lively university town of Leiden is packed with interesting museums including the country's foremost archaeological museum, Museum van Oudheden. There is a delightful botanical garden and plenty of student cafés for relaxing in.

Leiden is famous for taking a brave stand against the Spanish in the sixteenth century. Approaching starvation, the besieged town was finally saved when William of Orange opened the dikes to flood Central Holland and changed the battlefields into a sea for his navy. The Spanish reputedly left in such a hurry that they left their dinner simmering on the fire. Even today every year, on 3 October, the locals celebrate over steaming pots of stew. William offered the town permanent tax exemption or a university and wisely they chose the latter – the university is the most prestigious in the country.

A short distance from the station you will see the **Museum de Valk** (open Tues–Sat 10 a.m.–5 p.m., Sun 1 p.m.–5 p.m. Admission f3), a working windmill complete with grinding stones, millers'

OUT OF THE CENTRE AND GETAWAYS

rooms and mechanical models. It's a steep climb up, not suitable for small children or arthritic joints, but the view of Leiden from the top is worth it. Not far away is the municipal museum **De Lakenhal** Oude Singel 32 (open Tues–Sat 10 a.m.–5 p.m., Sun 1 p.m.–5 p.m. Admission f2.50). The splendid old cloth hall is largely intact, but includes architectural features and entire rooms rescued from the old *Stadhuis*. The brewers' room upstairs, complete with murals of hop cutters, beer making and barrelling is fascinating. There are also some fine furniture and tiles and a good collection of paintings, a rather pastel-toned *Last Judgement* by Lucas van Leyden being among the better of them. Upstairs is a unique wall tapestry from 1574, depicting a map of the area and the movements of the Spanish and Dutch within it at the time.

Top of the list of Leiden's museums is the **Rijksmuseum van Oudeheden** at Rapenburg 28 (open Tues–Sat 10 a.m.–5 p.m., Sun 1 p.m.–5 p.m. Admission f3). This archaeology museum contains objects from ancient civilisations, as well as some Netherlandish finds. The huge Egyptian *Temple of Taffeh* makes a striking centrepiece in the main hallway. Upstairs the Egyptian mummies attract hordes of kids looking for something dead – lines of schoolchildren ogle at rows of mummified people, dogs, cats, an ibis and a crocodile. There is some fine Greek pottery and a splendid golden Roman warrior's helmet among the rooms of sarcophagi and temple fragments. Behind the museum is the fifteenth-century **St Pieterskerk** (open 1.30 p.m.–4 p.m. daily) which dominates a rather dishevelled square full of scavenging cats and socialising students. It's worth popping in to see the dried-up body found in a secret room under the pulpit. No one knows who it is, how it got there or how old it is.

Between 1609 and 1620 a group of English Puritans and their preacher, John Robinson, settled in Leiden. It was the same group of Pilgrim Fathers, minus their preacher, who went back to England and boarded the *Mayflower* at Plymouth and set out for the New World. For a slide show on the course of events visit the **Leiden Pilgrim Collection**, Vliet 45 (open Mon–Fri 9.30 a.m.–4.30 p.m.) which is close to the botanical garden.

The university's **Botanical Garden** (open Mon–Sat 9 a.m.–5 p.m., Sun 10 a.m.–5 p.m.) is one of the oldest in Europe, planted in 1594. Clog-wearing gardeners lovingly tend every tiny plant, but none will let on when it is that the giant water lily *Victoria Regia* is likely to flower. This immense specimen, capable of supporting three men on a single pad, flowers for one night only in the year.

Getting There Take the train from Amsterdam's Centraal Station for a 30-minute journey to Leiden; the station is a short walk from all the sights.

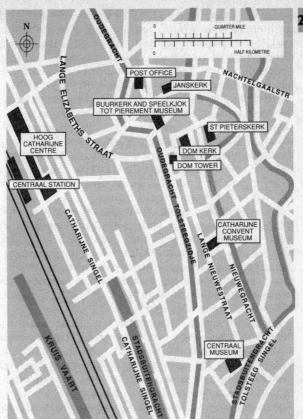

UTRECHT

As you get off the train direct to Utrecht from Centraal Station you are plunged into a busy, vast and unattractive shopping mall which is enough to make you turn tail and head for home. Don't. Utrecht may not be stunning, but it is a lively place where the streets sit high above sunken canals, shoppers dash around cobbled streets and the sights are both unusual and even unique. The museum 'From Carillon to Barrel Organ' is one of the most entertaining in the country. The convent of St Catharine has an enormous collection of Netherlandish religious artefacts which is a rare sight in this ardently Protestant country, and the Central Museum has some terrific works of art.

From the station follow signs to the VVV and this will take you out of the shopping mall. For an invigorating start go to the **National Museum van Speelklok tot Pierement** (from Carillon to

Barrel Organ) at Buurkerkhof 10 (open Tues–Sat; guided tours on the hour 10 a.m.–4 p.m., Sun 1 p.m.–4 p.m. Admission f5; English spoken if requested). Set in an old church, the museum traces the development of mechanical instruments from the eighteenth to the twentieth century. The tours are taken by amusing, entertaining and handsome music students who operate many of the instruments, play others, sing to some and dance when prompted. Children love the mechanical rabbit peeping from his cabbage and the musical chairs which pipe up when sat on; ancient juke boxes play catchy oldies and an extraordinary 'Phono Liszt Viola' (a pianola with three pneumatic violins) has a good crack at orchestral sounds. By the time you reach the marvellous display of barrel organs and ball-room organs you will be in the mood to join in. Children are allowed to help work some of them.

Just round the corner is the sturdy **Domtoren**, Domplein (open for guided tours on the hour from April–Oct, Mon–Fri 10 a.m.–4 p.m., weekdays noon–4 p.m., mid-Oct–March, weekends only noon–4 p.m. Admission f3). It's a long steep climb to the top, but you do have a chance to catch your breath at various levels as the guide explains the history of this austere fourteenth-century tower. It is not suitable for small children and even a reasonably fit person will suffer from wobbly legs by the end.

Opposite the city's cathedral, the **Domkerk** was separated from the tower by a massive earthquake in 1674 which brought the nave crashing to the ground. However the elegant choir, built between 1254–1321 in the style of Cologne Cathedral is evidence of the cathedral's former glory. Whether you are interested in religious memorabilia or not, it is worth paying a visit to the large **Rijksmuseum het Catharijne Convent**, Nieuwe Gracht 63 (open Tues–Fri 10 a.m.–5 p.m., weekends 10 a.m.–5 p.m. Admission f5) which concentrates on the history of Christianity in the Netherlands. Among lots of rather dreary paintings lie a few real treasures, including some exquisite medieval ivories and illuminated manuscripts in the basement and some fine renaissance sculpture by the Utrecht artist, Jan van Scorel.

The **Central Museum** in Agnietenstraat (open Tues–Sat 10 a.m.–5 p.m., Sun 1 p.m.–5 p.m. Admission f3, Bus 2) is a little further out of the centre, about 20-minutes' walk from the cathedral. Housed in a convent it is an eclectic mix of sculpture, painting, armour, costume, ceramics, decorative arts and period rooms, punctuated with contemporary art and photography, so be prepared to spend some time here and skip anything that doesn't appeal. The museum has works by Utrecht masters Abraham Bloemaert, Gerard van Honthorst and Jan Both. The twentieth-century collection includes works by Mondrian and the Dutch magic Realists Carel Willink, Pyke Kock and Charley Toorop (see p.166). Downstairs in the period rooms keep an eye out for a wonderful ceramic piece *Where Babies Come From* by contemporary artist Rhonda Zwillinger – a writing mass of arms, legs, placenta and organs set on the table like a bowl of fruit. Before leaving, take a look at the enchanting seventeenth-century dolls' house complete with ornamental garden, oil paintings, tortoiseshell mirrors and fine china table settings.

While long-term residents struggle to find even a tiny apartment to live in Amsterdam's tourists are spoilt for choice with lots of hotels and hostels, many situated along the most prestigious streets and canals, all within easy walk of main sights and attractions.

There are no bargains in the city, but with prices ranging from f15 for a dormitory bed to f700 for a room in the most expensive hotel in the Netherlands you can't fail to find something suitable.

Seventeenth-century travellers tended to stay in the old heart of the historic city where they tolerated, or enjoyed, the variety of brothels, inns and eating houses around Dam Square, but didn't have to contend with the traffic and neon lights that invade the area today. A few hotels in the Spui area capture something of the waterfront views that so impressed our predecessors and are well situated for excellent restaurants just around the corner. Many people dream of staying in a quaint little canal house along the Grachten Gordle with views along the canals and there are a number to choose from. Bear in mind that most converted seventeenth-century canal houses have incredibly steep and narrow stairs, small rooms, low beams and a lot of rooms that don't overlook the canal. They are often unsuitable for disabled and elderly people and, if beautifully furnished, you can guarantee that children won't be welcome. Many package tours use hotels in the quiet residential streets of the Museum Quarter. While they are close to all the major galleries and museums there is not such a concentration of restaurants in the area and you may find you have to walk a little further for your dinner. Apart from the lack of noise, the other main advantage of staying here is its proximity to Vondelpark for morning jogs and evening walks.

Hotels are star graded and priced by the Benelux Hotel Classification (Belgium, Netherlands and Luxembourg) according to their size and facilities, but this gives no indication of their character. Apart from giving a rough idea of price the stars say little – a large anonymous chain hotel will be awarded five stars for elevators, minibars, a trouser press and a shower cap while a small one-star canal house may be beautifully furnished with fine antiques, fresh flowers and Persian carpets. All hotels in this guide have been selected for their character, position, safety and suitability for women, old or young, alone or accompanied, or travelling with children.

The price of a room usually includes breakfast and Dutch breakfasts are good. Expect cheese, ham or salami (spam), an egg, rolls and tea or coffee in even the cheapest hotels. Breakfast is often charged as an extra in the larger hotels and it is advisable to take it if you are hungry since cafés and bars tend not to open much before 10 a.m.

The Dutch are notoriously clean and efficient so you can expect a clean room whatever price you pay. Bathrooms in cheaper hotels usually consist of a shower and WC and little more; at the end of the season don't be surprised to find paint peeling. Many of the cheap hotels have flimsy metal fold-away beds. You basically get what you pay for – the few exceptions, where you get more than is expected, tend to be in hotels run by gay men who put themselves out to make you welcome, comfortable and happy.

The majority of package tours use large hotels which are part of a chain and may be good value. Where companies use hotels listed here, the packages are very cheap and much better value than booking independently. That said, it is worth bearing in mind that customers booking through a package will probably be allocated the least attractive rooms.

If you wish to stay independently in the hotel of your choice book well in advance, particularly if you are there for New Year or between March and September. It is best to telephone to discuss what rooms are available; canal rooms can be pretty but noisy and it is often better to overlook a garden at the back. Proprietors are generally honest and are unlikely to encourage you to take a room if they know it won't suit when you arrive. You will be asked to pay a deposit and if they don't take credit cards (which is likely) you will have to send it by post. Prices, especially in the large hotels, are always negotiable during winter months or slack periods, so it is worth asking.

If you prefer to leave the booking to someone else use the National Reservations Service which is a free service for booking hotel rooms anywhere in the Netherlands. Write to them at PO Box 404, 2260 AK, Leidschendam, NL or telephone 070 320 2500 (from abroad tel. 31 70 320 2500). If you are planning to stay in a hostel it is a good idea to book in advance – a number of beds are allocated for reservation and it saves a scrum when you get there. If, however, you wish to leave accommodation arrangements until you arrive use the Amsterdam Reservations Service run by the Tourist Office VVV on Stationsplein (see p.13). For f3.50 they will find you somewhere to stay, but on busy days can only offer what is left. That usually means expensive or out of town, but staff will do their best to help. If you arrive late at night with nowhere to stay it is best to ring one of the hostels listed below.

Single travellers are not well catered for in Amsterdam. Single rooms are often poky, have shared bathrooms and you can be sure the room will be next to them. All this comes for around 80% of the price of a double room or more, so always check your room before you take it and if you don't like it say so. If on business it's a good idea to book a double room anyway to give you more space.

Businesswomen are generally better catered for in the large chain hotels, but those who don't need facilities and just want somewhere to relax may prefer something a little more intimate. The large hotels are frequented by businessmen and their escorts and working women are better off slouched in front of the telly in their rooms. No hotel offers lounges or dining rooms specifically for women.

The city has no hotel exclusively for lesbians despite the number of hotels for gay men. Some lesbians choose to stay in gay hotels, but find them predominantly geared for male visitors selling condoms, shaving cream and showing homosexual films on the hotel video programme. You should have few problems booking a room with a double bed in Amsterdam but some hotels are more receptive to lesbians than others. Hotels popular with lesbian visitors are *Quentin* (currently changing hands but the new owners plan to maintain its reputation) and *De Admiraal*.

Children are surprisingly unwelcome in a number of Amsterdam hotels which limits your choice, but at least means that hotels accepting children actually like them. Most of the larger hotels belonging to international groups have family rooms and offer good rates for families out of season. Cheaper places can usually put up extra beds for family members and most hotels rent cots for around f15 a night. Many families find the cheapest and often easiest options are to stay in a hostel or to rent a houseboat or studio room. Babysitting is not offered by many hotels, but there are good childminding agencies in the city (see p.308).

If you intend to stay for a week or more it may be worth considering renting a houseboat or apartment; neither are cheap but they offer far more independence at a similar price to a hotel. A number of cafés also hire out rooms and studios – look for signs outside or discreetly placed inside. If you have decided to stay on in the city, it is well worth asking over the bar of your favourite café – they may just have a little studio upstairs.

Students are well catered for in hostels, budget hotels and large shared hotel rooms. Also, most hotels have at least one family room for up to five people, well worth considering if you can't abide by curfews and communal showers.

Staying Alone

Despite the lack of facilities for single people in small hotels, they are definitely the best place to be if alone in the city. Staff have time to chat, they are keen to help you enjoy your stay and can recommend decent places to eat in the evening, introducing you to any other solo travellers who may be looking for company. Hotels in the Grachten Gordle area are all well suited to single travellers with restaurants close at hand and entertainment not far away. It is not advisable to stay in the Red Light District and lone businesswomen staying in the larger hotels around Dam Square may find the immediate area somewhat intimidating.

Staying on Business

As the city grows as an international business centre, more hotels are providing the basic facilities for businesspeople – faxes, telephones, meeting rooms, conference rooms, temps and translators – all at extra cost. All tend to be at the top end of the scale, the *Amstel* and the *Krasnapolsky* being definitely the best for people with serious work in hand. If you just happen to be attending a conference in Amsterdam, but have free time rather than office time to spare, it may be more enjoyable to take a smaller three- or four-star hotel.

BEST OF THE BUNCH

Luxury: **Amstel** (p.237)
Moderate: **Canal House** (p.239), **Wiechman** (p.240)
Inexpensive: **Agora** (p.236), **De Filosoof** (p.243), **Prinsenhof** (p.242)
Families: **Acacia** (p.240), **Arthur Frommer** (p.239), **Impaia** (p.241)
Businesswomen: **Krasnapolsky** (p.236), **Ambassade** (p.238)

Unless otherwise stated you can assume that your room will have a phone in each room, 24-hour reception or keys given to the guest, breakfast, bar and fax.

Map grid references given refer to their location on the detailed maps given in this book. Prices refer to the cheapest single to the most expensive double. The cheapest double is usually very close to the single price.

HOTELS

The Historic Centre

If you are in Amsterdam on business you are likely to be accommodated in the historic centre. Dam Square is noisy, touristy and on the edge of the Red Light District, but also a stone's throw from some excellent restaurants. Towards Spui brings you closer to the more salubrious night life and is central to all the sights.

ACCOMMODATION

GRAND HOTEL KRASNAPOLSKY
*****

*Dam 9, 1012 JS. Tel 554 9111. Fax
622 8607. Telex 12262 KRAS NL.
Tram 1, 2, 5, 13, 14, 16, 17, 24 to
Dam Square. On KLM Bus route
from Schipol or a 5-min walk from
Centraal Station.*

If you are organising a conference in
Amsterdam this is the place to do it.
The enormous hotel in the centre of
the city has the best business facilities
in town with a business centre, a
convention centre for up to 2,000
people and numerous smaller rooms
for meetings. An abundance of
flunkies dash around the striped sofas,
chairs and pot plants in the foyer with
messages, drinks and smiles, directing
people to their rooms, shops, meetings
and restaurants. Breakfast, banquets
and anything you wish for can be taken
in the famous winter garden, amid the
giant palms under the vast glass and
cast iron roof. Alternatively, tuck into
sushi in the Japanese restaurant, roast
quail in the plush Le Reflet d'Or or
swig Dutch beer in one of the many
bars. Rooms are tastefully decorated
though the soft pastel shades are
somewhat monotonous. There is a
beauty parlour and swimming pool.
All 317 rooms have air conditioning,
minibar, TV, coffee and tea-making
facilities. Rooms f350 to f425. Credit
cards: Master, Visa, Amex, Diners, EC.

HOTEL DE L'EUROPE *****
*Nieuwe Doelenstraat 2–8, 1012 CP.
Tel. 623 4836. Fax 624 2962. Telex
12081. Tram 4, 9, 14, 16, 24, 25 to
Muntplein.*

Excellent position overlooking the
Amstel with its own riverside terrace
and all the facilities and efficiency one
would expect from the renowned
Relais and Chateaux group, but little

of the old world charm that the
external architecture implies. All
rooms have private facilities, TV,
minibar, hairdrier and there is a health
centre and swimming pool for letting
off steam, plus business facilities for
working guests. In-house babysitting
facilities. Rooms f445 to f620. Credit
cards: Amex, Diners, Master, Visa,
traveller's cheques and Japanese cards.

DOELEN KARENA ****
*Nieuwe Doelenstraat 24, 1012 CP.
Tel. 622 0722. Fax 622 1084. Tram 4,
9, 14, 24, 25 to Muntplein and next
door to the Europe.*

Famous as the place where Rembrandt
painted the 'Night Watch', this
venerable building has been a hotel for
a hundred years. Rooms are
disappointingly small and the musty
decor could be brought up to date. At
least the canalside rooms have good
views, especially the corner suites
which look over water in three
directions. Business facilities,
bathrooms, minibars and TV in every
room. Rooms f280 to f345. Credit
cards: Amex, Diners, Master, Visa.

AGORA **
*Singel 462, 1017 AW. Tel. 627 2200.
Fax 627 2202. Tram 1, 2, 5 to Spui
and the hotel is on the opposite side of
the Singel, close to the flower market.*

The eighteenth-century canal house
was recently renovated to create a
modern and comfortable environment,
though carefully chosen fabrics,
beautiful antiques and the abundance
of fresh flowers in the communal
rooms maintain a genteel atmosphere.
Run by two of the most charming men
you will meet in Amsterdam, the
Agora is comfortable, friendly and
brilliantly situated. Breakfast is
accompanied by classical music in the

bright breakfast room and there is plenty of good art on the walls to keep you interested. Some rooms are fairly small, most have private facilities and all have a TV. There is a very nice family room in the attic. Rooms f100–f190. No bar. Credit cards: Amex, Master, Diners, Visa.

The Grachten Gordle

Most of the city's more charming hotels are situated in the Grachten Gordle, occupying historic canal houses with pleasant views and authentic fittings. The quieter hotels tend to be on one of the three main canals – Herengracht, Keizersgracht or Prinsengracht – the more cheap and cheerful places tend to be closer to the two centres for night life, Rembrandtsplein and Leidseplein. All are within easy reach of the main sights and good restaurants.

AMSTEL INTERCONTINENTAL
*****

Prof Tulpplein 1, 1018 GX. Tel. 622 6060. Fax 5808. Telex 11004. Tram 6, 7, 10 to the Amstel Hotel.

The grand Amstel Hotel recently reopened after a f70 million facelift, making it the most luxurious and expensive hotel in the Netherlands. Smart doormen discreetly welcome pop stars, politicians and millionaires into the vast galleried hallway with sweeping staircase, marble floor and deep leather sofas. With no expense spared you should find everything you need here. Businesswomen will find a personal fax and telephone answering machine in their bedrooms and plenty of desk space for working. If that is not enough there are office rooms and conference rooms available. Downstairs a beautician is on duty at the health club from 7 a.m.–11 p.m. or you can lounge around in the swimming pool, watching the boats float by on the Amstel just outside. Trips into town are easy in the hotel's Rolls Royce or motor yacht. This is the one place where you can expect to be pampered and rooms have everything you can think of. Rooms f700 to f925; suites f1400 to f4000. Credit cards: Amex, Diners, Master.

PULITZER *****
Prinsengracht 315–331, 1016 GZ. Tel. 523 5235. Fax 627 6753. Telex 16508. Tram 13, 14, 17 to Westerkerk.

The Pulitzer is run by the excellent CIGA chain who have a good reputation for high quality accommodation in historic surroundings. Twenty-four seventeenth-century canal houses on the Prinsengracht and the Keizersgracht have been carefully converted with the garden in the middle providing a peaceful retreat. The buildings are connected by a maze of passages, stairways and lifts. The restaurant is one of the best in town; its wine list is the longest and the chef is something of a master when it comes to sugar decoration. Peach quilted covers and matching upholstery are standard, but the decor varies according to the nature of the room, whether it is a beamed attic or a sedate *Sael*. Contemporary works of art add the final touch to each room, all of which have private bathrooms,

TV, minibar, hairdrier and safe. Communal rooms and conference rooms are elaborate. Rooms f395 to f525; suites f975; extra bed f70; breakfast f32. Credit cards: Amex, Diners, Master, Visa, EC.

AMERICAN ****
Leidsekade 97, 1017 PN. Tel. 624 5322. Fax 625 3236. Telex 1540 CBO NL. Tram 1, 2, 5, 6, 7, 10 to Leidseplein.

The uncompromising Art Deco building on the edge of busy Leidseplein was built as a hotel at the turn of the century and the café was once a gathering place for the city's literati. Today the plush hotel is run by a division of Intercontinental Hotels offering good facilities and little atmosphere. While it does have function rooms and basic business facilities working women may find it a bit soulless and the café is always teeming with non-residents trying out a posh place. All rooms have TV, minibar, hairdrier and private facilities. Fitness suite. Rooms f345 to f495; suites f1150 to f1725; breakfast f30. Credit cards: Amex, Carte Bleu, Diners, Master, Visa.

DIKKER EN THIJS ***
Prinsengracht 444, 1017 KE. Tel. 626 7721. Fax 625 8986. Telex 13161. Tram 1, 2, 5 to Prinsengracht.

You could spend all day working your way through the menus in the excellent restaurants on the ground floor or munching goodies from the famous Dikker and Thijs delicatessen next door, but the harsh black, grey and pink decor in the rooms is not exactly restful. All rooms in this small hotel have private facilities, minibar and TV. Rooms f250 to f365; breakfast f10.50 to f25; extra bed f75. Credit

cards: Amex, Master, Diners, Visa.

ESTHEREA ****
Singel 303–309, 1012 WJ. Tel. 624 5146. Fax 623 9001. Telex 14019. Tram 1, 2, 5 to Paleisstraat.

A rather soulless hotel which is popular with groups. Made up of eight pretty canal houses, the inside is disappointingly average with long dingy passages, plastic flowers, thick velvet curtains and reproduction prints on the walls. Rooms overlooking the canal are the only ones worth staying in. All rooms have private facilities (with bath and shower), TV, safe and hairdrier. Rooms f155 to f325; family rooms f250 to f425. Credit cards: Amex, Master, Diners, Visa.

SCHILLER KARENA ****
Rembrandtsplein 26–36, 1017 CV. Tel. 623 1660. Fax 624 0098. Telex 14058. Tram 4, 9, 14 to Rembrandtsplein.

For years the hotel was frequented by artists, writers and friends of the artist proprietor, Fritz Schiller, whose paintings hang throughout the hotel. A pianist plays old favourites in the lobby by day and moves into the popular restaurant at night. The staff are friendly, efficient and discreet about visiting pop stars. Rooms are small but comfortable. Good business facilities and all the services one would expect from a chain hotel, but the square is very noisy well into the early hours. Rooms f190 to f335. Credit cards: Amex, Diners, Visa, Master.

AMBASSADE ***
Herengracht 341, 1016 AZ. Tel. 626 2333. Fax 624 5321. Telex 10158. Tram 1, 2, 5 to Herengracht.

Eight seventeenth-century patrician houses along Amsterdam's grandest canal make up this popular hotel. They have been carefully converted to incorporate, where possible, the original rooms and fittings. Some rooms are very small, but all are elegantly decorated in quiet colours, pretty floral fabrics and furnished with antiques. A good choice for businesswomen looking for something more intimate with a very comfortable drawing room where you can peruse the papers from plush, silky salmon sofas under crystal chandeliers, or watch the boats go by on the canal outside. Some suites are entered through your own front door on the canal – rooms overlooking the water are by far the best and always in demand. The size and character of rooms varies enormously so always check the details when booking. All include TV, safe and private facilities. Rooms f215 to f265; suites and apartments f365 to f450. Credit cards: Visa, Amex, Master, Diners.

MERCURE ARTHUR FROMMER ***

Noorderstraat 46, 1017 TV. Tel. 622 0328. Fax 620 3208. Tram 16, 24, 25 to Prinsengracht.

No longer the 'five-dollar-a-day' establishment that was intended, this former complex of weavers' workshops is tucked away in quiet backstreets between canals and the museums. Run by the Mercure/Altea group, it is a fairly standard chain hotel but offers very good deals for families. Rooms f150 to f255; children under 16 free if sharing parents' room and in low-season weekdays, up to three children under 16 get a free room to themselves. All rooms have private facilities, TV and minibar. Credit cards: Amex, Master, Visa, Diners.

CANAL HOUSE ***

Keizersgracht 148, 1015 CX. Tel. 622 5182. Fax 624 1317. Telex 10611. Tram 13, 14, 17 to Westerkerk.

This has the atmosphere of a stately home where guests are made to feel as if they are joining a private house party. It's a beautifully converted canal house complete with intricate stucco work on the ceilings, marble entrance hall furnished with crystal chandeliers, Persian carpets and fine antiques taking you straight back to the seventeenth century. The huge breakfast room is magical with views over a pretty garden and a grand piano for guests to tinker on. Rooms vary in size, but all are impeccably decorated, furnished with period antiques (including the beds), homely, warm and very comfortable. All rooms have private modern bathrooms. No TVs since they are not in keeping with the atmosphere and no children under 12 for fear they might disturb the peace. Rooms f175 to f240. Credit cards: Amex, Diners, Master.

PRINSENGRACHT ***

Prinsengracht 1015, 1017 KN. Tel. 623 1666. Fax 627 4946. Tram 16, 24, 25 to Prinsengracht.

At the turn of the century it was the home of the Association for the Interest of Young Women. Today's hotel is equally welcoming to lonesome women but prices are a little high for the small rooms. All have private facilities and TV. Rooms f135 to f200. Credit cards: Amex, Master, Visa.

TOREN ***

Keizersgracht 164, 1015 CZ. Tel. 622 6033. Fax 629 9705. Tram 13, 14, 17 to Westerkerk.

An imposing seventeenth-century canal house in which Abraham

Kuyper, once Prime Minister, lived until 1923. Heavy pink bedspreads or satin look quilts, kitsch pictures, soft drink dispensers and a microwave in the passage contrast sharply with the grand breakfast room with chandeliers, marble fireplace and painted cherubs floating around on the ceiling. All rooms have private facilities, TV, hairdrier and safe. Rooms f135 to f185; family rooms f210 to f250. Credit cards: Visa, Master, Diners.

AMSTERDAM WIECHMANN **
Prinsengracht 328–330, 1016 HX. Tel. 326 3321. Fax 626 8962. Tram 13, 14, 17 to Westerkerk.

This impressive canal house was once a boarding house for actors and actresses performing at the Stadsschouwburg theatre just around the corner on Leidseplein. Today it is a comfortable family-run hotel lavishly furnished with antiques and ancient gadgets that would impress even a modest collector. The reception alone boasts a suit of armour, an old cannon and a gilt Russian Samovar. It generally attracts an educated bunch and is also a good option for families looking for something a cut above the average in this category. All rooms have private facilities. Rooms f135 to f250; family rooms for f250 to f300. No credit cards.

ACACIA *
Lindengracht 251, 1015 KH. Tel. 622 1460. Fax 638 0748. Tram 13, 14, 17 to Rozengracht.

A good cheap choice for families. The small hallway is crammed with umbrellas, buggies and coats. It is a family-run hotel, situated in a corner house on the edge of the lively Jordaan area. Whitewashed rooms contain the bare essentials (literally a bed), but all

have private shower and loo and some afford spectacular views down the canal. There is a wonderful corner room which sleeps up to four. Cots are provided free. Rooms f90 to f120; family rooms f220. For anyone wanting more space and cooking facilities studio rooms start at 140f and for the ultimate Amsterdam experience try the houseboat for 150f. No bar. Credit cards: Master, Visa.

ADOLESCE *
Nieuwe Keizersgracht 26, 1018 DS. Tel. 626 3959. Fax 627 4249. Tram 9, 14 to Waterlooplein.

Rosella, the resident parrot provides the entertainment in the lobby of this newly decorated (gutted) canal house where accommodation is basic, but good value for groups and families. Heavy-duty carpets, breeze block walls and minimal decor gives little to complain about, little to destroy and little to enjoy. It is a short walk from the centre and not as nice as the Fantasia just a few doors down. Some rooms have private facilities. Rooms f75 to f145; quads f175; dorms for five f200. Credit cards: Visa, Amex, Diners.

DE ADMIRAAL *
Herengracht 563, 1017 CD. Tel. and fax 626 2150. Tram 4, 9, 14 to Rembrandtsplein.

Once a brothel, the Admiraal is now a homely laid back sort of place, with an eccentric air about it. The breakfast room, reception and bar consist of a comfortable front room furnished with ancient pieces of furniture, a china cabinet, and a model of the ship *De Admiraal*. A mass of pictures hang from the brown carpeted wall and silver sugar bowls, candlesticks and the daily papers are scattered around the tables. Upstairs whitewashed walls, worn carpets, houseplants and wicker chairs give a scruffy but comfortable feel. Being just round the corner from Rembrandtsplein it is noisy at night, but it is great if you want to be out late yourself. Breakfast is particularly good here. Rooms have safe and TV. Rooms f75 to f155; triples and quads f50 to f70 per person. Room 6 is the best quad room you will find in the city with stunning views down Reguliersgracht and Herengracht. No official bar. Credit cards: Master, Amex.

SEVEN BRIDGES *
Reguliersgracht 31, 1017 LK. Tel. 623 1329. Tram 16, 24, 25 to Keizersgracht.

This small hotel on one of Amsterdam's most picturesque canals is cheerfully decorated with contemporary art, scattered rugs, pot plants and jolly bed covers. Every room is different, all comfortable and the atmosphere is so relaxed that it would be easy to spend the day lounging around in your room instead of seeing the city. Some rooms have bathrooms and TVs and breakfast is served in the rooms. Price f105 to f170; family rooms f170 to f280.

FANTASIA *
Nieuwe Keizersgracht 16, 1018 DR. Tel. 623 8259. Fax 622 3913. Tram 9, 14 to Waterlooplein.

A larger than average canal house on the 'other side' of the Amstel so it is close to the Opera House and a ten-minute walk to Rembrandtsplein. Good basic accommodation if rather dull decor. An overdone breakfast room with gas lamps, fake panelling and deep brown carpet sets the tone. Efficiently run by a friendly family who keep it spotlessly clean. Two rather mean single rooms are the only ones without shower and WC. Rooms

f75 to f145; triple f165; quad f200. No bar. Credit cards: Visa, Master.

DE HARMONIE *
Prinsengracht 816, 1017 JL. Tel. 622 8021.

A tiny family run canal house hotel close to Rembrandtsplein on a quiet stretch of canal which is best loved for the welcome rather than the facilities. Accommodation is cheap, cheerful, cramped and clean and no rooms have private facilities. Floral curtains, ageing bedspreads and checked table-cloths from the family collection liven up rather shabby rooms. Breakfast is served in the rooms, the staircase is very steep and there is no reception area due to lack of space. Ask for a canal view. Rooms f70 to f110; triple f150; quad f180. No bar. No credit cards.

HEGRA *
Herengracht 269, 1016 BJ. Tel. 623 5348. Fax 623 8159. Tram 1, 2 to Dam, Royal Palace.

A small family-run hotel close to Dam Square, offering basic accommodation in yet another converted canal house. You'll find steep stairs, worn carpets and textured paint, plus rooms barely large enough to swing a cat, but it is the cheapest hotel on Amsterdam's grandest canal. (There is a small Red Light District in the streets behind towards N.Z. Voorburgwal, but it is not intrusive.) Some rooms have showers. Price f65 to f145. No bar. Credit cards: Visa, Amex, Master.

IMPALA *
Leidsekade 77, 1017 PM. Tel. 623 4706. Fax 2–41216. Tram 1, 2, 5, 6, 7, 10 to Leidseplein.

Few hotels are as welcoming to families as the Impala, where even the breakfast room has a box of toys for walkabout

ACCOMMODATION

toddlers. Decor is scruffy, rooms are basic but a good size and the proprietors are kind and helpful. The street is lined with rather impersonal hotels and just off the busy Leidseplein, but the water frontage keeps noise levels low. TV in the breakfast room which doubles up as reception and bar. Rooms f70 to f100; family rooms f160 to f200. Credit cards: Visa, Mastercard.

VAN ONNA *
Bloemgracht 102–108, 1015 TN. Tel. 626 5801. Tram 7, 10, 13, 14, 17 to Rozengracht.

A budget hotel on one of the prettiest canals in the Jordaan. Worn carpets, peeling paint, uncomfortable beds and hideous selection of nylon bedspreads, but a jolly proprietor who has been here for years. The newly built house next door should offer some cleaner more up-to-date rooms in 1994. Rooms f50 per person. No bar. No credit cards.

PRINSENHOF *
Prinsengracht 810, 1017 JL. Tel. 623 1772. Fax 638 3368. Tram 16, 24, 25 to Prinsengracht.

If you are looking for something quaint, comfortable, quiet and extremely good value you couldn't choose a better hotel than the Prinsenhof which is a cut above anything else in this category. This genteel little canal house is beautifully decorated, furnished with antiques and numerous *objets d'art* and run by two charming men and a few of their friends. Curtains, covers and scatter cushions come in richly printed textiles, every room has deep wicker seats or plump upholstered chairs for relaxing and breakfast is served in a delightful blue breakfast room with central chandelier. Some rooms have private bathrooms. Rooms f75 to f165; triples f165 to f190; quad f230. No bar. No credit cards.

QUENTIN *
Leidsekade 89, IS. Tel. 626 2187. Tram 1, 2, 5, 6, 7 to Leidseplein.

This converted riverside villa has been a popular hotel with lesbians in recent years, but is changing hands in January 1994. Present owners and the faithful clientele are hoping it will continue to be the same peaceful, friendly place that it has been in the past. Prices cannot be predicted.

Museum Quarter

The Museum Quarter is full of hotels; towards the New South there is a concentration of expensive business hotels around Apollolaan and around the museums numerous smaller ones offer basic accommodation with no frills, many of them used by tour companies. There are some exceptions, well worth considering. The small area between the museums and Overtoom is particularly pleasant being close to Vondelpark, the flashy shopping street P.C. Hooftstraat and the theatres and nightlife on Leidseplein. Gourmets may find they have a little further to walk for a good meal if you wish to avoid the tourist traps in the immediate vicinity. If you are travelling with small children this is a good area to choose, close to playgrounds and running space in Vondelpark and on streets rather than canals.

HILTON AMSTERDAM *****
Apollolaan 2, 1077 BJ. Tel. 678 0780. Fax 662 6688. Telex 13647. Tram 5, 24 to Apollolaan.

This curvilinear concrete monstrosity is situated a short tram ride from the centre in the upmarket residential area of the New South. Apart from having all the facilities one would expect of the Hilton chain it is rather dull unless you fancy a night in the room where John Lennon and Yoko Ono staged their 'Bed In', surrounded by Beatle memorabilia with the first five bars of *All You Need is Love* painted on the ceiling. Not a good choice for businesswomen who will find the bar full of international businessmen and their escorts, and not great for tourists who will need transport into town. All rooms have TV, bathrooms, hairdrier and minibar. Rooms f390 to f630. Credit cards: Amex, Diners, Master, Visa and traveller's cheques.

MEMPHIS ****
De Lairessestraat 87, 1071 NX. Tel. 673 3141. Fax 673 7312. Tram 16 to Jacob Obrecht Straat.

A good choice for businesswomen who need a hotel in the vicinity of the Hilton, but prefer something smaller and more intimate. Rooms are comfortably decorated with floral print curtains and matching covers and upholstered furniture, generous hanging cupboards and marble bathrooms. A good bar for relaxing in and friendly staff. Main drawbacks are the piped music and the busy road running alongside, but it is close to small restaurants for eating alone and Vondelpark for evening and weekend walks. All rooms have TV and minibar. Rooms f285 to f450. Credit cards: Amex, Visa, Master, Diner.

AALDERS ***
Jan Luykenstraat 13–15, 1071 CJ. Tel. 662 0116. Fax 673 4698, Tram 2, 3, 5, 12 to Van Baerlestraat.

Just around the corner from the Van Gogh Museum and a stone's throw from P.C. Hooftstraat for upmarket shopping and people watching, the Aalders is a comfortable, friendly place in an excellent position. Rooms f95 to f185. Credit cards: Visa, Amex, Master.

OWL HOTEL ***
Roemer Visscherstraat 1, 1054 EV. Tel. 618 94 84. Fax 618 94 41. Tram 1 to the first stop on Overtoom.

A stuffed owl peers from a glass case on the façade – a reference to the wise lawyers who once lived here. Inside it is modern, comfortable and verges on clinical. A generous patch of lawn and proximity to Vondelpark and the main museums make this a good choice for families wanting to avoid the stress of the city centre; however, the babysitting is not cheap at f1.16 per hour. All rooms have bathrooms and TV. Rooms f115 to f190; triples from f250; extra beds f30; cots f15. Credit cards: Visa, Master, Amex.

HOTEL DE FILOSOOF **
Anna vd Vondelstraat 6, 1054 GZ. Tel. 683 3013. Fax 685 3750. Tram 1 from Central Station to Overtoom.

Ex-air steward and philosophy teacher, Ida Jongsma, runs one of Amsterdam's most attractive and distinctive hotels which is as much a centre of philosophy as a unique place to stay. Each room carries an intellectual theme: behind the painted sun on the door of Room 21 the names of great metaphysicians run around the frieze and across the curtains while a picture of Rodin's thinker reflects a contemplative mood; the Aristophanes room (No. 27) has clouds painted across the ceiling, quotations from the play float around the walls and a seagull mobile sways in the breeze. Breakfast is served on the covered verandah overlooking the garden with Vondelpark beyond. The hotel has another building across the road where the spacious Japanese or Persian rooms are particularly good for families or anyone wanting to be detached from the main hotel. The hotel bar and dining room host local philosophy and women's groups as well as the Dutch Labour Party, so there is no shortage of intelligent conversation. Ida's group of Practical Philosophers have a European reputation and they even offer *Diners Pensants* in the hotel, so you can enjoy a good meal while discussing your chosen query with a member of the group. Book early. All rooms have TV; some have bathrooms. Rooms f90 to f205; family rooms from f255. Credit cards: Amex and Visa.

HOTEL ENGELAND **
Roemer Visscherstraat 30, 1054 EZ.

Tel. 612 9691. Fax 618 4579. Tram 1, 2, 5, 6 to Overtoom.

One of a row of nineteenth-century houses designed to illustrate seven national architectural styles – German, French, Spanish, Italian, Russian, Dutch and English. It is a pleasant, small hotel with garden in a quiet street close to the museums, Vondelpark and Leidseplein. All rooms have TV; some have bathrooms. Rooms f785 to f195; family rooms f155 to f275. No bar. Credit cards: Amex, Master, Visa.

ACRO **
Jan Luykenstraat 44, 1071 CR. Tel. 662 0562. Fax 675 0811. Telex 10415. Tram 2, 3, 5, 12 to Van Baerlestraat.

Clinical, no frills modern accommodation which is well maintained and in an excellent position for a weekend's sightseeing. All rooms have private bathrooms and there is a TV lounge, bar and self-service restaurant. Rooms f100 to f150; family rooms for three/four f180 to f240. Credit cards: Amex, Master, Visa.

BUDGET: YOUTH HOSTELS, DORMITORIES AND CAMPING

There is no shortage of cheap, basic bunk-bed accommodation in Amsterdam but as hundreds of backpackers will testify, the quality varies enormously and your experience usually depends on who you are sharing with. Not all are ideal for women and if you are travelling alone it is best to avoid mixed dorms to ensure a hassle-free night. All those listed below are in excellent locations and have women-only dormitories. The main drawbacks of hostelling are curfews, daytime closures and rules. You may prefer to spend a little more for an anarchic budget hotel. Book early for all hostels.

The Dutch Youth Hostel Association (NJHC) has two good hostels in the city. To stay you should be a member of the International Youth Hostel Federation (IYHF) or you can pay an extra f5 a night. Visitors should be under 35 but, like everything in Holland, staff are usually flexible.

Hostels

STADSDOELEN (NJHC)
Kloveniersburgwal 97, 1011 KB, C.
Tel. 624 6832. Tram 4, 9, 14, 16, 24,
25 or 15-min walk from Central
Station.

Large single-sex dorms (sometimes mixed in busy periods) with canal views, good communal rooms, bar, restaurant and tiny open air courtyard. Near to the Red Light District, but in an excellent position and only a minute away from the University mensa for cheap grub. Good if you are on your own. Rates are f21.50 (sheets f6); f24 July and August.

VONDELPARK (NJHC)
Zandpad 5, 1054 GA, OW. Tel. 683
1744. Tram 1, 2, 5 to Vondelpark.

Great situation on th edge of Vondelpark, close to museums and Leidseplein. Slightly better facilities than the other NJHC Hostel, but bigger dorms and less personal. Costs f23 (sheets f6).

EBEN HAEZER (CHRISTIAN YOUTH HOSTEL)
Bloemstraat 179, 1016 LA, IW. Tel.
624 4717. Tram 13, 14, 17 to
Rozengracht.

Cheapest in town, in the lively Jordaan area, but early curfew at midnight weekdays and 1 a.m. weekends is frustrating. Religious wall decoration and prayer sessions (not compulsory) are not intrusive, but evident. Cheap food and nice courtyard garden. f15.

ADAM AND EVA
Sarphatistraat 105, 1018 GA, IE. Tel.
624 6206. Tram 6, 7, 10 to
Sarphatistraat.

Not a great location but worth trying if you can't get into the others. No curfew. f21.50 (sheets f6).

BOB'S YOUTH HOSTEL
N.Z. Voorburgwal 1012 SG, C. Tel.
623 0063. Tram 2, 5, 13, 17 or 5-min
walk from Centraal Station.

Only stay here if you are desperate; not recommended for lone travellers. f20.

Dormitories

UNIVERSAL BUDGET HOTEL
Leidsegracht 76, 1016 CR. Tel. 624
2784. Tram 1, 2, 5 to Leidseplein.

If you can't abide by rules, like to drink, smoke and play music into the night and don't mind small mixed rooms this is for you; cheap, cleanish and in the Jordaan close to the night life. Staff are laid back and friendly. f30 per person in four-bedded rooms.

Camping

Despite the weather in the Netherlands camping can be fun and there are a number of campsites within striking distance of the city. For a full list contact the VVV in Amsterdam.

HET AMSTERDAM BOS
Kleine Noordijk 1, 1432, Aalsmeer.
Tel. 641 6868. Fax 640 2378.
Reception open April–Oct 8 a.m.–10
p.m. Bus 171, 172.

Probably the nicest for families and
the quietest. Situated in the park,
Amsterdamse Bos, with the added
attractions of water sports and horse
riding close by, and a 30-minute bus
ride into town. Price includes car,
pitch for your own tent and showers
per person, per night. Adults f7.30,
4–12s f3.65, under 4s free. Electricity
f3 per night. Four-person cabins f46,
two persons f27.50 (take bedding).

VLIENGENBOS
Meeuwenlaan 138, 1022 Amsterdam.
Tel. 638 8855. Bus 32. Reception
open April–Sept 8 a.m.–11 p.m.

A small site, only ten minutes by bus
from Centraal Station, close to the
River Ij and popular with young
people, so it can get noisy. Over 30s
f6.75, 14–30s f5.75, 3–14s f4.50,
under 3s free. One person plus car
f8.75; camper plus two people f15.50;
showers f1.50.

Apartments and Houseboats

Apartments and houseboats can often work out cheaper than booking hotel rooms if you intend to stay for any length of time. If you
are looking for somewhere to stay permanently see p.51, but for
short stays the following agencies should be able to help. Be
warned: you are liable to heavy commission fees and tax on top of
the price quoted, so confirm the final total before committing yourself. Many of the smaller hotels and cafés also have apartments or
houseboats to offer or can put you on to others who do. (See *Acacia
Hotel* and *Lucky Mothers Café*.)

RIVERSIDE APARTMENTS
Amstel 138, 1017 AD. Tel. 627 9797.
Open Mon–Sat 9 a.m.–5 p.m.

Luxury furnished flats cost around
f4,500 a month for two to three
persons. Available for a minimum of
one week.

GIS APARTMENTS
Keizersgracht 33, 1015 CD. Tel. 625
0071. Open weekdays 10 a.m.–5 p.m.

Mainly luxury flats for visiting
businesspeople, but you may be lucky
and find them letting a private flat for
owners on holiday. Expect to pay over
f600 per week for a short-term let.

AMSTERDAM APARTMENTS
N.Z. Voorburgwal 63, 1012 RE.
Tel. 626 5930. Open Mon–Sat 9 a.m.–
5 p.m.

Rates start from f600 per week for a
studio flat or small apartment.

EATING AND DRINKING

EATING

There is no shortage of places to eat in Amsterdam, but choosing where to go can be a problem. The Dutch eat early so many restaurants close their kitchens by 10 p.m. or even 8 p.m. and booking is essential for most good restaurants which for weekenders means a phone call before you leave.

The choice is enormous. Unless you specifically wish to try Dutch cuisine you can sample food from almost any country under the sun whether it is Indonesian, Mexican or Japanese. French is considered the best, as it has been since the Napoleonic era but, whatever the cuisine, you will find that most kitchens are subject to various international influences. This applies especially to menus in the more refined restaurants. While Thai and Japanese places are currently in vogue, the most tantalising are the Indonesian restaurants whose presence here dates back to colonial days.

By international standards, eating out in Amsterdam is particularly good value with an average meal costing less than f50 without drinks. Even better value and atmosphere is found in the numerous brown cafés and designer bars which usually designate an eating area away from the bar and offer interesting menus mixing local and international dishes. For snacks and light lunches there are also plenty of cafés and coffee shops.

Eating alone in any city can be a little daunting, but in Amsterdam you will find plenty of places where you can relax and enjoy a meal without feeling self-conscious or hurried. If you walk into a restaurant to find no one sitting on their own it is probably because they have a singles table (not as bad as it may sound); if you want to be alone choose a place that has tables for one, bar seats or single seats staring out of the window. Remember to look confident, happy and assertive when it comes to dealing with waiters. If you don't like the table say so – remember you are a customer and you should get what you want.

It is a good idea to take a book with you or some postcards to write to keep you busy or the wait for courses can seem endless. If you don't feel comfortable in a place quietly notify the waiter that you don't want to eat there after all and leave. You are unlikely to be hassled by anyone – if the Dutch have a meal in front of them you are likely to be the last thing on their minds. If, however, you find yourself next door to a group of leering men and the waiter doesn't offer you another seat just ask to move or leave the restaurant. Restaurants are not really the place for making friends, but if you are lonely it is worth going to the smaller cheaper ones where tables are so close that you can't fail to talk to your next door neighbour. Vegetarian restaurants are usually full of friendly single people.

Eating Indonesian food in a group is a highly enjoyable experience, sharing dishes or dipping into the mass of different dishes that make up a *Rijstafel*. Eating Indonesian food alone can be a bit depressing as most of the full meals on the menu are usually for two and you end up eating *Nasi Rames*, which is a basic meal on a plate for one. It may be good, but you miss out on the multitude of tastes that make Indonesian food so exhilarating.

Eating out with children should not pose a problem. Most restaurants welcome children and many have high chairs and children's menus to help you out. It is best to choose a place with these facilities to avoid being turned away by frosty waiters and, if booking, check that children are welcome. Taking small babies is more difficult because of lack of space for carrycots or buggies in many restaurants and dense smoke in the bars and cafés. When booking it is best to check the seating arrangements and no smoking areas. Changing facilities in restaurants are almost universally non-existent and the loos are invariably tiny. If you are breastfeeding choose a corner seat where you can swing arms and feed comfortably and discreetly without elbowing the people on the next door table. The high-backed pews favoured in some places are a godsend. For all children pancake restaurants are great while Italian restaurants are the most welcoming.

Eating on a shoestring in Amsterdam is relatively easy and needn't be boring. Snacks from raw herring to hard boiled eggs and cones of chips, are readily available on street corners, from street dispensers and in bars. A bowl of soup may not sound sustaining, but when you have downed your first bowl of pea soup for around f5 you will understand the meaning of substantial. Unbelievably cheap meals can be had at the mensa which, unlike most university food halls, is quite a trendy and pleasant place to eat despite very early closing at 6 p.m. If you want to splash out you should be able to get a decent meal at a brown bar, a bowl of *fondue*, a pizza or a delicious vegetarian concoction for under f25.

DRINKING

With 1,402 cafés and bars in Amsterdam you are spoilt for choice whether you want a quick shot of caffeine, a cool frothy beer or an ice-cold genever. Some sell food, some not, some alcohol and some are primarily places for smoking dope.

If you are looking for a good place to relax over the papers with a coffee try one of the bright designer bars like *Puccini* or *De Americain*, the women's bar *Françoise* or the dark intellectual atmosphere in the brown café next door to the library, *Het Molenpad*. People watching is always fun around lunch time from the cool veranda of *De Kroon* on Rembrandtsplein or the lively patio outside the *Vertigo* café in Vondelpark. For a view over the city go to the top floor of the department store *Metz*. For the best cream teas choose *Greenwoods* on the Singel. For writing letters the quiet *Sluyswacht* near Waterlooplein is unbeatable – when you have finished join immaculate transvestites, tatty hippies and a theatrical bunch at *Tisfris*, just across the road. For early evening drinks the best *genever* is to be had at *De Drie Fleschjes* (along with the best chat-up lines) and the place to meet people is at the *Luxembourg* in Spui. If you want to experience your first smoking coffee shop, but are not sure if you have the courage then head for *Lucky Mothers* where you could drink coffee and watch the canal out of the window without needing even a whiff of marijuana to make you feel good.

Drinking alone is quite normal in Amsterdam; if you find it boring then choose somewhere with live entertainment like the *Engelbewaarder* where they have live jazz every Sunday afternoon or you may prefer a gallery café like *Leg Af*, where you can sip coffee while taking in the latest art exhibition on the wall. Women are less often seen alone in the ancient drinking houses known as *proeflokaalen* where there is usually standing room only and the idea is to drink a quick genever and then leave. If alone, expect a few annoying but harmless jeers from the clientele.

You can usually tell as you enter a place what it is like and who is drinking in there. Always take a quick look around before ordering your drink and if you don't like what you see leave; if you feel embarrassed make an excuse such as looking for a friend. Some bars, especially around Dam Square and the Red Light District, are particularly dodgy – full of pimps, drug dealers and sleazy looking businessmen who make it quite clear that they don't want company as soon as you show your face around the door. Don't go any further. It is not worth stirring trouble for the sake of a few drops of liqueur. It's best to steer clear of this area altogether when it comes to solo drinking.

One place you will always be welcome are the women's cafés. *Café Sarrein* in the Jordaan is currently the most popular and hub of the lesbian scene, *Vive la Vie* attracts a sociable bunch off Rembrandtsplein and *Café Vandenburg* in the Jordaan is great if you want to combine a drink with a meal.

One warning: Don't get drunk anywhere alone – an inebriated female is asking for trouble.

Coffee, Tea and Chocolate

Coffee is served throughout the day in bars and cafés until around 11 p.m. when many stop serving it altogether. Espresso is thick, strong and black served with evaporated milk or *koffiemelk* and very rarely with fresh milk. If you want a larger white coffee you need to ask for *koffie verkeerd* (literally coffee wrong) in which case you will get a 50/50 mixture with fresh milk. Many bars and restaurants also serve cappuccino. Tea is seldom served with milk unless you ask for it, but most cafés have a good selection to choose from, including herbal teas and infusions. Expect to be given a pot of water with a bag on a string to dangle in it. Chocolate, hot and cold, is deliciously rich, thick and dangerously addictive in cold weather. For a real treat order it with piles of whipped cream (*slagroom*) on the top. Children can spend hours spooning it off, sprinkling sugar into it and stirring it in. Another popular warmer is *anijsmelk*, warm milk with aniseed flavouring.

Soft Drinks

As a nation obsessed with beer and gin or more warming hot drinks, the Dutch have little time for special soft drinks, but consume large quantities of Pepsi and Fanta in hot weather. Prices for soft fizzy drinks (*frisdranken*) are roughly the same as beer. Fruit juices (*vruchtensap*) are available in most bars as is water, still or sparkling. Expectant mothers will be lucky to find non-alcoholic beers on menus and in bars, but it is worth asking.

Alcohol

Women have always drunk beer in Amsterdam and have been in the business from the start. In 1592, a formidable woman named Wijcher Elders opened one of the first, if not *the* first, commercial brewery in the city at the Port van der Cleve behind Dam Square. Beer (*bier*) means lager and is usually referred to as *pils*. Heineken, Amstel, Oranjeboom, Riddler and Grolsch are all widely available. It is usually served in a small glass with at least an inch of head on the top and costs around f2.50. In the summer people tend to drink the lighter lemon beer (*witbier*) served with a slice of lemon. Heineken also do a nutritious darker beer, *Oude Bruin*, similar to Guinness and recommended for breastfeeding mothers. Other darker beers – draught and bottled and usually Belgian – are available for people who prefer bitter; Trappist and Kriek are among the strongest.

One thing everyone should try is *genever* or *jenever*, the local gin which is made from molasses and flavoured with juniper berries,

drunk neat from tiny glasses filled to the brim. It comes in different
ages, *jong*, *oud* and *zeer oud* (young, old and very old), the flavour
mellowing the older it is. In Amsterdam they refer to them as *jong*
and *oud borrel*. Prices start at around f2.50 a glass. There are also
lots of flavoured versions, lemon *citroen-genever* and a sweet black-
currant *bessengenever* being the most popular. A strange herb-
flavoured one (*schelvispekel*) is worth a try if you are feeling
adventurous. Genever is not as strong as English gin, but certainly
strong enough to treat with caution. Don't have another until you
have felt the effects of the first. If you are looking for total collapse
order a *kopstoot* (knock on the head) which is pils with a genever
chaser.

Sweet liqueurs are also popular at the end of a meal. *Advocaat*
or eggnog is the best known, blue *Curacao* is the most colourful and
there are numerous fruit brandies to choose from. The Dutch
brandy, *Vieux*, is not up to French standards, but drinkable. Other
non-Dutch spirits are sold everywhere but can be very expensive
especially in clubs. If you stick to Dutch beer and gin you can drink
relatively cheaply and both cost very little in supermarkets.

Wine is not a very popular drink and most restaurants have disappointing lists with an abundance of German labels. Bars and
restaurants usually offer a drinkable (just) house wine (*wijn*, *rood*
or *wit*). Wine is not cheap.

Street Snacks and Fast Food

If you have a severe hangover the Dutch swear by gulping down a
raw herring and onions from one of the many street stalls to be
found all over the city; the shock of one wet salty fish early in the
morning seems to do the trick, but you may find it difficult to get
rid of the taste for the rest of the day. The better stalls will also have
mussels, mackerel rolls, smoked eel and the more palatable pieces of
deep-fried cod. If you are in need of something sweet, similar stalls
sell waffles (*stroopwafel*) or pancakes covered in maple syrup. A
more filling alternative is *poffertjes*, little dough balls served with
butter and rolled in icing sugar, or *oliebollen*, greasy doughnuts
with apple filling. At Christmas they sell a heavy currant bread with
marzipan in the middle which comes out again at Easter as *Paas
Brood*. Those unwilling to buy off the street will soon smell a baker
where you can pop inside and buy *amandelkoek*, special biscuits
filled with almond paste, or soft cinnamon biscuits known as *speku-
laas*.

The Dutch have got fast food down to a fine art – consuming
large quantities of chips from a cone with globs of mayonnaise
(*fritesaus*) seems to be a national pastime. If you don't like mayonnaise try them with goulash or curry instead. Another popular
snack is *kroketten* or croquettes in which cheese or meat are

mashed into a gluey paste, rolled in breadcrumbs and deep fried. These are available in every fast-food joint and if you are in a hurry buy them from a street dispenser where you select your item, pay around f1.50 and wait for the revolving display to deliver a cardboard carton with the greasy contents. For Dutch fast food, Febo is the largest chain but you will also find a smattering of international names like McDonalds and Burger King. Alternative Indonesian fast-food joints selling sate and noodles are dotted around the city, but for seriously good ethnic snacks try the snack bars at the Albert Cuyp market.

Main Meals

While you are eating your way through an enormous breakfast in your hotel most Amsterdammers are probably starting the day on a cheese roll and a cup of coffee. Lunch for most people is a quick snack, another roll or a slab of applecake; a hot lunch as we consume in America and England is virtually unheard of in the Netherlands. Instead, around 6 p.m., a ravenous nation tuck into their main meal of the day – between 6 p.m. and 8 p.m. the streets seem strangely quiet while the chink of cutlery and chatter drifts from open windows and doors, and the city's restaurants are full.

Be warned: to eat a three-course meal in any restaurant you have to be very hungry. Portions are enormous so it is wise to order one course at a time or you might be overfaced, not forgetting that the desserts are often the best part of a Dutch meal. Many restaurants also serve bread with garlic butter before the meal. The Dutch are not renowned for their culinary skills. Seventeenth-century visitors were appalled by thick stews and tasteless broths, surprised by the quantity consumed in one sitting and amazed at the Dutch capacity for alcohol. Abbe Satre reckoned that at a banquet lasting over five hours some guests, men and women, drank as much as fifty glasses of wine each and, while gaining a ruddy complexion, none of them was actually drunk. If you wish to try Dutch food for yourself *hutspot* (hotchpotch) is a thick, rather dull stew of meat and vegetables including huge lumps of watery potato. *Erwtensoep*, thick pea soup with sausage in it and a side dish of raw smoked bacon and pumpernickel bread is good for cold winter days and *Uitsmijter*, a slab of bread with fried eggs and cheese, ham or beef on top is a nourishing if unexciting experience. Among the most delicious fish starters try eel, usually smoked and presented in thin slices with a piece of lemon. For good Dutch food the fish dishes in Dutch restaurants (as long as you steer clear of stews) are usually very tasty. Vegetables are usually overcooked to the point of being soggy, large quantities of mashed or boiled potatoes are served with most meals and salads often include a generous amount of grated carrot and sweetcorn.

If you decide not to eat Dutch don't be surprised to find international dishes greatly tempered for Dutch tastes. Dishes that sound refined may well come piled high with mashed potato in a bland sauce and the combination of vegetables is often unusual. Few Indonesian restaurants serve authentic cuisine, but have developed something a little more palatable for Dutch taste-buds, usually meaning less hot.

If you decide to try real Indonesian food it is best to order *ristafel* (literally a rice table) made up of a number of delicately prepared, beautifully presented dishes which you should work through in gradual degrees of heat. Start with the mild selection and work your way up to the very hot. Waiters should explain where to start and what you are eating as they bring it to the table. Don't tuck into the hot immediately as it could deaden your taste-buds for the rest of the meal, and be warned, if they say hot they mean hot; even a harmless looking lettuce leaf can blow your head off.

Brown Cafés and Designer Bars

Gezelligheid, meaning cosy, comfortable and welcoming (in a Dutch way) is one of those words most commonly associated with cafés, bars and eating places. The Dutch are masters at making a place feel welcoming and comfortable. Apart from a few exceptions around Rembrandtsplein and Leidseplein, nearly all the cafés in the city are relaxed places to be, whether they are full of well-groomed young things, middle-aged hippies or old men playing chess. The brown cafés are unique to the Netherlands in a way that pubs are to Great Britain. Invariably dingy, with smoked-stained walls, wooden floors and the day's papers strewn across the tables they are usually relaxing by day and busy by night. These cafés started out as drinking houses, and for many people they still are, but many now offer food, from light snacks to three-course meals, earning them the name, *eetcafés*. Most offer a very good dish of the day (*dagschotel*) for around f15. Apart from lower prices there is little to distinguish some of them from restaurants, other than a bar crammed with locals every night. They can be especially good places to eat on your own and if you choose one with live music you will have entertainment laid on as well. Bars which haven't given in to providing food often have a pool table in the back room. The drink-only variety are less busy and although quite safe for single women they tend to be more popular with men.

In contrast to the brown cafés are the designer bars – chic, clean establishments frequented by smart young people, media names and tourists who are worried about the health regulations in the brown cafés. Music is usually very loud and the clientele as clean cut as the fittings. These cafés are equally suitable for single people and great for reading the papers, people watching, eating and killing time.

One thing brown cafés and designer bars have in common is that you can spend as long as you like over a single drink without feeling obliged to buy another. Cafés are about relaxing and socialising; both serve alcohol but the clientele determines the nature of the booze. Generally people drink beer, gin or wine in the brown cafés while in designer places you are more likely to see exotic cocktails and spritzers lining the bar. Most cafés with or without a restaurant have a variety of nibbles to stave off hunger – peanuts come in their shells, *bittenballen* are similar to croquettes, served with mustard and *chorizo* sausage or tortilla chips are popular alternatives.

As with restaurants, if you want to eat in a brown café booking is advisable and be warned: the kitchens often close as early as 9 p.m.

Cafés and Coffeeshops

'Coffeeshop' in Amsterdam usually refers to a sedate little tea house selling non-alcoholic beverages and delectable cream cakes, light lunches or handmade chocolates. It can also refer to the 'Smoking Coffeeshops' where people go to buy and smoke marijuana (see below). The two are easily distinguishable, but the gentle version provides wonderful bolt holes for women in the city with comfortable seating, gentle music (usually classical) and scrummy things to eat, mainly in the company of other women. Particularly recommended are *Greenwoods, PC* and the delightful women's café, *Françoise*.

Smoking Coffeeshops

If you want to get stoned this is where to do it. If you smoke marijuana in other cafés you are likely to be asked to leave or put out your precious joint. Smoking coffeeshops are easily recognisable by psychedelic colours painted on the windows, marijuana plants, obligatory playing of Bob Marley over the hi-fi and a string of mellowed people staring into space. Ask at the bar if you want to see the catalogue of dope for sale. Apart from selling marijuana some are licensed to sell alcohol. In general those that don't have a nicer atmosphere – if alone, choose between *Lucky Mothers* and *Rusland*. Some can be quite daunting if you are sober and female. If you have kids in tow *Lucky Mothers* is the only suitable one that we have found. Space cake (cake laced with the weed) is becoming something of a rarity these days due to tourists overdosing on it, but if you don't want to smoke and wish to try it be careful; ask what is in it and preferably don't try it alone. For information on drugs and the law see p.28.

Proeflokaal

Once free drinking houses for sampling wares before buying barrels of hooch, the *proeflokaalen* are among the oldest drinking houses in the city. Primarily for genever drinking, today there is seldom seating and the idea is to drop in for a shot of alcohol and leave (after paying). They are not really a women's domain but worth popping into, if only to get a glimpse of ageing barrels, gleaming brass taps and a load of drunken Dutchmen.

CHOOSING, BOOKING AND OPENING HOURS

You can eat full meals in restaurants, eetcafés, and some brown cafés, designer bars and cafés, so the following places are listed with full meals, snacks and drinks to help you differentiate. Confusingly, lunch is not considered a main meal in the Netherlands so you will find many places do not do full meals at lunch time but snacks, from filled rolls to applecake, are available almost everywhere. Dutch people eat early so many kitchens close by 10 p.m., even if the venue stays open until 1 a.m.

Booking

Always book your restaurant either on the day or preferably a couple of days before, and turn up on time. If taking children inform the restaurant when booking. Tipping is not necessary, but a small tip (around f5) is polite.

Opening hours

These vary considerably but most **restaurants** serve dinner from 5 p.m. to 10 p.m., staying open a little later on Friday and Saturday nights.

Brown cafés and designer bars are generally open from 4 p.m. to 1 a.m., and later at weekends, but some open from around 11 a.m. Those offering full meals tend to serve food from 5 p.m. to 10 p.m. Unlicensed cafés and coffeeshops open around 10 a.m.–6 p.m.; licensed ones tend to start later and stay open until 1 a.m. *Proeflokalen* open around midday till 8 p.m.

EATING HIT LIST

Mid-morning coffee and cakes – **Françoise** (p.269), **Pompadour** (p.269)
Full lunch – **De Gouden Reale,** (p.273) **Beddingtons** (p.270)
Snack lunch – **Het Karbeel** (p.258), **Backstage Boutique** (p.269), **PC** (p.271)
Tea – **Greenwoods** (p.263), **Metz** (p.295), **Françoise** (p.269)

For dinner

Expensive – **De Gouden Reale** (p.273), **Silveren SpiegeL** (p.256), **'T Swarte Schaep** (p.266)
Moderate – **Helmese Modder** (p.271), **Toscanini** (p.264), **Sluizer Vis** (p.266), **Belhamel** (p.262)
Cheap – **Eeetuin** (p.265), **Luden** (p.261), **Van den burg** (p.265)
Very cheap – **Atrium mensa** (p.259), **De Vilegende Schotel** (p.264), **Keuken van 1870** (p.257)
Trendy – **Pacifico** (p.257), **Kantjil** (p.260), **Paris Brest** (p.264), **Huyschkamer** (p.268)

Brown bars – **De Engelbewaarder** (p.258), **Van Puffellen** (p.263)
Indonesian – **Tempo Doeloe** (p.267), **Speciaal** (p.264)

For kids
Pancake Bakery (p.262), **Bollebeer** (p.259), and any Italian restaurant listed
Late night
Homolulu (p.268), **Bojo** (p.267)

Around Dam Square and Red Light District

Restaurants

DE SILVEREN SPIEGEL

*Kattengatt 4–6, tel. 624 6589. Open
Mon–Fri 12 a.m.–2 p.m., 6 p.m.–10
p.m., Sat 6p.m.–10p.m., closed Sun,
f100.*

A delightful step gabled house built by
Hendrick de Keyser in 1614, the tiny
rooms inside, complete with Delft tiles
and panelled walls, are still intact.
Excellent French cuisine includes such
delicacies as terrine of pigeon with
sweetbreads of veal and marinade of
shallots, warm lobster salad, scallops of
wild spinach, and the warm cheese tart
for dessert is out of this world. The food
is complemented by a good wine list.

1E KLAS

*Platform 2b, Centraal Station, tel. 625
0131. Open Mon–Wed 9.30 a.m.–11
p.m., Thurs–Sat 9.30 a.m.–11.30 p.m.,
Sun 10.30 a.m.–10.30 p.m. Lunch
noon–2 p.m, dinner 5.30 p.m.–10 p.m.
daily, but stays open till 10.30 p.m.
Thurs–Sat. Meals, snacks, drinks,
dinner f50.*

Beautifully restored nineteenth-century
first class waiting room in Central
Station. Tuck into *à la carte nouvelle
cuisine* and try to imagine the trains
outside are steam powered. One of the
few good restaurants in historic
surroundings with access and loos for
disabled people.

DE BLAUWE PARADE AND BLAUWE POORT

*Hotel Port van Cleve, N.Z.
Voorburgwal 178–80, tel. 624 4860.
Open Parade Mon–Fri noon–2 p.m.,
6 p.m.–10 p.m., Sat–Sun 6 p.m.–
10 p.m. f65, set f65; Poort daily
noon–9.30 p.m. f45, set f41.50.*

Since it opened in 1870 this beer hall
has expanded into two large
restaurants (the Parade is a little more
formal than the Poort). Both
restaurants offer genuine Dutch food
on such a large scale that they have
served nearly six million of their
trademark steaks; each one is
numbered and the recipient of every
thousandth wins a bottle of wine, a
good gimmick that attracts the
tourists.

HET MELKMEISJE

*Zeedijk 19, tel. 625 0640. Open
5.30 p.m.–11 p.m., closed Tuesday.
f60.*

It is not a good idea to venture down
Zeedijk on your own at night, but if
you have company excellent fish and
Dutch specialities are to be had in the
cosy and eccentric ambience of this
converted eighteenth-century dairy.
The bar is a transformed fairground
organ.

BREDERO PANCAKE HOUSE
O.Z. Voorburgwal 244, tel. 622 9461.
Open daily 10 a.m.–9 p.m. (winter),
9 a.m.–midnight May–Sept. f25.

A neat, small pancake house on the edge of the Red Light District. Not as good as the Pancake Bakery (see p.262) but more intimate atmosphere. Huge portions.

DE KEUKEN VAN 1870
Spuistraat 4, tel. 624 8965. Open
Mon–Fri noon–8 p.m., weekends
4 p.m.–9 p.m. f12.

Set up as a soup kitchen in 1870 and still serves basic, cheap Dutch food. Dish of the day varies from sausage and mash to jugged hare with cranberries. Aproned waitresses deliver huge platefuls to communal tables. Usually full of workmen, vagrants and students wanting a cheap bellyful.

Argentinian

TANGO
Warmoestraat 49, tel. 627 2467.
Open 5 p.m.–midnight. f50.

For serious meat eaters this is a small intimate restaurant on the edge of the Red Light District where huge steaks sizzle on a charcoal grill. Served in every conceivable way with chips or with delicious corn-based *humitas*. Best seating upstairs.

Mexican

CAFÉ PACIFICO
Warmoestraat 31, tel. 624 2911.
Open Tues–Thurs, Sun 5.30 p.m.–
11 p.m., Fri–Sat 5.30 p.m.–midnight,
closed Mon. f30. Look for neon light.

For a fun night out join the crowds for a Corona over the bar and tuck into the best Mexican food in town.

Whitewashed walls display old Sol ads and a little tiled sink in the corner gives it an authentic touch. Friendly waiters, nice people and excellent food. Don't be put off by its proximity to the Red Light District.

Spanish

CENTRA
Lange Niezel 29, tel. 622 3050,
11 a.m.–11 p.m., f20.

Fluorescent lighting and formica tables in the heart of the Red Light District make this an unlikely choice for dinner, but it seems to have got the vote from Spanish ex-pats for the best food in town. Don't venture out alone, but if you are looking for a good cheap meal it is well worth it.

Vegetarian

SISTERS
Nes 102, tel. 626 3970. Open
Mon–Fri noon–9.30 p.m., weekends
2 p.m.–9.30 p.m. Unlicensed. Full
meals f20 and drinks.

Every night this cosy restaurant is crammed with punters perched on bar stools, standing around the entrance or enjoying the relative comfort of the closely packed tables. Papers and magazines are passed around and the bowls of fresh flowers gradually get pushed to one side. Food is colourful, tasty and fun. Popular with women, but not exclusive as the name might suggest.

EGG CREAM
St Jacobstraat 19. Tel. 623 0575.
Open 11 a.m.–8 p.m. Closed Tues.
Unlicensed. Meals f20.

Famous, earthy and not exclusively vegetarian. Menus are provided by a different cook each day and are always tasty, authentic and different. Cramped conditions make this a good place to meet fellow travellers.

Brown Cafés and Eetcafés

DE ENGELBEWAARDER
Kloveniersburgwal 59, tel. 625 37 72. Open Mon–Thurs noon–1 a.m., Fri–Sat noon–2 a.m., Sun 2 p.m.–1 a.m. Full meals f18–30, snacks and drinks. Live jazz 4 p.m.–6 p.m. Sun.

Expect to meet interesting people in this friendly relaxed bar renowned as Amsterdam's 'literary' café. The place is packed on Sundays for the jazz sessions but there is extra seating on the barge outside if you can't get in.

FRASCATI
Nes 59, tel. 624 1324. Open bar Mon–Thurs, Sun 4 p.m.–1 a.m., Fri 4 p.m.–2 a.m., Sat noon–2 a.m., kitchen 5.30 p.m.–10 p.m. daily. Full meals f20–35, snacks and drinks.

A brown café with wine bar atmosphere, popular with theatre goers and students. Pastas, soups, steaks and salads are nearly always on offer, but you will find more exotic variations chalked on the blackboard.

CAFÉ LA STRADA
N.Z. Voorburgwal 93, tel. 625 0276. Open bar in winter Mon–Thurs, Sun 4 p.m.–1 a.m., Fri–Sat 4 p.m.–2 a.m.; in summer earlier at 3 p.m. Kitchen open daily 5.30 p.m.–10 p.m. Full meals f15–35, snacks and drinks. Vegetarian options.

Popular with lesbians and women who work in the centre of town, this split-level café is imaginatively decorated by a different artist each month and the food, mainly French, is terrific.

HET KARBEEL
Warmoestraat 58, tel. 627 4995. Open 10 a.m.–midnight; dinner 6 p.m.–10 p.m. Full meals f15–35, snacks and drinks.

Once a cheese and wine house, you can't fail to miss it by the hams, salamis and cheeses in the window. This is a perfect place for single women by day or night despite being in the Red Light District. Excellent for brunch and snack lunches (crusty rolls made up on the spot) or try one of their excellent fondues for dinner. One is big enough for two people unless you are very hungry.

T'GASTHUYS
Grimburgwal 7, tel. 624 8230. Open Sun–Thurs 10 a.m.–1 a.m., Fri–Sat 10 a.m.–2 a.m. Full meals f20, drinks and snacks.

A loud and lively narrow bar with a small area for eating upstairs at the back and a quiet canalside terrace at the front. Always full of students and plenty of seating for singles – a good place to meet people.

NIEUWE KERK CAFÉ
Eggerstraat 8, tel. 627 2830. Open 8.30 a.m.–6 p.m. Full meals f15–35, snacks and drinks.

This has the feel of a cathedral café, full of well-heeled middle-aged ladies and mothers laden with shopping wanting a rest. Uniformed waitresses talk in soft voices and hungry kids howl from their buggies. Neither the food nor the decor is particularly inspired, but they offer adequate breakfast, lunch and tea and a wide range of snacks at reasonable prices; there's also a cheap children's menu. Seating outside on Dam Square is noisy.

De Doelen

*Kloveniersburgwal 125, tel. 624 9023.
Open 10 a.m.–1 a.m. Sun–Thurs,
10 a.m.–2 a.m. Fri–Sat. Drinks and
snacks.*

Students, prostitutes, kids and ageing
hippies chat around the bar or gaze
out of the huge canal side windows
while old men play pool in the vaulted
room at the back or smoke their pipes
around the tiled fireplace. Pavement
seating is great for people watching.

Café Karpershoek

*Martelaarsgracht 2, tel. 624 7886.
Open Mon–Fri 7 p.m.–1 a.m., Sat
8 p.m.–1 a.m., Sun 9 p.m.–1 a.m.
Drinks and snacks.*

This bar has been serving apple pie and
coffee to salty dogs since 1629. Quiet
ambience except when the telly goes
on for major soccer matches and the
weekly draw of the national lottery.

Designer Bars

De Jaren

*Nieuwe Doelenstraat 20, tel. 625
5771. Open bar Mon–Thurs, Sun
10 a.m.–1 a.m. Fri–Sat 10 a.m.–2 a.m.,
kitchen: 5.30 p.m.–10 p.m. daily. Full
meals f20–30, snacks and drinks.*

Huge café overlooking the Amstel
with tiled floors, exposed brickwork,
chart music and trendy clientele. Sit on
the sunny terrace and watch the boats,
play chess, read a paper in a quiet
alcove or eat dinner in the restaurant
upstairs. Service can be hurried and
food a little mass produced.

Mensa

Het Trefcentrum Atrium

*O.Z.Auchterburgwal 237, tel. 525
3999. Open Mon–Fri 9 a.m.–7 p.m.*
*(lunch noon–2 p.m., dinner 5 p.m.–
7 p.m.). Full meals f10, snacks and
drinks.*

A buffet/self service restaurant where a
full meal of soup and choice of fish,
meat or vegetarian dish costs around
f8.50. Set in a glass pyramid in the
courtyard of the former hospital, it
also makes a good place for snacks
and drinks with coffee downstairs and
a bar upstairs. Anyone is welcome and
it is large enough not to feel self-
conscious. Good for children and
there is a small playground outside for
post prandial play.

Cafés

Bollebeer

*Kloveniersburgwal 38, tel. 624 3102.
Open Mon–Fri 9 a.m.–7 p.m., Sat
9 a.m.–5 p.m., Sun (July–Sept only)
10 a.m.–5 p.m. Light meals, snacks
and drinks.*

The only café in the city geared for
small children, where teddy bears –
old, new and well loved – outnumber
the seats. Visiting children will be well
supplied with bear related books,
puzzles, games and bear-shaped
biscuits and wine gums. Menu ranges
from omelettes, chips, and burgers to
cheese soufflé and snails.

Smoking Coffeeshops

Grasshopper

*Oudebrugsteeg 16, tel. 626 1529.
Open 8 a.m.–1 a.m. daily. Drinks,
snacks and dope.*

Large, loud, brash and expensive and
not solely for dope smokers. The bar
upstairs is a hot favourite with the
young set and a good place to meet
fellow tourists if you are travelling
alone. Sit at the bar or at the windows

for great views across the water. Smoking room downstairs can get a bit seedy, probably because most people here smoke 'skunk', fifty times stronger than normal grass.

RUSLAND
Rusland 16, tel. 627 9468. Open 11 a.m.–9 p.m. daily. Drinks, snacks and dope.

Small, intimate and a popular local haunt with a pool table, magazines and a friendly chat. They also have one of the best selection of teas in Amsterdam.

Around Spui

Restaurants

D'VIJFF VLIEGEN
Spuistraat 294–302 tel. 624 8369. Open 5.30 p.m.–midnight; sometimes opens at lunchtime with a promotional 'cheap' f45 menu. Entrance down the adjoining alley, Vliehendesteeg 1. f100.

This restaurant, once famed for its cooking, is now better known for its high prices though the so-called 'New Dutch Cuisine' is an interesting concept, using fresh Dutch produce wherever possible and portions considerably larger than the name suggests. Spread over five small, immaculately restored seventeenth-century houses, the restaurant is smart but intimate.

LUCIUS
Spuistraat 247, tel. 624 1831. Open daily noon–midnight. f80.

A classy fish restaurant where the food is better than the welcome. A cheaper

Proeflokaalen

DE DRIE FLESCHJES
Gravenstraat 18, tel. 624 8443. Open noon–8.30 p.m., closed Sun.

This narrow bar has the air of a gentleman's hatter until you notice that the wall is lined with padlocked barrels that have held Heindrik Bootz liqueurs since 1816. This genuine *proeflokaal* has served Amsterdammers since 1650 and is usually full of businessmen and stockbrokers, popping in for a quick shot of genever.

tourist menu operates till 7 p.m., but it is well worth waiting for the place to fill up and paying the extra.

HAESJE CLAES
Spuistraat 273–75, tel. 624 9998. Open 12 a.m.–10 p.m. f40.

A large restaurant made up of lots of smaller panelled rooms in typical Dutch style. Extensive menu is exclusively Dutch; the eel and the salmon with lobster sauce are exceptionally good. Traditional style makes it a hot favourite with groups of tourists, but don't be put off. Ask to sit downstairs and if directed upstairs to the stark 'tourist' room say you will wait for a downstairs table.

Indonesian

KANTJIL EN DE TIJGER
Spuistraat 291–93, tel. 620 0994. Open 4.30 p.m.–11 p.m. f45.

If you don't mind a Dutch interpretation of Indonesian cooking this seems to be the place to come. Slick black designer interior, massive pot plants and platefuls of steaming food attract hordes of designer people every night. Small tables for singles and large ones for groups and, unlike most restaurants, there is lots of space.

Italian

CASA DI DAVID
Singel 426, 1017 AV, tel. 624 5093. Open 5–11 p.m. f30–50.

Crisp white tablecloths and smartly dressed waiters add a sophisticated touch to this delightful restaurant. The smell of roasting peppers, garlic and freshly baked pizza invades the candlelit arches where families, lovers and single people enjoy the excellent fare. Good for a feast or a bowl of pasta, plus interesting salads. The wine list offers welcome alternatives to the poor house wine.

Brown Cafés and Eetcafés

BRASSERIE LUDEN
Spuistraat 304–06, tel. 624 5906. Open 11 a.m.–1 a.m., Sun 4 p.m.– 1 a.m. Full meals f45, bar meals f15, snacks and drinks. Booking essential for restaurant.

Bar meals are excellent value in this relaxed, trendy brasserie. There is good seating for singles and plenty of glossy mags, papers and a selection of Asterix to keep you entertained. The adjacent restaurant attracts an informal cultured crowd. Slightly public exit for the loos which are up a spiral staircase in the middle of the room – embarrassing when sober and lethal when drunk.

DAVID AND GOLIATH
Kalverstraat 92, tel. 623 6736. Open 9.30 a.m.–4.45 p.m. Light lunches, snacks and drinks.

A bright airy café adjoining the Amsterdam Historical Museum, with seating extending outside into the courtyard. A huge wooden Goliath soars into the rafters with a wimpy David at his feet (both rescued from the Amsterdam Pleasure Garden). A good place to take children for a midday meal.

LUXEMBOURG
Spuistraat 22, tel. 620 6264. Open bar Mon–Thurs, Sun 10 a.m.–1 a.m., Fri–Sat 10 a.m.–2 a.m., kitchen 11 a.m.– 11 p.m. daily. Snacks and drinks.

High ceilinged and genteel, this is definitely the place to be seen. Popular with local executive crowd and the class of clientele is reflected in the up-market snacks – the giant club sandwiches and dim sum are legendary.

HOPPE
Spui 18–20, tel. 623 7849. Open Mon–Thurs, Sun 11 a.m.–1 a.m., Fri–Sat 11 a.m.–2 a.m. Snacks and drinks.

Amsterdammers have been socialising here since 1670 and it is still as popular as ever. Single women will probably find it less male orientated next door at the Luxembourg. Both have a terrace onto the street.

TAPAS BAR CATALA
Spuistraat 299, tel. 623 1141. Open 4 p.m.–11.30 p.m.; closed Tues. Snacks and drinks.

A small tiled bar on the corner, for roasted peppers, marinaded anchovies, lobster claws and other Spanish delicacies. Drop in for a quick bite or make a meal of it. Most dishes are extraordinarily inexpensive.

Designer Bars

ESPRIT
Spui 10, tel. 622 1967. Open Mon–Wed, Fri 10 a.m.–10 p.m.,
Thurs 10 a.m.–midnight, Sat 10 a.m.–7 p.m., kitchen closes at 9 p.m. Mon–Wed, 10 p.m. Thurs, 6.30 p.m. Sat. Snacks and drinks.

The clean, sleek glass and aluminium café is run by the clothing chain next door. A popular coffee stop for shoppers off Kalverstraat which serves huge rolls, good salads and sticky cakes.

Grachten Gordle: Western section from Brouwersgracht to Leidsegracht

Restaurants

BELHAMEL
Brouwersgracht 60, tel. 622 1095. Open 6 p.m.–10 p.m. daily. Full meals f50. Drinks.

A pretty canalside restaurant with subtle art nouveau decor, brilliant views, handsome waiters and good French food; try the marinaded prawns. Always brimming with the arty crowd who live up here and if you can get in (always book well in advance) you are guaranteed a good meal. Ask to sit upstairs for spectacular views.

T'ZWAANTJE
Berenstraat 12, tel. 623 2373. Open 4.30 p.m–11 p.m. f30.

A traditional-style restaurant with Persian carpets strewn across the tightly packed tables, candles flickering from the corners and street views through lace curtains. Huge portions of spare ribs and French fries, thick stews and slabs of steak at reasonable prices.

THE PANCAKE BAKERY
Prinsengracht 191, tel. 625 1333. Open noon–9.30 p.m. f15–25.

A huge selection of sweet and savoury pancakes are cooked on an old Dutch griddle by a very hot chef. Marble-topped tables stretch the length of this low beamed cellar. Toddlers play with the sand on the floor while their parents pick at the enormous pancakes they left behind. Soups and omelettes also available (high chairs provided). Huge portions.

Greek

FILOXFENIA
Berenstraat 8, tel. 624 4292. Open 5.30 p.m.–11 p.m, closed Mon. f30.

Set in a quiet street full of restaurants, Filoxfenia tends to take some time to fill but is popular with locals wanting a fix of taramasalata, dolmades and Retsina, accompanied by some cheery Greek music and a very hairy proprietor.

Vegetarian

BOLHOED
Prinsengracht 60, tel. 626 1803. Open Mon–Fri noon–10 p.m., weekends 10 a.m.–10 p.m. f25. Situated on the edge of the Jordaan, just south of Noorderkerk.

Psychedelic walls, wooden floors, gentle folk music and a toothbrush dispenser in the loo. The reason most people come here is for the imaginative vegan menu. It is also one of the few vegetarian restaurants to be licensed and to stay open until 10 p.m.

Brown Cafés and Eetcafés

HET MOLENPAD
Prinsengracht 653, tel. 625 9680. Open bar Mon–Thurs, Sun noon– 1 a.m., Fri–Sat noon–2 a.m., kitchen noon–3.30, 6 p.m.–10.30 p.m. Full meals, snacks and drinks. f35.

Intellectuals and academics hog the papers and businessmen entertain their foreign associates over lunch. Interesting menu marred by packet soup and meagre sandwiches, but generally a good bet for an evening meal.

VAN PUFFELEN
Prinsengracht 377, tel. 624 6270. Open bar Mon–Thurs, Sun 2 p.m.– 1 a.m., Fri–Sat 2 p.m–2 a.m. Kitchen summer 6 p.m.–10 p.m., winter 4 p.m.–10 p.m. daily. Full meals, snacks and drinks. f45.

A very popular brown bar with a restaurant in the back for good Dutch food under a rather bizarre ceiling, where naked women float among the clouds. Booking essential.

'T SMACKZEYL
Brouwersgracht 101, tel. 622 6520. Open Mon–Thurs, Sun 11.30 a.m.– 1 a.m., Fri–Sat 11.30 a.m.–2 a.m. Drinks.

Dingy, dark brown bar with good views and local customers.

Cafés

LEG AF
Oude Leliestraat 9, tel. 624 6700. Open Sun 4 p.m.–1 p.m., Mon–Thurs noon–1 a.m., Fri–Sat noon–2 a.m. Drinks and snacks.

A good place for a quick snack and a chat. Rows of sauce bottles, steel tables and regular art exhibitions make an unlikely combination, but it works. Good omelettes and burgers and delectable crab salad in French bread.

CAFÉ DE KLEPEL
Prinsenstraat 22, tel. 623 82 44. Open Sun–Thurs 4 p.m.–1 a.m., Fri–Sat 4 p.m.–2 a.m. Drinks and snacks.

De Klepel, with its sponged blood red walls, piano in the corner and fresh flowers stuffed into a fish bowl on the bar, is always full of women drinking thick strong coffee, smoking Gitanes and reading the papers.

CAFÉ TER KUILE
Torensteeg 8, tel. 639 1055. Open Sun–Thurs 10.30 a.m.–1 a.m., Fri–Sat 10.30 a.m.–2 a.m. Drinks and snacks.

Huge windows, bright lights and mirrors and loud music that competes with a constant burble from the cappuccino machine and a frenzy of young trendies popping in for a quick drink.

GREENWOODS
Singel 103, tel. 623 7071. Open Mon–Fri 9.30 a.m.– 7 p.m., weekends 11 a.m.–7 p.m. Snacks and drinks (unlicensed).

This simple café is renowned for its excellent Devonshire cream teas, American-style club sandwiches and, in case you are missing it, baked beans on toast. The informal atmosphere and often English conversation is great if you are feeling lonely, and there are usually a few English papers hanging off the paper rack.

Designer Cafés

PARIS BREST
Prinsengracht 375, tel. 627 0507. Open bar 2 p.m.–1 a.m. closing later at 2 a.m., at weekends; kitchen 6 p.m.–midnight and opening earlier at 4 p.m. on weekends. Full meals f35, snacks and drinks.

If you wish to mix with the Amsterdam cool set Paris Brest has established itself as *the* designer bar for designer people. Lots of gleaming glass, shiny stainless steel and hi-tech lighting effects, most often seen through dark glasses.

Proeflokaalen

DE ADMIRAAL
Herengracht 319, tel. 625 4334. Open Mon–Fri 4 p.m.–midnight, Sat 5 p.m.–midnight, closed Sun. Drinks.

Unlike most *proeflokaalen* you will find comfy sofas and chairs amidst barrels and taps and the place stays open till midnight. This is Amsterdam's last remaining independent distillery and you will find, among the long list of spirits, a number of obscenely named concoctions like *pruimpje prik in* – all very potent, hence the chairs.

The Jordaan

Restaurants

Italian

TOSCANINI
Lindengracht 75, tel. 623 2813. Open 6 p.m.–11.30 p.m., closed Tues. f50. Credit cards accepted. Booking essential.

The best Italian food in Amsterdam is prepared in an open kitchen at the far end of the large whitewashed warehouse. Always full of Italians, always good and always booked up well in advance. Thick creamy risotto, best buffalo mozzarella, rabbit, steaks, fresh fish and piles of rucola, basil and plump red tomatoes. Poached egg on asparagus is exceptionally good, as are the *biscotti di Prato* washed down with sweet vin Santo for dessert. Singles table is usually crammed with people who eat here virtually every night.

Indonesian

SPECIAAL
Nieuwe Leliestraat 142, tel. 624 9706. Open 5.30 p.m.–11 p.m. daily. f50. Credit cards: Amex, Visa, Master.

If you want a really memorable *rijstafel* this is the place to come. It may look tiny from the outside, but it opens up at the back where a couple of ceiling fans struggle to keep everyone cool. It is one of the most popular Indonesian restaurants in Amsterdam and the food usually comes up to expectations.

Vegetarian

DE VLIEGENDE SCHOTEL
Nieuwe Leliestraat 162, tel. 625 2041. Open 5.30 p.m.–10 p.m. Full meals f15–25.

Very basic cheap vegetarian restaurant with a good menu and friendly management in a dilapidated one-storey building. Good fondue, pastas and salads. Order your food before you sit down. Singles usually congregate around one table.

Brown Cafés and Eetcafés

VAN DEN BERG
Lindengracht 95, tel. 622 2716. Open Mon–Thurs, Sun 5 p.m–1 a.m., Fri–Sat 5 p.m.–2 a.m., kitchen closed Sat. Full meals f15–25. Snacks and drinks.

A pleasantly informal café for women though men are welcome, as are the rest of the family. Excellent vegetarian/sea food includes calamares, prawns with garlic butter, mussels, sate, fondue and enormous salads. Homely atmosphere and extra seating outside for sunny evenings. Good for eating alone and ideal for single mothers.

EETCAFÉ DE EETTUIN
2e Tuindwarsstraat 10, tel. 623 7706. Open 5.30 p.m.–11.30 p.m. daily. Full meals f25. Drinks.

Dark traditional eetcafé with long communal tables down the middle and a smattering of smaller ones around the sides. Fringed lampshades, patterned tablecloths and a creaky old dumb waiter set the scene. Food is simple, generous and cheap, ranging from spare ribs to Boeuf Bourguignonne, and the place is always packed. Children's menu comes with 'surprise'.

DE REIGER
Nieuwe Leliestraat 34, tel. 624 7426. Open bar Mon–Thurs, Sun 11 a.m.–1 a.m., Fri–Sat 11 a.m.–2 a.m.;

kitchen daily 6 p.m.–10.30 p.m. Full meals f30. Snacks and drinks.

This typical brown café is currently the 'in' place in the Jordaan. Good for a quiet read in the day, but by night bursting with local trendies. If you want to eat get there early or be prepared to wait for a table.

CAFÉ PAPENEILAND
Prinsengracht 4, tel. 624 1989. Open Sun–Thurs 11 a.m.–1 p.m., Fri–Sat 11 a.m.–2 p.m. Drinks.

A little step gabled house on the edge of the Jordaan where candles burn on old wooden tables, a log fire crackles and locals chat gently over a drink. Delightful place to unwind.

CAFÉ THIJSSEN
Brouwersgracht 107, tel. 623 8994. Open Sun–Thurs 9.30 a.m.–1 a.m., Fri 9.30 a.m.–2 a.m., Sat 7.30 a.m.–2 a.m. Drinks and snacks.

A good place for a snack lunch on the northern edge of the Jordaan. Lots of seating outside, crowds of young people and nice views down Brouwersgracht.

CAFÉ SMALLE
Egelantiersgracht 12, tel. 623 9617. Open Sun–Thurs 10 a.m.–1 a.m., Fri–Sat 10 a.m.–2 a.m. Drinks and snacks.

A firm favourite with Jordaaners. Excellent soup, hors d'oeuvres and applecake, no music and terrific terrace seating in summer.

NIEUWE LELIE
Nieuwe Lelie 83, tel. 622 5493. Open Mon–Thurs 2 p.m.–1 a.m., Fri–Sat 2 p.m.–2 a.m., closed Sun. Snacks and drinks.

A friendly Jordaan brown bar where locals read, chat or challenge one another to a game of chess.

De Tuin
2e Thindwardsstraat 13, tel. 624 4559. Open Mon–Thurs 10 a.m.– 1 a.m., Fri–Sat 10 a.m.–2 a.m., Sun 11 a.m.–1 a.m. Snack and drinks.

Stone floors, large wooden tables and poster covered walls and always someone to talk to. Mainly frequented by local Jordaaners reading papers, playing chess or chatting to the bar staff. If there are too many men for comfort head down the road to the Sarrein.

Women's Cafés

Café Sarrein
Elandsstraat 119, tel. 623 4901. Open Mon 8 p.m.–1 a.m., Tues–Thurs, Sun 3 p.m.–1 a.m., Fri–Sat 3 p.m.–2 a.m. Drinks.

Check out for an introduction to the women's scene in Amsterdam. A little bit of a club but it won't take long to feel accepted over a game of darts, billiards or pool, or a quiet drink on the upper level. Lots of good magazines and all the info you could wish for.

Grachten Gordle: Eastern section from Leidsegracht to the Amstel

Restaurants

'T Swarte Schaep
Korte Leidsedwarsstraat 24, tel. 622 3021. Open noon–11 p.m. f70. Credit cards: Amex, Visa, Diners, Master.

If you can manage the steep staircase you will be rewarded with a refined eclectic menu (traditional Dutch, nouvelle and post modern cuisine), an excellent wine list and a pretty oak-beamed dining room furnished with antiques.

Dikker and Thijs
Prinsengracht 444, tel. 625 8876. Open 8 a.m.–10.30 a.m., 12 a.m.– 3 p.m., 6 p.m.–10 p.m., closed Mon. f90. Booking essential. Credit cards: Amex, Diners, Master, Visa.

The brasserie is a popular haunt for local politicians and media stars. Stylish, slick interior and an excellent menu which changes frequently. Good

takeaways available from the deli next door.

Sluizer Visrestaurant
Utrechtsestraat 45, tel. 626 3557. Open Mon–Fri noon–midnight, weekends 5 p.m.–midnight. Children's menu. f50. Credit cards: Amex, Diners, Master, Visa.

A busy, cheerful restaurant for fish lovers. Fish soups, patés, mousses and marinades are followed by a variety of fresh fish grilled, poached, pan fried or delectably baked *en papillote*. Sponged yellow walls, fresh flowers and cultured conversation make this an intimate and enjoyable experience.

Sluizer
Utrechtsestraat 43, tel. 626 3557. Open Mon–Fri noon–midnight, weekends 5 p.m.–midnight. Children's

menu. f40. Credit cards: Amex, Visa, Masters, Diners.

A lively restaurant where students gather for parties, lovers introduce their parents and businesspeople entertain clients. It is light, airy, simply decorated and always full. The interesting menu, mainly French and Italian, is let down by Dutch interpretations of the dishes. (Gravy and mash are used in abundance.) Excellent value.

DE BLAUWE HOLLANDER
Leidsekruisstraat 28, tel. 623 3014. Open 5 p.m.–10 p.m. daily. f25.

Cheap Dutch food in a tiny restaurant in the middle of the tourist traps around Leidseplein. Walls are strewn with clogs, chopping boards and postcards from satisfied customers. You can't get more authentic, but you are likely to find the place full of fellow travellers and a long queue of the same outside.

Mexican

ROSE'S CANTINA
Regliersdwarsstraat 38, tel. 625 9797. Open Mon–Thurs, Sun 5.30 p.m.– 11 p.m., Fri–Sat 5.30 p.m.–11.30 p.m. f25. Credit cards: Amex, Master, Visa.

Lethal margheritas and tasty food in lively, noisy and sociable surroundings. Solos might feel a bit left out and will definitely have to remind the waiters of their existence from time to time.

Indonesian

TEMPO DOELOE
Utrechtsestraat 75, tel. 625 6718. Open 6 p.m–11.30 p.m. f60. Credit cards: Amex, Master, Visa, Diners.

One of the best Indonesian restaurants in the city. The entry bell and warm welcome gives you a sense of 'coming to dinner'. Blue silk curtains cascade down the peach walls and exotic flower arrangements reflect in the mirrors around the room. Take your time to enjoy the mix of flavours, textures, and fragrances. The *Istemewa* is exciting, invigorating and unforgettable. Booking advisable.

BOJO
Lange Leidsewarsstraat 51, tel. 622 7434. Open Sun–Thurs 5 p.m.–2 a.m., Fri–Sat 5 p.m.–6 a.m. f25.

This tiny bamboo-lined restaurant is useful for night owls at weekends because it stays open all night but the food tends to be insipid, dull and mass produced.

Japanese

SHIZEN
Kerkstraat 148, tel. 622 8627. Open 5 p.m.–10 p.m., closed Mon. f40. Credit cards: Amex, Diners, Master, Visa.

Affordable Japanese food like this is difficult to come by, but here you can enjoy macrobiotic food for a reasonable sum. No meat, but lots of fish and unbelievably beautiful and tasty vegetables. Tatami seating to the left and table and chairs to the right.

Vegetarian

GOLDEN TEMPLE
Utrechtsestraat 126, tel. 626 8560. Open daily 5 p.m.–9 p.m. f25.

The last surviving Golden Temple in the world. Seriously good vegetarian food is served by turbanned waitresses dressed entirely in white, while the men cook and field children in the kitchen beyond. The light atmosphere and unobtrusive live music make this a popular choice for people eating alone.

Lesbian

HOMOLULU
Kerkstraat 23, tel. 624 6387. Open Tues–Thurs, Sun 10 p.m.–4 a.m., Fri–Sat 10 p.m.–5 a.m. Restaurant attached to club. Full meals f60.

Run by lesbians, the gay club has a good restaurant overlooking the dance floor, usually full of gay men but a good place to be for the women-only nights on the first Sunday and third Friday of the month. (See Entertainment p.281.)

Designer Cafés and Eetcafés

CAFÉ AMERICAIN
Leidseplein 28, tel. 623 4813. Open 7 a.m.–1 a.m. daily, breakfast from 10 a.m., lunch 11 a.m.–2 p.m., dinner 6 p.m.–11.30 p.m. Buffet available all day f30; dinner f50. Reduced prices available for kids.

A grandiose art nouveau extravaganza which has attracted artists, writers and cultured types since the turn of the century. Can get rather full of tourists these days, but it's worth popping in for a coffee just to appreciate the decor and get off Leidseplein.

DE KROON
Rembrandtsplein 17, tel. 625 2011. Open bar Sun–Thurs 10 a.m.–1 a.m., Fri–Sat 10 a.m.–2 a.m.; kitchen lunch 10 a.m.–6 p.m., dinner 6 p.m.–10 p.m. à la carte. Full meals f50. Snacks and drinks. Look for doorway next to Escape club and go upstairs.

This huge colonial style café offers the best views over the square and a genteel atmosphere not to be found anywhere else. Marbled walls, wicker chairs, brass fans, outsize pot plants and a sunny terrace. A great place for a morning read, midday or evening drinks rather than evening meals. Because of its unmarked entrance it tends to be full of Dutch people.

SCHILLER
Rembrandtsplein 26, tel. 624 9846. Open bar 4 p.m.–1 a.m., closing 2 a.m. Fri–Sat; kitchen 6 p.m.–9.30 p.m. daily. Snacks and drinks.

Legendary art deco bar attached to the Schiller Hotel. A comfortable place to relax, often with live piano playing in the background. Good for single women.

CAFÉ HUYSCHKAMER
Utrechtsestraat 137, tel. 627 0575. Open Mon–Thurs, Sun, 3.30 p.m.–1 a.m., Fri–Sat 3.30 p.m.–2 a.m. Full meals f15–30. Snacks and drinks.

Once a male brothel; the talented present owner, Paul Suyl, has designed the quirky decor from painting effects to decaying classical architecture, stencilled floor and cast-iron seating. Popular with arty gay crowd who come here for the food, as well as the decor, which runs from simple Italian salads to delicacies like cured venison with hazelnuts and strawberries.

PALLADIUM
Kl Gartmanpints 7, tel. 626 6566, open Sun–Thurs 10 a.m.–1 a.m., Fri–Sat 10 a.m.–2 a.m. Snacks and drinks.

A large glitzy bar just off Leidseplein where beautiful people hang out. By day it is a quiet, civilised place for coffee and cakes, but as the night wears on the bouncers appear, the music gets louder and the pre-club brigade preen themselves for the next venue.

Cafés

BACKSTAGE BOUTIQUE
Utrechtsedwarsstraat 67, tel. 622 3638. Open 10 a.m.–6 p.m. daily. Snacks and drinks.

A wacky boutique cum café run by the Christmas twins, Greg and Gary. Psychedelic decor and knitwear to match, huge tuna sandwiches and scrummy cakes. A good place for a break and the twins are ace at entertaining the kids.

POMPADOUR
Huidenstraat 12, tel. 623 9554. Open Mon 1 p.m–6 p.m., Tues–Sat 9 a.m.– 6 p.m. Coffee, cakes and chocolates.

One of the best chocolatiers in Amsterdam whose elegant little shop doubles up as a tea room at the back where you can devour chocolates and cake in style.

ARTEMIS
Keizersgracht 676, tel. 623 2655. Open Mon–Sat 10 a.m.–3.30 p.m. Coffee only.

Coffeeshop attached to the arts centre where you can sip coffee and watch the dance classes, often led by dancers from the National ballet.

Women's Cafés

FRANÇOISE
Kerkstraat 176, tel. 624 0145. Open Mon–Sat 9 a.m.–6 p.m. for drinks, snacks and light lunches.

A relaxed, informal café run by warmhearted Françoise. Local artists exhibit their works on the walls and a heavily laden noticeboard advertises the latest info for Amsterdam's women. Enjoy thick frothy cappuccino, devour slabs of chocolate cake or apple crumble and relax to classical music.

CAFÉ VIVE LA VIE
Amstelstraat 7, tel. 624 0114. Open Mon–Thurs 3 p.m.–1 a.m., Fri–Sat 3 p.m.–2 a.m., closed Sun. Drinks.

Just off Rembrandtsplein, and popular with lesbians – old and young. Decor lacks atmosphere and the music is generally loud, but the clientele is usually very friendly towards both straight and lesbian women who are new to the city.

Smoking Coffeeshops

LUCKY MOTHERS
Keizersgracht 665, tel. 622 9617. Open 9.30 a.m.–8 p.m. daily. Snacks, drinks and dope.

A delightfully sunny room overlooking the canal, with fine plasterwork on the ceiling, pretty little white tables and a friendly proprietor who fills bagels with cream cheese and smoked salmon one minute and explains the differences between 'skunk' and hash the next. It is a pleasant atmosphere for both smokers and non-smokers and there are lots of pocket-sized games to keep you occupied.

EATING AND DRINKING

Restaurants

DE KNIJP
Van Baerlestraat 134, tel. 671 4248.
Open Mon–Fri 12 a.m.–3 p.m.,
5.30 p.m.–12.30 a.m., evenings
only at weekends. f65.

Its proximity to the Concertegebouw
and late opening makes this a popular
choice for theatre goers. Don't be put
off by the unassuming façade on a
busy street; inside the noise is
forgotten. Seating is arranged on three
levels so there is plenty of scope for a
romantic evening, solo eating or going
as a group. Friendly staff work behind
a wine laden bar and the food is
wonderful. Dishes offer a wide range
of contrasting flavours, textures and
combinations, among them oysters,
warm goat cheese salad, marinaded
lamb with honey and thyme sauce,
calves' liver with sweet and sour leek,
and goose in port sauce.

BEDDINGTON'S
Roelof Hartstraat 6–8, tel. 676 5201.
Open noon–2.30 p.m., 6 p.m.–10.30
p.m., closed Sun. Set lunch f55, set
dinners from f80. Credit cards: Amex,
Diners, Master, Visa. A 10-min walk
from the Concertegebouw or take
tram 3, 5, 12, 24.

Englishwoman Jean Beddington
combines French, English and
Japanese cooking to produce an
exhilarating meal every time. The
modern decor is a little barren, but the
sumptuous food makes up for it.

Italian

MIRAFIORI
Hobbemastraat 2, tel. 62 3013. Open
noon–3 p.m., 5 p.m.–10.30 p.m.,

closed Tues. f65, Credit cards: Amex,
Masters, Visa.

A classy Italian restaurant for good
food and attentive waiters in a grand
setting, but lacks the spirit of
Toscanini in the Jordaan.

QUATTRO STAGIONE
Johannes Verhulstraat 32, 1017 KM,
tel. 662 0071. Open Mon–Fri noon–3
p.m., 5 p.m.–midnight; weekends
evenings only. In the residential area
east of Vondelpark behind the
Concertegebouw. f30.

A lively, if cramped, trattoria for
pizza, pasta and simple but good
Italian fare. Excellent for children, but
fills up early with local families. As
they clear out the place attracts
romantic couples, singles and the
neighbours who can't be bothered to
cook.

Vegetarian

DE WAAGHALS
Frans Halstraat 29, tel. 679 9609.
Open 5 p.m.–9 p.m., closed Sun–Mon.
f30.

In the de Pijp area close to Albert
Cuyp Straat De Waaghals has regular
clientele who enjoy organic produce at
reasonable prices. It is one of the best
veggie venues in town, but a bit of a
hike if you are staying in the centre.

Brown Cafés, Designer Bars and Eetcafés

DELIKT
Valeriusstraat 128 B, tel. 676 4647.
Open 4 p.m–1 a.m.; meals served 5.30

p.m.–11 p.m. *Full meals, snacks and drinks. f30.*

An excellent find if you are staying in the area. Tassled lampshades, wooden floors, candles and printed red tablecloths, and a blackboard displaying the day's menu. Food is Dutch/French/Italian mix with a number of seasonal specialities.

CAFÉ VERTIGO
Vondelpark 3, tel. 612 3021. Open Sun–Thurs 11 a.m.–1 a.m., Fri–Sat 11 a.m.–2 a.m. Light lunches, snacks and drinks.

Film buffs tend to hang out in the Vertigo, alongside the film museum with good terrace views of the Vondelpark cruisers and special theme menus that tie in with whatever is showing next door.

WILDSCHUT
Roelof Hartplein 1, tel. 673 8622. Open 9 a.m.–1 a.m.; meals served noon–5 p.m., 6 p.m.–10 p.m. Full meals f15–30; snacks and drinks.

A brown bar cum brasserie which tends to fill with stripey shirts and ties in the evenings, but a good, if rowdy,

place for a cheap bite to eat in this upmarket area.

Cafés

HOLLANDSE MANEGE CAFÉ
Vondelstraat 140, tel. 618 0942. Open Mon–Fri 8.30 a.m.–1 a.m. weekends 8.30 a.m.–6 p.m. Drinks and ice creams.

Children love to suck ice lollies and drink their juice from the balcony while the horses and riders plod around the arena below. The café, like the riding school, is nicely dilapidated in its grandeur (see p.170).

P.C.
P.C.Hooftstraat 83, tel. 671 7455. Open Mon–Fri 10 a.m.–7 p.m., weekends 10 a.m.–6 p.m.

Whether you are shopping in the street or slogging around the Van Gogh museum nearby, P.C. is a good place to take a break. Comfortable seating inside or on the pavement and a good range of snacks, from stuffed ciabatta to sticky cakes and the frothiest cappuccino around.

Jewish Quarter: Around Waterlooplein

Restaurants

HELMELSE MODDER
Oude Waal 9, tel. 626 1085. Open 6 p.m.–10 p.m., closed Tues. f45. Booking essential.

Delightfully relaxed restaurant offering interesting, sophisticated food, much of which is vegetarian. Marinaded herring on spinach or lemon soup make good starters and don't forget to try the deep rich chocolate mousse – 'Heavenly Mud' –

from which the restaurant takes its name. A current favourite with Amsterdam's women.

Indonesian

ANDA NUGRAHA
Waterlooplein 339, tel. 626 6064. Open 5 p.m.–10 p.m. daily but closes 9 p.m. Mon.

A small family affair where Dad cooks

and Mum waits the six tables, with batik tablecloths and mean masks hanging on the walls, stainless steel sauce pots and Duralex glasses. If you can face the eerie walk across Waterlooplein at night it is a great place for solo eating, serving cheap *Rijstafel* and a great Sunday special of mussels with bamboo in hot sauce.

Brown Cafés and Eetcafés

PETIT CAFÉ DE SLUYSWACHT
Jordenbreestraat 1, tel. 625 7611. Open 10 a.m.–6 p.m. Drinks and snacks.

A wonky little house opposite the Rembrandthuis. Terrific cappuccino and applecake, classical music and friendly proprietor. Go upstairs to the attic for good views down the canal. A great place for a quiet drink with a good book.

ENTREPODOK
Entrepodok 64, tel. 623 2356. Open Sun–Thurs 11 a.m.–1 a.m., Fri–Sat 11 a.m.–2 a.m.; lunch 12.30 p.m.–2.30 p.m., dinner 6 p.m.–10 p.m. Light lunches and dinners f25, snacks and drinks. Close to the zoo.

A small café in the trendy Entrepodok frequented by the arty crowd that work down here and the houseboat owners who live on the water. A quiet place to stop for lunch or an evening drink if you are in the area. Nice terrace spills across the street to the water's edge.

Designer Bars

DANTZIG
Zwanenburgwal 15 (corner of Stadhuis on Waterlooplein) tel. 620 9039. Open 10 a.m.–1 a.m.; kitchen closes 10.30 p.m. Full meals, snacks and drinks. f50.

Large café with terrace overlooking the Amstel. A good place for coffee, but the poor service and small portions can be annoying if you are there for a full meal.

TISFRIS
St Antoniesbreestraat 142, tel. 622 0472. Open bar 10 a.m.–1.30 a.m. daily; kitchen 5.30 p.m.–9.30 p.m. daily. Full meals, snacks, drinks. Meals f18–30.

Psychedelic decor, loud music and good wholesome food includes pasta, *enchilladas*, salads and sumptuous cakes. You can expect to find young trendies, beautiful transvestites, hippies and dishevelled travellers. Good terrace on the bridge where kids can wave to boats, singles have lots to see and there are plenty of interesting conversations to tune into for the wicked.

Coffeeshops and Cafés

JEWISH HISTORICAL MUSEUM CAFÉ
Jonas Daniel Meijerplein 24, tel. 626 9945. Open 11 a.m.–5 p.m.

You don't have to visit the museum to use the café which serves scrummy kosher snacks and good coffee in a pleasant modern café cum bookshop.

PUCCINI
Staatsraat 21, tel. 626 5474. Open 9 a.m.–6 p.m.

A light patisserie café with good window seats and the most delicious selection of cakes, pastries and chocolates made next door. Lots of glossy mags as well as the daily papers.

DE GOUDEN REAEL
De Zandhoek 14, Westerdok, tel. 623 3883. Open noon–2 p.m., 6 p.m–10 p.m., evenings only at weekends. f80 but set menus for f50. Take tram 3/bus 28 or splash out on a water taxi.

It may seem a little way out, but the superb French cuisine, good wines and terrific welcome should be worth it. This seventeenth-century quayside house with a waterside terrace for sunny evenings is the perfect setting for a romantic evening. Chef Miek Blommestein specialises in French regional food and introduces a new region every three months to keep the regulars impressed. If you have a day in hand, lunch at De Gouden Reael would be a perfect end to a morning stroll around the islands. You can spend the afternoon sleeping it off on the waterside seats outside.

MENU
Basics

Dranken	Drinks
Voorgerechten	Starters
Hoofdgerechten	Main courses
Nagerechten	Desserts
Visgerechten	Fish dishes
Vleesgerechten	Meat dishes
Doorbakken	Well done
Half doorbakken	Medium
Rood	Rare
Warm	Warm
Proost	Cheers
Asbakje	Ashtray
Naif	Knife
Spoen	Spoon
Foark	Fork
Menu	Menu
Kinder menu	Children's menu

A–Z Dutch Food and Cooking Terms
A

Aardappalen	Potatoes
Aardbei	Strawberry
Appelgebak	Applecake or tart

B

Banaankoek	Layers of bananas and cream on pastry base with coconut on top
Biefstuk (hollandse)	Steak

Biefstuk (duitse)	Hamburger
Bier	Lager/Beer
Bitterballen	Balls of meat purée in breadcrumbs, deep fried
Bloemkool	Cauliflower
Bonen	Beans
Boter	Butter
Brood	Bread
Broodje	Roll

C

Champignons	Mushrooms
Citroenjenever	Lemon gin

D

Daging	Beef
Doorbakken	Well done
Dranken	Drinks
Drop	Dutch licorice

E

Eend	Duck
Eiren	Eggs
Erwten	Peas
Erwtensoep	Pea soup

F

Framboos	Raspberry
Fricandel	Frankfurter
Fricandeau	Roast Pork
Frisdranken	Fizzy drinks
Frites	Chips
Fritesaus	Mayonnaise
Framboos	Raspberry

G

Gebak	Pastry
Gebakken	Fried or baked
Gebraden	Roasted
Gekookt	Boiled
Gegrild	Grilled
Gehakt	Minced meat
Genever (jenever)	Gin
Gerookt	Smoked
Gestoofd	Stewed
Groenten	Vegetables

H

Haring	Herring
Haringsalade	Herring salad

Honig	Honey
Hollandse saus	Hollandaise sauce
Huzarensalade	Egg salad
Hutspot	Beefstew

I

Ijs	Ice cream

K

Kaas	Cheese
Kabeljauw	Cod
Kalkoen	Turkey
Kalfsvlees	Veal
Karbonade	Chop
Kip	Chicken
Kipkurrie	Chicken curry
Knoflook	Garlic
Koekjes	Biscuits
Koffie	Coffee
Koffiemelk	Evaporated milk for coffee
Komkommer	Cucumber
Kopstoot	Beer and genever chaser
Krab	Crab
Krabsalade	Crab salad
Kroket	Meat paste in breadcrumbs

L

Lamsvlees	Lamb
Lever	Liver
Loempia	Spring rolls

M

Mosselen	Mussels
Melk	Milk

O

Oliebollen	Doughnuts

P

Paling	Eel
Pannekoeken	Pancakes
Peer	Pear
Peper	Pepper
Perzik	Peach
Pinda	Peanut
Poffertjes	Small pancakes
Prei	Leek

R

Rijst	Rice
Rijstaffel	Collection of dishes served at Indonesian restaurant
Rookvlees	Smoked beef

S

Schelvis	Haddock
Schol	Plaice
Sinaasappelsap	Orange juice
Sla/salade	Salad
Slagroom	Whipped cream
Spek	Bacon
Spiering	Whitebait
Stokbrood	French bread
Stroopwafels	Waffles
Suiker	Sugar

T

Taai Taai	Honey cake
Thee	Tea
Tong	Soul
Tostis	Toasted sandwiches

U

Uien	Onions
Uitsmijter	Ham or cheese with eggs on bread

V

Varkensvlees	Pork
Vers	Fresh
Vis	Fish
Vla	Custard
Vlaai	Fruit tart
Vlees	Meat
Vruchten	Fruit
Vruchtensap	Fruit juice

W

Wijn	Wine
Worst	Sausage
Wortelen	Carrots

Z

Zalm	Salmon
Zout	Salt
Zuurkool	Sauerkraut

ENTERTAINMENT

Amsterdam may not be one of Europe's foremost cultural centres, but the variety and extent of entertainment is virtually inexhaustible and you will find that, if it isn't free, you pay very little. Everything revolves around cafés where Jazz, Blues or South American bands entertain the customers for nothing. If you want to dance there are lots of clubs from which to choose, from sedate little clubs and cash induced tourist bop houses to exotic gay jamborees, folkloric hip hops and illegal house parties.

The city may not be on the agendas of touring rock megastars, but it is the place to get to know the up and coming bands of the future. Classical music fans will find themselves in one of the best places in the world to catch good early music concerts, but will probably choose to forgo a night at the Opera for a glimpse at one of the exhilarating dance companies working the city's venues. English-language theatre is currently all the rage so you should find a good selection, too, and film buffs have an enormous choice, from tinted silent movies to the latest blockbuster – nearly all English-language films are subtitled rather than dubbed.

Entertainment is cheap, venues are almost entirely clustered around the city centre and women alone should have few qualms about doing exactly as they wish without feeling intimidated, self-conscious or unwelcome.

For complete listings of what's on visit the AUB Uitburo, Leidseplein 26 (tel. 621 1211) or the VVV booking office on Stationsplein 10 (tel. 626 6444). Of the magazines *Time Out Amsterdam* has the most information available in English, but the free *Uitkrant* in Dutch is fairly comprehensible. *Agenda* is good for pop music, as is the national *Oor*. For lesbian entertainment it is always best to ring the Gay and Lesbian Switchboard on 623 6565.

There are few cities with so relaxed an attitude to nightlife as Amsterdam. Few clubs are guarded by hunky men searching for the right kind of faces, funky clothes and fat wallets – in fact there is only one, the Roxy, which has a strict membership policy. Instead you will find amiable bouncers controlling the flow of people rather than the quality. The only time you are likely to find yourself spurned is when you've got the wrong night and the place is being used for a concert rather than a disco. While there are obviously a number of glitzy establishments around Leidseplein and Rembrandtsplein created for tourists and out-of-towners, there are plenty of places where you can rub shoulders with the locals.

For most people a night out means drinking in a bar until it closes around 1 a.m. and then club hopping until you find what you want, whether it be the right music, a dishy DJ or a partner for the night. Fortunately all the clubs are relatively central and close to one another so this is not as absurd as one might think. Admission prices, though higher at weekends, are extremely low and drinks tend to be reasonably priced too, as long as you keep off the spirits.

The mainstream clubs tend to offer chart music, but you will find a variety from hip hop to reggae, indie and an abundance of house. Some of the smaller clubs even host one night events, theme nights and live shows.

Clubbing alone in any city can be a little unnerving, but at least in Amsterdam you are not throwing away vast sums of money if nerve fails you. Whether you dress up, down, wild or straight, you should feel OK, but a touch of leather, denim or skin-tight lycra will all be equally suitable for taking to the dance floor and not sticking out like a sore thumb. It is perfectly normal for a woman to dance alone so if the mood takes you don't refrain – you are far more likely to be hassled, picked up or spoken to sitting in the wings waiting for something to happen. Whether you are looking for a good bop or a partner for the night you should not be disappointed and the two should not be dependent on one another.

One entertaining sideline to club life is the gay scene. Whether you are gay or straight the gay discos can provide the best entertainment, music and hassle free evenings around. Many gay clubs have a mixed night which tends to be a glorious cross section of glamorous gays, exotic transvestites, a few lesbians and a smattering of straights.

The only club exclusively for women is the much publicised, always on the move *Clit Club* where dyke goddesses go go dance on the bar, erotic images are projected around the walls, live performances are inevitably sexy and there's a lot of groove on the dance floor and grope in the backroom. It has to be said that the city's lesbians make up 90% of the customers, but it is geared as a women's club for femmes of all ages, statements and sexual persuasions. It is something of a breakthrough for Amsterdam's lesbians who till now have had no women-only venue in town. Lesbians bemoan the lack of clubs in comparison with Amsterdam's male gay scene and rely on the lesbian nights at various clubs and discos for their entertainment.

An alternative to the city's clubs and discos are the all night house parties or raves which have grown around the ever increasing popularity of house music. Mainly illegal, there is one almost every weekend in some deserted warehouse or building for about f25–f50 a ticket. The authorities have come to tolerate the system, so you are unlikely to be subjected to the kind of problems with police often associated with their English equivalent. Expect a house party to last well into the next morning and 90% of the participants to be popping pills throughout the event. (For details of these and smaller house parties look for leaflets in the local record shops or drop into the clubwear outlet, WILD, on Kerkstraat.)

A few tips   Wherever you go, don't arrive early, nothing happens before 1 a.m. or 2 a.m. Don't arrive inebriated, always tip the doorman on the way out (they will expect around f5) and watch out for rogue taxi drivers who hang out outside busy clubs and threaten to take you into the unknown if you don't empty your pockets. Single women are very vulnerable so if you need a taxi go to the nearest taxi rank – ask the doorman for directions.

Trendy Bars

These are a few ideas on where to go before you hit the clubs. You should find them buzzing until around 2 a.m. and full of people in party gear and party mood. A lot of picking up seems to go on here, before anyone ever reaches the dance floor.

LUXEMBOURG
Spuistraat 22, tel. 620 6264. Open Mon–Thurs, Sun 10 a.m.–1 a.m., Fri–Sat 10 a.m.–2 a.m.

Throbs with slightly older executive crowd and people looking for club mates.

DE KROON
Rembrandtsplein 17, tel. 625 2011, Open Bar Sun–Thurs 10 a.m.–1 a.m., Fri–Sat 10 a.m.–2 a.m.; kitchen lunch 10 a.m.–6 p.m., dinner 6 p.m.–10 p.m.

à la carte. Full meals f50. Snacks and drinks. Look for doorway next to Escape club and go upstairs.

Amsterdam trendy set mingle beneath the purr of the ceiling fans, pose against the vast expanse of mellow marbled walls and sip genever from wicker seats.

PALLADIUM
Kl Gartmanpints 7, tel. 626 6566, just off Leidseplein.

Fills with seriously beautiful young

people, neatly turned out – flashy clothes and flashy partners.

DE JAREN
Nieuwe Doelenstraat 20, tel. 625 5771.

Huge café/restaurant popular with the younger partying crowd.

PARIS BREST
Prinsengracht 375, tel. 627 0507. Open weekdays 2 p.m.–1 a.m. and weekends 2 p.m.–2 a.m.

The place to be seen for Amsterdam's coolest customers.

Clubs

BUNNIES
Korte Leidsedwarsstraat 26, tel. 622 6622.

Fairly staid clientele and small venue make this a safe bet for a pleasant night out.

DANSEN BIJ JANSEN
Handboogstraat 11, tel. 620 1779.

For chart music and an informal evening with the best part of Amsterdam's student population. You may be asked to show a student card.

MAZZO
Rozengracht 114, tel. 626 7500.

This relaxed club in the Jordaan is many people's favourite. No dress restrictions, good dance floor and plenty of places to sit. Features international guest DJs and live bands.

MELKWEG
Lijnbaansgracht 234, tel. 624 8492.

Once the live bands have finished playing at weekends there is usually a general bop to various dance music.

RICHTER
Reguliersdwarsstraat 36, tel. 626 1573.

Smart civilised membership club, but if you dress up and look good you have a good chance of getting in. Shattered mirrors on the walls and good soul/disco music.

ROXY
Singel 465, tel. 620 0354.

The current favourite among Amsterdam's serious club set probably because they have a strict membership policy to ward off tourists at weekends. If you look trendy you stand a chance of getting in during the week but be prepared to bop because there are few places to sit.

ESCAPE
Rembrandtsplein 11, tel. 622 3542.

Amsterdam's largest disco, mainly frequented by tourists and locals on the pull, but an easy-going place with an excellent sound system, good laser and video screens and plenty of places to sit. No jackets.

IT
Amstelstraat 24, tel. 625 0111.

A big gay disco popular with lesbians and straights for outrageous clientele, festive atmosphere and occasional drag and strip shows. Acid and house music.

Lesbian Clubs

Although there is no lesbian club many clubs and women's groups organise one nighter discos of which most seem to be crumbling under the pressure of competition from the Clit Club. As venues and times change frequently it is always worth checking with the Gay and Lesbian Switchboard (tel. 623 6565) when you arrive in the city. Start the night in either Café Sarrein or Vive la Vie (see p.269) and then head for whatever is scheduled for that night. A few regular women's nights which seem set to stay are:

CLIT CLUB
Web Club, O.Z. Voorburgwal 15–17, tel. 624 8764. Friday nights only.

They opened in September 1992 and have been struggling to find a venue since, but have had little difficulty picking up a faithful following. Entertainment ranges from glamorous go go dancers to strippers and public clit piercing. Fierce music and a fiery dance floor.

COC AMSTERDAM
Rozenstraat 14, tel. 623 4079. Women's disco Saturdays only.

A certain youth club atmosphere is highly appealing to first timers in Amsterdam. Drinks are bought on strip cards and there is a friendly rather tame atmosphere.

HOMOLULU
Kerkstraat 23, tel. 624 6387. Women's night (ring for details).

Gay disco with good restaurant attached, overlooking the dynamic dance floor.

ROXY
Singel 465–67, tel. 620 0354.

See above. This popular club has recently started an early evening women's party, 'Roxy Lady', on Sundays 4 p.m.–10 p.m. Phone for details.

Gigs

There is no difficulty in hearing live music in Amsterdam – instead you will find it hard to avoid. Buskers occupy every available pavement, many bars have live bands over weekends and in the summer the parks and squares host free festivals. There are numerous small clubs and music bars and several larger venues, but not one with enough capacity to host international tours of the great bands who end up going to Rotterdam. The result is an excellent cross section of small, unknown bands – some good, some appalling – sharing the venues with a few better known bands who feel some affinity with the Amsterdam scene. The city has become something of a mecca for jazz with excellent artists filling the brown bars at weekends and an eclectic mix of travellers and residents holding some exhilarating jam sessions. If jazz is too mellow for you there are an increasing number of South American drinking and dancing venues for trying your paces until you drop on your feet.

Rock and Pop and Folk

The raunchy saxophonist Candy Dulfer, described in Dutch *Elle* as the 'Netherlands' best known export' is a familiar story of Dutch talent. The draw of contracts with Prince and Dave Steward was too much to keep her in her home country for long, but the Dutch have a certain loyalty that brings them back to the home crowd from time to time, Dulfer included. Some artists, such as the dyke fantasy Mathilde Santing, will occasionally pay homage to her own people and grace the stage in Amsterdam, but you are more likely to find the weekly listings splattered with young British bands making the most of small venues and a receptive audience. Often the most interesting gigs will be held at the multi media centres, the **Melkweg** and **Paradiso**. Both products of the 60s and 70s they have sufficiently good subsidies to bear the brunt of a box office failure and can offer an exciting programme of old, new and untested bands.

To find out what's on the national mag *Oor* has a complete listing of gigs going on throughout the Netherlands while the AUB in Amsterdam, Leidseplein 26, have a free pop *lijst* for things going on in town. *Time Out Amsterdam* will also have a listing and may give you more information about the artists. (See also clubs p.280.) Tickets available from the AUB and the venues.

MELKWEG
Lijnbaansgracht 234, tel. 624 8492. Enter over drawbridge.

A converted dairy, hence Melkweg (milky way), run on a co-operative basis for drama, dance, film and live bands. Saturday night gigs are usually American and British bands (mainly indie rock) and Friday night is Roots Rhythm night for live South American or African music. The separate café/bar, one of the first cafés in the city to sell marijuana, is a great place if you need a break.

PARADISO
Weteringshans 6–8, tel. 623 7348.

This old church is a great venue for better known touring bands and local talent with a strong emphasis on reggae and latin music.

AKHNATON
N.Z. Kolk 25, tel. 624 3396.

Recording studios with rehearsing facilities and a lively programme of entertainment which includes ethnic poetry reading, dance sessions, and live jazz, ethnic and folk music.

CAFÉ HAASJES
Hazenstraat 19, tel. 639 1094.

Hot, sweaty blues bar for live music every night and local stars on Sundays.

KORSAKOFF
Lijnbaansgracht 161, tel. 625 7854.

Rock and heavy metal haunt with live bands on Wednesday.

PH 31
Prins Hendriklaan 31, tel. 673 6850.

Ex-squat bar in residential area, now a one-room venue for local bands and usually very noisy.

REMBRANDT BAR
Rembrandtsplein 3, tel. 623 0688.

If you don't mind the beer-drinking tourists of Rembrandtsplein this is a good place for Dutch folk music.

SLEEP IN
's-Gravensandestraat 51, tel. 694 7444.

Multi-bed hostel which surprisingly hosts local and foreign bands and endless student discos.

STRING
Nes 98, tel. 625 9015.

Small intimate bar for blues and folk.

VONDELPARK
Summer entertainment in the park is endless and crowds pour in to hear local groups and personalities perform on the main podium. Keep an eye out in the listings for passing stars.

Jazz

Jazz fans will have a heyday in Amsterdam, not only because there is a lot going on but also because the city is packed with ardent jazz followers. You can relax in a smoke-filled brown bar and listen to fine sounds over a beer or visit the famous Bimhuis, the city's main jazz venue close to the Rembrandthuis. An afternoon in a bar with a live band is an excellent way to spend some time in the company of others if travelling alone, and it is a great way of entertaining the family if you are with older children.

If you are there at the right time it would be worth taking a trip to the Hague for the **North Sea Jazz Festival,** one of the best jazz festivals in the world, which takes place in the Hague Congresgebouw over three days in July. For good local jazz it is worth bearing in mind that October is jazz month with extra concerts and small festivals all over the country.

For information check out the listings at the AUB, in *Time Out* and keep a sharp eye open for posters in bars. You could always ring the Jazzline on 626 7764 for an update in Dutch. There is rarely an entrance fee at jazz bars, but you will find the cost of drinks a little higher than elsewhere.

ALTO JAZZ CAFÉ
Korte Leidsedwarsstraat 115, tel. 626 3249.

One of the best jazz pubs in town in the busy Leidseplein area with live music every night, featuring superstar saxophonist Hans Dulfer on Wednesday evenings.

BIMHUIS
Oudeshans 73, 623 1361.

One of the few places to charge an extrance fee (f10–f20) rewarding you with big acts from overseas and a mix of avant garde and experimental jazz. The place for serious jazz followers – plain interested might feel a little left out.

BAMBOO BAR
Lange Leidsedwarsstraat 115, tel. 624 3993.

A loud, usually crowded, late night blues and jazz bar.

DE ENGELBEWAARDER
Kloveniersburgwal 59, tel. 625 3772.

A scruffy brown bar which attracts Amsterdam's students and media set. Live jazz every Sunday starts around 4.30 p.m. Good if you are alone.

HET HEERENHUYS
Herengracht 114, tel. 622 7685.

A very nice club for regular jam sessions with local artists.

DE HEEREN VAN AEMSTEL
Thorbeckeplein 5, tel. 620 2173.

You may catch saxophonist Candy Dulfer hosting a Sunday evening jazz-funk session when she is not jet-setting across the world. Food served.

RUM RUNNERS
Prinsengracht 277, tel. 627 4079.

A glitzy Caribbean bar/restaurant which hosts latin bands at weekends and consequently gets very crowded.

Classical Music and Opera

While Amsterdam is only just finding its feet in the opera world, having opened its first and only Opera House in 1988, it plays a leading role in the authentic music movement (early music and baroque) which has brought musicians and conductors from all over the world to live and work in the city.

Check out the listings in *Time Out Amsterdam* and *Uitkrant* or drop into the VVV or AUB for information on the classical scene. The **Concertegebouw Orchestra,** under the present conductor Ricardo Chailly, has an excellent string sound and less impressive brass, and the glowing acoustics in the Concertegebouw itself are among the best in the world. For great performances **Gustav Leonhardt** gives harpsichord concerts around town and regular organ recitals in the Nieuwe Kerk. Conductor **Nicolaus Harnoncourt,** pioneer of the authentic movement in Amsterdam, is worth looking out for. Flautist Frans Bruggen's **Orchestra of the Eighteenth Century** gives exhilarating performances and Ton Koopman's **Amsterdam Baroque Orchestra** is at the core of the early music scene. A rare treat would be a chance to hear violinist **Isabel van Kuelen** performing in her home town. If early music is not your thing, **Lois Andriessen** is the contemporary composer taken most seriously.

While tickets are relatively inexpensive you can always catch a free **lunch-time concert** on Wednesdays at the Concertegebouw and Tuesdays at the Muziektheater, both starting at 12.30. Contact the respective box offices for information. For something really Dutch, **carillon concerts** are held at Westerkerk (West Church) most Wednesdays at noon and at Oude Kerk (Old Church) most Saturdays at 4 p.m.

For information and booking from abroad it is best to call the AUB Uitburo (tel. 020 621 1211). They charge f2 to book for you or you can book directly with the concert hall. Credit cards are accepted at the Concertegebouw, Muziektheater and AGA Zaal. If you are in Amsterdam visit the AUB (saves time queuing at box offices) or ask your hotel reception to book for you.

AGA ZAAL AND WANG ZAAL
Beurs van Berlage, Damrak 213, tel. 627 0466.

Home of the Netherlands Philharmonic Orchestra, the former Exchange building has been sympathetically converted. The acoustics are surprisingly good and while the orchestra is torn between three functions as a Chamber Orchestra, Opera Orchestra and Symphony Orchestra, it is a good place to hear young up and coming soloists.

CONCERTEGEBOUW
Concertegebouwplein 2–6, tel. 671 8345.

Glowing acoustics and a world-class orchestra make this the best place to hear orchestral works and recitals by major artists. Recitals and chamber ensembles are also held in the Small Hall in the same complex.

ENGELSEKERK
Begijnhof 48, tel. 624 9665.

Informal concerts featuring local and visiting artists, ensembles and choirs happen four times a week. Lunch-time concerts in July and August.

IJSBREKER
Weesperzijde 23, tel. 668 1805.

Centre for contemporary music which has weeks dedicated to specific composers or instruments.

MUZIEKTHEATER
Waterlooplein 22, tel. 625 5455.

Home of the Netherlands Opera Foundation and the Opera Orchestra, the National Ballet and the Netherlands Ballet Orchestra, this is the only place to see large-scale opera in Amsterdam. The appalling acoustics are something of a joke to all but those who designed the building, so choose your seat carefully, front row of the first balcony is best.

NIEUWE KERK
DAM, tel. 626 8168.

Brilliant organ recitals by visiting organists and the resident superstar harpsichordist/organist, Gustav Leonhardt.

OUDE KERK
Oudekerksplein 23, tel. 625 8284.

Very cold and a little musty, the Oude Kerk hosts organ recitals and chamber music concerts.

WAALSEKERK
O.Z. Achterburgwal 157, tel. 625 0078.

Good for chamber music, early music and choral concerts.

Dance
If you want to see dance in the Netherlands, Amsterdam is the place to be. Home of the National Ballet and the Netherlands Dance

Theatre there are also numerous smaller avant garde groups living and working in the city. Since the opening of the Muziektheater in 1988, the city has played host to more visiting companies from around the world.

The **National Ballet** is particularly flexible but tends to concentrate on classical ballet with over twenty Ballanchine ballets in repertoire. The more modern **Nationale Dans Theater** also has a splinter group **NDT2**, made up of younger dancers. For a rare treat try to see a performance by the brilliant modern dance company **Dansgroep Krisztina de Chatel**. Performers to keep an eye out for include **Maria Voortman, Lisa Marcus** and **Angelika Oei**.

If you're a dancer and interested in taking classes in Amsterdam, check out **Artemis Kunstcentrum**, Keizersgracht 676 (tel. 623 2655) who run classes for professionals at f12 a time, often led by members of the National Ballet. The coffeeshop is also a good place to learn about the city's dance scene.

Book all tickets direct with the venues or through the AUB Uitboro (tel. 621 1211).

MUZIEKTHEATER
Waterlooplein 22, tel. 625 5455.

Amsterdam's most lavish performances tend to happen here. Performances by visiting companies as well as home-based groups, but the stage is more often than not occupied by the National Ballet or the Netherlands Opera with whom they share the building.

DE STADSSCHOUWBURG
Leidseplein 26, tel. 624 2311.

Experimental theatre, modern dance and full blown musicals.

DANSWERKPLAATS AMSTERDAM
Overamstelstraat 39, tel. 694 9466. Outside city centre; tram 8.

For a glimpse at the new – often avant garde and always different.

BELLEVUE
Leidsekade 90, tel. 624 7248.

A small theatre often featuring good modern dance companies.

CAPTAIN FIDDLE
Kloveniersburgwal 86, tel. 623 0363.

A fringe theatre where many new companies make a start.

FRASCATI
Nes 63, tel. 622 7860.

A venue for more established dance companies.

HET VEEMTHEATER
Van Diemenstraat 410, tel. 626 0112. Tram 3, bus 28.

A long way out in the port area, but has some good mime performances.

Theatre

Anyone travelling to Amsterdam for a glimpse of Dutch theatre should really plan to go in June during the **Holland Festival** and its fringe, the **Off Holland Festival**, when every venue in the city is packed with both Dutch and international performers. For the rest of the year Amsterdam's theatres are equally packed, but the choice is not quite so extensive. Whenever you go there will always be something in English as a constant stream of English-speaking companies perform in the city.

Outdoor performances in Vondelpark are always fun and if you happen to be there for the week of **Uitmarkt** (see p.6) you will find Museumplein covered with stages and free performances taking place day and night.

Dutch theatre had its heyday in the seventeenth century under such playwrights as **Vondel, Hooft** and **Bredero**, whose plays are still performed today. Even then, Dutch theatre toured Europe and Amsterdam's theatres welcomed touring companies. By the end of the nineteenth century theatre had become an elitist concern, allowing little scope for development.

The emergence of the alternative Mickery Theatre in a farmhouse just outside the city in 1965 was the beginning of Amsterdam's progressive theatre. Three years later saw the famous *Action Tomaat* (tomato action) in which members of the audience hurled tomatoes during performances of the Comedy Theatre over a period of six months in protest against the rigid hierarchical state of drama in the Netherlands. As the Comedy Theatre closed, Amsterdam became a mecca for experimental theatre in the 60s and 70s. By the 80s a serious revival of the play was in hand dominated by the smaller avant garde companies. Sadly in the 90s government cuts continue to squeeze the smaller companies, forcing them to merge or even close. It seems that the larger cabaret/revue shows are now gaining popularity.

There is no national theatre company as such, but the chief companies are the **Toneelgroep Amsterdam**, based at the Stadsschouwburg, for fairly stolid safe productions, and the **Stadhouderij** which produces reputable contemporary works. For works by Dutch women playwrights it is probably best to check out the listings for the Holland Festival.

Women playwrights have fought hard for recognition over the past century, but since the 80s there seems to have been renewed interest in their work and, more importantly, some works are being translated into English. **Judith Herzberg** is by far the best known; her writings include *Perverse Pleasure* (1982) and *Scratch* (1988). Other women writers to look out for are **Theo Doelwijt** (*A Fat Black Woman Like Me*, 1984 and *Iris*, 1988), **Hella S. Haase** (*A Thread in the Dark*, 1963). Writers-cum-playwrights worth looking out for are **Luisa Treves** and the multi-talented **Annie M.G. Schmidt** who, apart from TV plays, children's books, musicals and radio plays, has written three major plays: *What About Me* (1969), *A Tear's Fallen on the Cream Slice* (1979) and *Los Zand* (1989).

Their plays are well worth a shot if you can catch a performance.

For theatre listings check out the listings in *Time Out Amsterdam*, the free news-sheet *Uitkrant* or call AUB Uitburo (tel. 621 1211) or the VVV booking service (tel. 626 6444). Bookings can be made through the VVV, the AUB or directly through the theatre box offices. (For Holland Festival see p.6.)

DE STADSSCHOUWBURG
Leidseplein 26, tel. 624 2311.

The seventeenth- and eighteenth-century theatres here were destroyed by fire and the present large, grand building dates from 1894. Female director, Cox Habbema, is intent on nurturing traditional theatre, hence the annual production of plays by Vondel. She also welcomes national and international companies. English productions are often staged in the former prop room, the Bovenzaal.

DE STALHOUDERIJ
1e Bloemdwarsstraat 4, tel. 626 2282.

The tiny converted stable is the home of an international collective of artists who stage contemporary English-language plays and offer courses in English. A very good atmosphere if you are going alone.

FRASCATI
Nes 63, tel. 626 6866.

The complex has three auditoriums often showing new work. English-language performances are rare.

'T FIJNHOUT THEATER
Jacob van Lennepkade 334, tel. 618 4768.

Small theatre that often plays host to English-speaking touring companies.

KONINKLIJK THEATER CARRE
Amstel 115–25, tel. 622 5225.

The Christmas circus is a must for children if you are there in December. For the rest of the year the large theatre tends to host international money-spinning musicals like *Cats* and *Les Misérables*. Also has revues, cabaret and folk dance.

SHAFFY THEATER
Felix Meritius building, Keizersgracht 323 131, tel. 626 2321.

Struggling to stay alive but you may be able to catch an English touring company on the way through. A very beautiful auditorium.

DNA
Spuistraat 2, tel. 627 8672.

Multi-cultural work including story telling, major touring productions, experimental theatre and a range of entertainment for all ages.

MELKWEG
Lijnbaansgracht 234a, tel. 624 1777.

Multi-media centre whose theatre is a prime spot for new international groups and solo performers. Exciting range from gay, lesbian, ethnic, to experimental and gestural theatre.

ROB VAN REIJN
Haarlemmerdijk 31, tel. 627 9988.

Range includes English-language plays, but don't be surprised to find a transvestite evening instead.

VONDELPARK THEATER
Vondelpark, tel. 523 7700. Walk to the centre of the park to the fountain.

Open air theatre runs from June to September offering selection of concerts, drama, cabaret and children's programmes.

Cinema

Dutch film directors have made little impact on the international scene. Not surprisingly Paul Verhoeven, director of *Basic Instinct, Robocop, Total Recall* and *Turkish Delight*, is considered a national hero and the successes of Georg Sluizer's *The Vanishing*, Fons Rademaker's *The Assault* and Dick Maas' *Flodder in Amerika* give the natives something to be proud of.

That said, the Dutch people's thirst for good films is unquenchable. Cinemas throughout the city are invariably packed, queues stretch the length of the street for some bills and new cinemas are being built rather than destroyed as in the video cultures of England and America. Amsterdam may not be the place for premieres, but its cinemas range from converted canal houses to art deco extravaganzas. Prices are reasonable (f10–f15), only one venue, De Uitkijk, refuses to have an obligatory fifteen-minute interval and smoking is not permitted anywhere.

Most films are shown in their original language (invariably English) with Dutch subtitles. If the English film has been dubbed you will notice 'Nederlands Gesproken' written on the publicity.

You can't fail to miss what's on as most cafés are plastered with the weekly showings and listings are given in *Time Out Amsterdam* and the free *Uitkrant*, the Wednesday edition of *Het Parool* and the film mag *De Filmkrant*.

TUSCHINSKI
Reguliersbreestraat 26, tel. 626 2633.

A very beautiful cinema and Amsterdam's most prestigious (see p.133). Seven screens, but if you are going for the art deco choose screen one, whatever is showing.

DE UITKIJT
Prinsengracht 452, tel. 623 7460.

A small converted canal house with a slow turnover of films. Intimate, pleasant no pause and no refreshments.

RIKS BIOSCOOP
Reguliersbreestraat 31, tel. 626 2633.

A 'Dollar cinema' where last year's movies run a constant loop and the cost of tickets is no more than a beer – f2.50.

KRITERION
Roetersstraat 170, tel. 623 1708.

Slick cinema run by volunteer students with kids' matinees on Wednesday, Saturday and Sunday, plus cult American movies and erotic French late-night bills.

CALYPSO/BELLEVUE CINERAMA
Marnixstraat 400, tel. 623 4876.

Large, plush and comfortable.

ENTERTAINMENT

CITY
Leidseplein, tel. 623 4579.

The biggest complex in town with seven screens and an audience capacity of 2,094, yet they still have queues at weekends.

RIALTO
Ceintuurbaan 338, tel. 662 3488.

Good for sci-fi, animation and children's films.

FILM MUSEUM
Vondelpark 3, tel. 589 1400.

Tinted silent movies and various other delights from the archives (see p.169) as well as more modern releases.

HEALTH AND SPORT

Amsterdammers enjoy their sport. In winter skating is the talk of the town unless the local soccer team Ajax happens to be playing, and in summer their enthusiasm shifts to tennis and cycling. The city is well equipped with sports facilities and health clubs and more seem to open each year. Joggers head for Vondelpark or the more picturesque and testing routes in Amsterdam Bos. You can practise your basketball and skateboarding for free on Museumplein, provided you can find a spare court or ramp. If you want to try something new, Korfball, a cross between netball and volleyball, is gaining popularity in the Netherlands. The main advantage of the game is that the sexes compete on equal terms as they are only allowed to mark opponents of the same sex – ask at the sports clubs.

For information on sports and leisure facilities and fixtures, telephone the Sports and Leisure Department on 522 2490.

Spectator Sports

AJAX (SOCCER)
Middenweg 401, tel. 694 6515.

Ajax reached second place in the 1992 league table, but won the UEFA cup in the same year. The Dutch reputation for football violence is similar to that in Britain. Ajax matches are reasonably safe, but always heavily policed. It is advisable to buy seat tickets.

WAGENAAR STADIUM (HOCKEY)
Nieuwe Kalfjeslaan, tel. 640 1141.

Your chance to watch both international and league hockey matches played every Sunday from January to May and August to December. Women play at 12.45, men at 2.30 p.m.

APOLLOHAL (BASKETBALL)
Stadionweg, tel. 671 3910.

Basketball is practised in every park in the city, but for a first division match watch the first division, Canadians Amsterdam. Matches every Saturday 8 p.m. from September to June.

Participation Sports

Amsterdam Bos has a wide range of outdoor sports facilities (see p.212) and there are open air tennis courts in Vondelpark. Skating is free on the outdoor rink in Leidseplein over the winter; skates can be hired from the Hoopman Bodega café alongside the rink for f6.

DORCHLAND
Borchlandweg 8–12, tel. 696 1441. Metro Standuliet.

The only large sports centre for tennis, squash, ten-pin bowling and badminton.

SQUASH CITY
Ketelmakerstraat 6, tel. 626 7883. Bus 18, 22.

Squash, weights and art deco sauna.

AMSTELPARK
Karel Lotsylaan 8, tel. 644 5436. Bus 26, 48, 63, 158.

Indoor and outdoor tennis courts.

JAAP EDENHAL
Radioweg 64, tel. 694 9652. Tram 9.

Ice rink open October to March.

MARNIXBAD
Marnixplein 9, tel. 625 4843.

A large indoor swimming pool, water slides, whirlpool and sauna.

MIRANDABAD
De Mirandalaan, tel. 644 6637. Tram 15, 69, 169.

Sub-tropical swimming pool complete with stone beach and wave machine. Separate pools for children and a nice outdoor pool for summer.

ZUIDERBAD
Hobbemastraat 26, tel. 679 2217. Tram 1, 2, 5.

A popular old fashioned swimming pool for basic training.

SPLASH
Looiersgracht 26, tel. 624 8404. Tram 7, 10.

Fitness centre includes aerobics classes, weights, massage and sauna.

SAUNA KYLPY
Mercatorplein 23, tel. 612 3496. Tram 7, 13.

Women's sauna.

SHOPPING

 The abundance of markets and tiny specialist shops in Amsterdam make shopping a real pleasure. Unlike many other Dutch cities, Amsterdam has not yet, and probably never will, fall victim to international high street uniformity. There are few department stores, a sprinkling of international competitors and a mass of small family run businesses and co-operatives.

Second-hand shops, alternative beauty treatments and health food are all the rage so don't shy away from the alternative second-hand look, but make the most of what's on offer from funky Afghans to 1950s toasters.

Classy businesswomen and jet setters admit that Amsterdam is not the place for haute couture and European chic. With Paris only a short flight away most of them save serious clothes shopping for a Parisian weekend. Caught short and they head for the most upmarket, yet still low key, P.C. Hooftstraat where the range of designers is better than the choice in stock.

For good reasonably priced fashionable clothes for both work and casual wear *Sissy Boy* and the *Laundry Industry* are the best of the high street shops by a long way. Both have stores around Kalverstraat which tends to be the busiest and less attractive shopping street, but is good for essentials and second-hand books. For similar shops in a better atmosphere visit the new shopping mall, Magna Plaza, on N.Z. Voorburgwal 182, which also has a brilliant top floor devoted to children.

If you are into period clothes or the alternative look then you are in one of the best cities in Europe. You will find plenty to choose from if you move between Waterlooplein flea market and the specialist shops around the Jordaan, taking in some of the second-hand shops along the way. Students tend to stick to Waterlooplein market or bargain baskets outside the alternative shops, but anyone can dress well, in a funky sort of way, for very little money.

Amsterdam is renowned for fine diamonds so if you have something to celebrate or a particular passion for sparklers you should be able to find something you like at a good price. For cheap and cheerful jewellery the markets have great selections of both ethnic and traditional pieces and there are some good contemporary designers about. Earrings are everywhere and even the tackiest looking shops often have some stylish numbers.

Most of the souvenir shops tend to be along Leidsestraat and Damstraat, both of which are crowded with tourists and pickpockets. China windmills, clogs on keyrings and dolls in national costume seem to be standard fare; for something more authentic you would be better off wandering around the Jordaan or checking out the tiny streets that run between the canals like Huidenstraat, Runstraat and Hartenstraat.

For antiques, Delft tiles and prints the Spiegel Quarter is the best place (see p.139) but if you are more interested in authentic kitsch the Monday morning market at Noorderkerk (North Church), attached to the Lapjesmarkt, is excellent and the daily book market of Oudemanshuispoort has very cheap prints.

Books are prohibitively expensive in the Netherlands so buy any holiday reading before you go or check out the second-hand departments. If, however, you wish to read Dutch works in translation and have failed, as is likely, to find anything at home be prepared to splash out and head for W.H.Smith on Kalverstraat.

Despite a number of sumptuous local bakeries, butchers and food shops most Dutch people use supermarkets for their daily food. This means that the small food shops that do exist offer excellent quality in order to maintain regular customers. Around Easter and St Nicolaas' Day on 5 December you will find chocolate shops and patisseries brimming with delicately decorated chocolate novelties and marzipan figures, ideal for popping in a bag for the journey home.

THINGS TO TAKE HOME
Bottle of genever (Dutch gin)
Round of Gouda cheese (wrap it up in newspaper and it will last)
Earrings
Antique Delft tiles
Old print of the city
Fabric for patchwork or home-made clothes
Bulbs for planting back home
Clogs
Funky period clothes
Dope pipe/clay Dutch pipe
Fantasy condoms from the Condomerie

OPENING HOURS

Most shops open around 9 a.m.–6 p.m. Some are closed on Monday or open late around 1 p.m. Many stay open late until 9 p.m. on Thursdays and they generally close early on a Saturday around 5 p.m.

Credit cards are accepted at most department stores and larger shops for bills over f50, but be prepared for the smaller shops to want cash.

Warning: Many pickpockets work in the main shopping areas in the centre. Keep a hand on your bag, don't put money or a purse in your pockets and never wait at a till with your purse, money or credit card in one hand, poised to pay. Take it out of your bag as you reach the till.

Markets

ALBERT CUYP MARKET
Albert Cuypstraat, Mon–Sat 9 a.m.–5 p.m. Tram 2, 16, 24, 25.

The best local market for fresh herbs, fish, vegetables and more exotic food, wacky fabrics, second-hand and new clothes, and household goods.

BOERENMARKET
Westerstraat/Noorderkerk, Sat 10 a.m.–3 p.m.

Organic farmer's market which is good for health foods, local crafts and fresh produce.

LAPJESMARKT
Westerstraat/Noorderkerk, Mon 9.30 a.m.–1 p.m.

Brilliant market for fabrics, second-hand clothes and general junk, from sequined sofas to antique prams.

WATERLOOPLEIN FLEA MARKET
Waterlooplein, Mon–Sat 10 a.m.–5 p.m.

Enormous flea market, good for funky clothes and leather jackets with a few antique stalls and a few more specialist stalls ranging from theatrical costume to wheelchairs.

NIEUWMARKT
Nieuwmarkt. General food market Mon–Sat 9 a.m.–5 p.m.; antiques Sun 10 a.m.–5 p.m. (May–Sept).

A good local food market with excellent cheese stall and, on Sundays, fine antiques.

LINDENGRACHT
Sat 9 a.m.–4 p.m.

A good local food market.

FLOWER MARKET (BLOEMENMARKT)
On the Singel between Muntplein and Koningsplein. Mon–Sat 9 a.m.–4.30 p.m.

Cut flowers, bulbs, pots and bonsai.

BOOK MARKET
Oudmanshuispoort (off O.Z.Auchterburgwal, bottom end in enclosed passage).

English-language books are occasionally on sale, but old postcards, posters and prints might make an original souvenir – all very cheap.

STAMP AND COIN MARKET
N.Z.Voorburgwal 276. Wed, Sat 11 a.m.–4 p.m.

Specialist market for stamps, coins and medals.

Department Stores

DE BIJENKORF
Dam 1.

The Bijenkorf (the Beehive) is the best-known department store in the country with a good range of cosmetics, clothes, jewellery, shoes, accessories, toys and linen. Excellent book department has a good selection of English-language titles for both adults and children.

HEMA
Nieuwendijk 174, Reguliersbreestraat 10 and other stores all over town.

Budget store offering surprisingly good quality adult and children's clothes, underwear, accessories, stationery, household goods and some food. Good on baby gear and accessories.

METZ
Keizersgracht 455.

Expensive gifts, designer furniture, ornaments and scented soaps.

VROOM AND DREESMAN
Kalverstraat 201.

Slightly more upmarket than Hema, but selling everything from cosmetics and casual clothes to gardening supplies.

Designer Clothes

REFLECTIONS
Stadhouderskade 23/P.C. Hooftstraat 66.

A useful fallback for the chic who have not time to go to Paris. Armani, Farhi and other exclusive names.

JOHN AND VERA HARTMAN
P.C.Hooftstraat 36.

A good range of designer labels from Armani, Katharine Hamnett, Kenzo and Dutch labels. People of the Labyrinth for funky flowing numbers or Just B for casual beachwear.

PUCK AND HANS
Rokin 62.

A good range of young designer fashion includes Katharine Hamnett and Jean Paul Gautier.

ANTONIA
Gasthuismolensteeg 12.

An outlet for top Dutch designers like Gletcher and Imps. Swimwear from True Falsies and shoes from Lola Pagola.

MAX MARA
P.C.Hooftstraat 110.

Quality tailored suits, coats and separates in safe colours and classic cuts.

KHYMO
Leidsestraat 9.

Trendy gear from Katharine Hamnett, Jean Paul Gautier and less well-known labels.

Haute Couture

EDGAR VOS
P.C.Hooftstraat 132.

Suits and smart gear for international businesswomen.

FRANK GOVERS
Keizersgracht 500.

Frank Govers has a faithful clientele willing to pay enormous prices for beautiful clothes. Ready to wear start at f1000 and haute couture at f5000.

High Street Fashion

SISSY BOY
Kalverstraat 210.

Trendy clothes in seasonal colours, cuts and fabrics at moderate prices.

LAUNDRY INDUSTRY
Magna Plaza, N.Z. Voorburgwal 182.

Simple, stylish and fashionable clothes in mainly natural fabrics and the wackiest changing rooms in town.

Second-hand and Offbeat

DAFFODIL
Jacob Obrechtstraat 41.

Second-hand haute couture for women with numerous designer labels selling for less than half the original price.

ROSE ROOD
Kinkerstraat 159.

A wonderful shop selling period clothes from 1700 to the 1960s at very reasonable prices. Worth going to whether you intend to buy or not.

SISTERS
Lauriergracht 110, in the Jordaan.

Hippies rejoice! This small shop sells second-hand 60s and 70s clothes and also makes clothes to order in flowery, psychedelic and tie dye prints. Flares, sequinned jackets and Afghan coats and a terrific selection of clothes for hip children too.

ZIPPER
Damstraat 10.

Second-hand American clothes.

LADY DAY
Hartenstraat 9.

Quality second-hand clothes for women and children from sophisticated dresses to old jeans.

PASSAGE CENTRAL
Nieuwendijk 25–27.

Second-hand clothes sold by the kilo, so clothes come cheap at around f25 for a complete outfit. Great collection of original hippie gear, flares in leather, suede and flowery fabrics. Kaftans and lots of photoprint denim.

RETRO TWEEDE
Constantijn Huygenstraat 57.

This is one of the best places for seriously offbeat and eccentric clothes. If you are looking for an outfit for one night it is possible to hire.

ROXY
Kalverstraat 224.

Trendy second-hand gear, including a great selection of groovy footwear.

BEBOP
Nieuwendijk 164.

Second-hand party gear for exotic, eccentric and hideous ensembles.

Lingerie

VICTORIA'S SECRETS
Leidsestraat 32.

Expensive silky numbers.

TONY TOLO
Kinkerstraat 161.

The best stocked shop in town for glamorous designerwear or a price pair of knickers.

Large sizes

DUCO
Overtoom 167a.

Bright clothes for sizes 18–26 British, 16–30 American.

ONADUR
Spiegelgracht 6.

This little boutique carries a good range of larger clothes among its selection of classic cuts and knitwear.

Clubwear

WILD
Kerkstraat 104.

This tiny basement shop stocks a small supply of clubwear and sportswear ranging from lycra bodysuits to T-shirts, mainly from local designers. The back doubles up as a hairdressing salon for cheap and trendy haircuts.

NEW IMAGE
N.Z.Voorburgwal 351.

If you need something in a hurry the in-house designer will help you out in a matter of days – otherwise take your pick in the club shop.

THE FABULOUS SHOP
Eerste Jan Steenstraat 149.

A more upmarket clubwear shop for designer dressed clientele who want a one-off number for their next date.

Children's Clothes, Toys and Baby Equipment

See p.316.

Hats

DE HOED VAN TIJN
Nieuwe Hoogstraat 12.

Hats line the walls, hang off the ceiling and spill out of chests. Some stunning antique hats, outrageous old ones and a few new classics. Milliners come here for felt, ribbons and second-hand moulds.

Shoes, Leather, Luggage

DONKERS
P.C.Hooftstraat 108.

This is currently the 'in' place for footwear with a good range of sturdy boots and DMs.

STEPHANE KELIAN
P.C.Hooftstraat 99.

For beautiful classic shoes in classic colours.

BIG SHOE
Leliegracht 12.

All kinds of shoes in large sizes – British 8½–13½, American 10–15 – from trainers to stilettos, boots and classic court shoes.

HESTER VAN EEGHEN
Hartenstraat 1.

A small outlet for this talented Dutch bag designer who works from Italy, but whose bags are actually made in the Netherlands. Innovative shapes, styles and colours and some brilliant briefcases for women. Prices for bags start at f250.

FAÇADE
P.C.Hooftstraat 79.

Cardin and Gucci feature highly in this traditional outlet for gloves, diaries, briefcases and wallets.

CARINA LEDERWAREN
Nieuwendijk 95.

As well as more classy leather goods

they also stock cheaper rucksacks, school bags and reasonably priced suitcases.

Diamonds

If you are looking for diamonds there are plenty of outlets in Amsterdam and the cost of even a small stone should be considerably less than it is at home. It is worth shopping around to find a stone, setting and price that you like. The following are just a few of the reputable outlets.

COSTER DIAMONDS
Paulus Potterstraat 2–6.

GASSON DIAMOND HOUSE
Nieuwe Uilenburgerstraat 173–5.

VAN MOPPES
Albert Cuypstraat 2–6.

ROKIN DIAMONDS
Rokin 12.

Jewellery

Earrings are sold everywhere, on the street by passing travellers and in shops all over the city. The standard of local craftsmanship and ingenuity of local designers are extremely high and you may find a bargain if you keep your eyes open.

BEAUFORT
Grimburgwal 11.

Run by the talented designers, Liseth van As, Rita Burgersdijk and Bep Peters, this small shop is a great place for quality contemporary work. The styles of the three vary enormously so it is likely that at least one will appeal to you.

DIVA
Nieuwe Hoogstraat 12.

Earrings, brooches and hair decorations are all reasonably priced. Earrings range from Gothic danglers to hand-crafted gold studs.

CEDILLE
Lijnbaansgracht 275.

This earring cum toy shop has a wide range of cheap earrings in a variety of

materials – a good place for souvenir shopping.

Fabrics and Haberdashery

CAPSICUM
Oude Hoogstraat 1.

Woven cottons from India and Thai silks in sumptuous shades. Capsicum specialises in natural fibres and has plenty of choice, from lightweight dress materials to coarser weaves for bedspreads and wall hangings.

DE AFSTAP
Oude Leliestraat 12.

Vast selection of patchwork materials, many in traditional Dutch patterns, sold in small quantities. Rowan wools and an exhaustive selection of embroidery patterns and sets.

McLennan's
Hartenstraat 22.

Silks from China, Thailand and Mongolia in rich colours and bold prints.

Knopenwinkel
Wolvenstraat 14.

Buttons in every conceivable shape, style, colour and size – and a wonderful window display.

Health and Beauty

The traditional beauty parlour in the Netherlands is beginning to lose customers to the popular holistic healthcare centres, the healing arts like massage, acupuncture, reflexology are proving to be something of a hit in the capital. While brand name cosmetics are available in the department stores and chemists you will find there is a strong emphasis on natural products.

Jacob Hooy & Co
Kloveniersburgwal 12.

Established in 1743, this old fashioned apothecary sells herbs, spices, natural cosmetics, homeopathic remedies and health foods.

The Body Shop
Kalverstraat 157.

The full range of Body Shop products – soaps, shampoos, bath oils and makeup – for twice the price one would pay in England.

The Hair Shop
Antoiniesbreestraat 124.

As well as haircuts they offer a wide range of good hair and skin products, plus vegetable soaps.

Palais des Parfums
Van Baerlestraat 74.

A popular pamper parlour with a wide range of top brand perfumes and cosmetics. Five salons upstairs for treatment: manicure f27.50; massage f70; and facials start at f70.

Beauty Form
1e Oosterparkstraat, tel. 694 4957.

Beauty parlour offering a 'traveller's special' for f55 which includes epilation, peeling, massage, mask and compresses.

Centrum de Roos
Vondelstraat 35–7.

One of the city's best therapy centres offering massage, acupuncture, aromatherapy, chanting, tai chi, meditation, yoga and many more holistic treatments.

Tanya Balkera
Nieuwe Keizersgracht 23, tel. 624 5623.

Homeopath and herb doctor, Tanya uses iridology (eye diagnosis) to assess you and offers hourly treatment sessions for f75. Appointments only.

Ego Soft
Nieuwe Kerkstraat 67.

If you have always wanted to try out a brain machine to relax your confused brain and tired limbs then Ego Soft have all the latest equipment.

Haircuts

DE BIJENKORF
Dam 1, tel. 261 8080

Slick salon in this well-known department store will wash and set for f37.50, wash, cut and dry for f62.50; kids start at f25.

HAIR GALLERY
Hartenstraat 2, tel. 622 7693.

Seriously good cuts for the young and trendy. Cuts only.

WILD
Kerkstraat 104, tel. 626 0749.

Trendy hairdresser in the back room of the clubwear shop. Cuts f35 and colour f45.

BEREGOED
Buitenveldertsein 120, tel. 646 2660.

Children's hairdresser kitted out with the wherewithal to amuse the little ones while cutting. The only exclusively kids' place in town.

Sex

NVSH
Blauwburgwal 7–9, tel. 622 6690.

Women friendly sex shop for vibrators, contraceptives and advice on anything concerning sex. Sells Femidoms and Dental Dams.

CONDOMERIE
Warmoestraat 141. Opens 1 p.m.–6 p.m., closed Sun & Mon.

Condoms for everyone – designer condoms, sweet wrapped, flavoured, coloured and fantasised and every brand available.

MAIL FEMALE
Mail order, Postbus 16668, 1001 RD.

For the erotically enlightened this mail order lingerie company has recently expanded to include a range of women's love toys and erotic videos covering fetish, classics from the 40s and 50s and the Velvet label made by women.

Tattoo and Bodypiercing

Tattooing is big business in Amsterdam and the tattooists are real experts. All shops are checked monthly by the local health authorities so they are hygienic. Most shops are in the Red Light District, but many women choose to go to the exception, Skin Deep, in the Jordaan.

SKIN DEEP
2e Goudsbloemdwarsstraat.

The best place for body artistry, nipple, lip and eyebrow piercing. Evening appointments available for tattoos in intimate places if you are worried about people looking through the window.

Bookshops

W.H. SMITH
Kalverstraat 152.

Carries all the latest English-language magazines and lots of English books, fiction, children's and non-fiction. It also has the best collection of Dutch books in translation in the city.

THE BOOK EXCHANGE
Kloveniersburgwal 58.

Second-hand English books are bought and sold here.

THE ENGLISH BOOKSHOP
Lauriergracht 71.

British mags and books at Dutch prices.

ATHENEUM NIEUWSCENTRUM
Spui 14–16.

Most people come here to browse through the magazines, but it is also a good bookshop.

AMERICAN DISCOUNT BOOK CENTER
Kalverstraat 185.

Relatively cheap books in English.

KOOKBOEKHANDEL
Runstraat 26.

The brainwave of Jonah Freud who has collected this feast of cookery books from all over the world.

Children's

DE KINDERBOEKWINKEL
N.Z. Voorburgwal 344.

Books, many English, are arranged according to age.

FANTASTICO BOOKS
Magna Plaza, N.Z. Voorburgwal 182.

Children's books in Dutch and English, and helpful staff.

See also W.H. Smith and De Bijenkort department store (see pp.300, 295).

Women's and gay bookshops

ANTIQUARIAAT LORELEI
Prinsengracht 495.

Huge selection of second-hand books for, about and by women. There is usually a good choice of English titles whether you are looking for a holiday novel or a heavy tome on feminist theory. Good notice board.

VROUWEN IN DRUK
Westermarkt 5.

Extensive collection of books concerning women and by women – many in English.

XANTIPPE
Prinsengracht 290.

The prime women's bookstore for recent publications, old favourites and feminist classics. Good handout on women's venues in Amsterdam is available over the counter.

VROLIJK
Paleisstraat 135.

Gay and lesbian bookshop which also has a huge stock of international magazines.

Music

VIRGIN
Magna Plaza, N.Z. Voorburgwal 182.

Mainly CDs and videos and a coffeeshop for checking out the latest sounds.

CONCERTO
Utrechtsestraat 54–60.

New and second-hand albums and CDs for everyone, whatever their taste in music. Listening booths available.

JAZZ INN
Vijzelgracht 9.

Jazz through the ages – enthusiasts should not leave disappointed.

Antiques, Crafts and Collectors' Items

Serious antique buyers head for the Spiegel Quarter around Nieuwe Spiegelstraat which is packed with quality antique shops (see p.139), but there are a number of other outlets specialising in period items and also the popular Looiers indoor antiques market in the Jordaan.

LOOIER INDOOR ANTIQUE MARKET
Elandsgracht. Mon–Thurs 11 a.m.–5 p.m., Sat 9 a.m.–5 p.m.

A total mix of quality pieces and ageing junk, but a fascinating collection of stalls offering furniture, maritime instruments, china, silver and general bric-a-brac.

GALLERIA D'ARTE RINASCIMENTO
Prinsengracht 170.

Collectable pottery, antique tiles, repro tulip vases and exquisite clock cases.

FOCKE & MELTZER
P.C.Hooftstraat.

European china, crystal and glass, including Leerdam crystal and Porceleyne Fles Delftware.

COLLECTORS
Muiderstraat 21.

A large shop close to the botanical garden jammed with juke boxes, model ships, dentist's chairs, dinky replicas and classic cars. A must if you are going that way and not far from Waterlooplein if you feel like a walk.

FIFTIES–SIXTIES
Huidenstraat 13.

Jammed full of period pieces from toasters to teas-mades, lamps and furniture. Everything is authentic and everything works.

TESSELSCHADE – ARBEID ADELT
Leidseplein 33.

Local handicrafts made by a non-profit making association of Dutch women. Toys to tea-cosies.

Speciality Shops

MARANON BV
Herengracht 265.

Beautiful hammocks from South America for indoors and out in attractive styles and colours. Vast double hammocks are irresistible and very reasonably priced. They also stock wall brackets.

VLIEGERTUIG
Gasthuismolensteeg 8.

Kites, kites and more kites for adults and children in vibrant colours, sophisticated designs and hard-wearing materials at reasonable prices.

P.G.C. HAJENIUS
Rokin 92–6.

Tobacco specialist selling traditional Dutch clay pipes.

KRAMER
Reestraat 20.

Candles down one side and dolls on the other – both exhaustive collections.

WITTE TANDEN WINKEL
Runstraat 5.

A tiny shop selling nothing but toothbrushes in every conceivable shape, colour and size and flavoured toothpastes which are always a hit with the kids.

THE HEAD SHOP
Kloveniersburgwal 12.

Drug taking equipment. A good selection of pipes from around the world.

T'KLOMPENHUISJE
Nieuwe Hoogstraat 9a.

FOOD AND DRINK

Treats and gifts

VAN GELDER FRUITGESCHENKEN
Parnassusweg 3.

One of the few places where you can buy *kandeel*, a mixture of wine, milk, sugar, egg yolk and cinnamon, which is the traditional gift for pregnant women to keep the evil spirits away. Special gift boxes start at f14.50.

EICHOLTZ
Leidsestraat 48.

Deli selling souvenirs like chocolate tiles and Dutch as well as English and American specialities.

HENDRIKSE
Overtoom 472.

The best cakes and tarts in town – it is not surprising to find that they supply the royal family.

OLDENBURG
P.C.Hooftstraat 97.

Cakes, chocolates and exotic creations to salivate over in the window.

Clogs and souvenirs.

1001 KRALEN
1e Bloemdwarsstraat 38.

Beads, beads and more beads.

MINIATURE FURNITURE
Prinsengracht 293, tel. 626 7863.

Appointments are needed to see this beautiful selection of hand-made dolls' house furniture.

HARRISON'S
Kinkerstraat 339.

Cakes, cake decorations and custom made cakes to order (they can even be sent abroad).

POMPADOUR
Huidenstraat 12.

Great chocolates in pretty packages.

Delicatessens

DIKKER AND THIJS
Prinsengracht 444.

The best deli in town with an excellent take-away service.

Health Food

MANNA
Spui 1.

Everyone's most favourite organic foodstore with a bakery attached, take-away meals and a good range of cosmetics and aromatherapy oils, as well as things to eat.

Tea and Coffee

GEELS AND CO
Warmoestraat 67.

The city's oldest tea and coffee specialists with a good range of brewing equipment.

KEIZER
Prinsengracht 180.

This coffeeshop has an exquisite interior and sells excellent beverages. Also sells tiles made of pressed tea which make unusual presents.

Cheese

Dutch cheese is not dull. Most people think of the bland red rinded Edam as Holland's primary contribution to the world of cheese, but you will find Dutch cheese comes hard, soft and in a variety of interesting combinations. Whether flavoured with coriander, cumin and clove, garlic or nettle, all are delicious. For creamy cheese ask for *jong* or young; the old, *oude*, is generally harder and sharper tasting. *Goudse* is the most popular cheese from Gouda, followed by *leidse*.

WEGEWIJS KAAS
Rozengracht 32.

Dutch cheese shop offering over a hundred varieties of local cheese. Tasting is all part of the buying process.

Drink

WATERWINKEL
Roelof Hartstraat 10.

A hundred bottled mineral waters from around the world. Dead sea mud is sold as an acne remedy.

DE CUYP
Albert Cuypstraat 146.

Specialises in miniature and giant bottles. A good place to buy gift bottles of genever.

WIJNKOPERIJ
Utrechtsestraat 51.
Over 600 varieties of wine with tasting sessions on Saturdays.

DE BIERKONING
Paleisstraat 33.

Stocks 750 brands of beer.

Amsterdam is not somewhere one would automatically associate with family holidays and many parents are wary of the drugs and sex image of the city. They shouldn't be. If you arrive on spec you will be disappointed by the lack of obvious facilities for children, but an evening's planning can ensure the whole family will have the holiday of a lifetime. The city is a great place for children over six provided you plan ahead and make the most of the city's numerous children's activities, from circus workshops to open air concerts. Teenagers could have a really good time. As in all cities, small children are not so easy to entertain and you will have the constant worry of open canals to contend with. That said, there is plenty to keep them occupied for a few days and in the summer you have the added attraction of the beach only a short journey away.

If you are worried about the frankness of the sex industry, don't be. Yes, your child may come face to face with a window full of dildos because sex shops are all over town. Young children won't notice, older ones probably won't unless you look embarrassed and it is very easy to distract children in a foreign city. You would be advised to steer clear of the Red Light District unless you feel it is time for your children to address issues like prostitution and pornography. Some of the tourist streets do have an abundance of sex shops, so you may wish to avoid the top end of Nieuwendijk, Damrak and Damstraat.

Dutch children are fortunate enough to experience an old fashioned lifestyle in which they walk to school, talk to strangers and are allowed to trust people. Dutch parents find the abductions and molestations of children in England and America almost incomprehensible. You will find, at street level, people enjoy children. They will be offered sweets, biscuits and tasty cuts of cheese in many local shops, people smile at them, buskers perform to them and weirdos dance for them. The average family in the Netherlands has three children, but since the rise of the divorce rate in the 80s one third will have divorced parents. Women tend to have children in their late twenties and many choose or are forced to bring them up alone, so there are a large number of single mothers.

You won't see many kids out at night in Amsterdam, probably because parents find it easier to stay in. Most cafés and restaurants welcome children, offer special menus and have high chairs. Hotels generally welcome children too, and provide cots for babies at a small charge, but you will find that some have a no children policy. If taking babies and toddlers to Amsterdam you will need a buggy and, if your child likes to walk, a pair of reins (even if you detest them) is not a bad idea to avoid losing them in a canal. A papoose would be the easiest way to carry a baby because prams tend to be too big and cumbersome for many cafés, shops, restaurants and sights. Breastfeeding in public is perfectly OK provided you respect the general comfort of the people around you, as you would any-where. If in company it is polite to ask if anyone minds – if you ask as the baby takes first gulp they can't really say no. You will find few baby changing facilities in the city; the station and department stores offer a meagre corner in the public toilets and charge 50c for using them. You won't find special feeding rooms anywhere.

City children need entertainment and Amsterdam's kids have a lot to choose from. There's plenty of hands-on entertainment if your children don't mind joining the natives and being spoken to in Dutch. They can join a theatre workshop, perform in their own cir-cus or cook at the children's restaurant. They can scrub the deck or stir the pea soup on the old ship *Amsterdam* at the Maritime Museum, join ethnic dancers at the Tropenmuseum children's annexe (TM Junior) or make giant soap bubbles at the NINT Technology Museum.

For less taxing pursuits the zoo is a good family outing what-ever the weather, urban farmyards provide easy entertainment and there are terrific swimming pools and a good winter open air ice rink right in the centre of town. Canal boat trips are a good way of killing an hour if your child doesn't succumb to seasickness and a climb up one of the church towers is a good way to exhaust even the most energetic youngsters.

Amsterdam can be good for kids all year round. December seems to be their month with shops brimming with little treats and Christmas goodies, the arrival of St Nicolas on 5 December, who parades the streets on horseback watched by thousands of children and the famous Carre Circus which is the highlight of any child's Christmas. In spring they would enjoy Queen's Day on 30 April provided you spend the day in Vondelpark, which is reserved for family entertainment. Children from all over town join adults in setting up stalls selling old toys, face painting or playing Twinkle Twinkle Little Star on the school violin. Over the summer there are more buskers on the streets, further free entertainment in Vondelpark, regular Punch and Judy shows on Dam Square and generally better weather for enjoying the parks and playgrounds.

Over 12s

Many teenagers dread family holidays with the prospect of boring hotels, stuffy restaurants, family friction and hours of forced entertainment when they would rather be at home with friends. Amsterdam is a great place for teenagers provided the parents are prepared to make the most of the city too. Family holidays are not cheap, but if you take advantage of the 'children for free' offer at the Arthur Frommer Hotel (see p.239) you can do it relatively inexpensively.

Dutch teenagers are treated like mini adults. They officially become adults at 18 although the age of consent is 12 (parents are allowed to intervene if the partner is over 16). They may buy beer at 16 and spirits at 18, but kids are allowed into bars at any age. The police tend to turn a blind eye to under-age drinking unless youngsters are obviously disruptive.

Obviously all children have their personal preferences, but a live jazz session in a brown bar, a rummage through the funky clothes at Waterlooplein flea market or a look at a professional dance session in the Artemis café are always popular. Visiting the Heineken brewery is boring, visiting the Cannabis Info Museum (p.94) is not, while Anne Frank's House (p.124) may seem an obvious choice for people of her age, the Resistance Museum (p.177) may be more enlightening. Open air theatre may be tedious, but open air rock concerts won't be – both happen throughout the summer in Vondelpark (p.168). Film freaks can watch the latest releases or catch some old movies (often to live music) in the Film Museum (p.169). Children interested in going into the theatre would enjoy the guided tour around the Muziektheater (p.185) where dancers perform in Hollywood style practice salons, make-up artists apply wigs and face packs in the dressing rooms, and costume makers put the final touches to glamorous outfits while technicians programme the sophisticated revolving stages. Classical music fans may find an evening concert too long, but a lunch-time one entertaining.

Whatever your family's interests Amsterdam is an exciting, nicely laid back place where young adults can come to little harm and have lots of fun.

Information on Children's Events

The free monthly *Uitkrant* has listings for children's events in the *jeugd* section. The VVV tourist information offices (see p.13) should be of help, but, in our experience, they are not particularly reliable or helpful. If they tell you there is nothing on they clearly don't know so you will have to ring around yourself. Many of the venues have an answerphone message in Dutch which won't be enlightening but leave a message in English or wait until you catch someone in. Many events are organised by the neighbourhood centres, listed under *Buurthuis* in the telephone directory. It is worth calling them.

Child Helplines

Kindertelefoon, tel. 622 4455 (open 2 p.m.–8 p.m. daily) is a child helpline for trivial inquiries like doll repair to more serious matters of abuse. This is not an information service. **Kinderrechtswinkel** (Children's Rights Shop), Brouwersgracht 44 (tel. 626 0067) gives information on children's legal rights and the responsibilities of teachers and employers.

Babysitting

Some hotels will have their own babysitting facilities, but there are other reputable companies available. It may sound the perfect answer to a peaceful night out, but not all parents find it easy to leave a total stranger in charge of their kids in a strange city. Be assured that the companies mentioned have been going for years, they choose sitters carefully and the babysitter is likely to speak a little English. Be warned that men and women work for them and you may not always be able to specify by sex. If you are not happy about going out when the sitter arrives don't be afraid to say so; if necessary cancel the evening out. Constant worrying only means you won't enjoy your evening. If you are out after midnight you may be asked to call a taxi to take your babysitter home.

OPPASCENTRAL KRITERION
Roetersstraat 170, tel. 624 5848. Book between 5.30 p.m. and 7 p.m daily. Rates f4 an hour to 7 p.m., f5 per hour till midnight, f7 from midnight–3 a.m. and f10 per hour from 3 a.m.–7 a.m.; f2.50 supplement for Fri and Sat.

Use male and female students and may, in our experience, promise a female sitter and send a male, but otherwise the most reputable company in town.

BABYZITCENTRALE BABYHOME
Tel. 616 1119. Book Mon–Thurs 3–5 p.m.

Cheaper than the Kriterion, but they haven't been going so long. Only use female sitters.

Planning a Holiday

Transport as a Treat

Canal Boat Trips

Canal boat trips are an excellent way of combining your wish to see the city with your child's desire to go on a boat, but it is important to choose a short trip or small children can get very irritable and occasionally seasick. Make sure that your child has been to the loo recently because few boats have toilets on board.

Trams

Children love trams. Try to sit up front where you can see the driver working the levers. The screeching brakes, screaming bells and breakneck speed of Amsterdam trams cause lots of excitement. Riding on trams is less easy with a buggy because of the steep steps and narrow door – always remember the doors only stay open if

you are standing on the bottom step, so put the buggy in first.

Pedalos

(see p.59) Splashing around in a pedalo is a great way to entertain children. You can relax better if they are reasonable swimmers. Most children over ten should be able to pedal and steer a pedalo on their own, but you need to tell them to keep to the right.

Ferry Trips Across the Ij

The free ferry leaves from behind Centraal Station to Amsterdam North every ten minutes.

Bike Hire

(see p.60) Hiring a bike to get around can be fun for families with older children or if you have very young children small enough to travel in the baby seats provided by some companies.

Markets

Amsterdam's markets can get very crowded so if you take small children keep hold of them or be prepared to put them on your shoulders. The city flea markets are a trendy teenager's dream.

Waterlooplein

(see p.184) Good for hip clothes and jewellery.

Noordermarkt

(see p.144) Great cheap junk for teenage bedrooms, good fabrics and nice clothes for small children.

Albert Cuyp

(see p.173) A bit crowded, but good fast food stalls and well worth combining it with a run around Sarphatipark.

Flower Market

(see p.134) A picturesque place for holiday snapshots for the parents.

Museums and Sights

Nint Museum of Science and Technology

Tolstraat 129, tel. 570 8110. Open Mon–Fri 10 a.m.–5 p.m., weekends noon–5 p.m.; closed 25 Dec and 1 Jan. Take tram 4. Admission f7.50 adults, f5 under 13s, under 6s free.

Young kids enjoy bombing around and pressing buttons, but the museum is intended for 6–12-year-olds. Don't expect too much but there are a good range of exhibits concerned with optical illusions, pneumatics, energy, holography and the more local task of building dikes and dams. Computer fanatics will have a great time upstairs where computers ask you to play and all have menus in English. A good café for snacks and children's meals.

TM JUNIOR
Linnaeusstraat 2, tel. 586 8233.
Mon–Thurs. Book in advance.

TM Junior run organised tours around the Tropenmuseum (see p.198) for children aged 6–12, telling stories and answering questions along the way. The tours and the weekend workshops are very popular so you need to book at least two weeks in advance, but it is well worth it. If you can't make a tour, the Tropenmuseum is suitable for all children and adults.

MADAME TUSSAUDS
(see p.79) The Amsterdam branch of the London waxworks display is not as extensive or as good as its sister branch, but a good family outing if you don't mind paying the steep entrance fee.

TRAMLINE MUSEUM
(see p.213) A chance to take a jolly antique electric tram into the Amsterdam Bos (see p.212).

MARITIME MUSEUM
(see p.201) The museum can get a bit boring, but kids love the replica ship *Amsterdam* moored outside, where they will be put to work scrubbing the deck for a growling sea captain or stirring the soup for the ship's chef. Take the museum boat to get there and it becomes a real adventure.

ARTIS ZOO AND PLANETARIUM
(see p.197) A good family day out and enough to see under cover on a wet day. There is also an urban farm on the site for fondling cuddly mammals and a playground for letting off steam. There is usually a chocolate egg hunt at the zoo over Easter.

HISTORICAL MUSEUM
(see p.108) Only worth visiting if your children want a go at playing the carillon bells in Room 10, where they can make a lot of noise and have a lot of fun.

SCHIPOL AIRPORT MUSEUM
(see p.213) Plane spotter's paradise with some old models to sit in.

POEZENBOOT
(see p.122) A boat full of good natured cats for feline fanatics.

DE KLOMPENBOER
(see p.75) Clog making demonstrations and a few hens pecking in the sawdust.

DIAMOND CUTTING
(see Coster diamonds, p.160) Older children may enjoy watching a short demonstration if you are passing, but don't make a special journey.

RESISTANCE MUSEUM
(see p.177) A fascinating insight into resistance work, spies and heroes which is imaginatively displayed and appeals to older children interested in the war and the underground.

ANNE FRANK HOUSE
(see p.124) An interesting insight into the plight of Anne Frank and an eye-opener into current nationalism in Europe. More educational than enjoyable.

MUZIEKTHEATER

(see p.185) Guided tours backstage at the Opera House. Good for teenagers interested in the theatre, but they need to ask questions if they start to get bored.

TOWER CLIMBING

Everyone likes a challenge and the following churches have towers open for just that: Zuiderkerk (p.101), Oude Kerk (p.90) and Westerkerk (see p.123).

See also Hollandse Manege and Artemis in Cafés below.

Tackling the Art Galleries

Few art galleries are made for children – they can't touch, they can't swing on the barriers, they can't see the pictures because they are hung too high or adults push them aside for a better view. Children need to fight back because art can be enjoyable for everyone.

Parents wanting to visit galleries should bear in mind that an hour is probably enough for any child and, however much you would like to spend a few more, few kids can be conned by a token present at the end. Families can enjoy galleries if you all go prepared. Always explain to your child why they can't touch (a very old picture would be worn away if everyone did the same – don't use the alarm bell excuse because it becomes rather appealing). Arm your child with a small pad and paper for copying something they like; this gives them a reason for being there. Most of all listen to what they have to say. Children can be extraordinarily perceptive – an interested youngster may well have something to teach you.

RIJKSMUSEUM

(see p.151) Although large, young children would probably find this the most interesting. Choose a few pictures to look at with them and you will enjoy it too. Flower paintings (Room 206) are fun for spotting beetles and bugs and the *Portrait of a Little Boy* dressed as a girl by Jacob Willemsz Delff is also quite amusing. There is a wonderful *Winter Scene* by Avercamp in Room 208, full of fallen skaters, pony-drawn sleighs and festive characters. Let the child draw you to animals and party scenes along the way and stop at Rembrandt's *Night Watch* which appeals because it is big, there are guns going off, funnily clad people, a pretty little girl and lots of hidden details looming in the darkness.

RIJKSMUSEUM VINCENT VAN GOGH

(see p.160) Older kids love the tragic, mysterious biographical details of Van Gogh, images of a fanatical artist trudging through the mud in search of gnarled peasants, the difficult child, the prostitute's friend, the madman who cut his ear off and went to the lunatic asylum, the shot that nearly missed and left him dying for three days. Make sure they know this before they go and they will enjoy the different images of him and his world along the way. Younger children may initially enjoy the vibrant colours, but you may be better off persuading toddlers to snooze in the free buggies provided at the door while their older siblings sketch *The Bedroom* and compare it with their own.

CHILDREN

STEDELIJK MUSEUM
(see p.163) The Stedelijk collections will probably appeal most to children who study art or art history and already show some interest in different art forms. A number of classics from the permanent collection would obviously appeal, like Matisse's *Parakeet and the Mermaid* and works by Manet, Toulouse Lautrec, Degas, Chagall, Picasso and Mondrian. The temporary exhibitions are likely to provoke serious family discussions which may be entertaining. Young kids would probably love it, too, but unless you have particularly well behaved children you may find it a frustrating couple of hours, keeping them away from tempting installations or scattering piles of artistically arranged sand.

Cinema

Special children's programmes show at the Rialto and the Kriterion (see p.289) and the Film Museum runs a good programme of children's entertainment (see p.169). Most films for the under tens will be dubbed into Dutch (*Nederlands gesproken*), but the family orientated films are more likely to be sub-titled. Look out for *kinder matinees* in the listings.

Theatre, Puppets and Circus

KINDERTHEATRE ELLEBORG
Passeerdersgracht 32, tel. 626 9370. Open to non-members alternate weekends; sessions 1.30 p.m.–5 p.m. Sat and 10.30 a.m.–4 p.m. Sun.

Anyone aged 6–16 can learn circus skills from riding a unicycle, juggling and tightrope walking to make-up skills and conjuring tricks. Volunteer staff speak English, but the majority of participants are Dutch. Children with disabilities are welcome. Always very busy.

CARRE THEATRE
(see p.000) Spectacular circus every Christmas.

DE KRAKELING
Nieuwe Passeerderstraat 1, tel. 625 3284. Separate performances for over 12s and under 12s are held on Wed, Sat and Sun at 2 p.m. and at 8 p.m. Fri.

Language need not be a problem if you go to one of the many mime or puppet shows.

POPPENTHEATER DIRIDAS
Hobbemakade 68, tel. 662 1588.

Using either marionettes or glove puppets the theatre puts on a show for the under 5s on Sunday at 11 a.m. Shows for over 5s at 3 p.m. on Saturdays and Sundays will be in Dutch, but if you inform the puppeteer that you are there he will give you a rundown of the plot before it starts.

PUNCH AND JUDY
There are free performances of Punch and Judy over the summer every Monday on Dam Square, starting at 11 a.m., but check with the tourist board VVV to be sure as the time changes from year to year.

VONDELPARK OPEN AIR THEATRE
Summer open air theatre hosts many programmes for children.

Cooking

KINDER KOOKUCAFÉ
O.Z. Achterburgwal 193, tel. 625 3257.

A novel idea whereby the chefs are aged between 6 and 12 and the diners are kids too. It is very popular so you need to book at least two weeks in advance. Few tourists go there because of the booking procedure, but if you are in Amsterdam for any length of time the kids will love it. Children can either cook (under supervision in the specially adapted kitchen) and wait on the tables or they can eat there at the child size tables and chairs. It is strictly a children's restaurant, but parents can accompany them as long as they keep out of the way!

Sports, Parks and Children's Farmyards

Swimming

MIRANDABAD
De Mirandalaan, tel. 644 6637.

(see p.291) Wonderful pool with a wave machine, slide and also an outdoor pool.

MARNIXBAD
Marnixplein 9, tel. 625 4843.

(see p.291) Whirlpool, slides and decent sized pool.

If the weather is good the beach is only half an hour on the train.

Skating

Free skating on a small ice rink in Leidseplein is popular with teenagers. Skates can be hired from the Café Hoopman Bodega in the square for f6 a pair.

Parks

VONDELPARK
(see p.168) The easiest to get to with plenty of space, an abundance of buskers, open air entertainment in the summer and a couple of playgrounds, three cafés and a few animals fenced in the middle.

SARPHATIPARK
(see p.173) A tiny park with a couple of poor playgrounds, lush grass and ducks to feed. Combine it with a trip to Albert Cuyp market.

AMSTELPARK EUROPALAAN,
Bus 8, 48, 49, 60, 158, 173.

Situated in the South it is good for children with excellent playgrounds, a miniature train and pony rides.

AMSTERDAM BOS
(see p.212) It may be half an hour out of town, but your child could spend days discovering all the attractions. The goat farm is a real hit if you go in springtime when animals outnumber children tenfold and children can bottlefeed the kids.

Playgrounds

Small playgrounds are dotted around the city and usually consist of a sand-pit, slide and climbing frame with rubber matting underneath. None is impressive, but can satisfy the needs of small children for a while. In the parks they tend to be fenced off to ward off dogs.

A few useful ones are: **in the Centre,** behind the Atrium Mensa, OZ Achterburgwal 237; **Grachten Gordle,** Herenmarkt, square off Brouwersgracht; **Jordaan,** Noordermarkt (North Church), not Mondays because of the market; **Karthuzerplantzoen,** in the middle of the Jordaan, better equipped than most; and, in the **Museum Quarter,** Museumplein is not very appealing, but across the road from the Van Gogh Museum one block away, where Jan Luikenstraat crosses van de Veldestraat, is a small walled area used by the children at the primary school opposite.

Excursions
If you are in the city for a few days it may be worth planning a special trip to see some of Holland's prime children's attractions or combine a day out for you with something for them.

DE EFTELING, KAATSHEUVEL
Europalaan 1, Kaatsheuvel, Noord Brabant, tel. 04167 8811. Situated 110 km from Amsterdam, off A261 just north of Tilburg. Daily excursions from Central Station are available which include all rides. If you want to stay overnight there is a hotel, tel. 04167 8200, on the site.

One of Europe's most imaginative, but little known theme parks where rubbish bins thank you for your contribution, carpets fly and fairies flit around the enchanted forest. The brainchild of illustrator Anton Pieck, the animated theme rides are superb and the funfair well maintained. This is well worth the journey from Amsterdam if you want to treat your children to something really special.

MADURODAM
Haringkade 175, Den Haag, tel. 070 355 3900. Around 57 km from Amsterdam. It is easiest to take the train to Den Haag and tram 1 or 9 straight to Madurodam. Admission f12.50 adults, f7.50 under 11s, under 2s free.

This extensive miniature village/city features most of the country's most

prominent buildings in minute detail. Planes taxi around Schipol airport, the congregation sings in Amsterdam's New Church and cars stream along the busy roads. Stay on till dusk when the street lights go on.

KROLLER MULLER MUSEUM AND HOGE VELUWE NATIONAL PARK
(see p.220) Children love the extensive sculpture garden and bike rides across the park. A good trip for combining your needs with theirs. Take a picnic.

UTRECHT
(see p.229) The National Museum 'from musical clock to street organ' is much enjoyed by children. Guided tours allow them to help operate the numerous musical instruments, from a motivated rabbit in a cabbage musical box to a ballroom barrel organ.

LAND VAN OOIT
Parklaan 40, Drunen, tel. 04163 77775. The easiest way to get there is to take a NS day excursion ticket from Central Station which includes train, bus and admission. Open Easter–Oct daily 10 a.m.–6 p.m. Entrance f18 adult, f14 under 11s, under 4s free.

Old fashioned fantasy park with lots of rides, but no machine powered ones which makes them very safe for little children as long as they have the energy to pedal a pie-shaped pedalo, climb over a giant and into a tree house café. Lots of dressed up actors swanning around as princes, princesses and other fairy tale characters, of whom a few speak English if invited to do so.

Children's Food

Choosing somewhere to eat or drink with children is not really a problem in daytime Amsterdam as most cafés offering light snacks will be able to rustle up an omelette, pancake or croquette for a hungry child. The places listed below are recommended because they have something good to look at or are especially geared towards catering for children. You will find the *kinder menu* usually means a croquette and chips, followed by ice cream and washed down with a fizzy drink.

BOLLEBEER
(see p.259) Friendly café with a bear theme.

THE PANCAKE BAKERY
(see p.262) Best pancake house in town with exotic sweet, umbrella, treat covered ones for special occasions.

BREDERO PANCAKE HOUSE
(see p.257) Small pancake house.

DAVID AND GOLIATH
(see p.261) Good children's menu and safe open air seating.

ARTEMIS CAFÉ
(see p.269) Good café for ballet loving teenagers.

HOLLANDSE MANEGE CAFÉ
(see p.271) Antiquated café overlooking the riding school.

DANTZIG
(see p.272) Large café overlooking the Amstel and next to Waterlooplein.

TISFRIS
(see p.272) Relaxed, slightly hip bar close to Waterlooplein with good seating on the bridge.

CASA DI DAVID
(see p.261) Good Italian for an evening meal.

QUATTRO STAGIONE
(see p.270) Family haunt near Vondelpark.

EETCAFÉ DE EETTUIN
(see p.265) Cheap and cheerful Jordaan restaurant.

CAFÉ PACIFICO
(see p.275) Good for teenagers.

ROSE'S CANTINA
(see p.267) For trendy teenagers.

ENGELBEWAARDER
(see p.258) For a family (with older children), brown bar supper or jazz session.

GREENWOODS
(see p.263) For the child who wants baked beans.

CAFÉ HOOPMAN BODEGA
Leidseplein 4.

Sit outside on a nice day or watch the skating from a window in the winter.

HAAGEN DAAS ICE CREAM
Leidseplein 1–3.

Yummy ice creams.

BURGER KING
Leidseplein 5.

Fast food joint.

MCDONALDS
Kalverstraat … and around town.

Kids' favourite burger bar.

PUCCINI
(see p.272) Nice café. Stop to watch chocolates being made through the window next door.

Clothes and Baby Equipment

The department stores Hema, De Bijenkorf, and Peek and Cloppenberg (Dam Square) have good children's clothes departments, but the best place for clothes, unusual toys, books etc. is the top floor of the new shopping centre, The Magna Plaza, which is almost entirely devoted to children's shops.

HEMA
(see p.295) Excellent children's clothes and baby equipment.

DE BIJENKORF
(see p.295) Upmarket department store with good clothes, toys and books, beakers and baby equipment.

PEEK AND CLOPPENBURG
Dam Square.

Department store with very colourful, reasonably priced kids' clothes, and holds good sales.

BAMBAM
Magna Plaza, N.Z. Voorburgwal 182.

Everything for the designer baby. Cradles, cots, buggies, kids' furniture, pots and lots of present ideas from toothbrush starter packs to tartan suitcases for two-year-olds. Beautiful bed linen and clothes and a few maternity garments.

MOWGLI
Brouwersgracht 56.

Children's clothes (0–4) made on the premises in exotic ethnic fabrics. Hats, dungarees, shirts, scarves, bags and purses for kids.

WAMPIE
2e Angeliersdwarsstraat 19.

Cheerful clothes, all original designs for kids up to 7.

'T SCHOOLTJE
Overtoom 87.

Expensive clothes and shoes for kids up to 16. Carries designer labels like Oilily.

PRENATAL
Kalverstraat 79.

Clothes, toys and equipment for 0–5 year olds. A good range of maternity clothes. They also stock terry nappies.

BYZANTIUM
Tesselschaderstraat 1D.

Bright and cheerful furniture for
children from beds, bunks and desks
to comfy chairs and lamps. The place
for the child who thought he had
everything.

JULES POLMAN
Sarphatipark 16.

Just off Albert Cuypstraat, this
upholsterer also makes delightful
armchairs and sofas for children to
order. Plenty of fabrics to choose
from.

Toys

Expect to find most toy shops full of old fashioned toys rather than
the latest range of Fischer Price. Wooden toys, miniature dolls'
house furniture and puppets are all sold at reasonable prices and all
finished to a high standard. Children love to learn new languages
and younger kids enjoy coming to grips with a few words – a basic
ABC in Dutch is a good holiday present.

PINOKKIO
Magna Plaza, N.Z. Voorburgwal 182.

Wonderful wooden toys from intricate
dolls' houses and pedal cars to
stocking fillers. Good selection of
puppets.

BELL TREE
Spiegelgracht 10.

A large bear blows bubbles outside
this popular toy shop run by a devotee
of Rudolf Steiner. Good dolls' house
equipment and lots of small treats.

CEDILLE
Lijnbaansgracht 275.

Tiny shop selling wooden toys,
musical boxes, mobiles and puppets.

KRAMER
Reestraat 20.

(see p.302) Beautiful dolls.

VLIEGERTUIG
(see p.302) Kites for young and old.

MINIATURE FURNITURE
(see p.303) Dolls' house furniture.

For children's bookshops see p.301.

Holland's glittering trading past may have faded three centuries ago, but it never disappeared altogether. Today the country is the hub of the European community, controlling more than a third of the EEC's transportation. Rotterdam's immense port is twice as big as its nearest rival, New York, Schipol Airport carries 17 million international passengers a year, the country boasts excellent communications by road and rail into Europe and a convenient marriage of bonded warehouses and user-friendly customs allows goods to be transported and processed through the country without paying duty or VAT.

The easy movement of goods and finance is also encouraged by one of the world's most liberal trading environments. The virtual absence of import and export licences or restrictions on the flow of capital and profits has encouraged over 3,500 foreign companies to open offices here, including the EC distribution centres of many multinationals such as Nissan, IBM, Sony and ITT.

But the Dutch do not just shuffle other nations' goods. They export a massive 65% of Gross Domestic Product. A quarter of these exports are produced by an agricultural sector that exploits this fertile land with such mechanistic efficiency that only the farmers of the USA earn more in foreign exchange, and not even they can match the Dutch dairymen and poultry farmers. The other pillars of Dutch industry are food, drink and tobacco, petrochemicals and electrical engineering. Most Dutch companies, both private *BVs* (private limited companies) and public *MVs* (public limited companies) tend to be small, but three multinationals seem very familiar – Royal Dutch Shell, Phillips and Unilever.

However, the main area of growth is the service sector where more than half the population now earn their living. Major players in financial services include the ABN AMRO in banking and National Nederlandershe in insurance, while the Effectenbeurs (Stock

Exchange) lists 250 Dutch and 350 foreign companies. The Optien-beurs (European Options Exchange) is the largest of its kind, trading over 55,000 options in gold, silver, shares, bonds and currency a day. Tourism brings 8½ million visitors a year to Amsterdam alone.

Dutch women are poorly represented in the workforce. Thirty-three-year-old Ada van der Veer Vergeer has every reason to 'feel proud' as the sole woman bank director in the Netherlands – the financial sector is notoriously low on the list of female professions. Successful women are more commonly found in the arts and the thriving fashion industry, like Cox Habbema, director of the Stadsschouwburg theatre, and Margreet van Roemburg, the new director of Herome, a leading name in Dutch cosmetics.

Working women may not be a Dutch phenomenon, but with the many foreign companies to have set up Dutch offices the country is not unused to women sitting around the board table.

The first thing most foreign women notice when travelling to Amsterdam on business is the relaxed dress code. Look smart but comfortable. Power dressing does not really impress the Dutch as much as a smile and a good handshake. Obviously everyone chooses their outfit according to the work they do, but you are unlikely to find other women wearing very short skirts, dripping with jewellery and wearing excessive makeup. Choose smart, simple clothes, look good but not glitzy. There is little place for overt femininity in business – flirting and flaunting are not par for the course. When meeting people it is always polite to shake hands and to say your name; even if you have been introduced they will expect you to say your name as you shake hands.

Time is very important in the Netherlands. When making an appointment it is a good idea to say how long you need and expect to be given exactly that. Punctuality is crucial. If you arrive late expect your appointment to be cancelled or your meeting shortened to fit within the allocated time.

Don't expect to be invited out – families are as important as work to a lot of Dutch people. However, if the host company know you are alone you may well be invited out for an evening meal. Take a good look at the menu when ordering, bearing in mind that Dutch portions are huge, meat is often chewy (not good for conversation) and fish is a good bet if you are going for lots of courses. If you are entertaining remember that the Dutch eat early and if you want to go on somewhere the clubs open late. Tip taxi drivers, leave a small tip in restaurants and always give the club doorman around f5 when you leave.

Accommodation will probably be booked for you by your host company, but many businesswomen travelling to the city are disappointed at being accommodated just outside the centre, close to work but a long way from the sights and nightlife. If you feel you will have some leisure time and wish to see the city ask to be located nearer the centre. If you are booking for yourself there is a good range of business hotels and more intimate canal houses to stay at (see p.235). If you are worried about staying in a street level room always specify when booking, and it is a good idea to check if there is a separate work surface or desk in the room. The Dutch are avid smokers so if you want a non-smoking room ask when booking. Prices in all business hotels are high, but staff are often willing to negotiate. Expect a good concession over the winter, out of the tourist season, but don't be surprised if they won't negotiate in the summer.

If you have been posted to Amsterdam on business you may consider joining the Women's International Network (see below) who for a reasonable membership fee of f150 organise lectures and meetings for working women (as well as unemployed women), as well as providing useful business contacts. It can be an excellent way to meet other working women and come to grips with business in the Netherlands.

USEFUL ADDRESSES

Contact groups

Women's International Network. *(PO Box 15692, 1001 ND, tel. 679 9951)* Contact: Agnes Benjamin.

STEW
Weesperzijde 4, OE, tel. 665 5016. Open Mon–Thurs 9 a.m.–5 p.m.

Association has information on companies run by women throughout the Netherlands.

Temporary offices

World Trade Centre

Strawinskylaan 1, OS, tel. 575 9111/ fax 662 7255.

Offices can be hired for a day, a week or for longer periods. All office facilities available. Secretaries and translators can also be hired.

Euro Business Centre

Keizersgracht 62, IW, tel. 626 5749/fax 623 1506.

Offices in the centre for a minimum of three months. Some private offices can be rented for the day only.

Faxing

Faxes can be sent from most hotels or more cheaply from the **Telehouse** (see p.16) and some of the district post offices. Facilities also available at the World Trade Centre (see above).

Photocopying

Nearly all libraries have self-service photocopiers for readers' use. There are also a number of duplicating and printing shops around the city, many of which have metered photocopy machines which save time and use up loose change.

Multicopy *(Weesperstraat 65, IE, tel. 624 6208). Open Mon–Fri 9 a.m.– 5.50 p.m.*

Print and Company *(Utrechtsestraat 138, tel. 627 7116). Open Mon–Fri 9 a.m.–5 p.m.*

Equipment Hire

Ruad Computer Hire *(Kuiperbergweg 33, OSE, tel. 697 8191). Open 8 a.m.–5 p.m. daily.*

For computers, fax machines, photocopiers and car phones.

Decorum Verhuurg *(Jarmuiden 21, OW, tel. 611 7905). Open 8 a.m.–5 p.m.*

For office furniture.

Avisco *(Stadhouderskade 156, OS, tel. 671 9909). Open Mon–Fri 7 a.m.–6 p.m.*

For audiovisual equipment.

Translators and Interpreters

Some hotels will have their own translation service. See World Trade Centre and Euro Business Centre above or try: Berlitz Language Centre, Rokin 87 (tel. 622 1375/fax 620 3959). Open 8.15 a.m.–9 p.m.; Congrestolken–Secretariaat (Prinsengracht 993, IS, tel. 625 2535/fax 626 0501). Open Mon–Fri 9 a.m.–5.30 p.m. Specialist conference interpreting.

Couriers

International Couriers Amsterdam (Coenhavenweg Loods 610, Pier Europa tel. 686 7808). Open 24 hours daily; Bluesprint (JJ Viottastraat 37, tel. 664 4311). Open 24 hours daily.

Conference Centres

Grand Hotel Krasnapolsky (see p.236); RAI Conference Centre (see p.178); Beurs van Berlage (see p.73).

Office Catering

Florence Exotic Catering (Noordermarkt, I, tel. 699 0868). If you need to impress visiting clients/businesspeople Florence does authentic Surinamese buffets and dinners.

Car Hire

(see p.50) Europcar, Overtoom 51–3, OW, tel. 618 4595.

Travel Agents

NBBS, Dam 17, tel. 620 5071.

Taxi

Central Taxi Service, tel. 677 7777.

BACKGROUND

RECOMMENDED BOOKS

Many books about the history of the Netherlands are out of print, but available in public libraries and often found in second-hand bookshops. Dutch works in translation are rarely stocked in the bookshops but can be ordered. Alternatively, most of the books listed below should be available in Amsterdam. W.H. Smith in Kalverstraat has the best selection.

History

S.Shama, *The Embarrassment of Riches: an Interpretation of Dutch Culture in the Golden Age* (Abeville, 1975, presently out of print). A readable, entertaining and enlightening account.

Richter Roegholt, *A Concise History of Amsterdam* (City of Amsterdam PR Dept, 1992). An informative quick read available from the Amsterdam Historical Museum.

Christopher Hibbert, *Cities and Civilisations* (Weidenfeld and Nicolson, 1987, presently out of print). A fascinating chapter on life in the seventeenth century, much of it specifically related to Amsterdam.

Geoffrey Parker, *The Dutch Revolt* (Peregrine, 1988). Comprehensive history of the Revolt.

Adam Hopkins, *Holland* (Faber & Faber, 1988). A good introduction to the Netherlands, their history, people and culture.

Art and Architecture

Jakob Rosenberg, *Dutch Art and Architecture 1600–1800* (Pelican, 1991). Definitive work on the subject with lots of illustrations.

R.H. Fuchs, *Dutch Painting* (Thames and Hudson, 1978). Concise and entertaining read.

Eugene Fromentin, *The Masters of Past Time: Dutch and Flemish Painting from Van Eyck to Rembrandt* (Phaidon, 1981). A relaxed and informative read.

Paul Overy, *De Stijl* (Thames and Hudson, 1991). An excellent survey of the De Stijl movement.

Melissa McQuillan, *Van Gogh* (Thames and Hudson, 1985). A well-researched concise monograph.

Christopher White, *Rembrandt* (Thames and Hudson, 1992). Accessible and informative on the artist's life and works.

Annemarie Vels Heijn, *Rembrandt* (Scala, 1989). Discusses individual paintings in detail – many in the Rijksmuseum.

F. Hofrichter, *Judith Leyster* (Yale, 1993). Definitive work on one of the leading Dutch female artists, but too big to fit in your hand luggage.

Guus Kemme, *Amsterdam Architecture* (Thoth, 1992). An excellent architectural handbook with photographs of every historic building in the city, concise descriptions and good introductory chapters.

Manfred Bock, *Berlage in Amsterdam* (Architectura & Natura, 1992). Illustrated pocket guide to all Berlage's projects in the city.

Literature

Joost van den Vondel, *Lucifer* (Absolute, 1990). One of the few works by the master of Dutch literature translated into English. His most famous work, *Gijsbrecht van den Amstel* (Dovehouse Editions, Carlton University, Ottawa, 1989), is also available in translation.

Multatuli, *Max Havelaar: or the Coffee Auctions of the Dutch Trading Company* (Penguin, 1987). A classic about Dutch colonial corruption which shocked the nation when it appeared in 1860.

Harry Mulisch, *Last Call* (Penguin, 1985, currently out of print). A captivating novel examining national guilt over the lack of intervention on behalf of the Jews in the Second World War through the story of an elderly actor cast as Prospero in the Tempest.

Marga Minco, *Bitter Herbs* (Penguin, 1991). Like all the novels from this award winning writer it deals with life during the occupation. Marga Minco worked as a journalist, but her novels have become increasingly popular and are at last being translated into English. See also *Empty House* (Peter Owen, 1989), *The Fall* (Peter Owen, 1990), and *Other Side* (Peter Owen, 1993).

BACKGROUND

Cees Nooteboom, *In the Dutch Mountains* (Penguin, 1992). One of many witty novels from this popular Dutch writer. Try also *Song of Truth and Semblance* (Penguin, 1993).

L. Couperus, *The Hidden Force* (Quartet, 1992). A great novel set in nineteenth-century Colonial East Indies by one of the leading Dutch writers.

Nicolas Freeling, *Because of the Cats* (Penguin, 1963). Good detective novelist, Freeling was the creator of the BBC TV series Van der Valk. His books make good holiday reading and many are set in Amsterdam.

J. Holmes and W. Jay Smith (eds.), *Dutch Interior: Postwar Poetry of the Netherlands and Flanders* (Columbia University Press, 1984). A delightful anthology.

Biographies

Anne Frank, *The Diary of Anne Frank* (Pan, 1972). A moving account of life in hiding in Amsterdam during the Second World War.

Etty Hillesum, *Etty* (Triad Grafton, 1985). A lively and optimistic account of life in Amsterdam under Nazi occupation by a member of the Jewish Council.

Eva Schloss, *Eva's Story* (Castle Kent, 1992). A survivor's story which is well written and deeply moving.

Women's History

Gisela Kaplan, *Contemporary Western European Feminism* (UCL Press, 1992). Contains an excellent chapter on the Netherlands and carries a good bibliography.

Mineke Bosche & Annemarie Kloosterman, *Politics and Friendship: Letters from the International Women's Suffrage Alliance 1902–42* (Ohio State University Press, 1990). A fascinating collection of correspondence including lots to and from Aletta Jacobs.

Rudolk Dekker, *Traditional of Female Transvestism in Early Modern Europe* (Macmillan, 1993). A survey of female transvestites in the Netherlands, concentrating on women found to be working for the East India Company in Amsterdam.

Dineke Stam, *Sporen van Vrouwen* (Uitgeverij BZZTÔH 1987, presently out of print). A series of historical walks for women through the streets of Amsterdam. If you are going to be there with Dutch-speaking friends it is well worth buying a copy from one of the second-hand stores.

Hellen Halverhout, *The Netherlands Cookbook* (Driehoek, 1987). For those Dutch recipes you just can't live without.

At Home in Holland (The American Women's Club of the Hague, 1990). Everything you need to know if you move to the Netherlands, written by women who have done just that.

c. 1225	Fishermen settle on the Amstel.
c. 1270	A dam is built across the Amstel.
1275	Count Floris V of Holland grants the city exemption from tolls in an attempt to gain popular support against Gijsbrecht IV, but Floris is mysteriously assassinated.
1300	Amsterdam granted first charter.
1345	Miracle of the regurgitated host.
1419	Philip of Burgundy begins to unite the provinces.
1421	First Great Fire.
1425	First circular canal dug – the Singel.
1428	Philip the Good, Duke of Burgundy, acquires Holland from cousin Jacoba of Bavaria. The Pax Burgundia brings stability and prosperity to trading cities. Amsterdam thrives.
1452	Second Great Fire.
1477	Death of Charles the Bold. Mary of Burgundy succeeds and marries Maximillian, who becomes Holy Roman Emperor. Their son marries Juana the Mad, heiress to Castile and Aragon.
1500	Birth of Charles V.
1515	Charles V assumes control of Low Countries, Spanish and German territories.
1535	Anabaptist protests in Amsterdam.
1555	Charles V abdicates in favour of his son, Philip II of Spain.
1566	Iconaclastic riots against Catholicism.
1567	Duke of Alva sent to Amsterdam to quash anti-Catholic feeling.
1568	William of Orange leads the Dutch Revolt against Spain.
1576	Pacification of Ghent unites 17 provinces, but stalled on religious grounds.
1578	The Alteration. Amsterdam changes from Catholic to Protestant.
1579	Union of Utrecht unites seven northern provinces with William as Stadhouder. The southern provinces declare allegiance to Spain in the Union of Arras.
1585	Antwerp falls to the Spanish and refugees flock to Amsterdam.
1588	Defeat of Spanish Armada breaks Spanish naval power and heralds the beginning of the Golden Age.
1590	Amsterdam merchants start exploring trade routes to East.

1602	East India Company incorporated.
1603	Zuiderkerk, first Protestant church, is built in Amsterdam.
1609	First plans of the Grachten Gordle are drawn.
1609–22	Twelve-year truce with Spain.
1621	Dutch West India Company incorporated.
1626	Manhattan bought from the Indians and named New Amsterdam.
1628	Descartes settles in Amsterdam.
1632	University is established in Amsterdam.
1634–7	Tulip mania hits Holland.
1642	Rembrandt paints the *Night Watch*.
1648	Treaty of Munster concludes the Eighty Years War.
1652	First Anglo-Dutch war breaks out over the English Navigation Act.
1665	Second Anglo-Dutch war.
1672	Louis XIV invades the Netherlands.
1672–4	Third Anglo-Dutch war.
1685	Revocation of edict of Nantes brings flood of Huguenot refugees from France.
1688	The Glorious Revolution in Britain. Stadholder William III of Holland and Mary become King and Queen of United Kingdom.
1697	Czar Peter the Great in Amsterdam to learn shipbuilding.
1700	Start of decline of Amsterdam's trading role in Europe.
1701–13	War of Spanish Succession. Netherlands emerge free from French claims, but under control of Austrian Charles VI. Continuing friction between supporters of French ('Patriots') and Austrians ('Loyalists').
1734	War of Austrian Succession.
1747	French invasion, unrest in Amsterdam.
1778	Trade agreement with rebel American colonies angers British.
1780–4	Fourth Anglo-Dutch war.
1780	Unrest between Patriots and Loyalists.
1786	Patriots take control, ousted by Prussians.
1791	East India Company collapses, West India Company wound up.
1792–5	France defeats Austria. Batavian Republic established by Dutch radicals and French troops.
1806	Kingdom of the Netherlands established under Louis Napoleon, who converts Town Hall into Royal Palace.
1810	Louis abdicates, Holland annexed by France.
1813	Liberation of the Netherlands and creation of a kingdom under William I, uniting N (Holland) & S (Belgium) Netherlands for a short time.

1830	Belgium becomes an independent state following Belgian revolt.
1876	Construction of North Sea Canal brings new prosperity to Amsterdam.
1880	Bicycles come to Amsterdam. Ladies attend cycle schools.
1882	Aletta Jacobs opens world's first birth control clinic in Amsterdam.
1889	Centraal Station built.
1890	Wilhelmina crowned Queen.
1894	Formation of Association for Women's Suffrage.
1901	New Housing Act leads to better housing in Amsterdam.
1903	Berlage's Stock Exchange (*Beurs*) opens.
1914–18	First World War, Netherlands neutral.
1919	Women win vote in the Netherlands.
1928	Amsterdam Olympics.
1930s	Development of New South by architects of Amsterdam School.
1932	Building of Afsluitdijk, creating the Ijsselmeer.
1935	Women's archive IIAV founded.
1939	Second World War begins; Holland tries to remain neutral.
1940	Holland invaded by the Germans.
1941	Amsterdam's dockworkers strike in protest against the deportation of the Jews.
1943	Amsterdam Registry burnt by Resistance.
1944–5	Liberation of Holland.
1948	Queen Wilhelmina abdicates after 58 years on throne; Juliana becomes Queen.
1949	Dutch East Indies achieves independence.
1953	Zeeland flood disaster.
1965	Provo demonstrations and happenings in Amsterdam. Hippies flood the tolerant city.
1966	Provo riots. Provos win seat on Council.
1967	Provos disband.
1969	Dolle Mina feminists storm Gynaecologists' Conference.
1970	Kabouters follow Provos to win five seats in local government.
1970s	Riots sparked by the construction of the Metro.
1980	Metro opens.
1980–4	Squatters occupy vacant buidings, battles with police.
1986–7	Completion of Musiektheater and Stadhuis after protests during construction.

INDEX